The Emperor's Guest 1942–45

The
Emperor's Guest
1942-45

JOHN FLETCHER-COOKE

Pen & Sword
MILITARY

For my children Charles, Richard and Gillian and to M.L.B.
Without whose encouragement
the book would have never have been written.

First published in 1971 by Hutchinson & Co. Ltd
Republished in 1972 and 1994 by Leo Cooper

Published in Great Britain in 2013 by
Pen & Sword Military
an imprint of
Pen & Sword Books Ltd
47 Church Street
Barnsley
South Yorkshire
S70 2AS

ISBN:- 978-1-78340-072-0

Printed and bound in the UK by CPI Group (UK) Ltd, Croydon, CRO 4YY

Pen & Sword Books Ltd incorporates the Imprints of Pen & Sword Aviation,
Pen & Sword Family History, Pen & Sword Maritime, Pen & Sword Military, Pen
& Sword Discovery, Wharncliffe Local History, Wharncliffe True Crime,
Wharncliffe Transport, Pen & Sword Select, Pen & Sword Military Classics, Leo
Cooper, The Praetorian Press, Remember When, Seaforth Publishing
and Frontline Publishing.

For a complete list of Pen & Sword titles please contact
PEN & SWORD BOOKS LIMITED
47 Church Street, Barnsley, South Yorkshire, S70 2AS, England
E-mail: enquiries@pen-and-sword.co.uk
Website: www.pen-and-sword.co.uk

Contents

Foreword
by
Field-Marshall Lord Bramall, GCB, OBE, MC

This book is one of the classics of prisoner of war literature. To describe any book as a classic is not something which should be done lightly, for the word is easily devalued; nonetheless it is an appropriate term for *The Emperor's Guest*. Sir John Fletcher-Cooke was a man of great distinction, as his post-war career in the Colonial Service and as a Member of Parliament amply demostrated, but in some ways the most remarkable years of his life were those he spent as a prisoner of war, and this book is a still more remarkable chronicle of that time.

Becoming a prisoner of war must have been, for everyone who suffered the fate, a traumatic and frightening experience. Naturally, individuals reacted differently but few can have accepted their situation and responded to it as effectively as Fletcher-Cooke. In this he was helped by the companionship of his fellow prisoners, and most particularly by his diary, in which he recorded the events around him and his own reactions. The diary formed the source for the book, written 25 years later, and gives an immediacy and vividness to his picture of events. The most remarkable aspect, however, is the balance which the author displayed, both at the time and late on relfection. His realization that there were good and bad Japanese, just as there were good and bad prisoners, was a rare insight, displaying a tolerance of view which many of his fellow prisoners could not, or did not want to emulate. Throughout he retained his awareness that his captors were fellow human beings, even when they behaved inhumanely, and it was this that led him to want to meet them again after the war - something which he achieved and recorded in his Epilogue.

Ultimately, this balance and the all-round nature of the picture is what gives the book its lasting value. We live in a world in which hatred and hostility flourish, and Fletcher-Cooke experienced more than his fair share of both, but if there are lessons to be learnt from history then books such as this must continue to be read.

Preface

This is one man's story covering the four years December 1941 to December 1945.

Many thousands of my fellow-countrymen, as well as many thousands of our allies, had experiences similar to those recorded in this book.

Many of these suffered much more grievously than I ever did; many, too, never survived to tell their tales. Some who did survive were so damaged in body or mind that they could never have recorded all that they had endured, even if they had wanted to.

Throughout this period I kept very full diaries, notes and records of various kinds. These included letters which I wrote in captivity but which were never sent and, indeed, have never been seen by any eyes but my own. There are a number of references to these papers, and to my methods of concealing them, in the text of this book.

The last entry in these diaries is dated the 10th October 1945. It was written, many thousands of feet above the earth, in a Halifax bomber in which I was flying over 'the Hump' from Kunming in the Chinese Province of Yunnan to Calcutta in India.

Quite deliberately I never looked at any of these papers until I started to write this book just after Christmas, 1969.

In particular, I specifically refrained from perusing them before I paid my visit to Japan in August 1969 to which reference is made in the Epilogue. I was particularly anxious to meet my captors and to visit the camps without any prejudices, to which a re-reading of my diaries might have given rise.

The Epilogue was written in November 1969, after my visit to Japan and before I had looked at my diaries. A shortened form of this Epilogue appeared as an article published in the *Sunday Express*, London, of the 7th December 1969.

I trust that I have been fair to my fellow P.o.W.s, and to our captors, in all that I have written. There were good and bad Japanese just as there were good and bad P.o.W.s.

To the best of my knowledge and belief all the incidents referred to in this book occurred as described. Where they were not based on personal experience they were derived from information given to me, the veracity of which I had no reason to doubt.

It is possible that some, but not many, of the incidents described have been transposed in time.

The events of the last few weeks at Miyata (Chapter 11) were so extraordinary that in order to satisfy my own curiosity as to what really happened in Japan at that time I read the French edition of *Japan's Longest Day*, to which I have made a specific reference in Appendix II.

In the light of my own experiences and in the light of the events referred to above I am firmly persuaded that few, if any, of the P.o.W.s would have got out of Japan alive if the atomic bombs had not been dropped on Hiroshima and Nagasaki.

I say this for two reasons. In the first place the dropping of these terrible bombs re-kindled in the minds of the Japanese, and particularly in the minds of our guards, that dormant and indefinable fear of the P.o.W.s which they all possessed. The Japanese never began to understand us and it is natural to fear what one cannot understand (see page 135).

More important still, the dropping of the atomic bombs, and the threats of more to come, were the decisive factors which led the Japanese to accept capitulation. Did not the Emperor himself say, before the second bomb was dropped on Nagasaki, that Japan could not afford a repetition of Hiroshima?

It was these devastating bombs which ensured that when, finally, the Allies landed in Japan the 'invasion' was unopposed. If the Allies had been forced to make an 'opposed' landing the Japanese would undoubtedly have 'liquidated' the P.o.W.s, if for no other reason than that to guard and feed them would have interfered with the task of repelling the invaders, 'polluting the sacred soil of Nippon'.

There is no doubt in my own mind that these atomic bombs

saved many more lives than the tens of thousands they killed. They saved the lives of tens of thousands of P.o.W.s, of hundreds of thousands of Allied Servicemen and almost certainly of millions of Japanese—for, let there be no mistake, if the Emperor and his Cabinet had decided to fight on, the Japanese would, literally, have fought to the last man.

Why have I written this book at all? That is a question I have asked myself repeatedly, particularly since I embarked on my task. The war with Japan has now been over for nearly twenty-five years. The world has changed, Japan has changed and Great Britain has changed, but the variety of human natures has not changed.

The world is made up, as it always has been and always will be, of some men who are stronger, both physically and morally, than others, of some men who are kinder and more humane than others, of some men who are more sensitive than others, of some men who are more cruel than others and, above all, of some men who are luckier than others. The spectrum of human varieties and of human qualities is infinite.

P.o.W. camps, and particularly P.o.W. camps in Japan, were 'forcing beds' for such human varieties, and this applied not only to the P.o.W.s but also to their captors.

Many of us learnt, within a span of a few years—or did we only think we did?—more about human nature in all its forms than we had ever learnt before or would ever learn thereafter.

Those were the lessons which I wanted to pass on to my children and their contemporaries. It is they, the youth of the world, who will have to wrestle with the world's problems in the future; and they should realise that far more of these problems are caused by human nature than by Nature.

Many have asked me, since my visit to Japan in 1969, how I could possibly have brought myself not merely to return there but deliberately to seek out and entertain my captors and visit the camps.

My answer has always been, quite simply, that I wanted to. I wanted to learn more about these mysterious people. I wanted, if I could, to learn why they had behaved as they had. I have found it impossible to be bitter against the Japanese. I have found it equally impossible to avoid a profound distaste for the national system which had led to Japan's declaration of war and all that followed therefrom. But that was the system into which our captors

had been born; that was the system in which they had been nur-
tured; and it was that system, prostituted by a greedy and ambitious
militarist clique, which was largely responsible for the maltreatment
of P.o.W.s.

An evil system can never be condoned or pardoned. Individuals
whose actions have been conditioned by such a system may, perhaps,
be forgiven.

Forgiveness is an individual matter. It is not easy to forgive
those who have hurt oneself. It is much more difficult, perhaps
even beyond capacity, to forgive those who have hurt one's loved
ones. That I understand.

JOHN FLETCHER-COOKE

Lausanne, Switzerland

Prologue: The Bridge

The sun was just coming up. I moved cautiously, picking my way through the undergrowth skirting the single-track railway. I was cold, lonely and desperately afraid. Then, suddenly, the sun's rays caught it and I saw it, the bridge.

For the past eight hours I had thought of nothing but the bridge and there it was, I had never seen it before and I was never to see it again. I did not know then, I do not know now, exactly where it was.

There seemed to be little to distinguish it from the many other bridges, spanning rivers, creeks and swamps, which carried the railway line from western Java to Jogjakarta, the port away to the south. But I had no doubt that it was *the* bridge.

It was deathly still. The nocturnal noises of the jungle which had terrified me since ten o'clock the previous evening had died away; and the morning chorus of the birds, bringing reassurance that one was still alive, had not yet started.

I moved forward again. A burst of machine-gun fire flung me flat on my face. I tied my handkerchief on to a stick and wormed my way on my belly deeper into the undergrowth. Suddenly I came to a path running parallel to the railway. I walked slowly along the path in the direction of the river, carrying my stick in my right hand like a cavalry sabre, and for the first time in twenty-four hours I found myself chuckling.

A dozen years before I had joined the Cavalry Squadron of the Oxford University Officer's Training Corps with my great friend Denis Wright.* It was not that we were particularly warlike,

* Now Sir Denis Wright, K.C.M.G., Her Britannic Majesty's Ambassador in Teheran.

but, impecunious as we were, we both wanted free riding. We had
attended summer camps at Aldershot and Tidworth; we had galloped
over Port Meadow at Oxford at seven o'clock on cold spring mornings; and on one occasion I had disgraced myself.

My horse had run away with me while I was carrying my
cavalry sabre in my right hand and endeavouring to ride him
with my left. Recalling the counsel of our instructor, Sergeant
Rhimes of the 17/21st Lancers, 'if 'e bolts wiv yer, sir, try a sawin'
motion on 'is mouf', I brought my right hand in to grasp the off-side
reins, prior to sawing. The result was disastrous. The heavy sabre,
as it inclined inwards, nicked the tips of my steed's ears. Not unnaturally this infuriated him still further. I continued with my sawing and sabring, the effects of which seemed, alas, to be cancelling
each other out. As we thundered across the vast, unencumbered
and apparently unending expanse of Port Meadow, I wondered
why the War Office had never considered it as an alternative to
Salisbury Plain.

Whether it was exhaustion or loss of blood which brought
the runaway to a standstill I do not know. Certainly he felt better
standing still; it was some time before I could induce him to move
at all. By the time we had got under way, the rest of the squadron
must have completed unsaddling in the stables near Worcester
College.

Fortunately Sergeant Rhimes had left for his breakfast by the
time I returned. I was glad to be spared the rough lash of his tongue,
but my blood-flecked face and chest and the flagging ears of my
unfortunate mount called forth some ungenerous remarks from
the attendant grooms. I wondered what Sergeant Rhimes would
have thought if he had seen me, in R.A.F. uniform, walking slowly
along that jungle path. I suddenly wished he was at my side.

The path led, as I thought it would, to a little clearing on the river
bank. No doubt village women from some *kampong* in the jungle
behind me came there to do their washing and collect water. I
peered out cautiously to my left. Now I could see the bridge quite
clearly. I could make out the silhouettes of a couple of sentries.
Were they Dutch in their jungle green or were they Japanese in
dark beige? I could not be sure.

Another path led from the clearing along the river bank to
the bridgehead. I began to walk slowly along it. Two rifle-shots rang
out, apparently from the other side of the river. The two sentries

on the bridge turned towards me and I waved my stick, topped with its white handkerchief. By now, and to my great relief, I could see they were Dutch; as I got nearer I could see that one was from Holland and the other a Javanese. Keeping me covered with a machine-gun and a rifle, they beckoned me to approach.

Addressing them in Malay, for I could speak no Dutch, I asked to see the officer commanding the detachment guarding the bridge. One of them picked up a field telephone. I was then told to wait until an escort arrived across the bridge from the other side of the river.

Within a few minutes I was telling my story to the Dutch Captain in a little hut at the other end of the bridge, with a most welcome cup of hot coffee in my hands.

We had entrained at some point in western Java during the afternoon of the previous day. We had been told that our destination was Tjilatjap, where a ship would be available to take us to Australia. We were all R.A.F. Our informant had added that, as we were all key-men with specialist qualifications, we were to be afforded priority in the evacuation from Java. I could not forbear a wry smile as I heard these words. I had heard them before in Singapore on Friday the 13th February, after General Sir Archibald Wavell* had taken a similar decision just before he flew back to Java at midnight on Thursday, the 12th February. As one who had only been commissioned in the R.A.F.V.R., in Singapore on the 7th February, I felt no more of a key-man now than I had then. I knew virtually nothing about the R.A.F.; I had never been in an aircraft; in fact I felt a bit of a fraud, but I was to pay for this later. In Singapore, as in Java, I had been swept along by the Service machine, and who was I to argue with those who were apparently offering me the chance of freedom?

The train had bumbled its way across Java during the late afternoon and early evening. We were all in covered goods trucks; it was very hot and we had the sliding doors open on both sides. We were squatting on the floor, eating our hard rations or smoking. The train made frequent stops and this afforded opportunities for some to change places with others in different wagons. There was a happy end-of-term feeling. The horrors of the Japanese invasion of Malaya and the fall of Singapore were behind us. We were going to Australia.

* Later Field Marshal Earl Wavell.

We were passing through a peaceful countryside dotted with little *kampongs*. Where we stopped, the Javanese would offer us fruit and much liquor was purchased; where we did not stop, we had to be content with friendly waves. A rumour spread through the train that some of the more enterprising had persuaded pretty little Javanese girls to make part of the journey with them. They would find relatives further up the line with whom they could stay until an opportunity of making their way home again presented itself.

As dusk fell and parched throats were refreshed, there was singing, and probably dancing too, in many of the wagons. By now those hanging out of the doorways were given warning of approaching *kampongs* by the lights of village fires.

Between nine and ten the look-outs announced that we must be approaching a fairly large settlement, as many fires could be seen through the trees skirting the winding track; then the full fury of the Japanese ambush was unleashed.

The engine was toppled over, either by a mine or by a large mortar shell. The driver and the firemen were killed outright and the boiler exploded. Most of the wagons were derailed; many were burning. The Japanese brought automatic fire to bear, but apparently from one side of the railway line only.

My wagon had escaped comparatively lightly. One man had been killed outright and one or two others had minor injuries.

I jumped down on the blind side of the train and ran along to the wagon at the rear where I knew the officer in command of the train was travelling. It was a long train and the last wagons, which were on a curve at the time of attack, were relatively unscathed.

I found the officer, who was muttering to himself: 'It must be a mistake; there can't be any Japanese here.' He quickly gave orders to other officers who were with him and they went off on their allotted tasks. Catching sight of me he said: 'I've got a job for you. You were in Malaya; you can speak Malay. For God's sake get to the bridge before the Dutch demolish it. Tell them what has happened and prevent them from blowing it up until I can get this lot over.'

By this time the Japanese had disappeared from the scene. Perhaps it was just a patrol which had learned in the village that a train was coming and had decided to lay an ambush. Perhaps the patrol was as ignorant as I was as to what means of retaliation, if any, there were on the train.

The commanding officer took out a map and showed me the bridge which appeared to span a large river. 'You can't get lost,' he added, 'you've only to follow the railway track.' I had no time to ask how far it was, nor to enquire at what time the train would have arrived there, if its journey had not be interrupted.

Avoiding the engine which was still belching forth scalding steam, I passed through the small village which was in complete darkness. The Japanese ambush party had clearly lit a number of fires to create the impression that their strength was greater than it was.

I set off, more resolutely than I felt, along the track. I suppose I had covered five or six miles when I came to quite a large station. There were lights, and people moving about. Having satisfied myself, as far as I could, that there were no Japanese around, I knocked on the door of a lighted office and walked in. The Javanese station-master looked up from the form he was filling in. I quickly told him what had happened. He nodded; he had been expecting the train.

I asked him whether there was an engine with steam up which could take me along the track to the bridge. He replied that there were serviceable engines but that the drivers and their mates would not be reporting for another couple of hours. He added that there was a hand-propelled railway trolley available and that he would try to get two men to come with me. He invited me to wait in his office.

While he was absent I wrote out, in as glowing terms as I could muster, a tribute to Abdullah bin Hassan's great contribution to the Allied war effort. I only hope he had the sense to destroy my testimonial before the Japanese overran his station.

He returned a few minutes later looking rather crestfallen. He had found only one man, not two; and, as the Dutch guards on the bridge were known to be very trigger-happy, the reluctant railwayman would only come with me as far as a halt on the line, about five miles short of the bridge.

I settled for this immediately, but I had not the heart to amend my testimonial, though a casual reader might well have concluded that he had furnished me with an express train, complete with dining-car and sleeper. In an attempt to restore some sort of a balance, I urged him to send the first available engine, together with half a dozen wagons, down the line to meet the party which had been ambushed. This he undertook to do.

My Javanese companion and I eventually worked out some sort
of a rhythm on the trolley-car. I soon learned what I had always
suspected, that, on such machines, output is not a direct function of
input. A small input plus much knack produces the optimum
output. I tried, without much success, to imitate the flexible grace
of his lithe, slim body. What an admirable bow he would have made,
I thought, in an Oxford Eight.

Ali Mohamed's local knowledge was invaluable. He knew when
we could afford to slacken off a bit—what moments of bliss for my
aching arms; and he knew too, when we had to give a little bit more
to get up the, to me imperceptible, inclines.

The moon was nearly full. As the track turned and twisted
through the jungle, we continually passed from pitch darkness to an
eerie brilliance, as though some hostile searchlight was playing upon
us. Occasionally, and mercifully, he suggested a brief stop for a
smoke and a chat. He told me he was twenty-two and unmarried;
he added quickly that he had a girl. I asked him where she lived.
He replied with a broad smile that she lived quite close to our
destination. I realised then why he did not want to waste valuable
courting time accompanying me as far as the bridge. He added that
they planned to get married soon. I wondered if they ever would.

We were now on the last lap. Another ten miles and he would
be in his girl's arms and I would be alone in the jungle. Perhaps
my clumsy efforts at propulsion had improved; perhaps there was
now more downhill; we covered those ten miles in a flash.

The Dutch captain who had listened carefully to my story offered
me a cigarette and another cup of coffee. He looked at his watch
and said: 'It is now seven o'clock. Your train was supposed to have
been over the bridge by half past five. My orders were to blow the
bridge not later than six-thirty. How long will it take for your chaps
to get here?'

'I have no idea,' I replied. 'I don't know whether the station-
master managed to get a train down to meet them. What's the form
here? Are there any Japs in this area?'

The Dutch Captain thought for a moment. 'I don't know where
the Japanese are; I don't believe anyone knows. All I know is that
the bridge should have been blown up at least an hour ago and it's
my duty to blow it up now.'

I watched him carefully. The dilemma tortured him. If he blew
the bridge then he would cut off the escape route of several hundred

key-men. He knew that the train had been destined for a south coast port and its passengers for Australia. As a Dutch army officer he would have to stay and take the consequences. Why should he, at the cost of disobeying orders, facilitate the flight of others? If, taking a wider view of the conflict, he decided to defer demolition for as long as possible, the bridge might be rushed by the Japanese, with I knew not what consequential disruptions of the Dutch defence plans.

I was not faced with any such conflict. My orders were clear: 'For God's sake . . . prevent them from blowing it up until I can get this lot over.'

The Captain pondered and then he suddenly said: 'I shall blow the bridge at eight o'clock. Come and have some breakfast.'

As we sat down to bacon and eggs, coffee and rolls in a nearby hut, a plan formed in my mind. I thought to myself: 'If I can prolong the breakfast, if I can keep him talking for an extra ten, or even five, minutes, that might help.'

We talked, or rather I talked. I told him about my experiences during the retreat down the Malayan peninsula; I told him about the fall of Singapore; I told him about my voyage from Singapore to Tandjong Priok, the port for what was then Batavia. He glanced nervously at his watch every two minutes or so; I realised I was on the wrong tack. I tried again. I told him that although I had travelled widely on the Continent, I had never been to Holland; and I asked him questions about his country. This was a far better approach and soon he was in full spate. I hoped that our breakfast might continue until eight-thirty.

It must have been a few minutes after eight when an orderly rushed in and said something to him in Dutch. He leaped up from his chair and raced across the few yards to his H.Q. I followed him. He picked up the telephone and exchanged a few words in Dutch with whoever was at the other end. He then went into an adjoining room and barked out orders to a junior officer and some N.C.O.s. All this took about thirty seconds. He then returned to his office and removing a canvas cover, forced down a plunger into a black box. There was a terrific explosion and I was flung on the floor, as he was too. We picked ourselves up; and then he spoke to me for the first time since we had left our breakfast.

'Thank God I was in time. One of my outposts on the other side of the river reported that the Japs were preparing for a surprise

B

attack. They had not fired a shot but were massing in the jungle to rush the bridge and take it intact.'

I felt relieved. I had done my best to delay the blowing of the bridge; and he had blown it just in time to deny it to the enemy.

We went outside. I was a little surprised that everything was so quiet. I dodged about from one bit of cover to another, expecting a fusillade of Japanese bullets from across the river. As I dashed for another tree, I stumbled and fell. I had tripped on half a human body in R.A.F. uniform. I vomited.

The events of the next few hours are even now confused in my memory. As I picked myself up from the ground I could see human flotsam and jetsam all around me. Some I recognised, or thought I did.

I never did learn the full story. I believe the seriously wounded were left in the village, near the ambush, with a number of medical orderlies who had gallantly volunteered to remain behind. I believe the station-master did get a train down the line, but, on the return journey, the engine-driver, convinced that the bridge had already been demolished, refused to go beyond the halt, near which Ali Mohamed was locked in the embraces of his girl. I believe it was thus but I do not know.

The stragglers crossed the twisted wreckage of the bridge in comparative safety during the next few hours.

I felt intense sympathy for the Dutch Captain when he realised what had happened. But none of it seemed to matter much. Within a few days all of us, including the Dutch Captain, were Japanese P.o.W.s. Perhaps those who were blown to pieces on the bridge and those who were killed outright in the ambush were better off, after all. Who could tell? At least they had died as free men.

1

'Shangri-La'

Western Java—March 1942*

There were about eight of us, all junior R.A.F. officers, staking our claims to a small bed-space on the concrete floor of the garage. One was J.F., who, like myself, had been a member of the Malayan Civil Service and had joined the R.A.F. in Singapore. I had met him once or twice during the preceding four years. I did not know him well. I was soon to get to know him very well, in somewhat unusual circumstances.

As I unfolded my blankets, I tried to unfold my thoughts. I tried to recall how I came to be in the garage at all. I suppose I must have been suffering from shock. The demolition of the bridge and the events leading up to it had been very real. The events of the succeeding days appeared to have no beginning and no end.

I stretched out in my corner and when the single bare electric light had been extinguished I began to recall certain incidents.

After the stragglers had made their way across what was left of the bridge there was considerable confusion. I remembered spending a night in a tobacco factory to which we had been taken in Dutch army lorries. There were many Dutch soldiers and other R.A.F. personnel there. No one seemed to be in control of the situation; and small groups would arrive, and leave, indiscriminately. It was like an amoebaean dance seen under a microscope.

The next day I found myself in one of a convoy of three lorries taking R.A.F. remnants to Poerwakerta, a town north of Tjilatjap. By now I had a raging fever. I had been bitten by a monkey in a jungle village about a week earlier and the swollen glands under my arms were giving me hell. I wondered what the quarantine period

* See map 1, page 316.

for rabies was. I must have been delirious for the next twenty-four hours or so.

Then the scene shifted. Now I was one of a large group in a jungle clearing. We were being addressed by a senior R.A.F. officer. He told us that the Dutch High Command in Java had surrendered to the Japanese and that we were now prisoners of war. We were to dump all our arms in a pile at the side of the clearing. Some of the regulars demurred at this, but he retorted sharply that it was an order. They reluctantly complied.

As my turn came to drop my revolver on the pile, I realised that I had never been taught to use it by the R.A.F. I had only fired it once. When the Japanese had ambushed the train I had loosed off a few rounds in the direction from which the Japanese automatic fire had come. My revolver had comforted me during the whole of the long month I had been in the R.A.F. I was sorry to see it go.

We had remained in the clearing all that day and at dusk Dutch army lorries had arrived. In these we were driven to a tea estate. The senior officers were billeted in the manager's house, the junior officers in the outbuildings, and the other ranks in the tea-factory. I had not yet seen a Japanese in Java.

When we woke up the next morning—I believe it was the 12th March 1942—we started to exchange our stories.

For me, the long road to the garage on the tea estate had started in Downing Street. In 1934 I had entered the Colonial Office as an Assistant Principal, the lowest form of administrative life in Whitehall. I was very happy in the Colonial Office but extremely frustrated. I was dealing with peoples, places and problems at second-hand. I might as well have been in a 'think-tank' at the bottom of the sea, connected with the surface by a pipe. Down the pipe would come problems and up the pipe would go my miniscule contributions to their solution.

After a couple of years I had applied for a transfer to what was then known as the Colonial Administrative Service. I had hoped to go to Palestine, to fill a vacancy caused by the assassination of a British officer by Arab terrorists; but a Financial Commissioner chose that moment to report that the finances of Palestine were in such a parlous state that all vacancies would have to be left unfilled for the time being. And so it was that I had transferred to the Malayan Civil Service at the end of 1937. After various postings in the Federated Malay States and Singapore, I had arrived in Cameron Highlands in 1940, as District Officer in charge of the District.

Cameron Highlands was the largest and highest hill station in Malaya. The settlement itself was 4,750 feet above sea-level. All around there were tree-covered peaks, the largest of which, Gunong Batu Brinchang, towered another 2,000 feet towards the heavens. The only access road came up from Tapah, a small town in the plains to the south-west. Tapah, in the State of Perak, was strategically situated on the main road and railway line from Singapore to the border with Siam, as it was then called.

Cameron Highlands itself was just inside the State of Pahang, the administrative capital of which was Kuala Lipis, away to the east on the other side of the main mountain range. There was no road between Kuala Lipis and the Highlands. My predecessors had made it a practice, at least once during their tenures of office, to make the three- or four-day trip by raft down a series of streams and rivers from the Highlands to Kuala Lipis. This involved enlisting the services of the aboriginal Sakai who eked out a primitive and precarious existence in the mountains. During the summer of 1941 I had begun to make plans for such a trip and I had sent out emissaries to make contact with the Sakai headmen. I never did raft down to Kuala Lipis.

The peculiar geographical position of Cameron Highlands brought with it certain complications. For some purposes I was answerable to the British Resident, Pahang, for others, including police and defence matters, I came under the British Resident, Perak, who resided in Taiping away to the north-west.

On arrival in Cameron Highlands, I had found myself responsible for a scheme whereby the District was to be built up as a reception centre. It was assumed that if and when the Japanese launched an attack on Malaya this would take the form of aerial and naval bombardments of Singapore and the other principal towns of Malaya. We were to make ready to receive large numbers of refugees from these centres of population. Schools, hotels, and even private householders, had been encouraged to build up large reserves of food and other necessities. Plans were made, too, for an emergency hospital and substantial stocks of medical supplies were being accumulated. The Service authorities in Singapore, who had been discussing for some time past the construction of a large convalescent hospital in the Highlands, had at last reached a decision and work had started on this during the summer of 1941.

During that summer, Felix Ingold, the Swiss manager of the Cameron Highlands Hotel, had gone to Singapore to buy up the greater part of the cellars of the French liner the *Ile de France*, which was being converted into a troopship.

The telephone rang about six-thirty in the morning of Monday the 8th December 1941. It was Hugh Bloxham. Bloxham was to be a source of great strength to me during the following fortnight, as indeed he had been during the whole of my time at Cameron Highlands. He had been a regular soldier in his earlier days and then he had joined the Prison Service in Hong Kong. On his retirement he had built stables at Tanah Rata, on the road down to Tapah. There he kept his own, and other people's, horses. He was most public-spirited and could be relied upon to handle with great competence everything he undertook to do. At that time he was, among other things, the commander of the Highlands detachment of the Local Defence Corps.

He told me briefly of the raid on Pearl Harbour and of the Japanese landings on the beaches near Kota Bharu, a town on the east coast, in the State of Kelantan near the Siamese border. I invited him to join me at breakfast. We had much to discuss and to do.

While we were breakfasting, the telephone rang again. It was J. R. Neave, the Acting British Resident, Perak.

'You've heard the news, I suppose?' he said.

When I confirmed that I had, he went on crisply and to the point:

'You will now do two things. You will ensure that the Police and L.D.C. round up all the Japanese in your District. And you will bring into immediate operation the Air Raid Precautions plan. I will communicate with you again as soon as may be necessary.'

I had always liked and admired Neave, who had won an M.C. in World War I. In 1938 I had been his assistant at Klang, where he had been conspicuously successful in making all the arrangements for the state funeral of the old Sultan of Selangor and for the coronation of his successor. I knew I could count on him to give me clear and precise instructions, to the extent that the confusion in higher places would permit this.

My immediate compliance with his instructions made no contribution whatever to the war effort. We had had a number of

Japanese residents in the District. There were one or two photo-graphers and several vegetable gardeners; at least that is what they were supposed to be. When the Police went to round them up they were not there. All except a couple of aged crones had slipped away individually during the preceding week. In an outhouse belonging to one of the vegetable gardeners the Police found a lot of photographic equipment in a dark room and a large number of photographs of signposts, of cross-roads and of the approaches to the District Office.

We had an Air Raid Precautions scheme of which, indeed, I was the Director. But our generating station produced such a feeble flow of current that most people in the Highlands went to bed at the same time as the three or four hundred European children in the two boarding schools. In any event, a pilot who flew over the central mountain range by night at an altitude which would permit him to see our flickering candles and oil-lamps was far more likely to crash into one of the towering peaks than to pin-point our settlement. And had we not been assured that, as the Japanese did not eat enough carrots, they all suffered from night blindness and could never undertake bombing raids by night? Nevertheless my hard-working staff spent many hours, which could more profitably have been devoted to sleep, pounding round the District on their A.R.P. duties.*

In my mountain eyrie I felt very cut off from the momentous events going on all around me. I had no means of knowing what the true state of affairs was. Like others, I was mainly dependent on the wireless for news; and that was bad enough. Late in the evening of Wednesday the 10th December we heard that *Prince of Wales* and *Repulse* had been sunk. By the end of the first week European refugees were arriving from Kedah, Perlis and Northern Perak, and wealthy Chinese were flooding into the Highlands from all parts of the peninsula. At about the same time the Service authorities in Singapore must have decided to step up work on the Service conva-lescent hospital; 300 Bengali labourers arrived with masses of building equipment.

* It was not until November 1947 that I was able to certify that my admirable Malay Health Inspector, Abdul Majïd bin Lassim, had performed his duties as Deputy Divisional A.R.P. Warden to my entire satisfaction, and that he should be paid for these services in accordance with the prescribed rates. As I signed this certificate, I was glad to reflect that Abdul Majïd had survived the cataclysm with his strength as unimpaired as that of Financial Regulations.

It could only have been a matter of hours later that someone, somewhere, had taken the first of two decisions in an exactly opposite sense. The second was to be taken about ten days later.

It was, I believe, on Tuesday the 16th December that I received a second message from the British Residency, Perak. Neave did not speak to me personally on this occasion; it was one of his assistants. The message was to the effect that the reception centre egg was to be unscrambled immediately. This meant that our large stocks of food, medical and other stores were to be dispersed. The message added that all who could possibly leave Cameron Highlands were to be persuaded, and assisted, to do so and to proceed further south. The implications were clear; despite the encouraging tone of the official communiqués which were still being broadcast, some, at least, in high places realised that it was only a matter of time before Tapah and, therefore, the Cameron Highlands were overrun by the Japanese.

One day a party of military officers arrived at the District Office on another mission. There was every reason to believe, they told me, that the Japanese were planning to drop parachute troops on the golf-course. This must be prevented at all costs, they added. I took them out to inspect the course. It had been one of my duties as District Officer to maintain this from public funds. It was in magnificent condition, ready for the normal Christmas invasion. It was one of the great attractions for visitors to the Highlands. In happier times, I had played there almost daily. As the officers discussed the technicalities of our task, I recalled in particular the many games I had played there with J.B. He was a prominent figure in the banking world of Singapore. In his youth he had played golf for Scotland. Sympathetically tutored by him, I had reduced my handicap to quite a respectable single figure. J.B. had given me much sound advice about improvements to the course, and he was very close to me as its destruction was planned.*

With heaviness in my heart, and a notebook in my hand, I

* Like all of us, J.B. could have had no conception of how the war would affect his life. I believe his wife was drowned in one of the last ships to leave Singapore. He was interned. When he returned to Scotland in 1945 he needed clothes, which were very hard to come by. I gather that he answered an advertisement in the 'Personal' column of *The Times*. This advertisement had been inserted by a widow whose husband had been killed in an air raid. She wished to dispose of her husband's extensive wardrobe and the measurements were the same as those of J.B. J.B. called upon the lady, bought the clothes and in due course married her.

walked round the course with my visitors, as they sited the various obstructions which they deemed necessary.

For the next week I and my small hard-working staff were occupied twenty hours a day on these various tasks. Oil-drums and stakes were dotted all over the golf-course; lorries and vans were despatched with enormous loads of food and medical supplies to Kuala Lumpur; perishables such as rice were sold to local merchants; and the temporary hospital, which had been established at the Rest House barely a week earlier, was dismantled.*

At this time all those whose presence in the District was not essential to the continuation of a more or less orderly administration were urged to make their own arrangements to leave or to avail themselves, with one suitcase apiece, of the transport offered in the chartered, and far from comfortable, local buses.

It was Nature, and not man, who then rebelled. The road from Tapah had never had such a pounding. Lorries, buses and cars were going down with European women and children, and stores; lorries, buses and cars were coming up with material for the Service convalescent hospital, with rice for the Bengali coolies and for the wealthy Chinese refugees, whose large American cars never ceased to invade the District. My Sisyphean task was never-ending; as soon as I got someone or something away, someone or something arrived. It was then that Nature decided to protest at this confusion in high places. If those who should have taken clear-cut decisions would not, Nature would. With a rumble that could be heard for a considerable distance, a serious landslip occurred at the twenty-ninth mile which looked like putting an end to these unco-ordinated movements once and for all.

Again I was summoned to the telephone to take another message from the Perak Resident's Office.

'Hallo! old boy, how's it going at your end?' the anonymous voice enquired; and then added before I had a chance to reply: 'It's getting rather grim here.'

This masterly understatement was punctuated by what seemed to be the sound of automatic weapons. A temporary lull permitted the drawling voice of my imperturbable caller to resume.

'You know, these Nips are bloody awful when they're sober, but

* The credit for the rapid establishment of this excellent emergency hospital must be attributed to the professional skill and energy of the District Medical Officer, Dr. Molesworth, who subsequently, I believe, became one of the world's experts in the treatment of leprosy.

they're real buggers when they're tight. We've heard a lot of nasty tales from people who've come down from the North.'

After another extraneous interruption the voice continued: 'I believe you've got quite a lot of liquor up at C.H. You'll have to knock all that off before you leave; and you'd better get cracking on it now.'

Cursing Felix Ingold and his purchase, at knock-down prices, of the wines and spirits of the *Ile de France*, I wished my caller the best of luck and returned to my chores, to which another task had now been added.

For forty-eight hours we used all our available transport to collect the liquor. In addition to the very large stocks held by the three hotels, every private house, whether owned by a rubber planter, a tin miner or a business tycoon seemed to have almost limitless supplies.

The siting of the funeral pyre presented a number of problems. It had to be accessible by road so that the lorries could back on to the site and deliver their loads with the minimum of manhandling. It had to be in an area where there was no risk that the ensuing blaze would set fire to neighbouring dwellings. It also occurred to me that if a controlled (or so I hoped) bonfire of this magnitude could be sited so that the large numbers of children at the schools in Cameron Highlands, who needed a little cheering up anyhow, could witness it in safety, so much the better.

Not for the first time, nor the last, I found the Reverend Mother Superior of the Pensionnat de Notre Dame most receptive and sympathetic. I explained my problem and enquired whether I might use the ravine at the side of the Convent for this destructive act. I pointed out the many advantages of the site. As the wooden crates and bottles were tipped into the ravine, there was every prospect that they would break; and we had no man-power available to perform the preliminary part of the ritual. Again, 300 children in her care would be well placed to witness the blaze in perfect safety. Finally, perhaps she might be, and she was, willing to invite the children from the other school, Tanglin, to witness this unusual display.

Whether the pained expression which flickered across her otherwise radiant countenance was indicative of her revulsion at such a wanton waste of God's gifts I shall never know, but I recalled that on happier occasions she had always offered me a glass of wine and had sometimes partaken modestly herself.

The night chosen for the sacrifice was the night before all the chool-children would be leaving the hill.

At seven o'clock I stepped to the edge of the ravine and flung in a blazing brand from each hand. The roaring flame which leapt towards me drowned the acclamation of the audience and for some time to come I went about my business with substantially diminished eyebrows.

The following morning I went to see the Convent children off to a future which I could not predict but which did not seem to trouble them. At the last moment the Reverend Mother Superior and her second-in-command, Sister Sainte Rosalie, refused to leave.

'There will be much for us to do here when the Japanese arrive,' the Reverend Mother observed quietly.

The buses and escort were waiting, the children were impatient.

'I beg you to leave, Reverend Mother,' I replied, and added: 'These children will need you.'

She looked me straight in the eyes and murmured: 'These children have their parents. When you have gone, as go you must, I know, what parent will the people of this District have?'

I felt very small, but I had to persist and eventually the secular overcame the clerical.

As I waved the Reverend Mother and Sister Sainte Rosalie good-bye I thought to myself: 'I bet they'll come back, if they can.'*

Within another day or so all had been done that could be done; and I awaited the telephone call that I knew would come. It came very early in the morning of Tuesday the 23rd December. Neave himself instructed me to evacuate the District, to take all account books, important records and cash and deliver them to the authorities in Kuala Lumpur. All in Government service, irrespective of rank or race, were to be offered transport to Kuala Lumpur for themselves and their families. Those who elected to stay were to be paid up to date. The few remaining unofficials were to be warned that this was their last chance to leave.

* In February 1947 I received a letter from the Pre-Occupations Claims Officer in Kuala Lumpur with a query about payment for the large stocks of food taken over from the Convent and sent to Kuala Lumpur. An attached copy of a letter signed by Sister Sainte Rosalie, for the Reverend Mother, contained the following words: 'Three months later when Malaya was occupied, Reverend Mother, a few Sisters and myself returned to Cameron Highlands but no provisions were left, not even a tin of milk. We set to work at once to cultivate the ground and managed as best we could.'

Neave added ominously: 'Be careful at Tapah. Scouting parties of Japanese may well be in the neighbourhood by seven o'clock tomorrow morning.'

Tomorrow, I thought, would be Christmas Eve.

I had no idea from where he was speaking. I was never to hear his voice again. I was subsequently told in Singapore that he had been shot by the Japanese during their advance through Perak.

Many of the final party left for Tapah independently during the succeeding hours of daylight. Those who had to stay until the last minute still had some final tasks to perform. We blew up the Police Station, the telephone exchange and such transport as we did not require. We left the generating station for the benefit of the wealthy Chinese and those who had elected to stay behind. As the engineer-in-charge had disappeared without authority during the previous night, the generating plant would soon grind to a halt.

I left in the final convoy about midnight. We made two stops on the way down: one to release Bloxham's horses from their stables in Tanah Rata; and one to pick up the Ringlet Postmaster and his cash. We had mattresses strapped on our vehicles. We had been warned that the Japanese were continuously bombing and strafing the main road from Tapah to Kuala Lumpur.

Our greatest hazards on the way down the mountain road were the enormous lorries, many with trailers, still bringing up building materials for the Service convalescent hospital. I had tried, in vain, during the past ten days to get those in charge of this operation to cancel it. But Service mills grind slowly and it looked as though the work would go on long after the District had been officially evacuated.

As we passed through Tapah we heard sporadic firing in the distance, but we were not troubled. The road to Kuala Lumpur was choked with military and civilian traffic and progress was slow.

We were bombed and strafed from time to time but suffered no casualties or material damage.

The handing over, during an air raid, to the authorities in Kuala Lumpur of my books, records and cash marked the end of an insignificant chapter in the history of British colonial administration.

Time hung heavily on our hands in the garage. Service discipline required that one of us should be Duty Officer of the day, but as I left the camp before my turn came round, I never did discover what this involved.

The Duty Officer was our only contact with the world outside. We were strictly enjoined not to leave the garage unless we had a good reason to consult one of the senior officers in the nearby manager's house.

Gradually the rumours filtered in. An agreement had been reached between our Commanding Officer and the Japanese whereby we would administer ourselves; and the latter would confine themselves to guarding the perimeter of the tea estate. This agreement was to last for the duration of hostilities. Those who had seen something of the estate, painted a picture of Shangri-La. There were swimming pools, or at least a swimming pool. There was an open space which could easily be turned into a football pitch. There were shady paths, running between the tea plantations, which led up to little hills which afforded magnificent views of the surrounding countryside. Someone was already engaging in preparing the layout of a golf-course. Another, more enterprising, was said to be having preliminary conversations with the Japanese about a scheme whereby a number of carefully selected young Javanese girls would take up residence in a sort of summer-house on the estate. Some credence was unwarrantably lent to this latter tale by the fact that a view of what purported to be the roof of the summer-house, nestling among the trees, could be obtained by standing on tiptoe on a packing case in the garage and peering through a skylight.

As a result of these fanciful rumours, morale went up considerably. When would it all start? Why was no one getting cracking? A confined space certainly distorts one's powers of judgement.

A day or two later the Duty Officer returned with another piece of 'gen' which, to some of us at least, seemed a little more plausible.

'Listen, chaps,' he said. 'The old man has asked me to pass on a message.'

We all stopped doing nothing to listen.

He went on: 'The old man wants it known, but not talked about too much, that, before the Nips got us, a series of caches were buried in various parts of the island. He didn't say what was in them but I suppose it must be maps, weapons and food. If any of you chaps want to have a go, you'll have to see him.'

The Duty Officer paused, gratified at the effect his words were having on his audience.

He continued: 'But there are one or two other things he told me to tell you. He's got a helluva lot on his plate at the moment,

and the Nips are being bloody difficult. He hasn't time to listen to
a lot of crack-pot ideas; and he's only interested in chaps who can
speak Malay and who have been in this bloody awful part of the
world long enough to have become accustomed and acclimatised
to it.'

The spokesman for the C.O. was himself a gallant young pilot
who had won the D.F.C. in the Battle of Britain. He had come out to
Singapore about a month before the Japanese attacked; and his
ancient Buffalo had been blasted out of the sky by the first Japanese
Navy Zero he had encountered. No wonder he referred to the
'bloody awful part of the world'; quite clearly he could not himself
meet the C.O.'s qualifications.

I caught J.F.'s eye and soon we had a chance of a whispered
talk. We didn't for one minute believe all the bally-hoo about
Shangri-La. We had both seen and heard enough during the Malayan campaign to know that the unreal world of fantasy in which we
had been living for the last two or three days would soon be shattered
when it suited the Japanese to shatter it. As it was getting late, we
agreed to sleep on it and to beard the C.O. next morning, the 16th
March.

I did not sleep much that night. I turned it all over, over and
over again, in my mind. Did we have a chance? Even if we got to
the south coast, how could we ever get to Australia or Ceylon?
Would we be shot, or worse, if we were caught? And what would
happen if we just stayed where we were? I reached no conclusions,
but when morning came we were both determined to go.

We went to see the C.O. at 8 a.m. I don't think either of us had
ever seen him before; certainly he had never seen us. He was
already beginning to acquire that look which was to be stamped
indelibly on the faces of all those who had the misfortune to be the
senior officer in any Japanese P.o.W. camp. They carried an immense responsibility; they were faced with appalling decisions; they
took the brunt of Japanese fury; they were constantly beaten and
degraded; and behind them was a horde of fellow-prisoners, criti-
cising their every act. Whatever they did was wrong; if one stood up
to the Japanese authorities, the latter were capable of taking ten
men at random and torturing them or putting them in solitary
confinement without food or water, until the senior officer bowed
to their will. If, which was very rare, another showed signs of
weakness and permitted intolerable conditions to go unchallenged,
then his fellow-prisoners, ignoring the burdens he had to bear,

would taunt him, usually behind his back, with cowardice. All this lay in the future, but even then the pattern of that future was beginning to unfold.

J.F. and I introduced ourselves and told him that we thought we might meet his requirements. He listened carefully and asked a few questions. Then he said:

'The decision to go must be yours; and you must think very carefully about this before taking such a decision. It is the duty of every officer to try to escape; and, in theory at any rate, I cannot prevent you. In practice I have a veto. You wouldn't get anywhere, and you know it, having regard to the bloody mess we're in, unless I give you all the information I have about the caches. I am the only one here who knows this information and I am the only one here who cannot contemplate escaping because I am responsible for every man in this camp.'

He paused, and offered us cigarettes, lighting one for himself. 'I must tell you frankly that I don't think you can possibly make it. The very fact that we are all here indicates that the Nips have made much more rapid progress in their conquest of the island than ever we thought possible. By now they will be all along the south coast, and certainly in Tjilatjap and Jogjakarta.'

He paused for a moment, drawing on his cigarette, and then added: 'On the other hand there are a few pluses. The Japanese don't know how many of us there are here. I don't bloody well know myself. There has not been time for me to collect or, for them to demand, nominal rolls. This means that if you go now and are recaptured you can play stupid boys. You can deny that you have ever been in Japanese hands and they can never prove otherwise. Moreover, there are, I know, fairly large groups of Allied forces, with special tasks to perform, at large in the jungle and you might run into one of those. Some of them have radio transmitters and you might be able to whistle up a submarine. The nearest cache is not too far from here and God knows how long these bloody Nips will leave us in this tea estate. They are quite unpredictable. They might well move us tomorrow.'

Again he paused and there was a long silence. An orderly came in and reported that two of the wounded had died in the night. After the orderly had left the C.O. went on:

'Another thing, you should not find it too difficult, now, to get outside the perimeter. They can't spare many men as guards at the moment.'

I looked at J.F., but before I could get a reaction, the C.O. was off again:

'It will be a risky business. If a Nip patrol catches you, they may not bother to ask questions. You may not get out of this alive. But, then, how many of us who stay here will?'

Before we had time to say anything he dismissed us, saying: 'Go away and sleep on it, and come back and see me tomorrow morning. I am prepared to give you all the help and information I can. And I won't think any the worse of you if you decide not to go. I have many decisions to take, but thank God this is not one of them.'

We returned to the garage. Without saying a word to each other, we started to put a few belongings together as though the decision had already been taken. Perhaps it had been. We then decided we would disobey orders and go for a walk. We needed some air, and we thought we had better have a look at what we were escaping from, even though we could have no idea of what we were escaping to. We studiously avoided any talk about what was uppermost in our minds.

J.F. must have been about six or seven years older than I was, which would have put him then at thirty-six or thirty-seven. He had joined the Malayan Civil Service in, I believe, 1929, and had spent most of his service in the district administration. He spoke Malay fluently, far better than I did.

He was an extremely handsome bachelor of medium build. A well-shaped head, crowned with wavy hair, prematurely turning grey, framed a strong bronzed face, the most prominent feature of which were his deep-set dark brown eyes. An immaculately trimmed grey moustache completed a physiognomy of which a successful film star might well have been proud.

By disposition he was quiet, and somewhat introspective; outwardly he took a gay, if somewhat cynical, view of life, which he appeared to enjoy to the full. A slightly supercilious smile was rarely absent from his lips.

In his youth he had hurdled for Ireland. In this pursuit he had seriously damaged a knee which had been operated upon a number of times. This was to lead us to the brink of disaster later.

What paths had led him to captivity in the tea estate I did not know. He had not been with the party which was ambushed in the train, nor had he been involved in the incident at the bridge.

He had joined the R.A.F. in Singapore in much the same

circumstances and at much the same time as I had. It was quite fortuitous that he had been commissioned about a week before I was. I told him what had happened.

My medical examination had been held at the main R.A.F. airfield at Seletar. The Japanese were bombing the area at the time. At the crucial moment, when I was stark naked and when the medical officer was about to say 'Cough, please', we heard the whine of a bomb which appeared to be unpleasantly close. We both dived under tables as the bomb fell. When we had picked ourselves up from the rubble I found that all my clothes had disappeared. The medical officer found that a similar fate had befallen the records of his examination to date, and the samples of urine and blood which he had taken for analysis. Indeed, all his equipment had vanished out of the gaping hole in the wall. 'Sorry, old man,' he said, 'I am afraid we shall have to start all over again in a quieter spot. I'll get my chaps to fix up another appointment.'

About a week later I was summoned to report for another medical examination, appropriately enough in a lunatic asylum.

Now J.F. and I were approaching the summer-house, the roof of which we had seen from the garage skylight. We peeped in. It was like a Chinese summer palace, beautifully built and decorated. We supposed that it had been constructed by some wealthy tea-planter for entertaining. There was a large central hall for receptions or dancing and a considerable number of alcoves behind, opening out on to a wide verandah. We imagined the soft lights, heavy brocaded curtains and dozens of pretty Javanese girls which must have been taking shape in the mind of the entrepreneur, alleged to be engaged in his preliminary conversations with the Japanese authorities.

But however hard we imagined, we could not see it ever happening.

As we left, I touched J.F. on the arm: 'That might be useful,' I said, pointing to a short driveway which appeared to lead to a gate in the perimeter fence which itself opened on to a road.

He nodded. 'We might go that way,' he observed quietly.

We returned to the garage; we did not want to miss our only daily meal.

Once again I did not sleep. My mind was full of clichés: 'Out of the frying pan and into the fire.' The frying pan was not too bad; but how durable was it? 'Better the devil you know than the devil you don't.' But we didn't know the devil—yet.

By next morning I had, I thought, firmly made my mind up not to go. It was all so damned silly. I didn't think we had a chance in hell; hadn't the C.O. himself said so? Even if we did get through, what good would it do anyone? I was not the repository of secret information which would be of great value to the Allied war effort, if only it could be conveyed to the right quarters.

I hoped against hope that J.F. had reached the same conclusion. In fact he had, but neither of us disclosed our hands until it was far too late to turn back—even if we could ever have found the way!

At the appointed hour we called on the C.O. again. After two sleepless nights I didn't feel at all adventurous. My one idea was to curl up in my corner in the garage and sleep indefinitely, which, in the twilight world in which we lived, would have been both possible and permissible. As we entered the cubby-hole which served as his office, my cliché-ridden nightmare returned and all I could think of were the words: 'There is a destiny which shapes our ends...'

We both saluted smartly and, on invitation, sat down on two tea-chests. The C.O. looked at us across the table and said:

'Well, have you made up your minds? I suppose you're going.'

We both nodded, more from lack of sleep than anything else; and then, recalling the circumstances, we added briskly: 'Yes, sir.'

'I am glad,' he said, 'because there's one thing I forgot to mention yesterday. I have some information which I want you to pass on to the proper quarters, if and when you get through. I shan't give you anything in writing but I want you to listen carefully.'

He then gave us a résumé of the situation as it had developed during the days and hours leading up to the Dutch capitulation in Java, stressing certain important facts. He mentioned in particular that while, as I was well aware, the authorities in Malaya had applied a rigorous scorched-earth policy to deny resources and facilities to the invading Japanese, no such policy had been followed in Java, where everything had dropped into their hands like ripe plums.

We listened attentively to all he had to say and made mental notes of the matters to which he attached particular importance. He then enquired: 'When do you propose to leave?'

The previous day, the 16th March, J.F. and I had discussed this, so it came as no surprise to me when J.F. replied: 'Well, sir, today is St. Patrick's Day and as an Irishman I think that would be a good day to start. We thought of leaving at dusk tonight.'

'Very well,' the C.O. replied. 'I think you had better leave me now. I have many things to do. Come back about two o'clock and I will give you details of the caches and other information.' We left.

As I lay on my blankets, in the garage, I pondered on the information the C.O. had given us. On reflection, that information did not seem to me to be particularly important; and, in any event, I felt sure that most of it had already reached Australia, either through the selected few who were flown out at the last moment or by radio. Again, the C.O. was not the sort of man who forgot things. Why had he made no reference to this at our first interview the day before? Was it because he did not want to influence our decision which, as he had made clear, over and over again, was ours and ours alone?

Another possibility was taking shape in my mind. Perhaps, I thought, he had waited for our decision; and then, when he had learnt that we had decided to go, he wished to strengthen our resolve to get through by entrusting us with a mission. He was a wise man, the C.O.

At two o'clock we went back again to see him. He had clearly had a harassing morning.

'The bloody Nips have just left. They are an impossible people,' he said. Then he got down to business.

He had in front of him two copies of maps of the western half of Java. On both were marked the sites of the caches; on the reverse side of the one which he gave us someone had written, in a legible hand, details of the exact position of the caches, with compass bearings and references to large trees, rocks, streams and other identifiable physical features. We went through these with him in some detail. He pointed out the best road to the first cache which was in the foothills of Gunong Sawal, about thirty miles away to the east.

'In each of these caches,' he said, 'you will find more detailed maps, compasses, food, knives, revolvers, and so on.' He added: 'Be careful not to take more than you need. Before leaving, make sure that you have carefully replaced the earth, leaves and twigs. Others may have need of these things.'

'Is there a chance, sir, of getting transport for the first leg?' I asked.

'There are several Dutch cars on the estate,' he observed, 'and I will arrange for you to have one of these. When you have found the first cache, tip the car over a ravine if you can, or at least hide it in the undergrowth and make it unserviceable.'

He paused and lit a cigarette. 'Have you given any thought to how you are going to leave the perimeter?' he enquired.

I mentioned the driveway we had noticed near the Chinese summer palace.

'How do you know about that?' he retorted sharply. 'You know I have given orders that only those with specific duties outside are allowed to leave their billets.'

Shamefacedly we told him of our stroll in the woods the previous day. He let it pass and went on: 'Well, that's not a bad idea. I'll tell you what I'll do.'

He then explained that from time to time he had to send officers by car down the driveway with messages for the Japanese headquarters which were just outside the main gate. These cars always carried a large white sheet strapped over the bonnet. He would arrange for a white sheet to be on the car which he was to provide for our getaway. He would give us a message, of no great moment, for Captain Yamada. If we were stopped in the vicinity of the estate we were to ask for Captain Yamada, indicating that we had lost our way in the maze of roads and tracks which criss-crossed the estate. If we got away unchallenged we were to take an early opportunity of burying the sheet and destroying the message.

The C.O. then added: 'If you are caught after you have buried the sheet, and if you are brought back here, I do not know you and you do not know me. You have never been here before. There'd be hell to pay if the Nips thought you had escaped from here.'

He then wrote out a message for Captain Yamada and gave it to J.F. 'By the way,' he added, 'I'd better have a note of your next of kin. Are you both married?' J.F. replied that he was a bachelor and he gave the name of his sister who had, I think, been evacuated to Australia. I replied that I was married and that I had put L. on the S.S. *Afridi*, one of the last ships to leave for India just before the port of Singapore was closed to civilian transport. I had no idea whether she was alive. It was seven weeks since we had said good-bye. Ugly rumours had been circulating in Java about the bombing and torpedoing of the last ships to leave Singapore. I had spoken to one Dutchman who had come to Java from Sumatra. He had told me about the party of nurses who had been evacuated from Singapore. When their ship was sunk in the Straits of Malacca they had made their way in open boats to the coast of Sumatra. There they had been raped by the Japanese and then bayoneted to death. I gave the C.O. the address of my brother-in-law who was in the Indian Civil Service in the Punjab.

By now it was about half past three. The C.O. promised to send the car round to the garage at seven o'clock. I picked up the map. It had been agreed that it would be better if this was not found in J.F.'s possession as he had the message for Captain Yamada.

'If you run into trouble, destroy the map. That chain of caches may yet save other lives,' the C.O. repeated. He then wished us good luck and we left his office. I never saw him again.

2

Escapade

*Western Java—March 1942**

'I have always wanted to do that,' I said, as we peered through the darkness at the car crashing through the undergrowth towards the bottom of the ravine. Suddenly it was stopped by a large tree. We could hear the wheels spinning. Presumably it was upside down. We had hoped that it would have passed out of our sight, but we could still just make out its silhouette.

'Well, we'll have to leave it at that, anyway,' J.F. replied.

It had all seemed so easy. We had had no difficulty in passing through the gate by the Chinese summer palace. We had carefully studied the map before leaving the garage; and we had chosen a track which enabled us to give the Japanese at the main gate a wide berth. The track was sufficiently close to the entrance to the estate to have lent credence to our story that we had a message for Yamada, had we been stopped.

We were soon bowling along the road in the direction of the first cache. In a dark patch of jungle we buried the sheet and destroyed the note. We passed through several villages but saw few lights. The car made such a noise that we could not hear the barking of the village dogs; but we could see their eyes reflected in our headlights and their evil, snarling muzzles.

We were now approaching a cross-roads where we had to take a turn to the right down a narrow track which should lead us into the foothills of Mount Sawal. I was driving and J.F. had his torch ready to flash on to the signpost. Suddenly there was a severe jolt.

'I must have run over a dog,' I said. I stopped the car.

*See map 1, page 316.

We could hear no whimpering. J.F. flashed his torch out of the rear window.

'Whatever it is, it's a bloody sight bigger than a dog,' he replied.

We got out of the car and walked towards the huddled form in the road. It was the body of a young Dutch soldier who had been severely wounded. He had clearly been dead for some time. The traces of dried blood on the roadside showed how he had crawled out of the jungle to die; the same jungle that we were about to enter in an attempt to live. We could do no more than lay his body gently in a ditch and make a note of the name and number on his identification disc.

This reminder that our world was still at war, a fact from which we had been shielded in our 'Shangri-La' for nearly a week, shook us a bit. We were silent as we turned off the main road towards the mountain.

J.F. was studying the map and trying to identify such natural phenomena as he could see through the darkness. Suddenly, as we were crossing another track, he said: 'I think we'd better stop here and take stock.'

I pulled up. We got out. The night was clear and, as our eyes became accustomed to the darkness, we were able to relate our surroundings to the map.

'That's Gunong Sawal. Bang in front of us and just where it ought to be,' J.F. said.

We could see the outline of the top of Mount Sawal, nearly 6,000 feet above sea-level. It stood between us and· our ultimate goal, the south coast.

'And that must be Gunong Malabar,' I replied, pointing away to the west, to our right. We could just make out the peak of Mount Malabar in the distance, towering 8,000 feet into the darkness.

Between the two peaks ran the railway line and main road from Bandoeng to Tjilatjap and Jogjakarta. At some stage we would have to cross these two hazards, probably near Tjiamis where they both turned to the east, having completed their north to south passage between the peaks. At that moment Tjiamis was also 'bang in front of us', but separated from us by the great mass of Mount Sawal.

As I studied the map, I recalled my delirious night at Poerwakerta about ten days earlier. I was only about thirty to forty miles by road from Tjilatjap then. What a lot of ground we still had to cover, I thought. As if answering my unspoken question, J.F. interpolated:

'It must be more than a hundred miles to Tjilatjap from here, as the crow flies. But with all these bloody mountains around, it'll probably be nearer two hundred, perhaps more.'

We then concentrated on finding the first cache. It looked as though we had only another mile or two to go. Now our objective was a large tree at the side of a stream to our left. Our track was due to carry us over the stream on a wooden bridge.

We started off again very slowly. We didn't see the bridge, but as the wooden planks clattered beneath us, we both turned our heads to the left and saw the stream and the tree. We stopped and I manœuvred the car so that the headlights pointed towards the tree.

As I switched the engine off I heard an aircraft in the distance. I dowsed the lights immediately and we waited for about a quarter of an hour. When the aircraft had passed I switched on the lights again and we made our way to the tree.

We had brought a spade and a pick with us to be dumped with the car. We knew the instructions for the first cache by heart and with a quick look at the compass with which the C.O. had provided us, we started pacing off; twelve to the south and six to the east, from the base of the tree. By then we were just inside the light undergrowth.

A few jabs with the pick evoked a metallic ring. We soon had the lid of a large metal box uncovered. Inside we found almost everything we had hoped for: tinned food, matches, knives, maps, torches and a little solid-fuel stove. There were also two Sten guns, several revolvers and a number of other items. We made our selection.

We each took a revolver, a knife and a torch. We left the Sten guns as we had to travel light; and neither of us understood how they worked. We took as much tinned food as we could stuff into our packs; we also took the solid-fuel stove, one map, and a packet of first-aid dressings.

We were disappointed to find no boots. We were wearing the black leather shoes which formed part of our R.A.F. tropical uniforms; these were more appropriate for dancing than for ploughing through the jungle.

We closed the box and, we hoped, removed all traces of our pilfering.

Our success in finding the first cache so easily had put us in good spirits. We still had to find a place to dump the car, but, before coping with this problem, we decided to drink a toast to St. Patrick.

I turned off the lights of the car and stacked our stores on the back seat, while J.F. broached a bottle of whisky he had brought with him to the tea estate.

As we sat smoking and drinking on a heap of stones near the car, life looked good. We were free men again; and we were now equipped for at least the first part of our journey. It was a glorious tropical night; there was not a cloud in the sky. I regretted that my education had not included a study of the stars. I tried to identify the Southern Cross which, I felt sure, should be visible. J.F. was as ignorant about the heavens as I was.

We were enjoying our freedom and were in no hurry to move.

As we had approached the site of the cache, we had seen no signs of a suitable place in which to dispose of the car. We decided to continue along the track, towards the mountain. We hoped that something would turn up. We must have covered about seven miles before we came to the ravine where we decided to dump our vehicle.

As we left the scene, our impedimenta weighed heavily on our backs and shoulders. Our plan was to go up the mountain and skirt round its western flank at a fairly high level. There would, we thought, be less risk of discovery; but, more important still, we should have access to unpolluted water.

We started to climb, along a path which turned off the track. By now we were really in the jungle and the noises of the night began to play upon our nerves. The path led to a little hut, made of bamboos, with an *attap* roof and sides. We decided to spend our first night there. I suppose it must have been a wood-cutter's shelter.

We had had a meal before we left the tea estate and we were not hungry; but we decided to brew up some tea on the solid fuel stove. We then had a discussion as to whether we should take it in turns to sleep or whether we could both safely sleep at the same time. We seemed to be so remote from any signs of life and we were both so tired that we settled for the latter. We had two blankets and a rain cape apiece. We were making ourselves as comfortable as we could when we saw them. Our legs and arms were covered with leeches. We had to strip and burn them off each other with lighted cigarettes.

Eventually we settled down for what was left of the night. The jungle teemed with living things, unseen but not unheard. Some screeched, some grunted, some purred and some just moved. Why had I ever left the garage, where the snores of my companions had reassured me during sleepless hours?

The sun was up when we woke. We were stiff and it was much colder than I had expected. The surrounding jungle looked quite friendly as the sun's rays peeped through. We made some coffee and opened a tin of bully beef. I retired for a decent distance into the undergrowth. When I returned, J.F. was shaving. Perforce, I followed suit. We were not to shave again for some time.

We then had a good look at the map. There was another cache about fifteen miles away, on the south-western slope of Gunong Sawal. We could see through the trees a clearing about a hundred yards away which should give us a good view of the scene below. We strolled over to the clearing. There was so much rich foliage that we could not pick out as many landmarks as we had hoped to do. We could just make out the railway line, or so we thought, away to the west; and we identified a small township. We also found another path which appeared to lead in the general direction of the second cache.

We quickly packed up our kit and set off. The going was easier here as we were moving along one of the lower contours of the mountain which towered above us to the east. We crossed a number of little ravines on roughly constructed foot-bridges. About twelve-thirty we turned off the path into the jungle for a meal. The more we ate, the less we had to carry.

After lunch we started off again. Then suddenly we saw a dog on the path ahead. He barked furiously and out of the undergrowth appeared a little wizened Javanese. J.F. addressed him in his impeccable Malay.

'Where are the nearest Dutch or British forces? Are there any Japanese in the neighbourhood?'

The Javanese replied that he came from a *kampong* about a quarter of a mile away. He had seen no Japanese, though he had heard that they were moving up and down the main road about ten miles away to the west; and that the Dutch soldiers had all left. He had been cutting bananas when we disturbed him and he gave us a bunch.

We thanked him and went on our way, with his words of peace, '*Selamat Jalan*', ringing in our ears.

We were not unduly disturbed by this unexpected encounter. Even if he told any Japanese, who might visit his *kampong*, that he had seen us, it was most unlikely that they would bother to follow us. The Japanese had many more important tasks to perform. Our greatest worry was that we might run into a Japanese patrol, but this was unlikely until the time came for us to leave the protection of the mountains and make our dash across the plain to the coast. The position would be quite different if, and when, we ever got to the coast. There, no doubt, the Japanese had already terrified the local inhabitants and had made it clear, in their own inimitable fashion, that there would be big rewards for those who informed and severe penalties for those who did not.

We plodded on along the path and seemed to be making good progress. By sunset we must have covered nine or ten miles. We looked about for somewhere to spend the night. We were at a lower level, and therefore more vulnerable, than we had been the previous night. We took the next path up the mountain and after about a quarter of an hour found a reasonably clear and level patch. After a meal, and a leech-hunt, we turned in. We both slept better that night. Was it that there were really less nocturnal sounds or was it that we were desperately tired?

The following morning we were off shortly after sunrise, descending the slope to continue along the same path that we had been following the day before. We were anxious to reach the site of the second cache before dusk; and we reckoned that we only had about five or six miles to go. We saw no one and heard nothing. About half past two we started to look out for the physical features which would indicate that we were in the vicinity of the cache. We had memorised these during our midday meal. The most prominent were the two bush-covered hillocks with a single tree growing in the depression between them.

We took it in turns to walk ahead. J.F. was leading at the time and suddenly he held up his hand. We stopped in our tracks and slipped into the undergrowth. He had seen something moving on a track away to the right and lower down the hill. We listened. We thought we could hear the noise of a motor vehicle approaching. We peered through the undergrowth and saw a small Japanese scout car moving slowly along the track about 400 yards away. J.F., looking through the field-glasses, said softly:

'There are three Nips and what looks like a wounded Dutchman. Have a look.'

I took the glasses. They were the first living Japanese I had seen since the war began. I suddenly remembered the other one, but he had been dead. During the ten days or so I had been in Kuala Lumpur before moving on to Singapore I had joined the Local Defence Corps. We had been loading stores into a goods train when the Japanese bombers appeared. As I lay on my back between the rails, squirming deeper into the earth and praying, I had watched the bombers sailing overhead. There were no Allied fighters in the sky but the Ack-Ack guns were putting up a good show. Suddenly they had got a direct hit on one of the bombers which had exploded in mid-air. What was left of the body of one of the crew had landed quite close to me. But the screams I heard did not come from him; they came from a British officer trapped in a blazing car. As we rushed to the scene, he was pleading for someone to shoot him and put him out of his agony. I fingered my revolver but I did not have the courage. An army Major silenced his screams.

The Japanese scout car was now moving away from us. I handed the glasses back to J.F. My hands were trembling; and so were his. We were disturbed by this sign of enemy activity so near our immediate objective. We lay in the undergrowth for some time.

'We're wasting valuable time,' J.F. said suddenly. 'We must find the cache before nightfall.'

We moved off slowly along the path, and then, as we turned a corner, we saw the two hillocks with the single tree between them. They seemed to be some way away from the track along which the scout car had travelled; and we were momentarily encouraged. We quickened our pace and suddenly our path debouched into an open space where a number of tracks met. There were tyre marks on most of these tracks, and it seemed to be an unhealthy place to be. We turned quickly up the track to the left which clearly led to our goal. Now we were keeping as close as possible to the undergrowth, as we could see that a vehicle of some sort had passed down the track fairly recently.

We did not need to pace out the steps from the base of the tree. We could see the little mound of freshly turned earth only too clearly.

'We've had it,' said J.F.

I was too troubled even to reply. Hoping against hope, I crawled on my belly—it seemed safer that way—and looked into the hole. There was nothing there except the outline of a metal box similar to that which had been our salvation earlier.

I suppose we must have panicked a bit. Our one idea was to get back up the mountain. We had a choice of several paths and we took one at random. We moved as quickly as we could without speaking. Anything to get away from that spider's web of tyre tracks.

After about half an hour's stiff climbing we both stopped and flung ourselves on the ground on a level patch. I suppose it must have been about five o'clock. Without a word, J.F. opened his bottle of whisky and, detaching my metal cup from my belt, poured out two strong tots.

'Perhaps St. Patrick didn't get the first message,' he said. 'We'd better try again.' It was a stiff drink, even by Malayan standards, and if St. Patrick didn't get that message, I did. I suddenly felt much better.

I only just stopped myself saying to J.F.: 'We might have reached that cache in time if only we had not waited until St. Patrick's Day before setting off.'

Our only problem was food. We had our revolvers, maps and compass; we had our stove and matches; we even had half a bottle of whisky left; but we only had food for another forty-eight hours, and that would be stretching it a bit. As there was nothing we could do that night we decided to sleep with our problem. Without any discussion, but through some form of telepathic agreement, we went on up the mountain path, deeper and deeper into the jungle.

After another hour's climb we chose a place for the night. We had a smaller meal than usual. Then we turned in.

'I don't feel too good,' I said to J.F. 'How about you?'

'Oh! I've got a bit of a headache and my limbs ache all over, but I suppose that's all this pounding up and down this bloody mountain,' he replied.

I dreamed a lot that night. I was in Australia, where I had never been, and had just finished a magnificent round of golf. I was luxuriating in a warm shower. As I woke, I felt the rain beating down upon me. Even the foliage all around me afforded no protection. I was already soaked to the skin, for I had put down my rain-cape as a ground-sheet. J.F. was tossing and turning but seemed to be still asleep. I woke him up.

The rain continued relentlessly as we tried to brew up some tea. The sky, which we could just see through the fronds above us, was overcast, leaden and menacing. Everything had changed. We seemed to have woken up in quite a different place from that in which we had gone to sleep the night before. All around us there were rivulets and streams flowing down the mountainside. One of these was covering the path up which we had laboured.

We rigged up a shelter with one of our rain-capes and sat on the other one. We warmed our chilled hands on the little stove. We were not hungry and we ate nothing. We must have sat there shivering until midday; but there was no sun to signal the approach of noon.

We then decided that, if we did not move soon, we would never move again.

I suppose it was inevitable that we should disagree as to what our next move should be. We were tense, irritable and bewildered; and, although we did not know it then, we both had fevers. I felt that we should strike off across the plain for the coast and take our chance.

'Every day we put this off,' I argued, 'the Japanese will get a tighter grip on the coastline and our chances of getting a boat will diminish.'

'You must be mad,' J.F. replied. 'When we make our dash for the coast we must have enough food for four or five days. We'll have to avoid all human beings, even the Javanese, like the plague. Our move now must be to the next cache, on the south-eastern corner of the mountain.'

'But supposing we find that cache gone, like the last one; or supposing we don't find it at all,' I retorted. 'We shall have gone another twenty miles or so out of our way for nothing.'

'I don't agree,' he replied. 'Even if we don't find the cache, we are safer here on the mountain. And if we continue to skirt round it towards the south-east we shall be reducing the amount of open country to be crossed, when we do have to make a dash for the coast.'

'I see that,' I said, 'but if we don't find the cache we certainly won't find any other food on this bloody mountain. Our only hope will be to beg, borrow or steal something. And that means a *kampong* on the plain.'

And so the argument raged for an hour or so. Eventually he persuaded me. I was so tired. In any event, he was clearly right. As matters turned out, it would have made no difference, even if I had won the argument.

We studied the map. The nearest cache, by the quickest route, was at least twenty miles distant, fairly low down on the south-eastern slope of the mountain. We were about a third of the way up on the south-western slope. We took a compass bearing. We moved to the edge of the trees to see if we could identify any landmarks. The lowering clouds and pounding rain concealed everything.

We gathered our rain-sodden belongings together and started off in the general direction of the cache. It was impossible to pick out a path; we had to choose between half a dozen rivulets. If I had been alone I would have given up after about an hour and lain down, never to rise again. When eventually we did stop for the night, J.F. admitted that the same thought had passed through his mind a number of times. He had lost a shoe in the mud and it took us several minutes to find it in the swirling waters. Our sodden gear was twice as heavy; and, as we had eaten nothing at midday, we were soon exhausted. I doubt if we had covered more than a couple of miles when we stopped.

By now we both had raging fevers and sore throats. We could see nothing tempting as a place for the night, although it was getting appreciably darker. We decided to put through one more call to St. Patrick. We felt a little better after this. We then decided we would have to climb a little higher up the mountain, if only to find a drier spot to lay our heads. We might as well have spared ourselves the extra effort. If anything the rain was heavier and the ground wetter.

We made ourselves some hot soup, but the thought of bully beef nauseated us. After the soup we had some hot coffee. Thus strengthened, we embarked on our nightly leech-hunt. They had had a field day. We decided that our only hope of snatching some sleep was to strap ourselves by our belts to two trees. The ground was too steep to permit us to stretch out; and, in any event, it would have been like going to bed in a river. We rigged up a rain-cape between the two trees to afford us some protection from the incessant rain. Then, facing each other and strapped to the two trees as though we were awaiting a firing squad, we tried to sleep.

I remember saying to J.F. as I bade him good night: 'Well, we shan't hear any jungle noises tonight.'

I suppose there was a moment of time when one could have said that I woke up the next morning, but I could not identify it. Whether sleeping or waking my thoughts and dreams—or were they nightmares?—were indistinguishable. I was hot and cold alternately. Sometimes I felt that I was being burned at the stake; at others that I was being whipped naked in the snow. I struggled to control myself. Why were my hands tied behind my back? Had we been captured? Were we in some Japanese cell? Why did J.F., who faced me with his head lolling on his chest, look as though his neck was broken?

Eventually the human spirit reasserted itself. I struggled to

unfasten the belt which bound me to my tree. My fingers were stiff
with cold and I could not undo the buckle. As panic enveloped me,
I struggled again with no better result. Javanese wood-cutters would
find us years later, after this ghastly war was over, two skeletons
bound to two trees. 'Another Japanese atrocity,' they would say, as
they cut us down.

I decided to do nothing for five minutes and to compose myself.
I was desperately thirsty and my throat was full of hot coals. The
rain was still beating down; I opened my mouth to the heavens.

'Who was the bloody fool,' I thought, 'who put that rain-cape
up to deprive me of water?'

I must have subsided into unconsciousness again. When I came
to I undid my buckle the first time and rushed out to scoop up water
from the nearest pool.

Then I undid J.F.'s buckle, tweaking his ear at the same time.
I had learnt at school that that was the proper way to awaken
someone in a deep sleep. He slumped into the mud at the bottom
of his tree and for a moment I thought he was dead.

He moaned a bit, then opened his eyes, looked at me and closed
them again. I needed a cup of tea and it looked as though he did too.
I managed to get the stove going under the protection of the cape.
Selfishly, but justifying myself by the fact that J.F. was still sleeping,
I gulped down the first cup. Then I poured out another and tweaked
his ear again. Now he opened his eyes and took the cup, saying
'*Terimah Kasek*', as he must have said a thousand times thanking his
Malay boy in his District Officer's residence.

We were in pretty poor shape. We both had very high temperatures.
We forced ourselves to face the bully beef but we hardly did it
justice. I put the remains in my pack in a scrap of paper. The ants
ate it during the day. When we had collected ourselves we decided
to take another compass bearing before setting off. It was then we
discovered that the compass was missing, as well as the map with
the detailed instructions about the cache sites. We must have left
them at our previous night's stopping place. This was a major blow,
but we thought that we knew the general direction to take and
that we could remember, between us, the siting details.

Making doubly sure that we had left nothing behind, we set off
again, somewhat depressed.

An instinct for survival had now become our major motive force.
Although neither of us ventured to suggest to the other that our

ESCAPADE   31

chances of getting through to the coast were now virtually nil, we were both increasingly conscious of this.

Where, or quite how, we moved during the next few days I cannot recall. The only constants in the equation were the rain and the mountain. We were imperceptibly, and subconsciously, changing our plans. It was not so much a weakening of resolve as an acknowledgement of the fact that we were lost. We had not spoken to anyone, except to each other, since we took our leave of the Javanese ancient. We had not seen another human being since we had peered at the three Japanese and the wounded Dutchman through our glasses. We were no longer frightened at the prospect of being captured or even killed, but we were terrified by the idea of dying alone in the jungle, our fate unknown to anyone except to him who would be the last to die.

We must have stopped somewhere for our last night in the jungle, for I remember packing up, always in the relentless rain, the next morning. We must have eaten the last of our food for there was none left to pack. During our periods of more or less lucid consciousness we had agreed on a new plan. We would go down the mountainside by the shortest route; and as soon as we found a sizable stream, we would wade down it. Streams, we had learnt in our youth, sooner or later led to the sea; but long before we got there we would have come across human beings.

And so we set off, hand-in-hand, like schoolboys, rather than the heroes we had hoped to have been. We trudged through the mud, slithering down the slopes rather than risking a turn to right or left. Eventually we saw a stream and we waded in up to our knees. We plodded on and now the jungle was giving way to the secondary growth of the foothills. It was becoming difficult to keep our foothold, as the stream became a river and as the pressure of the current increased. Suddenly I was alone. J.F. had twisted his damaged knee and had disappeared into a deep hole in the river bed. His heavy pack weighed him down. I plunged down and fished him out. We were both gasping for breath as we emerged. He had lost his pack, his revolver and his blankets, but it didn't seem to matter much.

We dragged ourselves to the bank of the river to rest for a bit. I cut myself a stout stick and nearly cut the tip of my finger off in the process. It hardly seemed worthwhile to burn off the leeches which covered our bodies, even if we could have got our matches to strike.

C

After about ten minutes we entered the river again. We waded on with an energy of which neither of us thought ourselves capable. At dusk we hauled ourselves on to a grassy slope. We had seen no one and no signs of life. We lay down to sleep as we were, caring nothing for the rain which continued to beat down upon us.

I dreamed again of Australia, wonderful dreams of warm and dry open spaces, of women and children sunning themselves on sandy beaches. The harsh Australian accents beat upon my ears. I opened my eyes. The warm sun, caressing us, had chased the rain away. For the first time in days I heard the gentle song of birds. It was so warm and peaceful that for a moment I thought I was dead. Gingerly I tried to move my limbs. Here lay reality. My arms and legs ached so much I thought they must have been broken in several places. Although I was now fully awake my vivid dream continued and the Australian voices persisted. As full consciousness returned, I realised that there were Australian voices. I became tense and alert. Perhaps we had run into one of the specialised groups of Allied forces to which the C.O. had referred in the tea estate. I had visions of being carried on husky shoulders to the coast and gently transported into the womb of a submarine. No more decisions to take; someone else would worry about the compass and the maps. I was already lying between clean white sheets with a pretty nurse fussing over me.

J.F. was still asleep, or dead. I crawled up the grassy slope. It was only a few yards and then I could see them through the undergrowth in a clearing. There were about ten of them, stripped to the waist, loading timber on to two lorries. They seemed to me to be making a lot of noise for a specialised Allied jungle group. Suddenly I saw their two guards squatting under a tree; two evil-looking Japanese, one of whom had his rifle casually across his knees. It was a working party of Australian P.o.W.s. I watched them for about ten minutes. The P.o.W.s. seemed happy and healthy enough, joking with one another and making snide remarks about their somnolent guards.

I crawled back to J.F., woke him up and told him what I had seen. It was a hard decision to take. We were still free men. On the first occasion we had fallen into Japanese hands we had had no decision to take; we were just told by one of our senior officers that we were P.o.W.s. This time it was harder, as we had to take the decision ourselves.

Of course we had no choice. We had no food; we were racked with fever; we were so weak that we could only speak to each other in whispers. If we had let the working party leave without us, I doubt whether we could even have got into the river again. We would have just lain where we were until we died, first one and then the other.

It was soon decided. I threw my revolver into the river. I tore our remaining map up into little bits and watched it fall like confetti into the raging torrent. I filled a water-bottle and we both had a long drink. We kept our torches, knives and field-glasses, but not for long.

We then crawled up the slope again to my earlier vantage point. We could not have walked if we had tried. This time we crawled a few yards further into undergrowth, practically on to the edge of the clearing. We lay there panting for a few minutes. Then, as two Australians passed quite close to us carrying a log on their shoulders, I said softly, addressing their legs:

'Hi! cobber—give us a hand.'

They stopped, and the one in front, almost without turning his head, whistled out of the corner of his mouth to his companion:

'Did you hear that, Bert?'

Bert, equally astonished, indicated that he had heard something. They put the log down and peered into the undergrowth. Bert, who had flaming red hair, was the first to see us.

'Fuck me,' he said, 'if it isn't a couple of Pommie bastards.'

One of the Japanese guards, who must have seen the log put down, came rushing over shouting: '*Kura, kura.*' He gave Bert such a whack on his rump with his rifle-butt that Bert was nearly catapulted into our arms.

We were dragged out of our hiding place. The other Japanese guard and all the P.o.W.s crowded round. We were pulled to our feet, swaying from side to side. Then we fainted.

When I recovered consciousness a few seconds later, J.F. and I were both lying on the ground. The Australians looked about ten feet tall. The Japanese, reflected in the other mirrors of this fun-fair, looked about three feet tall. The Japanese were chattering away like monkeys as they examined our knives, torches and field-glasses, which we never saw again. One of the Japanese then gesticulated to a couple of Australians to take our clothes off. There were so many leeches on our bodies that we must have looked like currant suet puddings. These were burned off gently by the Australians with their cigarettes. Meanwhile the guards were going through our clothing and my pack. When they had satisfied themselves that there was nothing of importance in these, they were returned to us and it was made clear that we were to dress. This we could never have done without Australian help.

The guards then signed to the Australians to carry us over to the tree under which they had been sitting. The working party resumed its labours.

We lay there, dozing off from time to time, all the afternoon. The Japanese guards were watching us carefully and presumably they were discussing us. It was comforting to feel that we had no more decisions to take; but we were still a little apprehensive about what was going to happen to us. We thought it wise not to talk to each other.

We had both lost our watches. Whether we had lost them in the river or whether the guards had taken them I did not know. It must have been about three-thirty when two Javanese lorry-drivers arrived and reported to the guards. I suppose that they had been off to some neighbouring *kampong* for their midday meal and a rest. They took not the slightest interest in us.

One of the guards rose to his feet and shouted, '*Yasume*,' signifying the end of the day's work. The Australians brought their last loads to the lorries and some were detailed to lift us aboard. One of us was placed in each lorry and in each lorry there was one guard. Whenever any of the Australians tried to talk to us, the Japanese guard would box his ears. I was lying on the floor among muddy Australian boots and sweaty Australian legs. Mercifully, I dropped off to sleep.

3

The Darkness Falls

Garoet—Western Java—April 1942

I woke up on a mattress on the floor of what appeared to be a small school, turned into a hospital. A smiling Javanese nurse was bending over me.

'How do you feel?' she said to me in Malay. 'You have been very ill, pneumonia.' Before I could reply, she added: 'Your friend over there has got pneumonia too,' as though that would make me feel better. The index finger of my left hand, the tip of which I had nearly left in the jungle, was throbbing and I saw it was heavily bandaged.

'We had to stitch it up,' she observed.

Later in the day an elderly civilian Dutch doctor came round.

'Can you a bath take?' he asked in broken English. 'It will better be if you a bath take. Help you we will.'

Now that I was conscious I appreciated the reason for his insistence and I signified my assent.

The Javanese nurse was summoned and tried to get me on my feet. I could not help her much and a male Javanese orderly had to be called. We made our way down the corridor like the front row of a pack of rugger forwards looking for our opponents. As we turned a corner we found them—two Japanese soldiers supporting one of their comrades with a badly crushed foot. Narrowly avoiding a scrum, we shuffled around them; and I was piloted into a small room with two or three metal bath tubs full of warm and heavily disinfected water.

The Javanese nurse gently washed me all over. My body was a mass of sores where the leeches had had their fill. When I had regained my mattress she dressed these with some ointment.

Once more I was back in the world of make-believe, which reminded me of the garage on the tea estate. I was a P.o.W. again but the Japanese did not bother me. I rarely saw them and the kindness of the Dutch and Javanese hospital staff insulated me from the harsh world outside.

This illusion grew as the days slipped by and I regained my strength. Dutch ladies would call with old books and magazines, cigarettes and sweets. As I pondered on these things, I wondered if J.F. and I had got it all wrong. Perhaps even now football was being played at the tea estate; perhaps even now gay parties were being held in the Chinese summer palace.

One morning I was told that I would be leaving the hospital the following day. I had by then discovered that we were in the town of Garoet. J.F. had not mended quite as rapidly as I had. They told me that he would be staying in the hospital for another few days.

At the appointed hour a Japanese guard arrived and took charge of me. He led me out into the street and set off at a spanking pace down the main street. I was amazed to see British, Australian and Dutch servicemen mingling with the crowds and shopping freely. I began to wonder whether my delirium had really left me.

Arriving at the school my escort handed me over to a Japanese Sergeant in an outbuilding. The latter appeared to be expecting us; he made a tick against a cluster of Japanese characters which I presumed was my name, though I had no recollection of having given it to anyone since we had left the jungle. The Japanese Sergeant motioned me to go into the main school building.

There I saw a sign marked 'Adjutant's Office', so I knocked and walked in. I saw a Flight-Lieutenant sitting at a desk in the corner and I saluted smartly announcing, my name, rank and number.

'Damn it, man,' he said, 'don't you know you never salute without a cap on?'

It was only then that I realised that I was not in uniform. I was wearing a white shirt and green slacks. I supposed that the hospital authorities had very wisely burnt the rags in which I had emerged from the river. All I had to remind me of our failure was my stout Dutch Army pack, on it my name in white paint and in it a few personal belongings.

'I know you've had a rough time, old man,' the Adjutant said more sympathetically, 'but the C.O. insists on strict Service discipline here. Keeps up morale, you know.' He continued quickly:

'There's another thing you should know. We run ourselves here. The Nips keep out of our hair; and we keep out of theirs. That's the way it is; and that's the way we want it. By the way,' he added, 'all Nip officers, whatever their rank, have to be saluted.'

He then went on to explain the rules of the game. He told me about the meal-times; about the hours during which we were permitted to go out and shop: about the areas of the town which were out of bounds; and so on. I felt I was in the housemaster's study again. I half expected him to add: 'Now if you are interested in cricket, old boy, there are practice nets every afternoon between four and six.'

My mind began to reel again at the thought of little British communes springing up all over Java. Those in towns, such as Garoet, would have the benefits of shopping, as in Bath or Cheltenham; others, on tea estates, would be afforded such rural delights as might be found in Scotland or the shires. It didn't seem to make sense to me.

My musings were cut short by another outburst from the Flight-Lieutenant. 'We can't have you going about like that, old man. The C.O. would have a fit. Fortunately we have a spare P/O's uniform. Poor old Q* couldn't take it. He blew the top of his head off with a rifle a few days ago. Luckily he was wearing his pyjamas at the time. I'll get the Corporal to give you his uniform.'

He summoned a Corporal from an adjoining room and gave him some orders. 'Corporal Shrivenham will look after you now and show you around. See you in the Mess later,' he added gaily.

Corporal Shrivenham took me along a corridor where he unlocked a cupboard and handed me a well-laundered and neatly folded khaki tunic, slacks and shirt.

'Try the cap for size, sir,' he said, and then added persuasively: 'I hope it fits, sir; it's the only one we've got in stock at the moment.'

It didn't fit too badly; nor did the black shoes, from which I removed two neatly rolled khaki stockings. The Corporal relocked the now empty cupboard.

'Now, if you'll follow me, sir,' intoned the Corporal, like a museum attendant, 'I'll show you where the junior officers sleep.'

I followed him up some stairs and we entered what must have been a classroom. The room was empty and I assumed that all my fellow-officers were out shopping or having afternoon tea somewhere.

* Q (which was not one of his initials) was a planter in Malaya and I had known him slightly before he joined the R.A.F.

I selected an open space on the floor.

'I'll bring you a couple of blankets a little later, sir, now I know where you'll be,' said the Corporal.

I thanked him for his trouble and he left me with my thoughts.

The food was good at Garoet; and as I sat down to what might reasonably enough be described as dinner, wearing my newly acquired uniform, I felt good too. Among my fellow-officers I found a number I had come across previously. One was T., who had been a solicitor in private practice in Kuala Lumpur. When he went to Malaya he had, I believe, established his permanent home in New Zealand. He must have been about fifty at the time and he had always seemed to me to be kindly, wise and sensible.

I found that he had the bed-space next to mine and after lights-out I had a whispered conversation with him. I asked him what he made of it all. He agreed with me that the present situation couldn't last.

'As I see it,' he said, 'the Nips never expected to take any prisoners. No Nip, unless he is unconscious, is ever taken prisoner. They have, as yet, no organisation whatever to deal with the thousands of prisoners they have taken all over the Far East.'

He offered me a whisky from a bottle he had and then went on: 'There's another thing. When the Nips invaded Malaya they swept all before them in their advance down the peninsula from the north. They had got everyone bottled up in Singapore before the capitulation. Here, in Java, the position is quite different. They seem to have made a number of landings in different places. When the Dutch decided to capitulate there were dozens of Allied groups, all over the place, who had seen nothing of the Nips. Indeed, some of them may not, even now, have heard of the Dutch capitulation. So the Nips' plan has been to contain these groups wherever they have found them. They haven't, as yet, enough forces available to administer us directly. Indeed, they probably haven't yet decided what they're going to do with us or how they're going to do it.'

We sipped our whisky and our cigarettes glowed in the darkness.

'That's exactly what I think,' I replied. 'And this accounts for the fact that, at the moment, the Nips are content to leave us to our own devices. In the tea estate, here and no doubt elsewhere, they are following a policy of what might be loosely called "perimeter control". The exact details in each case are, I suppose, worked out between the senior officers on either side. But this can't last and those who think that these conditions are going to continue indefinitely are plumb crazy.'

As I turned over to go to sleep, I thought I had better do a little judicious shopping on the morrow.

The following morning I presented myself to the Adjutant's Office again and asked if I could have an advance of pay.

'Indeed you can,' the Adjutant replied. 'I want to get this stuff dispersed. When we move the Nips will grab the lot.'

I then enquired if I could go to the hospital and visit J.F.

'No, I fear that's not possible,' he replied, 'but if you'd like to send him a message I can see that it gets to him. In any case, we expect him here tomorrow or the day after.'

I scribbled out a note for J.F. and left it with him. I then went out into the town to do some shopping. I bought a couple of French books, an inflatable Lilo mattress and some razor blades. If I'd had my wits about me I would have bought a sewing kit and a spoon, but I never thought of those.

J.F. arrived on the Saturday morning, and I was glad to see him again. He looked desperately thin and his deep-set eyes seemed to have sunk further into his skull. But he was, as always, smiling. I put him in the picture and told him that he had arrived just in time for the camp concert, which was to be held that evening.

The concert produced a remarkable amount of individual talent. One dark young Flying Officer, who looked as though he had Italian blood in his veins, still had his guitar with him and treated us to a number of Italian love-songs. It was a long time before he was allowed to leave the stage. We were all desperately homesick and still sufficiently virile to miss feminine companionship.

He was followed by a Cockney Aircraftsman who did a soft-shoe routine with spoons, accompanied on the school piano by a Squadron-Leader. Then came two comics, dressed up as old women; was one of them Corporal Shrivenham? I wondered. There were the inevitable jokes at the expense of the C.O. and other senior officers. Most of these passed over my head, but I joined in the laughter just the same. A number of other turns preceded the finale.

The concert was held in the school-yard and the flickering lights cast huge shadows on the surrounding walls. I noticed a number of Japanese soldiers standing about in the background. I wondered what they thought of it all. Here were those whom they had vanquished, laughing and singing. Both we, and they, were far from our native lands. Were they wondering, too, as many of us were, how it would all end? Did they find us as strange as we found them?

Suddenly there was a roll on the piano and it was clear that this was the finale.

A young Corporal of Welsh origins, though he could hardly have been a dedicated Welsh Nationalist, was standing alone in the spotlights. In a beautifully controlled tenor voice he began to sing, very softly, 'There'll always be an England', and gradually the audience of two or three hundred joined in. They did not make their claim arrogantly; they did not shout, they did not open their lungs, as they would have done with 'Abide with me' at a Cup-final. Following the Corporal's lead they sang softly; their confidence was quietly expressed.

Although we did not know it then, this was to be our last night at Garoet and, indeed, our last night of twilight freedom.

Early the following morning the word went round that we were to pack, hardly an appropriate word in the circumstances, immediately. Shortly thereafter a large number of armed Japanese arrived at the school and bundled us into lorries. They were quite different from the Japanese we had seen in the streets of Garoet. Many of them were much larger; these, we subsequently learnt, were not Japanese at all but Koreans. No doubt many of them had suffered at the hands of the Japanese during the Japanese occupation of Korea. Now the time had come for them to work off their frustrations on others. Thus started the daily round of beatings which was to be our lot until we were released by death or by the Allies.

Within half an hour the state of mind of hundreds of men had been radically altered. As free men, we had been faced with the risks of war, risks which, though hardly predictable from one moment to the next, were at least capable of being comprehended. Then we had been anaesthetised for several weeks; we had lost our freedom in the widest sense, but within the little dream-worlds in which we lived we had a large measure of personal liberty and, above all, we were insulated against the grosser physical dangers. Now all had changed in a matter of moments. Our bodies, our personalities, our minds were to be at risk for months, for years, maybe for ever. We became the playthings of malevolent guards, frequently drunk, who appeared to be answerable to no one. Life had to be lived on the knife-edge of uncertainty. Nothing, but the unpredictability of it all, was predictable.

Our long journey seemed interminable. At midday we stopped on the roadside outside a Japanese army camp. As we stood about near the lorries, we were given two small rice-balls and a cup of weak tea. Then we scrambled into the lorries again, the last to arrive being cuffed and beaten by the guards. Eventually we arrived at a railway station where we waited for several hours. A goods train arrived and we were crowded into goods wagons with two or three guards to each wagon. At least, I thought, the prospect of this train being ambushed was very remote.

About three o'clock the following afternoon we arrived at the main station in Batavia, now Djakarta. There we were formed up and marched through the streets to Boei Glodok, a prison built by the Dutch for long-term Javanese prisoners. I think we must have taken a rather roundabout route; this was no doubt arranged to ensure that as many as possible of the inhabitants of Batavia witnessed our degradation and learnt the proper lessons from the brutality of our guards.

According to my reckoning it was four months to the day, since the 8th December when, at Cameron Highlands, I had learnt of the Japanese invasion of Malaya.

4

The Prison

Boei Glodok, Batavia—April–October 1942

The gaol could not have been a pleasant place for the three or four hundred Javanese long-term criminals who were its normal occupants. I don't suppose the Dutch ever intended that it should be. Before we arrived the Javanese had been concentrated in one half of the complex of buildings. This had its own entrance and was virtually self-contained. We had no contact with our fellow-residents. We, some 1,200 P.o.W.s, mainly R.A.F., were crammed into the other half.

There were several possible changes of scene. There were the barrack rooms where we slept, ate and spent most of our time; there were the indescribably filthy open drains where, even when racked with dysentery, we spent as little time as possible; and there were the solitary confinement cells where, if we could avoid it, we spent no time at all.

The senior prisoner officer was Group Captain C. H. Noble, known to us all as 'Beery'. His nickname took account not only of his rubicund countenance but also of his warm and refreshing personality, redolent of a good strong English brew. I believe that he had been a regular officer in the R.A.F. during the early thirties; and that, after he left the Service, he had joined Shell. He had been posted to Australia, I think, and he must have been on some reserve of officers, from which he had rejoined on the outbreak of war.

A number of R.A.F. P.o.W.s were already in the gaol when our party arrived and Beery and his staff had already made considerable progress in getting things organised. Flight-Lieutenant

C. McLaren Reid was both Adjutant and chief interpreter. I believe that Reid had had some R.A.F. experience before he joined the Malayan Customs Service.

Beery's policy was aimed at interposing himself between the rest of us and the Japanese Commandant. He tried, with a considerable measure of success, to ensure that it was he who gave us orders, not the Japanese. These were passed down the line by the other British officers. The Japanese, for example, would demand a certain number of men for working parties, but it was the R.A.F. orderly room which worked out the rosters and spread the load as fairly as possible.

The Japanese Commandant, and other Japanese, did make unannounced visits to the barrack rooms, but very rarely to the open drains, at all hours of the day or night. Beery tried to keep this practice to a minimum by enforcing a measure of self-discipline. Prisoners were expected, as far as possible, to conduct themselves as they would be required to do in an R.A.F. camp.

Such a policy required great courage, diplomacy and tenacity for its success and some of the other ranks, unaware of the daily battle of wits and wills, misunderstood what was going on.

'Why the bloody 'ell should I do that? I'm not in the fuckin' Raff now; I'm a poor, bleedin' P.o.W.—like 'im. 'Oose 'e to give me orders now? I 'ave to fuckin' well do what the Nips say, and that's enuff. 'E can go piss in 'is pants, for all I care.'

Fortunately those who thought thus were in a minority, but they did exist and they added to the problems of Beery and the other officers.

Within a day or two of our arrival I was out on a working party. Beery had already established the principle that the Japanese had no right to require officers to work and for the time being they had accepted this. But he had had to concede that junior officers should accompany the working parties. He had readily agreed to this because he felt, and rightly so, that the presence of their own officers might prevent some of the men from making fools of themselves. More important still, if any man, through no fault of his own, got into trouble with the Japanese guards, an officer might perhaps be able to defend and protect him. From the officers' point of view, although it was intensely boring to stand about for hours on end while the others were working, at least it made a break in the monotony of a life bounded by prison walls.

But Beery and the other senior officers were wiser men than many gave them credit for.

The junior officers who were detailed to accompany the working parties were summoned, one by one, into the C.O.'s presence. Each of us was then told that in view of the imminent recapture of Java by the Allies it was imperative that every possible piece of military intelligence should be collected. This would be invaluable when the time came. We were given some rudimentary instructions as to how to identify Japanese units, aircraft, tanks, guns and other machines of war. We were to keep our eyes and ears open for every piece of information, even rumours and gossip, which could conceivably be of value. Each of us was given the name of a senior officer to whom we were to report privately. We were required not to discuss this with, or even mention this to, any of our fellow junior officers. This, no doubt, was to create the impression that each of us had been hand-picked for this delicate assignment.

After my interview with Beery I recalled the secret information with which J.F. and I had been entrusted by the C.O. of the tea estate camp before we left on our abortive attempt to make contact with General Douglas MacArthur in Australia. I recalled, too, the circumstances in which it had been given to us. This time I was a little less cynical. To gather information is always interesting and it would give one something to do on working parties. Who could tell? The day might come when it just might be of value to the Allied war effort.

The working routine consisted of marching to the Batavia airfield and filling in the craters made by Japanese bombers during the opening stages of their attack on Java. The midday meal consisted of a small quantity of rice, washed down by water or, occasionally, weak tea. We usually finished about three-thirty and then marched back into the prison.

Among those who went on these working parties were a young R.A.F. Flying Officer and two Sergeant Pilots. As air-crew they had taken an intense professional interest in the Japanese aircraft which were already using parts of the airfield. They kept their intentions to themselves but the story was pieced together afterwards.

It appears that they had their eyes on a particular aircraft in which they planned to escape. One night they broke out of the gaol and made their way to the airfield. The story goes that they boarded the aircraft and succeeded in getting one of the two engines started. While they were struggling with the other one, the Japanese airfield guards, alerted by the noise of the first engine, rushed across to the plane and hauled them out.

It seems probable that they were then taken to the airfield guard house, to which the *Kempetei** were immediately summoned. There, it is said, they were tortured for several hours in an attempt to extract from them information about any others who might be involved in their escape plot. Finally, it was alleged, they were taken outside, to some open ground in a corner of the airfield, where they were forced to dig their own graves. Then they were bayoneted to death.

The disappearance of these gallant men cast a deep shadow over Boei Glodok, but there were more shadows to come. Shortly after this incident every man in the gaol was given a piece of paper by the Japanese. This was a formal undertaking, which each man was required to sign, that he would make no attempt to escape. Beery Noble issued an order that no one was to sign.

For a week or so the tension in the gaol was electric. The Japanese Commandant and his staff had, no doubt, been hauled over the coals by their own higher authorities for permitting three men to break out by night. They were in an angry mood; there was a substantial increase in the number of beatings.

Meanwhile Beery courageously pointed out to the Japanese Commandant that it was the duty of every P.o.W. to try to escape. He got a severe beating-up for his pains.

The Japanese became more enraged at the delay. It was clear that something would have to give.

One morning we learnt that the Japanese Commandant had given orders to the guards that the ten men whose names appeared first in the camp nominal roll were to be thrown into a solitary confinement cell and left there without food, water or any other attention until such time as every man in the camp had signed. Beery held his hand for a few days to see whether the Japanese meant business.

This must have been an appalling strain for him and his responsibility was a heavy one. When it was clear that the Japanese were prepared to go to any lengths to secure compliance, Beery formally gave an order to every man to sign, adding that as the signatures were being obtained under duress they were without effect. The atmosphere in the camp improved perceptibly. No

* Japanese Military Police.

doubt the Japanese thought they had won a great victory, but the real victor was Beery Noble.

The daily round of working parties continued. From the very beginning the monotony of these had been relieved by the efforts of a number of very brave Dutch women and girls, sometimes accompanied by friendly Chinese. These camp-followers would hang about behind the hedges and outbuildings surrounding the airfield and we could always find an excuse to make contact with them. They would then surreptitiously slip us fruit, eggs, cigarettes or sweets. The Japanese guards would beat-up brutally both the donor and the recipient whenever they could and even to the recipient this frequently seemed a high price to pay for his titbit. The gallant Dutch women, despite all the beatings, continued to turn up day after day.

On one occasion I encountered on the airfield a young Second Lieutenant who was escorting a working party from another P.o.W. camp in Batavia. I believe he came from the 'Bicycle Camp', as it was called. Normally parties from the 'Bicycle Camp' worked elsewhere, but occasionally their working parties were sent to the airfield.

The Dutch women and girls had been particularly bold that day and the guards had been beating them viciously.

'It makes me sick,' I said to my companion, 'to see these bloody Nips bashing women and children about like that. And there's nothing we can do about it. Those Dutch girls have got plenty of guts—more than many of their menfolk, I think.'

A glazed look came over the young officer's face. He couldn't have been more than nineteen or twenty.

'Do you know,' he enquired hoarsely, 'what they did the other day when I had quite a large party down here?'

I shook my head.

'I'll tell you,' he said, and I could see the muscles of his jaw become tense. 'There was the usual hoo-haa going on, with all the chaps dashing behind the hedges to go to the *benjo*. I must say they were rather overdoing it. At times there was hardly anyone working at all. The Nips were bloody mad, charging all over the place like bulls and bashing anyone in range. Suddenly, the Corporal-in-charge, a real bastard, appeared, dragging a young Dutch girl by the hair through the hedge. She must have been about fifteen or sixteen.'

He paused and swallowed hard. I thought for a moment that he could not bring himself to go on with his tale, but he did.

'Then the Corporal shouted at the other guards who rounded us up and formed us into a square facing inwards. He was still holding the poor girl by her hair. She was crying and moaning all the time.'

My companion turned his head away from me as he went on:

'The Corporal then posted four kneeling guards with loaded rifles inside the square facing outwards, that is facing us.'

His voice was barely audible now, but he was determined to go through with it. He continued, groping for words to describe his nightmare:

'Then the Corporal and two other bastards dragged the girl to the middle of the square . . . they spreadeagled her out . . . and tied her wrists and ankles to bayonets they'd driven into the ground. By now . . . she was screaming . . . screams which I shall never, never I say, forget.'

He turned his face towards me for a moment; I could see the tears in his blue eyes.

'It might have been my sister,' he whispered. I could find no words to utter, so I grasped his hand firmly, hoping he would not go on.

'Then, one after another, they raped her in front of us . . .', he continued, 'and when each one had finished with her, he took over from one of the armed guards, to let him have a go. The men growled and muttered. But we couldn't do anything, could we?' he enquired plaintively. 'One man did make a move but the guard cocked his rifle and he moved back into his place, shouting obscenities.'

He paused, and his grasp on my hand tightened. 'A couple of chaps fainted,' he went on relentlessly. 'I wanted to but I was the only officer there.'

A long pause followed. He was looking over to a distant part of the airfield, perhaps to the scene of this horror. He shuddered a little and then he added softly: 'I believe she was dead by the time the second one got into her. I hope so; I was praying so hard that she would die quickly.'

He relaxed his grip on my hand and went on as though he was talking to himself: 'When it was all over they carried her to a tree; it was more like a large bush really. Then they strung her up by her wrists and left her there.'

He took a sip from his water-bottle and spat on the ground.

Then he took a longer draught and swallowed it. 'But they're still here, as you can see.'

At that moment a Japanese guard approached shouting the all-purpose '*Kura, Kura*', which signified his displeasure that we should be talking.

We parted without saying a word and returned to watch over our respective flocks.

It was about this time that I succumbed to dysentery. I suppose I had picked it up during our wanderings in the jungle. J.F. came down with it about a week later.

I was one of the lucky ones. Our dedicated prisoner doctors, —Stoll, a Flight-Lieutenant, and Reilly, a Flying Officer—had managed to bring into the gaol a very limited number of emetin injections. My complaint was diagnosed, quite how I do not know, as amoebic dysentery, for which, I gather, emetin is the prescribed cure. It had been decided, before I became affected, that the first dozen or so P.o.W.s who got dysentery would be given full courses of emetin injections and I was one of those so treated.

Dysentery was certainly the greatest killer of P.o.W.s during the succeeding three and a half years. When it struck those who were already weakened by malnutrition and other complaints, when the pathetically small stocks of drugs had been exhausted, there was nothing that the doctors, or anyone else, could do, except comfort the dying.

There was no hospital in the gaol, but there were several long since abandoned and decrepit solitary confinement cells, normally used as storerooms to which the worst cases were transferred. I was removed to one of these.

In a crowded barrack room a dysentery patient is a particularly unpleasant person for one's neighbours to have to endure. Moreover, the open drains which served as *benjos*, and no doubt served to spread the complaint as well, were some distance from my barrack room. At least in my lonely stone cell I offended no one but myself.

I had my first emetin injection on the 28th April 1942 and my ninth and last on the 10th May. Having recovered from dysentery, I was struck down by dengue fever on the 18th May when I was again put in one of the stone cells. I made room for someone else on the 27th May. It was not until the 30th June that I was deemed to have recovered enough strength to go out with another working party. It was my first public appearance since the 19th April, the day I had met the young Second Lieutenant from the 'Bicycle Camp'.

The two and a half months I had spent within the prison walls, without seeing the outside world, were not, however, uneventful, either generally or personally.

Soon after we had entered the gaol we were all told we could write one letter each. I wrote a long letter to L. It was a difficult letter to write. So much had happened about which I could not write, and I did not even know whether she would be alive to read it. The scratching of pens and pencils all around me, and the long pauses, indicated that many of my companions were faced with similar problems.

Eventually the letters were collected and we all felt better. For the next few weeks we dreamed of the progress our letters were making. The optimists were expecting replies, almost by the next post.

About six weeks after the letters had been collected the news broke. The Japanese were making a bonfire of our letters in a corner of the prison grounds.

The long weary days were not without their brighter moments. Despite all the strippings and searchings of every P.o.W. who passed through the main entrance to the prison, a wireless receiving set had been smuggled into the camp in bits and reassembled. I do not know quite how this was done, for Japanese searches were very thorough. It was long before the days of transistors and mini-sets. The valves, I did learn, had been inserted into hollow bamboo poles, on which sacks of rice were transported into the camp.

The concealment of this set, once it had been reassembled, presented a number of problems. It had to be easily accessible to the brave Australian officer who operated it. Equally well, it had to be so concealed that if, by chance, it was discovered, the finger of suspicion could not be pointed at any particular individual or individuals. I was not privy, nor had I any wish to be, to the deliberations which led to the final decision. I do know, however, that the advice of the officers who had formerly been in the Malayan Customs Service was sought. What better experts could be found? They had spent their lives searching dingy Chinese junks for opium and other illicit cargoes; they knew all the likely, and unlikely, places of concealment in the hovels of Singapore's Chinatown.

The decision was finally taken on the basis of the belief that when not actually in operation the best place for the set would be right under the noses of the Japanese. But how to ensure that it would be accessible to the operator at the moment the B.B.C. news was broadcast?

The final solution was simplicity itself. The set was concealed in the false bottom of one of the large buckets in which rice was brought into the junior officers' barrack room by P.o.W. orderlies twice a day. For all but a couple of hours out of twenty-four the set was in the camp kitchen, effectively under Japanese control. As our evening meal coincided with the B.B.C. transmission, it was always available when required.

Thus it was that our spirits were raised, during the early months of 1942, by news of British successes in the Western Desert and elsewhere.

It was a moment of carelessness that nearly compromised this precious link with the outside world; it was also a moment that might well have cost brave men their lives.

It was the practice of the Japanese as of others who have had P.o.W.s in their charge, to conduct searches of premises, persons and property at unannounced hours. This was one of the few foreseeable dangers. If, for one reason or another, a P.o.W. elected to have prohibited articles in his possession, that was his concern, provided he did not put any of his fellows at risk.

In those early days many P.o.W.s kept diaries of a sort and most of these were quite innocuous. But when the Japanese found, in one of their random searches, a diary which contained a number of references to B.B.C. news bulletins they were not unnaturally interested. There followed another period of extreme tension throughout the prison.

This tension was a much more complex phenomenon than that which followed the mass refusal to sign the declaration not to escape. Then the prisoners formed a solid block; now there were all kinds of fissiparous tendencies at work.

The wretched owner of the diary was unmercifully pilloried by the herd, but least of all by those whom he had placed in the greatest danger. It was hoped that he would have the wits to cook up some explanation of his unfortunate jottings which would put the Japanese off the scent. This was not as great an impossibility as it might seem. He had, in fact, no first-hand knowledge that there was a set in the camp, nor did he know anything about those who might have been operating it.

He had merely recorded what other P.o.W.s had passed on to

him. It was just possible that he might persuade the Japanese that he had picked up this information from an outside contact while on a working party.

The C.O. was, not unnaturally, desperately worried, and let it be known that no one was to keep a diary in future.*

The Japanese were puzzled. The diary had fortunately made no specific reference to an illicit set in the camp. Despite their rigorous searches, the Japanese had found nothing incriminating; and they must have concluded that it was virtually impossible for a set to be operated in such circumstances. But they could not be sure. A puzzled Japanese was an angry Japanese.

A week or so later working parties reported that strange vans with aerials were moving about in the vicinity of the camp. It could not, of course, be confirmed or denied whether they remained there after dark.

Meanwhile, the news continued to be passed around by word of mouth, perhaps a little more discreetly, at regular, if not daily, intervals.

It was, I think, between my recovery from dysentery and my collapse with dengue fever that I had a personal brush with the Japanese.

From time to time individual P.o.W.s had been summoned to the Japanese Commandant's office, where they were subjected to questioning and to a certain amount of unpleasantness. Among these were half a dozen officers who had remained for some time in the jungle, on a special mission, with Laurens van der Post, after the bulk of us had been captured. Laurens van der Post had, I believe, been taken to a camp at Bandoeng.† His companions had been dragged into Boei Glodok and thrown into a solitary confinement cell. They had had a very rough time before they reached us and for several days they existed in appalling conditions, completely isolated from the rest of the P.o.W.s.

* I must confess that this was the only one of the Commanding Officer's wishes which I ignored. I justified my decision (to myself) by making two resolutions. First, that I would conceal my records in such a way that they would never be found; and they never were, despite the fact that I was stripped and searched on dozens of occasions during the succeeding three years. Secondly, that even if they were discovered, they would be quite unintelligible to anyone; I was equally successful on this second score, in the sense that, even now, I have the greatest difficulty in deciphering the hidden meanings, concealed in what purported to be lecture notes and musings on various innocuous subjects.

† See Laurens van der Post's *The Night of the New Moon*, 1970.

These Japanese invitations to individuals were, like so much else, quite unpredictable. Ugly stories circulated about the treatment meted out. One officer was said to have been strapped to a chair with wire and left there for forty-eight hours with a bright electric light shining in his face. This was a realm in which facts were hard to come by. Those who were invited did not want to talk about what had happened, and the rest of us went about our business, preferring to exclude these things from our thoughts.

With my heart pounding, I followed the Japanese Corporal, who had summoned me, to the Commandant's office. I had never been inside it before. The Commandant was not there.

I was taken into a small side office, where a Captain, who was, I believe, a member of the *Kempetei*, signalled me to sit down on a chair facing him across the table. He had a number of papers on his desk. Offering me a cigarette, which I took, he asked me in English whether I would like a cup of tea. I accepted and tea was brought.

We smoked and sipped our tea in silence. My only thought was that he would suddenly say, 'Why is your heart making such a noise?'

After a minute or so he leaned across the table and said very softly: 'Tell me a military secret. Any one will do.'

'But I don't know any military secrets,' I replied.

He smiled, and continued as he opened a file: 'I have your papers here. You were an Intelligence Officer in the Royal Air Force, in Singapore.'

'I am a prisoner of war in Japanese hands and you have my name rank and number,' I replied rather pompously.

There was another silence. I quickly reviewed in my mind the circumstances in which I had joined the R.A.F. in Singapore, so as to be ready for his next question. I had applied for flying duties and at the second medical examination in the lunatic asylum I had been passed fit for these. Since it was clear, at that late stage, that there was no prospect of my learning to fly in the immediate future, I was commissioned into the Administrative and General Duties Branch. I was hardly qualified to make much of a contribution to the work of the R.A.F. at the time, and I had, therefore, been posted to Air Headquarters, Far East, as a general dog's body. My intelligence duties, such as they were, consisted largely of translating documents written in Malay and of identifying various places on maps for the edification of my superiors.

'But you were attached to Air Headquarters in Singapore,' he stated, and then went on triumphantly: 'You must know something.'

The logic of his reasoning was unanswerable, but his conclusion was just not true.

I have always had the greatest admiration for those possessing military intelligence of value to the enemy who have withstood persistent questioning, and endured torture, rather than utter a word. My own quandary was rather different. How could I make him believe that I knew nothing?

'Come on,' he hissed, 'you must have some information to give me.' Then he added ominously: 'You know that we have ways and means of making you talk.'

I remained silent. If only he would ask me specific questions, I could say 'no' more convincingly.

I studied him carefully. He had tufts of black hair coming out of his ears and out of his broad nostrils. He had a deep scar on his left cheek. His two prominent front teeth were capped with gold. His appearance did not appeal to me.

He was clearly becoming angry and impatient. The soft tones of his offer of a cigarette and tea were things of the past. He shouted in Japanese and two guards rushed into the room. One pinioned my arms behind my back while the other punched me hard on the head and neck. The Captain ordered them to stop.

'Now will you talk?' he spat at me.

His gorillas remained on either side of me. It was at this stage that I decided to exceed the 'name, rank and number' limitation. I knew that whatever they did to me they would never get anything out of me, since I knew nothing. But I saw no reason why this charade should continue on his terms. I told him that I had only joined the R.A.F. on the 7th February, which he probably knew anyway, and that prior to that I had been a Government administrative officer in Malaya. He quickly looked at his file.

'You were an Intelligence Officer all the time,' he shouted, and added: 'pretending to be a civil administrative officer.'

As I shook my head, I remembered the Japanese vegetable gardeners and photographers at Cameron Highlands. The thought also passed through my mind that the only damage I was doing to the Allied cause was to raise doubts in my tormentor's mind as to the efficiency of the R.A.F. intelligence service.

He was clearly puzzled; all my replies presumably fitted such facts as he already had in his possession. But he was not yet prepared to give up.

He barked at the guards who forced me down into the chair. One held my right arm behind my back while the other forced my left arm on to the table, where he splayed out my hand. He then took a sharp knife from his belt and carefully made a deep incision across the base of my left index finger. I was terrified, but the pain was no worse than when I had nearly cut the top of the same finger off in the jungle, on the bank of the river.

There was a long pause as we all watched the blood oozing out. The *Kempetei* Captain, in particular, seemed mesmerised. Then he shouted at me again: 'Will you talk now?'

'I have nothing more to say,' I replied.

'Get out,' he snarled, 'and don't talk to anyone. I will send for you again.'

The gorillas hauled me to my feet, dragged me through the door and flung me down the steps of the building with the *Kempetei* Captain's last words ringing in my ears.

I washed the cut under a tap and tied my handkerchief round my finger. I then went to the prison sick-bay where a P.o.W. orderly bandaged me up.

'I cut myself,' I said lamely.

'You ought to have some stitches in that, sir,' he replied, 'but we've none left.'

I went back to my quarters and lay on my bed-space, shaking all over.

For the next few days I dreaded another summons. It never came. I suppose that my inquisitor was busy with those who knew something.

It was a clean cut and it healed fairly quickly. It was dressed regularly when I returned to the hospital cell with dengue fever. I did not make any note of this in my diary. I did not need to. I have the scar to this day.

It was now high summer and the Japanese P.o.W. organisation was slowly grinding into gear. We were issued with numbers to be sewn on to our shirts. My number was 23. We were all required to have our heads shaved. I borrowed fifty florins from a Flight-Lieutenant, R. D. Viner. I gave him a cheque for £6.10s., written on a scrap of paper and drawn on my account with Lloyds Bank, Finsbury Circus Branch, London. He must have survived, as the cheque was duly presented and honoured after the war.

The 7th August 1942 was the eve of my thirty-first birthday and of our seventh wedding anniversary. I had crept away to a quiet

corner of the walled-in 'officers only' exercise path. I had decided
to write a long letter to L.

Privacy was at a premium in the prison, unless one was in
solitary confinement, and there one would not have a pen and paper.
It was officially three o'clock in the afternoon. The Japanese had
introduced Japanese time, and much else, into the Greater East
Asia Co-prosperity Sphere. This was one and a half hours ahead of
old Javanese time. In reality then, it was 1.30 p.m. and the hottest
time of the day. I had deliberately chosen this moment, as I had
hoped the exercise path would be deserted. I had not, however,
reckoned with the concert party. I was not aware that they had been
given permission to practise in this secluded spot at a time when no
officer in his senses would wish to walk there, either with a companion or with his own thoughts.

They were rehearsing the 'Lambeth Walk' to the accompaniment
of a very loud piano-accordion. Such noises have never disturbed me
as much as crickets chirping or as people whispering in such tones
that one just cannot hear what they are saying.

I soon insulated myself from the intruding noise; and I lay
on my back in the shade on what was left of a patch of grass. There
were two small birds on the high boundary wall, pecking away
among the broken bottles.

I wrote my letter in an old exercise book. It was never intended
to be sent and it has never been read by anyone but myself.

I found it so difficult to convey a sense of all the contradictions
around me. The sounds of the piano accordion must have been the
last sounds heard by those dying of dysentery in the stone cells
close by; dying for lack of drugs and appropriate food. When the
concert for which the party was practising took place, Japanese
and Korean guards would stand around in the shadows on the
outskirts of the crowd. They would not be on duty but would have
been attracted by the sounds of those who were trying to forget,
for a brief moment, their days and months of misery. Many in the
audience might have been savagely beaten up, perhaps even the
same day, by some of the attendant guards. The Camp Commandant
or one of his officers might even be sitting on a bench in the front
row, next to the C.O. whom he had maltreated and degraded hours
earlier.

Nothing made sense any more. There were no longer any guide-
lines. Each day was, and had to be, sufficient unto itself. The past

was dead, and in many cases buried. The future—was there a future?

On my way back to the barrack room I called on J.F. who was suffering from a bad attack of dysentery in one of the stone cells.

As September succeeded August there were signs that something was about to happen. Our captors, who had never produced drugs for the dying, suddenly produced large quantities of injections for the living. We were injected in all sorts of places for, allegedly, all kinds of complaints. One series of injection purported to be a prophylactic against dysentery; the wise ones said there was no such thing. The cynics went further, contending that all these injections were devilish concoctions designed to emasculate us. Most of us thought they were just water.

This activity led to rumours that the camp was to be broken up; and so it proved to be.

A small party of Army P.o.W.s left on the 23rd September and the first R.A.F. party on the 10th October, both for unknown destinations.

Whether it was the Japanese injections or whether it was a sub-conscious wish not to have to face the unknown, I do not know; but during the first week of October I was again 'admitted to hospital' with a raging fever, the cause of which was never diagnosed.

A few days after I was discharged I was warned to be ready to move at twenty-four hours' notice. The Japanese had left it to the C.O. and his staff to make up the parties. The latter tried to ensure that there was a Malay-speaking officer with each party. It was hoped that he would provide a channel of communication with our Japanese guards, whoever and wherever they might be.

The party to which I was detailed consisted of about 380 Army P.o.W.s and about 120 R.A.F. The C.O. of this party was Colonel 'Copper' Saunders, R.A. As I learnt afterwards, he had particularly asked Beery Noble if I could be attached to his party as a Malay-speaking officer.

I had made friends with a number of army officers during my time at Boei Glodok. One of these, Bell, had been at Peterhouse, Cambridge, with my brother Charles, but he had left with the first army party in September.

Among the other army officers in Saunders' party were Alan Steele and Robin Black.* Robin, whom I had known in Malaya, had

* Later Sir Robert Black, G.C.M.G., O.B.E., Governor of Hong Kong.

been one of the half a dozen officers with Laurens van der Post in the jungle.* Another had been Len Cooper who was a Lieutenant-Commander in the Straits Settlements R.N.V.R. He, too, was in our party.

By now the rumours were flying thick and fast. We were going to the coal-mines in Japan. We were going to the forests of Borneo. We were going to work on the Burma–Siam railway.

There was much leave-taking of friends who were to be left behind—for the moment. I said good-bye to J.F. who was slowly recovering from his dysentery. He was earmarked to go, as the Malay-speaking officer, with a later party. I was never to see him again.†

On Sunday morning the 18th October we were all paraded with our kit; we were only allowed such kit as we could carry. In addition to my heavy back-pack, side-pack, blankets, ground-sheet and water-bottle, I had acquired a large Gladstone bag in which I had, among other things, a number of books.

We staggered out of the prison to a nearby football field where all our kit had to be laid out for inspection. It was so hot and I was so weak, having only just come out of 'hospital', that I nearly collapsed. I decided there and then to abandon my Gladstone bag and its contents; the loss of my books was a great blow and I had forgotten that it contained my lilo mattress. A Japanese searcher took away my torch, but neither he nor any of his successors found my diaries.

We stacked all our kit outside the prison, which we re-entered to have a meal, prior to departure. Some hitch must then have occurred; or perhaps it was all deliberately contrived. We remained in the prison for three nights, while our kit remained outside.

These were three particularly uncomfortable nights, with no bedding and no razor.

After lunch on Wednesday the 21st we marched out of the prison again. It was terribly hot. By the time we had sorted out all our kit and formed up, I thought I was going to faint. Several of my fellow-prisoners did.

Fortunately the march to the station was only about a mile; we were bundled into a train for the docks at Tandjong Prior.

* See page 51.

† I was told after the war that the party to which he had been assigned was sent to Borneo. The Japanese ship in which they were making the voyage was torpedoed by an American submarine and J.F. was drowned.

The *Yoshida Maru* was awaiting us, a Japanese cargo vessel of about 3,000 tons with four holds. The Boei Glodok party, about 500, was in the very small for'ard hold. Into the three other holds aft some 2,000 to 2,500 human beings were crammed. We had little contact with these but I believe they were Dutch P.o.W.s and Javanese slave labour destined for work on the Burma–Siam railway.*

The conditions were indescribable. The sides of the hold had been fitted with rows of rough shelves with a headroom of two feet. The majority of the P.o.W.s 'camped' on the wet ballast floor of the hold. No one, whether on the shelves or on the ballast, could stretch out his legs full length.

There were two steep wooden step-ladders, with armed sentries at the top, leading up from the bowels of the ship to the deck. There were no lights. In theory it was impossible for so many men to be in such a small space; in practice it happened.

The heat was unbearable. We were somewhat luckier in being for'ard. When the vessel was moving we could at least imagine that there was air. Those aft of the bridge structure got none. Many there were suffocated.

We spent the first night aboard tied up alongside. Without warning a sackful of loaves was thrown down the ladder into our hold. Men fought like animals for the loaves. Many loaves, and men, were trodden under foot. Many loaves were torn into fragments which were lost for ever among the ballast. Few men got anything to eat, and I was not among them. We would have to get something organised for the future, I thought.

Eventually we settled down as best we could for the night. As always happened when P.o.W.s were moved about, the strange guards had seemed more on edge and more brutal than those to whom we had grown accustomed. We had yet to learn their idiosyncrasies.

I tried to sleep, but like my companions I was restless and anxious. Where were we going to? What did the days and maybe years that lay ahead hold in store? I tried to take stock of the situation.

Whatever our destination might be, we would be going deeper into the heartland of the Greater East Asia Co-prosperity Sphere.

* In addition to the 16,000 or more Allied P.o.W.s (out of a total of some 61,000) who died on the Burma–Siam Railway, at least 100,000 Chinese, Tamil, Malay, Burmese, Javanese and Indische-Jongens (of mixed Dutch-Indonesian blood) impressed labourers also died there.

At Boei Gladok we had been buoyed up by the fantasy that the Allies would soon be re-taking Java. We had hypnotised ourselves into this frame of mind by our ludicrous attempts at collecting military intelligence whenever we left the prison walls. While this was an important strand in the fibre of our morale in Java, our sudden departure from the perimeter towards the centre deprived us of this support.

I thought, too, of the friendly faces behind the hedges and fences at Batavia airport. It lifted our spirits to know that there were some, close at hand, who wished us well and who had the courage to show it. Would we find any friendly faces where we were going? If our destination was Japan there would be no friends beyond the wire. We would be in a wholly hostile world.

But might there not be some compensations, even if we did go to Japan? Though there had been friends, there had been enemies too in Java, and Nature was the greatest of these. In the absence of any medical supplies we were all an easy prey to tropical complaints of all kinds. Surely, dysentery would be less rife, surely cuts and sores would have a better chance of healing, in the more equable climate of Japan.

When the Korean guards had been particularly brutal in Java, one would say to another: 'Well, of course, these bastards are allowed to do what they like here; they seem to be answerable to no one; they can, and do, get away with murder,' and the other would reply: 'Yes—I bet it would be different in Japan. With the Japanese brass breathing down their necks, these buggers wouldn't dare do what they do here.'

Wouldn't they? I wondered.

There is always noise in a ship, even when it is tied up alongside. As I turned these thoughts over in my mind I could hear the water lapping gently against the ship's sides. I could hear, too, raucous Japanese voices and the tramping of feet on the deck. The whine of cranes and winches, indicating that, like us, the rich loot of Java was to be carried away to some destination unknown.

I must have dozed off. When I woke again I could hear men marching on the deck above me and the harsh Japanese military commands. We knew that the Japanese had never ratified the Geneva Convention on the Treatment of Prisoners of War. I recalled that in Boei Glodok senior P.o.W. officers, who had waved copies of the Convention in front of the Japanese authorities, had received beatings for their pains. Once again the Japanese were showing their contempt for the Convention by transporting military personnel and stores in the same ship as P.o.W.s.

As dawn broke, the ship came to life. The guards again flung some loaves of bread down the ladder. By this time those in authority had worked out a system; and everyone got at least a mouthful of bread.

Then, ten at a time, we were allowed up on deck. There were two temporary wooden structures built out over the side of the ship. As most of the prisoners were suffering from dysentery or other intestinal complaints, these became unspeakably filthy in a very short space of time; and this was only the first day. The guards were chasing and chivying the while. If one was lucky, one got one's water-bottle filled, but there was always a risk that a malevolent guard, impatient to get the whole exercise over, would knock it out of one's hand.

Meanwhile, those below, unable to contain themselves, were shouting and crowding round the bottom of the ladder. Their fear, frequently realised, was that the Japanese would call a halt to this operation before they had had their turn. We would have to organise this too, I thought.

This shambles took about three hours. Then at 10 a.m. on Thursday the 22nd October 1942 we sailed out of Tandjong Priok.

5

Voyage to Japan

The 'Dai Nichi Maru'—October–November 1942*

We arrived in the roads off Singapore about midday on Sunday the 25th October. Our three days and nights at sea had been without incident, except for the chaos of the morning and evening scrambles on deck, which had proved much more difficult to organise than the distribution of a few loaves. A starving man can always be induced to wait for a few minutes if he knows he is going to get something in the end; sufferers from dysentery cannot.

Our greatest problems had been the presence of heat and the absence of water. After we had sailed we were not allowed any cold water at all. We were allowed three cups of hot water a day for drinking and one for washing. Very occasionally we were able, during our brief spells on deck, to get a douche under the sea-water hose. It depended on which guards were about. Much was the gravel, and many were the stones, which were then, unbeknown to us, forming in our kidneys.

The unrelenting heat was most oppressive and it was virtually impossible to sleep. If we persuaded the Japanese to leave the tarpaulin off our hatch it inevitably rained and we were soaked to the skin.

The Japanese Warrant Officer who was in charge of our hold was, surprisingly, as helpful and courteous as he could be. As interpreter, I saw a lot of him and of the cheerful little cook who was the only Malay speaker on the other side. He was also responsible for the rice and stew which occasionally replaced the bread.

The following day, Monday the 26th October, we tied up in Keppel Harbour. It was strange, as we steamed in, to see, under such

*See map 2, page 317.

different circumstances, the Singapore waterfront that many of us knew so well: Fullerton Building, the Supreme Court, and the Seaview and Raffles Hotels.

We spent another hot night on board and then on Tuesday the 27th October we disembarked. We spent most of the day in the broiling sun about 250 yards away from the *Yoshida Maru*. We watched, with interest, the unloading of a number of Bren-gun carriers from our ship.

Two incidents marked our day on the Singapore waterfront. The first was a most agreeable shower under a hose on the quay. For once we could stay there as long as we liked, and we did.

The other incident was less agreeable. We were lined up on the dock-side, facing the water, in groups of about fifty at a time. The order was then given to lower our trousers and bend over. To the great amusement of hundreds of Tamil coolies, a glass rod was then roughly inserted in each man's anus, revolved, removed and placed in a cardboard box on which, we supposed, our name, rank and number was duly inscribed. Quite what the purpose of this exercise was we never did discover. We presumed it was a medical test of some sort, but no results were ever made public.

Later in the afternoon, and when the unloading of cargo had been completed for the day, we returned to the *Yoshida Maru* to spend another unpleasant night.

The following day, Wednesday the 28th, our party finally left the *Yoshida Maru* and marched through the docks to a fumigation and disinfection centre. While we took baths in highly disinfected water, our kit was subjected to fumigation and pilfering.

That evening we went on board the *Dai Nichi Maru*, a much larger Japanese vessel of about 15,000 tons. Once again we were crammed down into a hold, where conditions were, if anything, worse than those in the *Yoshida Maru*. On the 29th we moved out into the roads and early on the 30th we sailed.

We did not know it then, but the voyage from Singapore to Moji in Japan, which was destined to be our landfall, was to be, perhaps, the grimmest part of our captivity. It was not that the Japanese were particularly brutal; on the contrary, they were, by and large, more considerate than when we were on dry land. But our conditions were such that many were to die en route; and many were to be led into depravities of which I, for one, did not realise the human race was capable.

There were other factors, too, which led to an ever-heightening sense of anxiety.

When we sailed out of Singapore, battened down in the stifling hold, we realised that we were not, as were those other unfortunates who had been in the *Yoshida Maru*, destined for the Burma–Siam railway. But we still did not know where we were going, except that we were going further and further away from the Allies. We knew, too, that by the latter half of 1942, Allied submarines had had considerable successes in sinking Japanese shipping all over the Pacific. Casual contacts with other groups of P.o.W.s on the dock-side in Singapore had confirmed this; some indeed were the survivors of such sinkings.

In order to limit the number of her children who go out of their minds, Nature has, I believe, contrived a mechanism which somehow detaches horrors from their actual surroundings. By blurring the edges of the frame of reality, certain memories, although vivid enough in themselves, seem wholly detached from the circumstances in which, one knows, they occurred. As the years pass, even the vividness of these horrors diminishes.

Thus I cannot recall whether the party which made the voyage to Japan in the *Dai Nichi Maru* was exactly the same as the party from Boei Glodok which had arrived in Singapore in the *Yoshida Maru*; or whether we lost some, and gained others, while we were in Singapore. I cannot recall quite how we organised ourselves. I do know that several other parties of P.o.W.s embarked in the *Dai Nichi Maru* in Singapore. I know, too, that we found few, if any, Malay-speaking Japanese on board; and it was this which made me determined to learn Japanese.

Our first port of call was Saigon, where we arrived about midday on Tuesday the 3rd November. Something must have gone wrong with the Japanese plans. We left in a great hurry, a few hours later, without, apparently, making any contact with the port. During the next twenty-four hours we were not allowed on deck at all. Our hold became the cess-pit it was to remain for the rest of our voyage.

It was on Armistice Day, Wednesday the 11th November 1942, that we buried the first of our dead at sea. His name was Glenister and I believe he was in the R.A.F. It was among the most impressive

D

funerals I have ever attended and it threw a new light on the Japanese character.

Once again the Japanese had ignored the provisions of the Convention on the Treatment of Prisoners of War. A substantial part of the ship was occupied by Japanese military personnel and there was a considerable amount of military equipment both on and below decks.

Having explained the circumstances and asked permission for the burial at sea, we were informed that all the Japanese senior officers on board would attend the funeral to pay their respects to our dead comrade.

At the appointed hour a small group of P.o.W.s assembled on the deck. A number of these were themselves to be buried at sea before the voyage was over. A Union Jack had been produced from somewhere and draped over the corpse, which was tightly bound in a shroud. There was no coffin.

We waited in silence and then one of the Japanese officers who was responsible for the P.o.W.s on board called us to attention with the command 'Kiotski'. Within a few moments a solemn procession appeared from amidships where the Japanese were quartered. Eight or ten senior Japanese officers in full dress, with immaculately laundered white gloves and wearing their samurai swords, were followed by four buglers, equally smartly turned out. Bringing up the rear were four soldiers bearing trays on which we could make out tins of condensed milk, rice-balls, fish, sweets and other Japanese dainties.

One of the senior prisoner officers read the burial service and concluded with an appropriate reference to the fact that it was Armistice Day. As the corpse slipped into the sea, the bugles spoke and the Japanese officers saluted smartly with their swords. Then, watched by a hundred hungry eyes, the Japanese officers, in turn, took food from the trays and cast it into the sea.

This bizarre ceremony formed the subject of many conversations in the hold that night.

'What did you make of all that?' my neighbour whispered to me as we settled down.

'The Japanese have great respect for the dead; they have an even greater respect for those who die for their country on active service,' I replied; and then added: 'They have no respect for P.o.W.s who, in their view, do not exist as human beings. To re-establish himself in their eyes it is necessary for a P.o.W. to die.'

'Yes, I know all about that,' my neighbour replied impatiently, 'but if they had only given some of that condensed milk to Glenister while there was still some hope he might never have died of dysentery.'

'I know,' I replied, 'but that is not the way their minds work. His spirit has claims on them. As a P.o.W. he had none.'

We buried many at sea during the succeeding days. The first few who died got the same V.I.P. treatment and then the senior Japanese officers and the buglers came no more. For a while the Japanese officer in charge of us would attend and cast overboard a token contribution for the sustenance of the departing spirit. Then even that ceased. By the end, the only representative of His Imperial Majesty was a slovenly Japanese guard who, as likely as not, would be smoking throughout the proceedings.

I had sat up with him for two or three nights already, in a foul-smelling corner of the hold. He couldn't have been more than twenty-one. He was an A.C.II, and he was suffering terribly from dysentery. For the first three nights I had persuaded myself he might survive. 'If only he would show some signs of wanting to live,' I thought, 'he might just make it.'

I had spent hours begging him to hang on and not to give up the struggle. Then on the fourth night, in a comparatively lucid moment, he turned on me.

'Why the hell should I live, sir,' he whispered hoarsely. 'I shall never be allowed to do what I want to do.'

I grasped his hand and asked him to tell me all about it.

'My father was a regular Colonel, sir. He retired a few years before the war. When I left England he had something to do with the Home Guard.'

He paused and gripped my hand more firmly; then he went on:

'Don't misunderstand me, sir. He's a fine man, my father, and I respect him very much. He was not a great soldier, you know, but it was his life; and he did what he did very well.'

There was another long silence and then he continued, 'I don't know how to say this, sir, but I must tell someone before I die.'

I offered him some water which he took avidly.

'It was always assumed in the family that I would go into the Army—Sandhurst, you know,' he whispered.

'And you didn't want to?' I enquired.

'Well, when I was young I didn't really think about it much

but I supposed that if that was what he wanted, that was what I would do.'

'What did your mother think?' I asked.

'I don't think Mum thought about it much. She followed Dad in most things. And I think she'd enjoyed her life as an army officer's wife.'

He paused for some time; and for a moment I thought he had lapsed into unconsciousness. Then he suddenly said:

'Have you got a cigarette, sir? I'd love to have a drag.'

I lit him a cigarette. One of the Japanese Sergeants who spoke a little Malay and through whom I had been making arrangements for the funerals had given me three cigarettes. I saw the cigarette glowing in the darkness.

'It all happened when I was about thirteen and went to my public school,' he said. 'I had learnt to play the piano when I was a kid, and I didn't play badly. It was quite fun really.'

There was another long pause while he puffed on his cigarette. The *Dai Nichi Maru*'s engines were throbbing away and all around me men were coughing, groaning and relieving themselves. I suddenly wondered what would happen if an American torpedo hit us.

'At my public school,' he went on, 'there was a wonderful music-master. When he learnt I could play the piano a bit, he encouraged and helped me. He gave me extra lessons for which he did not charge. And then, sir, I began to realise what music was all about.'

The dying boy beside me was now vibrant with life. In the light of the glowing cigarette I could see his eyes shining. Suddenly a look of intense sadness passed over his young drawn face.

'Does it hurt much?' I asked.

'No, sir, it's not that. I was just remembering when I told my father. It was at the end of the summer term. I was just seventeen and had another year to do at school.'

He then described the scene with his father. Returning home for the holidays, he had told his parents that he now knew what he wanted to do with his life. He wanted to play the piano professionally. 'The music-master says I can do it, Dad. He's been terribly helpful and encouraging. And that's what I am going to do.'

I could picture the reactions of the respectable elderly couple to this news. Suddenly all the father's hopes and aspirations for his son had been dashed to the ground. After an exchange of harsh words, the Colonel had marched out of the room shouting at his son:

'If you're not man enough to be a soldier, you had better go into something respectable, like a bank. But music—never!'

There was a bit of a movement in another part of the hold. A moment or two later a Flight-Sergeant touched me on the arm:

'Would you come over, sir. It's Briggs. I believe he's dying—or dead,' he whispered.

Picking my way through the recumbent forms in the darkness, I followed the Flight-Sergeant. Two of his companions were supporting the body, or the corpse, of their friend. He seemed to me to be dead, but I couldn't be sure.

'Well, there's nothing we can do till morning, anyhow. Keep an eye on him, Flight, and if he shows signs of life let me know. But I think he's dead.' It all seemed terribly callous, but there was nothing one could do. I don't recall that there was a prisoner doctor on board. A P.o.W. medical orderly would have to be consulted in the morning, and he could give nothing but advice, since we had no medical supplies.

I returned to the living.

'What was all that in aid of, sir?' he enquired.

'Oh! somebody with gripes in his belly,' I replied. 'He'll be all right,' I lied.

'Have you got another cigarette, sir?' he enquired. 'It helps me to talk a bit.'

I lit the second of my three precious cigarettes.

'My last year at school was hell,' he resumed. 'I refused to take the Sandhurst exam and that nearly broke Dad's heart. When I left school the music-master had fixed up for me to go somewhere for further music studies. I never went, of course. The war was on and I felt I ought to join up. I joined the Raff; and here I am.' He drew deeply on his cigarette. 'Of course, Dad was pleased when I joined up. He said that it would make a man of me. He suggested that I might transfer to the Army after the war, and try for a commission. He was still harping on the bloody Army, though I'd told him dozens of times that music was, for me, the only thing that mattered.'

By now he was getting weaker and I could see the tears welling up in his eyes.

'So you see, sir,' he whispered, 'what's the use of you telling me to hang on? Even if I do get through this, my father will do everything he can to stop me doing what I want to do—to play the piano.' He paused and then added pathetically: 'You can see, sir, that I should never make a soldier, and I don't fancy a bank.'

The butt of his cigarette was nearly burning his lips. I removed it and ground it out in the ballast. I had to find this by moving a corner of his blanket to one side.

'You'd better get some sleep now, and so had I,' and I added, as I moved off towards my shelf: 'I'll come and see you tomorrow night.'

I never did. He died in the early hours of the morning and I went to his funeral later in the day. As his corpse was cast into the sea, without even the music of bugles, I thought to myself: 'What a strange way to resolve human problems.'

The *Dai Nichi Maru* was now steaming along in the South China Sea. It was glorious weather and we were allowed up on deck in larger numbers and for longer periods of time. Below decks it was a different story. The dying were so weak that they could not get up the steep ladders and they fouled themselves where they lay. It was so dark that dead men, huddled in their blankets, could lie undiscovered for days.

It was about this time, mid-November, that we reached the port of Takao in Formosa, now Taiwan. We stayed there for three days and three nights.

The C.O. was desperately anxious to get the seriously ill off the ship; and the Japanese, no doubt fearful that the ship would arrive at its ultimate destination with nothing but corpses, were in no mood to argue.

I went ashore with the party of sick. We took with us a number of our dead and the funeral service was read before they were cremated.

On the dock-side I met a P.o.W. officer from another ship engaged in the same macabre task. He told me that 200 sick and twelve dead had been carried ashore from a single hold in his ship.

The port was very active and Japanese ships were continually entering and leaving. On the second day a party of Army P.o.W.s from Singapore were disembarked from the *Dai Nichi Maru* for work somewhere in Formosa. They were replaced by about 300 Americans and a mixed group from Singapore of some 200.

Among the latter I found two former members of the Malayan Public Works Service called Plunkett and Warren. We discussed the strange case of Group Captain R. L. Nunn who had been Director of Public Works in Malaya and who had left his post there without authority.*

The same afternoon I was leaning over the side of the ship trying to fill a bucket, attached to a rope, with sea-water. The rope broke and I lost the bucket. A Japanese guard saw me and lost his temper. It was the only beating-up I had on the voyage but the effects were with me for some time.

When we left Takao we made hurriedly for a group of very bleak islands to the west of Formosa, the Pescadores. We remained at anchor there in very rough seas for three nights. All the ship's lights were extinguished. This did not make much difference to us in the Stygian darkness of our hold, but a new element was added to our misery, seasickness. Those who had not been deemed by the Japanese to be sufficiently near death's door to leave the ship at Takao soon reached those gloomy portals and the burials at sea started again.

On the fourth day we left the Pescadores in convoy with five other ships and a destroyer escort. We sailed without lights for several nights. The Japanese on board were tense, irritable and anxious; one of the few Malay-speaking guards told me that we were passing through an area where many Japanese ships had been sunk by American submarines. 'Roosebelto no goodo,' he added for good measure.

Throughout the voyage the food had been of very poor quality and quite insufficient. After Formosa the portions of rice got smaller and smaller. What was far worse was the diminution in the quantity of water provided. For men racked with fever this was an unendurable deprivation. It was then that dying men drank each other's urine. It was then, or so it was alleged, that, shrouded in the merciful darkness, men would open each other's veins with razor blades and suck each other's blood. Many knew that they had but hours to live; many knew that they would never see the light of day again. Despite the ministrations of their comrades, there was nothing that the latter could do to alleviate their agony.

The contrasts persisted. Sunday the 22nd November was a glorious day. After two more funerals all who could came up on deck for a church service in the bright sunshine. The Japanese were in a better humour and became more friendly. They were approaching their homeland and they told us that we should soon be sighting Japan.

* See pp. 209–12 et al. of Noel Barber's *Sinister Twighlit—The Fall and rise again of Singapore* (1968).

On Monday the 23rd we sighted the first islands of Japan on the starboard bow. The sea was calm, but it was becoming increasingly colder. We were wearing all the clothes we possessed. The holds were hot and foetid; the decks were cool and fresh. During the day we passed many islands and dozens of Japanese junks. The fishermen waved in a friendly way at the strange white faces lining the ship's rail. That evening the Japanese issued us with soap, of which we had seen none during the voyage. We were not to pollute the sacred soil of Nippon.

It became increasingly cold that night and on Tuesday the 24th I woke up with a raging sore throat. In the afternoon we anchored in the roads off Moji, a port on the north-eastern corner of Kyushu, the southernmost of the four large islands which make up the mainland of Japan.

We remained anchored in the roads all night. It was bitterly cold. About four o'clock in the afternoon of Wednesday the 25th we steamed for about an hour into Moji and tied up alongside.

We were woken up by the guards at 2 a.m. on Thursday the 26th and told to prepare for a medical inspection on deck at 7 a.m. By now I had a raging fever. We stood about freezing on deck for several hours. 'At least,' I thought to myself, 'I shall die on dry land and not in that never-to-be-forgotten hold, where the dead and dying, indistinguishable from one another, had, perforce, been left.'

The medical inspection party never came, and at midday we returned to the hold for a meal. We took the opportunity of carrying those who were clearly dead up on to the deck.

In the afternoon those who could paraded on deck again. Anal orifices were pierced by glass rods; mouths were roughly prodded; and chests were examined. It was so cold that this medical inspection must have killed many more than it saved. The senior officers collected the personal possessions of those who had died and their foul clothes and blankets were distributed among the living. I succeeded in avoiding participation in this unappetising lottery. I thought it was too high a price to pay, even for increased warmth.

At half past three in the afternoon came the order to disembark. I now found myself the junior officer in a small R.A.F. party of about a hundred. The senior officer, Squadron-Leader 'Ricky' Wright, was a regular. A brave Battle of Britain pilot, he must have been about twenty-three or twenty-four when he inherited the heavy responsibilities of the senior officer in charge of a group of P.o.W.s. The next senior officer was Lieutenant-Commander L. L. Cooper, Straits

Settlements R.N.V.R.* A tough and somewhat taciturn Lancashire-man, he had worked for some years in Singapore with Guthries and had devoted many of his leisure hours to the S.S.R.N.V.R. He must have been about the same age as myself at the time. He sported a magnificent blond beard. He had plenty of guts. Number three in the hierarchy was Flight-Lieutenant 'Nippy' Knight. He had had long service in the ranks of the R.A.F. before obtaining his commission. He was dark and reserved. I put him down at between thirty-five and forty.

At the end of the line there were two of us, both Pilot Officers R.A.F.V.R. Tim Hallam was a most gallant fellow. A Carthusian, I seem to recall, he had seen active service during World War I. After the war he had emigrated to Australia, acquired a dairy farm, and then married, comparatively late in life. He must have been nearly fifty when war broke out in the Far East. He had three small daughters who had not yet attained their teens. Engaged, as he was, in food production, with a young family and over the call-up age himself, Tim could well have sat back and made some contribution to the Allied war effort in Australia. But that would not have been in character. I gather that he made life a misery to the authorities until he was sent overseas to what, they assumed, would be a quiet administrative job with the R.A.F. in Singapore.

I was to get to know my four fellow-officers very well during the succeeding twelve months.

In addition, we had with us two R.A.F. Warrant Officers. One, Pritchard, was quite first-class, not only as a W.O. but also as a man. He knew the R.A.F. backwards; he knew how to handle men; and he knew that discipline, particularly in a P.o.W. camp, had to be tempered with humanity. Cheerful and competent, intelligent and wise, he was a companion of whom to be proud in captivity.†

The other Warrant Officer was quite different. I will call him W. He was an 'old soldier' of the worst sort. Slovenly, lazy and always on the look-out for a 'scrounge', we could well have done without him. For all I knew, he may have had some highly specialised technical qualification, but it was not a qualification that was needed in captivity.

* See page 57.
† Pritchard was commissioned after the war. During the early fifties he turned up as a Squadron-Leader in Cyprus where I was glad to be able to entertain him and to talk over old times.

Our leave-taking with those who had made the cruise with us from Tandjong Prior was brief and the confusion on the dock-side was such that there were many friends to whom I did not say good-bye at all.

An American-speaking Japanese guard, who seemed to have some responsibility for our party, was pleasant and helpful. We were all given Japanese food in little wooden boxes. After the deprivations of the voyage it seemed like manna from heaven. Although simple, *hors d'œuvres* and rice, it tasted slightly better than, though it bore a close resemblance to, the insipid economy-class meals served in aircraft.

Our shirts and shorts afforded little protection against the bitter cold. Such knowledge as I had of Japan had been gained from travel posters; geishas, parasols, cherry blossoms, maple leaves, all shimmering in the heat of high summer. My geography was all wrong, I concluded; we must be closer to Siberia than I thought; and this was southern Japan.

We marched or rather shambled off. We were all weak and stiff from the long sea trip. Another long wait outside the ferry station; by now many were collapsing. Finally we embarked for the short trip across the straits to Shimonoseki, a large port on the southern tip of Honshu, the main island of Japan. It was the rail-head for the line that ran to Tokyo and beyond. The guards continued to be reasonably helpful and co-operative. 'This cannot last,' I thought, and it didn't.

Our first shock was at Shimonoseki. As we left the ferry, we were herded like cattle through specially constructed wooden passageways, with waist-high wooden barriers on either side. Beyond these there were hundreds of Japanese civilians, row upon row, bidden, no doubt, to see some of the spoils of war. We were on display. The crowd did not jeer; it did not roar; it was absolutely silent and inscrutable. The silence was punctuated by the gasps and groans of those, weakened by dysentery and malnutrition, who were collapsing. This was no part of the Japanese *mise en scène* and the brutality of the guards reasserted itself. Men were beaten and clouted unmercifully. If that did not serve to get them to their feet they were prodded and jabbed with bayonets. Some were now unconscious and would never move again. The cortège was not allowed to stop or even pause. If a man fell, towards the head of the column, his passing fellows might, with luck, haul him to his knees and drag him along; if he was at the rear, he had to be abandoned, for there was no turning back, nor even looking back. Whispers ran up the files that those who had fallen well behind were being bayoneted to death where they lay.

The atmosphere of friendliness and co-operation on the Moji side of the straits had evaporated into thin air in Shimonoseki.

Eventually we reached the railway station and those who did were hustled into not uncomfortable passenger coaches, with padded seats. Here, at last, it was warm; and here again the unpredictable guards, who no longer had a part to play, became reasonably friendly.

Few of us slept during the night journey. Those who were not constantly relieving their dysentery in the W.C. were kept awake by those who were.

We left the train at Onomichi at about seven o'clock in the morning. The station was colder, it seemed, than anything we had ever known. A second 'economy-class' meal in its little wooden box, though welcome, did not taste as good as the first one. The guards, however, continued to be friendly, bringing quantities of hot water with which to warm our empty stomachs.

About 11 a.m. we marched a short distance to the Onomichi ferry station and embarked in a tug. The officers were invited into the captain's cabin. This was the first and last sign of discrimination. For two hours we sailed through the islands of the Seto Inland Sea. We were now approaching a large dockyard, containing a number of vessels in the course of construction.

As the tug stopped at the little jetty of Habu on the island of Innoshima, the whole village seemed to have turned out, to see us, if not exactly to welcome us.

We marched through the narrow streets of the village and through a part of the huge dock-yard. No one fell out on the march. Those who had been seriously ill had been left dead or dying in the cattle pens of Shimonoseki. Those who had become ill during the train journey were being brought by a small boat from the jetty to the site of our new beach home, on the eastern perimeter of the dockyard. As the heavy gates of the camp closed behind us we wondered, as so often before, what lay ahead of us, and, above all, for how long.

6

The Dockyard

*Habu, Innoshima—November–December 1942**

Tim Hallam and I were marching briskly up and down the path which ran along the whole length of the single-storey wooden barrack block. Although we were together, each of us was alone with his own thoughts. We hardly exchanged a word. We preferred it that way. As we came to the end of the path, we did an about turn with such military precision as we could muster. We were trying to keep the cold at bay.

I was casting my mind back over the events of the past twelve months. I was trying hard to disentangle the weft and warp of the texture of life as a P.o.W.; and suddenly it came. The dominant feature of the design was contrast.

I supposed that in the ordinary life of a free man the same contrasting elements were ever present. But there they were overlaid by the hypocrisy of personal relationships and by a series of man-made devices to avoid extremes.

In the life of a P.o.W. the veneer of so-called civilised society was absent; the contrasts were sharpened; and their impact on the human spirit was enhanced. Never before had I come across so many saints and sinners; never before had I been so bored or so excited; never before had I known such extremes of heat and cold.

The sharpened contrasts were both spatial and temporal. I remembered the soft voices of the audience at Garoet singing 'There'll always be an England', while in the shadows lurked smiling Japanese who were to beat them unmercifully on the morrow; I recalled the men dying in agony at Boei Glodok with the sounds of

* See map 3, page 318.

the concert party in their ears; I re-lived the scene on the *Dai Nichi Maru* when the Japanese top brass had paid their highest tributes to the dead, whom they themselves had killed by neglect.

Now the contrast had moved into the sphere of time. After the *Dai Nichi Maru* the camp at Habu had seemed, at first blush, a not too disagreeable place. It was true that, whereas we had been perpetually thirsty, now we were perpetually cold. As the months went by, Nature would rectify this latter imbalance; but, at the same time, it would blur the horrors of the *Dai Nichi Maru* and thus sharpen the more unpleasant features of life at Habu of which we were, as yet, unaware.

Our first afternoon at the camp was spent settling in. We welcomed our sick at the little pier to which they had been brought in a small boat from the jetty at Habu village. Pritchard, as usual, was a tower of strength, both physical and moral. We carried them gently to one of the rooms in the gaunt bare barrack block, from which many of them were never to emerge, except in rough pine coffins.

We then enjoyed the luxury of a hot bath. After this we were each issued with two Japanese uniforms. One of these was to be worn whenever we went to work in the dockyard. This consisted of a paper-thin green silk tunic, with slacks to match. Perched on our heads were small green caps, rather like the old-style postman's hat, without the peak at the back. Round the crown of the cap we had to sew a band of red silk ribbon to indicate that we were P.o.W.s. As we were to discover later, the 20,000 Japanese dockyard workers wore similar uniforms without the red band.

Each man had to stitch on to the left breast of both his tunics a white piece of cloth with black numbers on it. Three black lines on either side of the number indicated that the wearer was an officer. My number, as the junior of the five officers, was 5.

Our working outfits resembled nothing so much as the bus conductor's or postman's uniforms that one used to buy on a card. They looked as though they would be just about as durable. They appeared to come in standard sizes only, but by a judicious series of exchanges we managed to look slightly less ludicrous than would otherwise have been the case.

All this trying on, taking in and letting out, interspersed with mutual comments on each other's appearance so reminiscent of a children's fancy-dress party, raised our spirits considerably and we had not yet lost the warmth of the hot baths.

A note in my diary records that the first evening meal in our new camp was good and that we had a little fish with our rice. The same entry records that the barrack room was bitterly cold.

There seemed to be a certain attractive amateurism about the arrangements at Habu. The Camp Commandant was Captain Akira Nomoto.* He was a slight, sensitive and rather timid man, about the same age as myself. He made up for his lack of self-confidence by a certain forced brusquerie. He never seemed to be quite sure what he ought to be doing or how he should do it. He came from a small village on the smaller of the four main islands, Shikoku. I doubt whether he had ever seen a European until we shambled into his camp. I am sure that he had never had a command before; and he was in no sense a *samurai* warrior.

On our arrival he had fussed about rather like a matron welcoming a lot of new boys to a boarding school. This, no doubt, reflected his true character, for he was essentially a kindly man. Then suddenly he would remember his position of responsibility, and that we were P.o.W.s, and he would bark and cuff with the rest.

His second-in-command was Sergeant Shigema Nagano. A true son of the soil, well-built, uncomplicated, with a coarse Rabelaisian sense of humour, Nagano could, and did, hit very hard; but he did not bear malice. In the fulness of time we came to refer to him as 'Smiler'.

The camp interpreter was a most unpleasant little Lance-Corporal called Nakano. Even on parade he looked dirtier and more slovenly than any of the P.o.W.s. He rarely shaved and he appeared to wash even less frequently, which was unusual for a Japanese. He seemed to bear a grudge against the whole world. His fellow-guards did not care for him much. He quickly learnt how to relieve his frustrations by beating up the prisoners. It was remarkable what strength this snivelling, stunted little fellow could command.

A number of other guards were capable of friendliness and even acts of kindness. One of these, known as 'George', had lost an arm during the Japanese campaign in China. Another had had the whole of the side of his face incinerated when the defenders of Singapore had sprayed burning petrol on the narrow stretch of water between Singapore and the State of Johore. His horrifying appearance earned him the name of 'Burnt Ears', but this sobriquet belied

* See also Epilogue in which I give an account of my meeting with Nomoto and others in August 1969.

his not ungentle character. It was only natural, I suppose, that those who had suffered themselves should have more sympathy with P.o.W.s than those who had never suffered.

The *éminence grise* of the camp was the so-called medical orderly. He was the owner of a small pharmacy in Habu village. Very early every morning he would come to the camp wearing a military uniform. He made no effort to heal the sick. He brought no medicine except a bottle of iodine. His sole task was to decide whether those dying of dysentery and malnutrition were fit to march to the dockyard and do a hard day's work there. I doubt whether this task placed any strain on whatever medical knowledge he may have had. Unless a man was virtually unconscious the verdict was inevitably 'fit'. We did not care for him much.

This was the human raw material which we had to try to mould into patterns of our own choosing. The prospects were not unpropitious. There were several factors working in our favour. We had been P.o.W.s in Japanese hands for over six months. We had acquired some knowledge of what made the Japanese tick; of their idiosyncrasies and of the unpredictabilities. To them we were unknown quantities. Surely this was something that we should be able to turn to our own advantage during the battle of wits to follow. Again, there were, as yet, no precedents governing the rhythm of life at Habu. We would have to try to ensure, so far as this might be possible, that such precedents as were created would be to our benefit. Anything that looked like being disadvantageous should be challenged and, if possible, changed before it hardened into a precedent.

It was only as the days went by that the full framework of our presence at Habu became clear to us.

In 1894 the Habu Dockyard Company had been formed. In 1911 it had been taken over as the Innoshima Branch Yard of the Osaka Iron Works. This latter company had been founded as long ago as 1881 by an Englishman, E. H. Hunter. During the years preceding the Japanese thrust to the south, there had been considerable developments at Habu. From 1937 a 50,000-ton dry dock, many buildings berths and other facilities had been constructed or expanded.

Our earliest visits to the dockyard clearly indicated that it had played a major role in implementing Japanese plans for the maritime penetration of South-East Asia.

The day was to come in 1943 when the Osaka Iron Works itself was to be absorbed by the giant Hitachi Zosen (Hitachi Shipbuilding and Engineering Co. Ltd.).*

'Why,' we asked ourselves, 'had a hundred or so P.o.W.s, already weakened by malnutrition and singularly lacking in the skills required for shipbuilding, been brought thousands of miles from Java to this little island on the Seto Inland Sea?'

The reason, we thought, was clear. We were not there to step up output; the Japanese labour supply seemed almost inexhaustible. We were there, it seemed to us, for one purpose and one only: to boost up the morale of the dockyard mateys. This was another fact of which we had to take account in our running battle with the Japanese authorities.

We took stock not only of the personalities of the staff but also of the physical features of the camp.

The camp, which was not yet finished, was being built, at the company's expense, by dockyard personnel on dockyard property. It was situated, agreeably enough, on some waste land between beach and the road which ran all round the island. On the far side of the road, opposite the camp gates, there was a grove of orange trees which were to bear forbidden fruit as the months went by.

On our arrival we had occupied the only completed barrack block. This was a single-story building constructed of roughly cut dwarf pine. Nothing fitted or met. There were large cracks in the walls and ceilings. The sliding doors and windows inevitably jammed when they were open rather than closed. There was no heating of any kind.

As a summer residence by the sea, it would have had its points. As a protection against the bitter Japanese winter, it was hardly adequate.

The block was composed of seven rooms, each about twenty-four feet square. A wooden shelf, with straw palliasses on it, ran along the whole of one side of each room, at a height of about eighteen inches from the ground. On this shelf slept fifteen or sixteen men, side by side, like sardines in a tin.

The few paper-thin blankets and the bullet-hard pillow, which appeared to be filled with scrap-iron from the yard, were not good advertisements for Morpheus.

The remaining furniture consisted of a long narrow table and benches.

* See also Epilogue.

The five officers and two W.O.s occupied the first room; the sick occupied the last.

At the other end of the camp two similar double-storey blocks were still under construction. There would ultimately be accommodation, by Japanese standards, for some 500 P.o.W.s.

A feature of captivity which had hitherto been absent was the call of the bugle. We soon learnt to recognise the various calls, and, as a result of constant repetition, I can remember them to this day.

The first of these shattered our day-dreaming about 6.15 a.m. on Saturday the 28th November. I don't think any of us were still asleep. The night had been bitterly cold. The water in a metal cup which one of us had left on the table was frozen solid. Most of us were suffering from oedema, that is wet beri-beri. We had made many trips to the latrines outside during the night, thus dissipating the tenuous warmth engendered by our thin blankets.

Dressing took no time at all. We all wore everything we possessed in bed. We merely had to put on our Japanese uniform over everything else and dash out into the cold darkness.

In the light of Japanese advances in electronics and in other similar fields their inability to count correctly, even a party of ten men, has always astounded me. They seemed to be equally astounded if, by any chance, they got it right the first time. This would inevitably lead to a second count which, equally inevitably, produced a different result. Roll-calls, even of very small groups, took a very long time.

After our first roll-call we did a little mild P.T. which at least got the blood circulating in our frozen veins.

The rest of our first day at Habu was devoted to administrative chores. We were all weighed and measured. I had lost over thirty pounds since I was weighed at the hospital in Garoet at the end of March and I had lost ten or fifteen pounds during my wanderings in the jungle before that.

All our personal belongings, or at least all our 'declared' personal belongings, were removed from us and sealed up in bags which were kept in the camp office. What was left of our kit was then sprayed with disinfectant, a process which was long overdue.

Each P.o.W. was then issued with a remarkable questionnaire. This included such questions as: 'What were your feelings when you first saw a Nippon warrior?' 'What thoughts flooded your mind when you first heard of the Greater East Asia Co-prosperity Sphere?'

'Give an account of your thoughts as you approached the sacred soil of Nippon in your ship.' 'What were your feelings when you entered Habu Camp?' 'Describe the circumstances in which you allowed yourself to be taken prisoner by the brave Nippon warriors.' 'What Nippon works of art do you most admire?'

I do not know whether this questionnaire was the work of Nakano's twisted mind or whether similar questionnaires were issued to other P.o.W.s in Japan. The compilation of the replies passed the time agreeably enough. Much fun was had in devising replies with double meanings. Many replied to the first question with the single word 'Unspeakable', or 'Indescribable'. Among the replies to the last question 'Habu Camp' or 'The latrines at Habu Camp' appeared frequently. As we never heard any more of this, our replies must have proved satisfactory to our captors.

During the course of the day, Nakano, with an ugly snarl, favoured me with the information that we would soon be going to work in the dockyard.

The following day, the 29th, started badly. About a quarter of the P.o.W.s were late for the 6.30 a.m. roll-call. Whether they had actually managed to get to sleep before the bugle went I do not know. Sergeant Nagano and the other guards were, not unnaturally, furious. As the stragglers arrived they were felled with rifle-butts. Those who had been on time were frozen stiff before the last of the sluggards arrived. Roll-call took an inordinate time that day. Ricky Wright let it be known that all were expected to be on time for roll-calls, and thereafter they were.

In the afternoon a Japanese Colonel and a number of dignitaries from the dockyard came to inspect us. Was it my imagination or did the dockyard dignitaries sniff a bit at the unprepossessing appearance of their new slaves?

Within seventy-two hours of our arrival at Habu three of our sick had died of dysentery. They had received no medical treatment whatever. After repeated requests a small charcoal brazier had been put in the sick-bay.

Nomoto produced some white cloth and some red and blue dyes. We spent the day making Union Jacks. Three simple and not very well-made dwarf pine coffins were brought into the camp. They must have been designed for Japanese, for they were not long enough for at least one of our comrades. *Rigor mortis* had already set in by the time the coffins arrived and his legs had to be broken before he could be fitted in.

The funerals were fixed for five o'clock in the afternoon, by which time it was quite dark. All the officers and the closest friends of each of the dead men attended the ceremony.

By the light of lanterns we walked up and down narrow mountain paths across a part of the island to a rocky promontory on the other side. We took it in turns to carry the lanterns and the coffins. On the promontory there was a small structure which served as a crematorium. We were to become quite familiar with it during the months of winter which still lay ahead.

Ricky Wright read the Church of England Burial Service. One of the dead men was a Roman Catholic. For him the appropriate service was read by Harry Radford, a large, tough and cheerful Sergeant. Harry had been employed by Spratts, makers of the famous dog biscuits, before the war. Perhaps this was why he had become the P.o.W. Sergeant in charge of the cook-house at Habu.

We placed each of the rude coffins in turn on the slab in the crematorium; there we remained until the Japanese attendants signified that all was over.

On our way back, no longer encumbered with our burdens, we marched through the narrow streets of the village. The little wooden dolls' houses lit by gay paper lanterns were the prettiest things we had seen in Japan so far. Some of the Japanese girls, squatting on the floors in gaily coloured kimonos, seemed even prettier.

The sudden death of our three companions so soon after our arrival seemed to have shocked Nomoto and his staff. A doctor visited the camp. Small quantities of fresh milk and of a liquid food called *rengiri*, as well as fresh apples, were promised for the sick. I cannot recall that the liquids ever appeared; and I do not believe that fresh fruit is normally prescribed for sufferers from dysentery.

The visit of this particular doctor, whom we were never to see again, was not, however, without result. Harry Radford's boundless energy and enthusiasm, which seemed to have been quite unimpaired by the rigours of life in the *Dai Nichi Maru*, were already cooking up another scheme.

'Why can't I have an oven to bake bread in my cook-house?' he had asked, very shortly after our arrival. To the rest of us lesser men it seemed a magnificent rhetorical question, 'such stuff as dreams are made on'. But Harry, who had been badgering the

Japanese staff incessantly, was not the man to miss a chance. He waylaid the doctor, and, with the charm and plausibility which have always stood him in good stead, got the visitor interested. When the doctor left he said that he would like to see plans of a bake-house. Nomoto was not to be allowed to forget that. In due course the days on which a small ration of bread was issued were days to be thought about, talked about and dreamed about, both before and after the event.

One other result of the doctor's visit was an arrangement whereby the seriously ill could be taken by us, by boat, to a small cottage hospital at Mitzonoshi, another little landing stage on the coast nearby. Few, if any, returned to the camp from that hospital, but at least they died in slightly less grim surroundings. We seemed to make as many trips to the hospital to collect and bury our dead as we did to deliver the dying. Sometimes we went all the way by boat from the hospital to the crematorium on the promontory. We could then see how wild and rugged many parts of the coastline were. Even the hardy pines could find no foothold. In places the sea was very rough. One day we put up a flight of wild duck in the marshes. They wheeled and crossed the watery sun. An old Japanese woodcut had come to life.

Nomoto was a numismatist. He would frequently wander round the barrack rooms, unannounced, to buy coins. He paid for his purchases in yen which were credited in our pass-books kept in his office. Many of the vendors begged him to buy razor blades, needles or threads with the proceeds of these sales. This, he replied sternly, was not allowed. We should just be proud to be possessors of valuable Japanese yen.

We encountered other patterns of Japanese thought which to us were incapable of any rational explanation. After enduring a week of biting cold, both inside and outside our barrack rooms, we were suddenly issued with thick warm overcoats. Our spirits soared at the very sight of them. Then we were told that they were never to be worn out-of-doors. They might be worn indoors, but only between the hours of 5 and 7 p.m.

Ricky Wright bearded Nomoto in his den to ask whether the overcoats could, at least, be worn for the morning roll-call. This had now been put forward to 5.30 a.m. to enable us, when we started work, to reach the dockyard by 6.30 a.m. Nomoto's reply was brief and to the point, if somewhat lacking in logic:

'No; it will get colder.'

By now we were getting accustomed to being thankful for the smallest of mercies. We could always fondle our overcoats, even if we could not wear them when they were most needed.

The sense of relief with which we had staggered through the gates of the camp a week earlier was now a thing of the past. All kinds of irritations were springing up like thistles to prick us at every turn.

Nomoto was not satisfied with what he elected to call our 'salutations'. We spent weary hours marching up and down practising saluting.

The water-pump was for ever breaking down, which resulted in water shortages and, what was almost worse, no hot baths.

We had been cut off from all news of how the war was going since we left Boei Glodok, and our illicit link with the outside world, more than a month previously.

We had all hoped to find letters from home awaiting us when we reached Japan but none had come.*

The very smallness of the camp, well under a hundred by now, although it had some advantages, had many disadvantages too. In Boei Glodok we could choose our friends among those with similar interests. There had also been a limited intellectual life which had helped to take the rough edges off our physical existence. Many had managed to bring books into the prison. I had been appointed Squadron Education Officer and had given, and attended, lectures on a variety of subjects. For the moment there was none of this at Habu.

Perhaps it was this general listlessness, coupled with intense boredom, which contributed to the fact that all of us, including my fellow-officers, suffered from minor complaints during our first ten days at Habu.

Tim Hallam was very much under the weather with a severe and very painful mouth infection. Len Cooper was wrestling gamely with his endemic dysentery. Ricky Wright and Nippy Knight had fevers of an unknown origin which laid them low from time to time.

The second Warrant Officer W. was so rooted to his bed-space

* Although I did not know it then, the first word that my family received that I was alive and a P.o.W. in Japanese hands was a telegram from the Air Ministry dated the 19th July 1943. Someone who had left Java just before the Dutch capitulation in March 1942 had, perhaps understandably, reported that he believed that I had been killed in Java.

at all times that it was difficult to say whether he was really ill or whether he was just lying low, like the old soldier he was, to avoid his duties and responsibilities. Only Pritchard seemed impervious to these various complaints. Catching him off his guard occasionally, I could see he was suffering with the rest of us, but he was extremely successful in concealing it. Pritchard was one of the best.

I myself had a fever and a severe sore throat. This was not improved by the torrents of rain which poured on to my bed-space through a crack in the roof during a severe storm. Even the medical orderly was impressed with my symptoms and I was given permission to stay in bed for a few days. But although he gave me his permission, priceless gift that it was, he gave me nothing to relieve my condition.

Then suddenly I remembered my snake-knife. I well recalled how I had acquired this in December 1937, just five years previously, before leaving London for Malaya. I had gone to one of those old-fashioned establishments which specialised in tropical equipment. I had asked the shop-walker, who, even then I believe, was wearing a morning coat, whether they stocked snake-knives.

Looking down his long straight nose he replied without batting an eyelid, 'I think you may find those on the fourth floor, sir. There's not much of a demand for them nowadays as you know, sir, but I believe we still have one or two left.'

I walked up the narrow stairs to the fourth floor. The aged shop assistant who was in charge of the 'Tropical Exploration Department' appeared to be so glad to have a customer that he could not have been nicer.

'Snake-knife, sir?' he repeated. 'Of course—invaluable in the tropics, if I may say so, sir.'

He spoke with all the conviction of someone who had spent most of his life within spitting distance of Wimbledon Common.

'I'm afraid we don't have quite the selection we used to have, sir. I remember in 1904 or was it 1906' (I could not help him), 'I had the pleasure of serving the Duke of Loamshire. His Grace was going out to India—tiger-shooting you know, sir.'

As I looked round the 'Tropical Exploration Department' I could see photographs of shooting expeditions, no doubt presented by satisfied customers. The voice droned on with its reminiscences of a more glorious past.

Rather rudely I looked at my watch. Even the Colonial Office only allowed two hours for lunch during the thirties. This shot brought my quarry down in his tracks.

'You're pressed for time, sir—I am sorry, sir,' he said, as he opened a drawer in the counter and produced what looked like a pencil-box. Sliding back the lid, he took out a slim pencil-like object which could not have been more than three inches long.

I must confess that I had no idea what a snake-knife looked like. The object in his delicate fingers did, however, look a shade on the small side for the sort of snakes that I expected to meet in Malaya. Before I had an opportunity of displaying my ignorance he was, fortunately, off again.

'This is the most popular model nowadays, sir,' he said. 'We sell a lot of these to gentlemen going to the tropics.'

I was determined to conceal my ignorance. I contented myself with taking the proffered bakelite phial from his outstretched hand and weighing it pensively up and down in my own, as though deciding whether I would have room for it in my extensive safari kit. I had not specifically said I was going to Malaya and for all he knew I could have been going to East Africa.

Perhaps he realised that I did not know what to do with it.

'It's really quite simple, sir,' he said, as he resumed possession of it, and then he added quickly: 'Perhaps I may show you, sir.'

I watched, fascinated, as he unscrewed a sort of miniscule cap at one end disclosing a sharp pointed blade.

'If you should have the great misfortune to be bitten by a poisonous snake, sir—though they're much more frightened of us than we are of them—just make a criss-cross cut on the wound with this little blade.'

He paused. I saw the saliva collecting round his lips and then he went on:

'When the blood is flowing freely, you rub some, but not too many, of these permanganate of potash crystals into the wound.'

At this stage he was struggling with a bakelite cap at the other end of the phial.

'A bit stiff, I think, sir. But we'll soon fix that.'

He fixed it all right, and a stream of the purple crystals shot on to the counter.

'Oh! I am sorry, sir. It's the heat, you know, that sometimes causes these caps to jam.'

As I was going to a hot climate, I immediately became suspicious.

Covered with confusion, he produced another phial from his pencil-box and removed the caps from both ends without difficulty, and without spilling the crystals.

'How about that, sir?' he said. 'And it's only a guinea.'

Although I thought the price was decidedly on the high side, his performance had been worth it. The bargain was concluded and I returned to the Colonial Office.

At tea-time I proudly showed my acquisition to my colleagues. They did not seem to be particularly impressed.

I only encountered three snakes in Malaya and on none of these occasions did I have my snake-knife with me. As none of the snakes bit me it did not matter much.

However, my snake-knife was one of the few personal possessions I had managed to keep with me during the whole time I had been in the R.A.F., both as a free man and as a P.o.W.

I poured some, but not too many, of the crystals into a metal cup full of water and gargled vigorously. My sore throat felt much better.

It was almost with a sense of relief that we learnt that we were to start work in the dockyard on Tuesday the 8th December 1942, the first anniversary of the Japanese attacks in South-East Asia.

The preliminaries to our new life as dockyard workers took place on the preceding day. Once again we were required to sign a declaration similar to that which we had all signed at Boei Glodok, discounting any intentions of trying to escape. As I signed, I thought to myself that the prospects of escaping from the Japanese mainland must have been absolutely nil. So far as I am aware no P.o.W. ever did escape from Japan.

We were then ordered to have our heads cropped again. This was done by barbers among our number, though it could hardly have afforded them any opportunity of practising their peace-time professional skills.

An inspection of the fancy-dress working uniforms, with which we had been issued on arrival, followed. As was foreseeable, many of these tawdry items had disintegrated and, amid cuffings, they were replaced.

We were then favoured by a lengthy speech from Nomoto, translated into an almost incomprehensible English by Nakano. It all passed over our cropped heads.

Then all the P.o.W.s who were reasonably fit, and most of those who were not, were paraded, prior to marching to the dockyard to inspect the places in which our labours would start the following day. Even W. was dragged off his bed-space by the Japanese to participate in this excursion, though neither we nor they, nor possibly even W. himself, really knew into which category he fell.

As always it was bitterly cold. But it was not the cold which made Nomoto shudder as he emerged in his beautifully cut dark green uniform, with shining black leather riding boots, to inspect the parade. It was the sight of rank upon rank of Michelin men.

As we were not allowed to wear our overcoats, every man had put on, under his green silk uniform, every other piece of clothing he possessed. Some even appeared to be wearing their overcoats under their work suits. Others had wrapped themselves up in a number of blankets before forcing themselves into their green silk sheaths.

Nomoto barked and shouted for nearly a minute. Nakano's antiphonal response was limited to the two words: 'No goodo.' We were dismissed and it was made clear that we were to parade again, in a less encumbered state, within five minutes.

It had already been established, as in Java, that all officers would accompany the working parties, allegedly in a supervisory capacity. Some of us were to find, in the days that lay ahead, that there was something to be said for participating in the work occasionally, if only to relieve the boredom of standing about for hours on end. One could always lend a hand when a group of prisoners were carrying something which was much too heavy for their emaciated bodies. One could, as I frequently did, have a go at riveting or welding and by a combination of ignorance and malevolence ensure that the work was badly done. With any luck, the faulty workmanship would only come to light when it was too late to do anything about it.

The dockyard authorities had decided to split us up into small groups for working purposes. In this way our propaganda value would be diffused as widely as possible throughout the yard. On this occasion, however, we were all marched round in a body, pausing briefly at the various sites where we would be working. I had been allocated to the timber-yard and saw-mill. I was introduced to the foreman and time-keeper but I had no time to size them up. I observed with some dismay that, as I had expected, no artificial heating was permitted in the saw-mill. My party noted with envy the furnaces and boilers in the shops in which other parties would be working. Even the welders and riveters, high up on the decks of the ships under construction, had little braziers dotted all over the place.

However, although we were cold in the timber-yard, we were not as badly off as those detailed for the shipbuilding yard. There the gang worked, for ten hours a day, knee-deep in the oil and bilge at the bottom of a ship. Perhaps it was poetic justice that Warrant Officer W. was in charge of this gang.

It was all the luck of the draw.

We marched back to the camp in the darkness. We were to have one more surprise that night. Before we were dismissed there was an issue of rubber-soled plimsolls. These, we were told, were compulsory wear for all parties working in the dockyard. Having seen the molten steel, the jagged bits of metal, the falling balks of wood and the nails which covered the ground at the yard, like so much confetti after a wedding, this was not a pleasant prospect. We protested but to no avail.

The first pair of plimsolls I tried on burst at the seams, which earned me a severe box on the ears from Sergeant Nagano. Although I only took size nine, there were no plimsolls large enough for me, or for many others. Our hope that it would be some time before the Japanese footwear industry remedied this situation was fulfilled.

The following morning the first bugle went at 5 a.m. for our first working day in the dockyard.

After breakfast, gobbled down to obtain such vestiges of warmth as still remained in the half a bowl of rice and accompanying cabbage water, we washed our bowls under a tap, just outside the barrack block. The tap was frequently frozen stiff. We also had to wash down the floors of our rooms. This latter task was quite unnecessary as the floors were still wet, or covered with a thin film of ice, from the previous day's washing.

Having arranged our blankets and pillows in the prescribed pattern, we emerged, into the pitch darkness, on to an open space on the seaward side of the barrack block. Since shortly after our arrival at Habu, no outside lights had been permitted in the camp, and heavy shutters had been fitted over the windows. We were naturally elated when we had been informed that this was necessary because of the ever-present risk of air raids. In the event of an air raid, we were to sit on the edge of our bed-spaces and await further orders. At any rate the shutters, psychologically at least, seemed to diminish the cold. But we knew we would have to pay dearly for these innovations; and so we did. The roll-calls in the darkness were even more indeterminate and prolonged. Such additional warmth as might have been engendered by the shutters was soon dissipated.

Whether it was deliberate or whether the Japanese N.C.O. of the day and interpreter really found it difficult to locate us in the impenetrable gloom, I do not know. It was late before the roll-call even started; it was very late by the time it finished.

Those who were virtually unconscious then returned to their barrack rooms; but even then they were not allowed to lie down on their palliasses, unless they had obtained dispensation the previous day, until the Japanese medical orderly arrived from his pharmacist's shop.

The rest of us then fell-in in our working parties. Despite the medical orderly's rigorous requirements, even he could rarely muster more than forty or so as fit for work. We then marched off along the sea-shore, strewn with flotsam and jetsam—another peril for those who were unlucky enough to have small feet—for about a mile and a half.

The martial music and patriotic songs, blaring from loud-speakers all over the dockyard, were in no sense intended to mark our adhesion to the labour force. Although perhaps louder and more insistent on this first anniversary of Japan's great adventure, we were to learn in the days to come that they were a regular accompaniment to the efforts of the 20,000 termites.

On this, as on every subsequent day, much time was lost in saluting, counting and checking. When our foremen and time-keepers finally led us off to our respective quarters of the underworld our escorting guards would disappear into the darkness, to spend the day, as we imagined, in untold delights. For us, at that time, untold delights meant eating and keeping warm, no more and no less.

The time-keeper for the timber-yard and saw-mill gang was a quite agreeable ex-soldier. He did not bother us much. The foreman was made of different stuff. A fussy little Japanese and a bit of a bully, he chivied us unceasingly.

The first shift was from 7 to 9.30 a.m. Then all the P.o.W. working parties trotted back to the original assembly point for a ten-minute break. Visits to the latrines were only permitted during these breaks, a serious hardship for those suffering from dysentery.

The second shift was from 9.40 a.m. to 12 noon. We had a thirty-minute break for the midday meal which had been sent up from the camp in barrels. It was invariably cold and invariably inadequate.

From 12:30 p.m. until 2.30 p.m. we worked again and then

broke off for another ten minutes at the assembly point. Officially the final shift lasted until 4.30 p.m. but some foremen would frequently keep the prisoners working until five o'clock or after. Those who had finished at the appointed hour then had to stand about until their comrades joined them.

The day ended as it had begun with much saluting, counting and checking. Our guards appeared from the darkness, into which they had disappeared ten hours previously, and resumed responsibility for us. We shuffled back to camp, to be faced with our evening meal which was none other than the cold rice and watery skilly which had revolted us at midday.

We had clearly been enjoying our hot baths too much, for on this, our first day at work, as on many subsequent days, there were no baths. When we did get a bath the routine was simple but agreeable. In traditional Japanese style, six of us would enter the small concrete tank and soak for a few minutes. While we were soaping and rinsing under taps on the surrounds, six more would take our places in the tank. When they were 'cooked' they would emerge for soaping and rinsing and we took their places for a final soak. This rhythm continued until all had bathed.

After the bath we put on the same clothes, and this meant everything we possessed, which we had been wearing, without a break, since we left Java. It was not until the spring came that we were able to indulge in the luxury of laundering our clothes.

Back to the icy barrack room, lit by a single bulb which would not have permitted reading even if we had had anything to read, we hung about until the final roll-call at 7.30 p.m. This inevitably took at least an hour, standing shivering, without overcoats, by our bedspaces. The N.C.O. of the day would decide who was fit for work the next day. But even if his untutored eyes could see that a man had a fever, the latter still had to get up for the following morning's roll-call and remain on his feet until the medical orderly certified that he was near enough to death to lie down.

We tumbled on to our palliasses about 8.30 p.m. and prayed for oblivion until the whole ghastly cycle started again at 5 a.m. Would all this never be brought to an end, except by death? we wondered.

I thought that the one-armed guard known as George would be my best bet. By now I had picked up quite a few words of Japanese and I had taken every opportunity of talking to him, both in the camp and on the way to and from the dockyard. I told him that I was anxious to learn to speak Japanese properly. I patiently explained that I was not going to try to learn the Japanese characters but that I wanted to learn romanised Japanese, that is *romaji*. I knew that that strange American, Lafcadio Hearne, who had settled in Japan at the end of the nineteenth century, had done a considerable amount of work to produce a romanised version of Japanese.

George was most receptive to my suggestion. He said he would try to get hold of some books in romanised Japanese. He was as good as his word; within a matter of days he brought me a couple of dictionaries and a grammar. They improved my morale considerably. I have them to this day.

There was little enough we could do in the camp to control our own destinies. Ricky Wright had shown great persistence in his protests to Nomoto. He had protested about the food, about the treatment of the sick, about the lack of baths, about the overcoats, about the futility of officers standing about in the dockyard without any control over their men; in short, he had protested about almost everything. Eventually, Nomoto had refused to see him. Undaunted, Ricky Wright was now engaged in preparing a written memorandum of all his protests.

We all knew what would happen. The memorandum would be referred to the interpreter, Nakano, who would be required to give Nomoto an oral summary of its contents. Experience had already taught us, and it was an experience which was to be confirmed in subsequent years, that, as a general rule, English-speaking Japanese were more evilly disposed towards P.o.W.s than those Japanese who knew no English. This was particularly marked among those English-speaking Japanese who had visited, or lived in, the United Kingdom or the United States. Perhaps they had memories of landladies slamming boarding-house doors in their faces; perhaps they recalled other insults. Now was their chance to get their own back and they took it with both hands.

It was thus a foregone conclusion that an English-speaking Japanese would almost always put a P.o.W. representation to the Japanese Camp Commandant in the most unfavourable light. The interpreter's influence in this respect was virtually unlimited. Knowing Nakano as we did, we did not hope for much in the way of results.

Not all Japanese camp staff were monsters. If handled correctly, Nomoto, and others, could sometimes be persuaded to make a few concessions. But this required that they should be presented with a proper statement of the case.

This was one of the main reasons which had led me to the decision to apply myself seriously to learning Japanese. There was another reason too. We could do nothing about the food; we could do nothing about the cold; we could do nothing about the conditions in which we worked. But there were two things we could do. We could do our best to keep our bodies fit and we could do our best to keep our minds sane.

There were, naturally, limitations to our efforts in both these directions. But the so-called fit man who lay on his bed staring at the ceiling, on every occasion that this was permissible, would soon be staring at the lid of his coffin, or go out of his mind. Mild physical exercise, even when this was not required by our captors, and self-imposed intellectual discipline were wonderful props in the struggle for survival.

I resolved to devote at least an hour every day to my Japanese studies.

1942 ended badly. We had several more deaths and several more trips to the crematorium on the windy promontory. The official cause of death, as recorded by the Japanese authorities, was invariably the same—'exhaustion'.

One of our sick was returned on foot, accompanied by a guard, from the cottage hospital at Mitzonoshi, on the grounds that there was not enough food to feed him there.

At the dockyard the mateys were rejoicing in a report that Churchill had been seriously injured in an air raid. P.o.W.s working in the ship-repairing yard reported that our old friend the *Dai Nichi Maru* had come in for a refit and camouflage.

Nakano, the interpreter, suddenly became very loquacious. He told me with malicious relish that as the island of Innoshima was a prohibited area we would never be allowed to send or receive letters. He added for good measure that the death rate in the other camps was much higher than at Habu and that we were very lucky to be in such a 'goodo campu'.

We continued to work all through the Christmas holidays. Christmas Eve was enlivened, not by Father Christmas, but by some para-military organisation of Japanese schoolboys who elected to hold their nocturnal manœuvres all round the camp. The occasion was at least marked by noise, if not by carols.

On Christmas Day we were all weighed again. I noticed that the two faces of the scales registered appreciably differently. I had dropped a few more pounds. What was far more disturbing was the fact that fifteen of the P.o.W.s now weighed considerably less than fifty kilos.

Somehow or other Harry Radford had managed to produce something that looked like Christmas puddings. The guards ate them all.

As usual the latrines were overflowing. I told the guard, Yama-sagi, who was responsible for the proper maintenance of the camp. In return for my information he told me that 400 British P.o.W.s and 200 Chinese would soon be coming to the camp. He did nothing about the latrines. If his story was true there would soon be nothing he could do.

We learnt that the dockyard would be closed on the 31st December and the 1st January. As we were cleaning up on the 30th the Japanese workers in the yard appeared to be particularly interested in their newspapers. The time-keeper in the timber-yard told me that two British 'battleships' had been sunk and that a Japanese ship bringing a thousand P.o.W.s from Hong Kong had been torpedoed by an American submarine.

The guards in the camp were preparing to make the most of the New Year's holidays. Several P.o.W.s reported seeing Japanese girls being smuggled into the camp for the night, by those guards who would be on duty. There was even more positive evidence that they were all drinking hard.

The heavy snow which had fallen on a number of occasions during the preceding week lay thick on the ground. New Year's Day 1943 was the coldest we had, as yet, experienced.

Harry Radford had baked some oatmeal cakes to mark the occasion, but Nomoto forbad their issue, saying that our digestions could not stand them. No doubt they suffered the same fate as the Christmas puddings.

For us, New Year's Day was marked by an issue of toilet paper and of ten cigarettes per man; the cost of the latter was to be deducted from our dockyard earnings, which we had never seen.

We had hoped that we might have had an issue of razor blades, even if we had had to pay for them from our earnings. Nearly all the officers and most of the men had managed to shave at least once every two days, even in the *Dai Nichi Maru*. We were determined to keep this up if we possibly could, but it would be difficult if we did not get blades soon.

We were glad to see the end of 1942.

7

Life at Habu

Innoshima—January–March 1943

The first fortnight of January 1943, marked by a number of severe snow-storms, was colder than ever. Fortunately we had acquired a new and more agreeable foreman in the timber-yard. Instead of trotting off to the assembly point at break times, we were permitted to 'relax' in a little hut with the foreman and some of his cronies. I had to detail members of my party, in turn, to light the stove in the hut a few minutes before each break period. After a little practice we got the stove so hot that within a few minutes the foreman and his chums were practically asphyxiated. They frequently dozed off and in this way we gained valuable minutes before resuming work.

The new foreman took a proprietarial pride in his gang of P.o.W.s. He produced needles and thread with which we were able to mend our tattered work suits; more important still he permitted us to take these invaluable tools back to camp.

He was most anxious to learn English and we tutored each other in our respective languages, which, for me at any rate, helped to pass the time and to improve my Japanese.

The foreman was also a keen poultry-farmer in his spare time. Occasionally I had to take some of the P.o.W.s. on board a ship in another part of the yard to collect rice and Indian corn for his birds.

On one of these occasions we were required to go aboard the *Arima Maru*. Eventually we found it—we were not hurrying—and the precious provender was duly collected. As we left the ship, I was bringing up the rear. The hook and chain of an enormous crane missed my head by inches and crashed on to the dock-side, with a bang which all but led me, in self-protection, to jump over the edge of the dock.

'You bastard,' I thought, as I peered up at the cabin of the crane, a hundred feet or more above me. There I saw the crane-driver gesticulating wildly. I couldn't make head or tail of the message he was trying to convey. He appeared to be signalling to me to approach the massive hook of his crane. I approached this very gingerly, fearing that at the crucial moment he would set his infernal machine in motion and whisk me up towards the heavens. But no! There was something tied to the hook by a piece of string. As I unfolded the package, five cigarettes tumbled out on to the ground— one for each of my party and one for myself. I saluted him as smartly as I could and rejoined my party which had been frozen into immobility by the loud bang. I distributed the cigarettes and formed my flock up into a semblance of a rank to give our smiling benefactor a smart 'eyes left'. I marvelled on the unpredictability of human nature.

My good relations with the foreman were nearly jeopardised by an incident which occurred a few days later. On the 12th January it was so cold that Nomoto surprisingly ordered that overcoats might be worn on the way to and from the dockyard. On arrival at the timber-yard all of us, including myself, shed our overcoats and put them in the hut. On our return to camp, I discovered that my fellow-officers, very wisely, had kept theirs on all day.

The following day, not wishing to break the common front, and because it was the sensible thing to do, I kept my overcoat on in the timber-yard. The foreman was furious, pointing out that he was not allowed to wear an overcoat. Why should I be allowed to? he argued.

The matter was settled when we returned to camp. Nomoto, who had no doubt been lobbied by my foreman, issued an order that no officer would wear an overcoat in the dockyard. Although my relations with my foreman resumed their cordiality, I noticed that my fellow-officers kept their distance for a day or two.

Occasionally the whole timber-yard party was temporarily shifted to another job to help the party normally engaged in that particular task. For a while we joined the charcoal party. This was a filthy job. The men had to carry heavy baskets of charcoal from one spot to another, and the officer normally in charge, Len Cooper, had established a precedent whereby he helped with the lifting of the baskets on to the men's backs. A few days of grime and dust and we were all glad to be back in the timber-yard.

E

On another occasion we found ourselves bolting plates together on a 12,000-ton vessel under construction. The noise of the mechanical drills and of the riveting was quite intolerable. We hardly noticed the high-pitched whining of the mechanical saws, to which we had become inured.

Everything was relative, I thought. There were no absolutes in the world. After the *Dai Nichi Maru*, Habu had seemed for a while, at least, almost bearable. A razor blade, which was discarded as useless after a week, when one knew one could get another one, could still be made to serve its purpose for months if necessary, when one knew one could not.

My fingers and toes, most of which were suppurating as a result of the bitter cold, were causing me considerable pain. It was only when I faced up to the fact that I was still alive and therefore, I supposed, relatively fortunate, that I could drag myself up from the morass of self-pity into which we all fell at times.

The Japanese in the yard were already counting the days to the 11th February which, as the anniversary of the birthday of the first Emperor of Japan, would be their next public holiday. We were counting the days to the end of the war or to freedom, though we realised that for us the first would not necessarily bring with it the second.

The dockyard was to receive two distinguished visitors during January. We looked forward to such visits because we always had a particularly good midday meal on such occasions. And so it was when the company director responsible for personnel favoured us with his presence. He made a long speech of which I understood not a word. Later the foreman explained the general tenor of his remarks. The visitor, it appeared, had made a number of references to the presence of P.o.W.s in the dockyard. We were there, he said, for two reasons.

The first was to bring home to the workers of Nippon how successfully and gallantly their brothers under arms were performing their duties at the front. We were, the director had apparently stressed, but a few of the tens of thousands of P.o.W.s who had fallen into the traps set for them by the brave and cunning Nippon warriors. Those traps had caught not only misguided soldiers, sailors and airmen but also high-ranking officers who formed an integral part of the Anglo-American imperialist clique. Many of these high-ranking imperialist officers were even now in the dockyard.

As the foreman imparted this information, I drew myself up to

my full height as a Pilot Officer and wondered whether notification
of accelerated promotion had somehow failed to reach me.

'But,' continued the foreman, bringing me back to earth with
a jolt, 'the Big Man also say one more thing. He say you officers
here to see how big and strong Nippon is; how Nippon cannot be
beaten; how you must stop to be arrogant.'

I thanked the foreman for this information and said I would
think it over.

The visit of the other distinguished visitor, a Japanese General
who was described by Nakano as 'a very rank officer', filled the
camp staff with forebodings. Virtually all the sick were told peremp-
torily that, however ill they were, they would have to go to work
in the dockyard for the day of the General's visit. It would not
do for him to see so many sick men in the camp. As if to give them
strength for their ordeal, the sick, so detailed, were told that this
was for one day only and that they would be permitted to return to
bed on the day after the General's inspection.

For the inspection itself, the cheerless barrack room which
served as a sick-bay was decked out with artificial flowers and gaily
coloured posters on which were inscribed various animated health
hints. One poster recorded that 'Cleanliness is next to Godliness'.
Many charcoal braziers, with steaming kettles, were introduced.
All these additions were immediately removed by the camp staff
as soon as the General had left. What a fraud it all was!

A rumour went round that officers were to be permitted to wear
their own uniforms in camp. I received this news with mixed feelings.
I was already wearing mine under my Japanese uniform; it was
still very cold.

In due course Nomoto issued the order and the rumour became a
fact. Ricky Wright, who was the only officer who had his R.A.F. blues
with him, looked resplendent in his Squadron-Leader's uniform. All
the Japanese camp staff, including Nomoto, regarded him with
admiration, touching every part of his uniform with curious fingers,
like children.

Tim Hallan and I only had very creased khaki tunics and rather
tatty slacks. I suddenly had to sew all the fly-buttons on my slacks.
Their absence when I was wearing them under my Japanese uniform
had not, of course, been apparent. We had no ties but managed to
achieve a certain *chic* with khaki stockings wound round our necks

like cravats. I now wore most of my Japanese uniform underneath my own.

Nomoto decided to inspect the camp, and particularly its occupants. For some reason which was never clear to us he took a particular interest in our fingernails. These were subjected to a most rigorous scrutiny. His second phobia was hair. He found my head insufficiently cropped and one of the prisoner barbers, a Sergeant Ravenscroft, whose trade in the R.A.F. was that of armourer, was immediately sent for. Those of my hairs which his blunt clippers would not cut were, or so it seemed to me, pulled out by the roots.

It was also rumoured that more P.o.W.s would be arriving very soon to occupy the new buildings at the other end of the camp. Every approachable Japanese guard had his own version and they were all different. It was clear, however, that something was about to happen. A number of new rice boilers arrived to be installed and a more or less serious effort to clean the *benjos* got under way. At this time, too, all the able-bodied guards were called up for active service overseas and we had to adjust ourselves to the idiosyncrasies of their replacements.

I took the opportunity of a day off from the dockyard to inspect the new barrack blocks. They seemed to be better built than the one we were occupying. Plywood ceilings had been fitted under the roofs; and instead of palliasses there were thin sorbo-rubber mats on the bed-shelves. The buildings, however, were far from ready for occupation.

I had a particular reason for wanting to have a sniff round unobserved. One of the rumours indicated that we were all going to move into the new blocks and I wanted to find a place to hide my diaries.

Even Nature seemed anxious to mark the impending change in the shape of things to come. Several earth tremors of moderate intensity occurred.

Nothing was ever to be the same again at Habu camp after Saturday the 23rd January 1943. During the following forty-eight hours many changes, almost all for the better, occurred.

In a sense it was the arrival in the camp of about ten gunny-wrapped bundles, clearly marked with a Red Cross on the outside, which was the most important of these events. We had no idea what was inside them, but we knew that even if all the contents were distributed among the prisoners, soon to be almost doubled in numbers, there would be precious little for each individual. And our experience with the Christmas puddings and the oatmeal cakes made it a foregone conclusion that the camp staff and guards would help themselves freely before any distribution to the P.o.W.s was authorised.

What was important was that someone, somewhere, in the Red Cross knew of the existence of our camp. The mental relief afforded by this knowledge would long outlast the physical relief to be gained, if we were lucky, from gobbling down a few goodies in a matter of hours. Those detailed to carry the precious bundles into the guard-house reported that some were marked 'American Red Cross' and others 'South African Prisoners-of-War Relief Fund'.

The optimists asserted that this was to be the first of regular weekly distributions, a hope which, alas!, was far from ever being fulfilled.

But even with all these doubts and reservations the very sight of this international symbol boosted our morale to heights never previously attained.

The second significant event was the arrival, about 4 p.m. on the 24th January, of one hundred British P.o.W.s who had been captured in Hong Kong. There was not a sick man among them, or, rather, they had all marched from the Habu jetty to the camp. There were no officers; they were led by an extremely pleasant and cultured Warrant Officer, Fabel, in the Army Education Corps.

They all seemed to us to be pretty fit and they all had warm clothes, overcoats and other comforts which had reached them from the Red Cross in Hong Kong. Many of them generously gave some of their clothing to those of us who were less well equipped. I was the lucky recipient of a large serge pull-over.

Most of them were members of the Hong Kong Volunteer Defence Corps; the rest were individuals who had become detached from their units, some army personnel, some R.N. policemen and the Bandmaster of the Middlesex Regiment, who was to prove an invaluable addition in the future.

Among those in the H.K. V.D.C. were members of the staffs of the Hong Kong and Shanghai, and the Chartered, Banks, whom I had known when they were previously working in Malaya. With one of their Sergeants, 'Bill' Williams, a Puisne judge, in Hong Kong,

I became particularly friendly.* Others in this cheerful group were businessmen, civil servants and at least one Professor at the University of Hong Kong.

This infusion of new blood into the camp put us all in high spirits. The whole atmosphere changed in a matter of hours. Those of us who had endured the *Dai Nichi Maru* and two months of a very hard Japanese winter were only too glad to forget these experiences and to learn from the newcomers about what had happened in Hong Kong.

The third event of importance was Nomoto's last-minute decision that all of us should move into the same new two-storey barrack block as the Hong Kong party. This decision brought joy for some but sadness for others.

We officers found ourselves in an upstairs room at the end of the block nearest the centre of the camp. We had a pleasant view over the beach and sea. It was a small room, with a bed-shelf running along one side only. As there were only five of us we had ample room for sleeping. More important still, we now had a charcoal brazier.

Our two R.A.F. W.O.s, Pritchard and W., occupied a similar small room, immediately below us, with the admirable R.S.M. Fabel. Their accommodation, too, was a great improvement on that provided in the old block.

The accommodation of the other ranks, which was similar to ours except that they occupied much larger rooms with bed-shelves on both sides, also afforded better living conditions than our party had had to endure in the old block.

Nomoto took advantage of the move to insist that all the P.o.W.s should sleep, side by side, in camp numerical order. This was indeed a hardship. In such conditions of close proximity the sharp edges of irritation and tetchiness are frequently softened by having congenial companions on either side. Now all these friendships were broken up and men found themselves sleeping next to their sworn enemies.

The two best rooms in the old block were set aside as the sick-bay, where, at least, the sick would be spared the interminable noise which now pervaded the newly occupied block.

All these movements and rearrangements proved to be such an exciting interlude in our drab lives that we cared naught for the

* 'Bill' Williams, who later became Sir Ernest Williams, Chief Justice of Borneo and Sarawak, died in 1965. On that occasion *The Times* published a letter from me containing a brief tribute to Sir Ernest's inspiring conduct in Habu.

fact that our new home was far from fit for occupation, and that, as the new rice boilers were not yet installed, we had even less to eat than usual for the next few days.

Nomoto, too, must have caught something of the new atmosphere. On the afternoon of the day after the new-comers' arrival, when we were all quite happily exchanging news and views, Nomoto ordered that there should be a concert—immediately. We were all hauled out, most reluctantly, to the open space between the two new barrack blocks and commanded to make merry. The British, when they are in the mood, can be as merry as the rest, but they cannot turn on merriment to order, particularly at two o'clock on a bitterly cold afternoon. To save our faces, some hardy souls stood up and put on quite a good show. One, Squires, gave Nomoto more than he bargained for. Concluding his rendering of 'She'll be coming round the mountain, when she comes', he bellowed, straight into Nomoto's face, 'They'll be flying in formation when they come', and 'They'll be dropping 1,000 pounders when they come'.

As these refrains were taken up by all present, Nomoto must have congratulated himself that the concert had been a resounding success.

We learnt much from the Hong Kong party. Some of them had already written three letters home and some had even had replies from their families. They too had had an illicit wireless set in Hong Kong and they gave us news of Allied successes in North Africa and elsewhere. All this rather went to the heads of the old Habu hands and many of us drafted, on empty cigarette packets, the telegrams we would send to our families when we were released.

Nomoto announced that the few cents which we had acquired, either by selling foreign money to him for his collection or from our labours in the dockyard, and which had been credited to us in pass-books kept in his office, might now be spent. A member of the camp staff came round to take our 'orders': these included sauces, razor-blades, combs, mirrors, slippers and pencils.

Cocoa and milk had been found in the Red Cross bundles and we had a cupful of this about once every ten days. We assumed that the Japanese guards did not care for it. The rest of whatever was in the Red Cross bundles remained firmly under Japanese control.

It was fortunate that our morale was now so high. Hardships which would have seemed intolerable a month or so earlier, before the arrival of the Hong Kong party, were now shrugged off as 'damned annoying' or 'typical of the Nips'. Although we now had braziers, the supply of charcoal ceased for weeks on end. It was 'typical of the Nips' that they should have chosen this particular moment to introduce the all-night fire-watch guard scheme. Although all braziers, when there was any charcoal, had to be removed from the barrack blocks before lights-out, the Japanese were, quite properly, very fire-conscious. Orders were therefore issued that the prisoners were to provide three fire-watch guards for each hour of every night. These were required to patrol the premises and to meet each other at prescribed spots. This meant that some twenty-seven weary men had their sleep interrupted every night. Indeed, as each 'sardine' emerged from his tin for his hour's vigil, the 'sardines' on either side of him would inevitably be woken up too. We never became reconciled to this cheerless task, particularly as armed Japanese guards were also patrolling the camp all night.

My fingers and toes had now ceased to suppurate but were wholly without sensation. The medical orderly was able to give vent to his sadistic impulses by sticking pins into them without my being any the wiser. He concluded that it was a form of pellagra and he gave me three white pills which he said contained vitamins A and C. They tasted like aspirin.

It was at this time, shortly after we were all installed in the two-storey block, that something occurred which caused us considerable anxiety, despite our buoyant morale.

During the somewhat amateur regime which had prevailed when we were occupying the old barrack block, Nomoto's inspections were casual and irregular. During his coin-purchasing excursions he would have a look around informally; and on formal occasions he was more concerned with fingernails and hair than with anything else.

It was now that we learnt that formal, and rigorous, camp inspections would be held regularly every twenty-first day, that is on our normal rest days from work in the dockyard. We had also learnt, from remarks dropped by the Japanese guards from time to time, that any tampering with, or damage to, the property of His Imperial Majesty was a very serious—some had even said a capital—offence. I myself could still recall the powerful punches of Sergeant Nagano, when I had, inadvertently, split the undersized plimsolls while trying them on.

When we had arrived at Habù from Java, at the end of November 1942, with little more than our jungle shirts and shorts, the more enterprising among us had promptly cut up one of the blankets issued to us and, by means of fish-bones and odd bits of string, had made suits to be worn in bed and, at work, under the green silk work-suits.

Just as one cannot unscramble eggs, so too one cannot re-assemble blankets which have been cut up and fashioned into suits.

We were full of forebodings on the day of the first of these new-look inspections.

Somehow or other we managed to establish a precedent whereby the inspecting party of Nomoto, Nagano and others should start with the upper storey. There they found, neatly folded at the foot of each bed-space, the prescribed number of blankets as issued, which, from time to time, they counted. As they descended the stairs at the end of the block, an incident was contrived to delay them. Before they had resumed their measured tread along the ground floor barrack rooms, an appropriate number of blankets had been thrown out of the windows of the upper storey, collected and neatly folded in the lower bed-spaces.*

Nomoto's attempts to run the camp more professionally were manifested in other ways too. The following notice was found pasted up in the officer's room on our return from work one day:

'The Principal of Management of this Camp.

'1.   To observe strictly the military discipline.
'2.   To maintain order in the camp.
'3.   To obey strictly the rules of salutations.
'4.   To make your life in the camp as comfortable as this camp.'

It was clear that Nakano the interpreter was slipping a bit; and the fourth 'principal' left us somewhat bewildered.

Like many other little men in big boots, Nomoto was a great believer in the personal touch. He also liked the sound of his own voice. After the 'success' of his impromptu concert he decided that he would 'expose' himself more often and, alas!, address us more frequently.

The first of these great occasions was held a few days before the Hong Kong party were due to start work in the dockyard. They had already been required to sign the 'no escaping' declarations, but the forms which they had signed had not included an under-

* See also Epilogue.

taking 'to make obedience in the factory', which we had also signed. Had Nakano overstepped the limit and had one of the 'very rank officers' hauled Nomoto and Nakano over the coals for this? We hoped so.

Nomoto soon got into his stride. He dwelt at length on the significance of the 'no escaping' declaration, which had clearly been initiated by the highest authorities, but he made no reference to the 'obedience in the factory' undertaking, as regards which he had clearly exceeded his powers.

He repeated, and elaborated upon, the four 'principals'. The fourth, he explained somewhat tortuously, replaced the earlier 'principal' of fire protection.

It was all so meaningless and confused that by now we had ceased to listen.

Then suddenly we pricked up our ears. In his final peroration he said that it was the policy of His Imperial Majesty, of the Japanese Government and of the Japanese armed forces, to treat all P.o.W.s in accordance with the accepted principles of international law. I made a mental, and subsequently a written, note of this which I thought might come in useful.

One of the matters exercising us all, and a rumble of discontent about this was now welling up from the ranks, was the non-appearance of the contents of the Red Cross bundles. We did not know exactly what was in these bundles but the magic words 'food parcels' were on everyone's lips.

Their delivery, only hours before the Hong Kong party had arrived, had complicated the position and had given rise to considerable argument. Were the new arrivals, who had already had a number of parcels in Hong Kong, to participate? Or were the parcels intended solely for the 'Java' men who had never yet seen one?

I came across a number, a very small number, of saints in captivity, whose selflessness commanded the admiration of us all. But most of us were made of baser clay and few starving men are capable of self-abnegation. It was unfortunate, too, that there were no officers with the Hong Kong party. The junta consisted solely of 'Java' men.

There was only one point upon which the whole camp was agreed, namely that the longer the Red Cross goods remained in the guard-house the less there would be for distribution to anybody.

I accompanied Ricky Wright to beard the Commandant in his office. By now I had acquired a modest fluency in Japanese, certainly enough to check any obvious misrepresentations which the evil Nakano might make.

Nomoto cleared the air immediately. The food parcels were intended for the 'Java' men only. As a result of our deaths, our numbers had now fallen to something in the eighties. Unfortunately the Red Cross had not sent enough parcels to provide for one per man. More unfortunately still, Nomoto added, the Red Cross authorities had ordered that a number of the parcels should be returned to them. That he really expected this remarkable statement to be believed I very much doubt, but there was nothing we could do about it. The upshot of this unfortunate concatenation of circumstances, Nomoto went on, was that it looked as though it might be just possible to make an issue of one parcel per two men of the 'Java' party.

A few days later the parcels were released to W.O. Pritchard. I shared one with Tim Hallam. Our box had inscribed on it, 'Prisoners' Parcels, British Red Cross and Order of St. John War Organisation, Bermondsey'. Another inscription read 'Kriegesgefangenerpost'. It was a pity that someone in Bermondsey had not replaced this latter by the equivalent in Japanese, but this seemed a petty thought to harbour, as we relished the contents.

I believe, and I certainly hope, that the 'Java' men found ways and means of repaying the 'Hong Kong' men for their open-handed generosity on their arrival, even if it was only a fifteen-second suck from a tin of sweetened condensed milk.

Now that the worst of the winter, or so we fervently hoped, was over, large wood-burning stoves were being fitted in the barrack rooms, but long before the installation was completed, notices were in place indicating that the stoves were only to be used between 5 and 7.30 p.m.

My timber-yard party had now been permanently transferred to shipbuilding. After a short time they were issued with 'Fs' to sew on their caps to indicate that they were now recognised as fitters. Our ship No. 1778 was progressing apace. It was then that I tried my hand at riveting and welding. I did my best to botch the work. For one who knew nothing about the mysteries, this was not difficult.

The midday meal at the yard had always been a shambles and those in the camp never sent up enough rice. With the working party from the camp now running at 130 or more, there was indescribable confusion. One day there were fifteen or twenty rations of rice short. On another occasion two men were observed sitting down on a bench opposite three portions of rice. In a trice, the middle portion had been divided between them and the empty plate slipped under one of theirs.

We were all struck at the yard by the deterioration in the clothes of the Japanese workers. The basic garments were now so patched and re-patched as to be hardly recognisable. Obviously Japan was beginning to feel the pinch.

The dockyard continued to buzz with rumours. Tokyo, Kobe and Osaka had all been bombed on one day. The Americans had bombed a Japanese hospital ship. The Japanese had been compelled to execute a 'strategic withdrawal' from the Solomons. The atmosphere in the dockyard became distinctly less pleasant.

One day fifty Japanese bombers flew over the yard in excellent formation. Twenty thousand Japanese throats cheered them to the echo, drowning the discordant imprecations uttered by a handful of British P.o.W.s.

These dockyard reactions to items of news unfavourable to Japan's cause, though understandable enough, disturbed us some-what. If any of us had ever had doubts about the final outcome of the war, these had long since evaporated. Though none of us could know how long it would take for the Allies to defeat the Axis powers, and particularly Japan, we were now, all, wholly convinced that the Allies would win. But there was another question which was never far from our thoughts. Would any of us survive the defeat of Japan?

As the weeks became months, and the months became years, many wondered how long, as individuals, they could survive such treatment and such conditions. By the end of January 1943 a process of natural selection had sifted those who had been endowed by their mothers with tough constitutions from those who had not been so blessed. The death rate, which had been high in Java, and very high on the voyage and during our first winter at Habu, was now dropping sharply. Of course, there would be many more deaths. Even strong men, after a prolonged period of malnutrition, become weak men and can fall an easy prey to complaints which they would probably have shrugged off if they had been reasonably well nourished. But for those with the will to live and the determination to endure there were other questions.

How would our captors behave when they realised they were beaten? Would we be killed in an Allied air raid? If the Allies had to make opposed landings on the Japanese mainland what would happen? If the Japanese Government and the Japanese Army disintegrated how would the Japanese civil population react towards us? If we were still at Habu, how would the dockyard mateys behave?

These were the thoughts which kept many of us awake at nights but which few of us dared to discuss with each other.

The answers to all these problems lay well in the future. To learn those answers we would have to survive the present and that meant living from one day to the next and doing our best to adjust to the ever-changing circumstances.

The Red Cross parcels were already things of the past. It was disturbing to reflect what very little impact they had really made on our physical well-being. There was plenty of evidence that even the strongest of us were now showing signs of prolonged vitamin deficiency.

Pellagra, beri-beri and other vitamin deficiency complaints were rampant. In some this took the form of weakened eyesight. The unhappy story went around the camp of two P.o.W.s whose eyesight was deteriorating rapidly and who had the misfortune to share a Red Cross parcel. They boiled a packet of biscuits for sixty minutes, having failed to distinguish it from a pudding and they had thrown away much tea and sugar with the paper wrappings which accompanied them.

Others were suffering from 'electric feet'. This was a particularly unpleasant complaint. When the feet became hot, and particularly when the owners were in bed, excruciating pains would develop. The unfortunate victims would leap out of bed and dance about in a vain attempt to relieve the pain. There appeared to be no cure, except a regular intake of vitamins.

Contracting foreskins and suppurating scrota caused others many hours of agony.

A large number of the P.o.W.s were developing symptoms of beri-beri. In its earliest stages, at least, these are obscene rather than painful. If a finger is pressed into a fleshy part of the body, the 'dent' remains there for some time instead of bouncing back, as it does in healthy tissue.

My feet and fingers were still completely numb but at times my feet began to ache intolerably. I feared the onset of 'electric feet'. My scrotum was sore and itched a lot. My reactions to the amateur's beri-beri tests were positive. What worried me most was my failing memory. I found myself making lists of my relatives and friends, in case I should forget their names.

Nippy Knight was the first of the officers to become really ill when the lower half of his body became paralysed. He had to be removed from the officers' room and put in the sick-bay.

Even W.O. Pritchard, who always seemed to be as strong as a horse, fainted when washing the floor of the Warrant Officers' room. Shortly afterwards he collapsed at work in the dockyard, with the same paralysis as Knight, and had to be carried back to the camp.

Another hazard of life was the risk of an accident in the dockyard. When I had been engaged in shipbuilding, four Japanese riveters had fallen from the side of a ship and had been killed. One of the R.A.F. prisoners, Squires,* had been knocked off a scaffolding and had fallen thirty feet. He had received serious injuries to both of his legs and to his left arm. A Hong Kong prisoner had lost the top two joints of one of his fingers. On at least one occasion there had been a serious explosion in the yard and several Japanese workers had been killed and many injured.

It was, perhaps, fortunate that just at this time, and quite accidentally, the medical advice available to us showed a marked improvement.

When the able-bodied old guard had left for active service overseas they had been replaced by a number of comparatively new, and very young, recruits into the Army. One of these, a Private Second Class, looked a cut above the others. I thought he would be a good person on whom to practise my Japanese. I was amazed when he told me, in quite adequate English, that he had recently qualified as a doctor in Tokyo. I asked him why he was not in the Japanese Army Medical Corps.

'You must have influence to get into the Medical Corps, and I have none.' Then he added, 'Many of those in the Medical Corps are not doctors at all, but they have influence.'

I then bethought me of a certain Dr. Miki, who had been

* In March 1969 I received a letter from Mr. Squires recalling the details of his accident. His spine had also been injured in the course of his fall, and when he had resumed his civilian occupation as an engineer, after the war, he had had to wear a spinal jacket. His condition was now deteriorating, a quarter of a century later, and he was considering applying for a disability pension. See also page 101.

visiting the camp, from time to time, as a Japanese Army doctor. I asked my new-found friend:

'Do you know Dr. Miki?'

'I have met him,' he replied.

'What do you think of him?' I enquired.

'He is a good doctor. In civilian life he is a rich coal-merchant. He has influence,' he answered.

I could hardly believe my ears at this *Alice in Wonderland* conversation. I began to wonder whether vitamin deficiency was affecting my brain, or my ears, as well as my feet.

The Japanese Private, Second Class, had other duties to perform and we took leave of each other.

Shortly afterwards I ran into Nomoto and after saluting him smartly, which I knew would please him, I engaged him in conversation. In the course of this I mentioned how glad I was to learn that we now had a doctor in the camp.

'You mean Dr. Miki,' he replied, 'who visits us from time to time. A very good man.'

'No, Commander,' I replied, 'I mean the new guard who is a qualified doctor.'

This was news to Nomoto. As, fundamentally, he was not ill-disposed towards the P.o.W.s, he was always ready to do what he could for them, within the scope of orders received from his superiors, of whom he was clearly in perpetual awe.

'I will see,' he said, as he strode off.

Within a day or two the Tokyo doctor was relieved of his normal guard duties and became the resident medical orderly. In a further conversation with him, I learnt that he was a Christian and that his first name was Luke.

This was a great improvement. Although Luke was inexperienced he at least knew the names of the complaints, which was more than Dr. Miki did. More important still, he was a dedicated healer, and always did his best to relieve suffering wherever he found it. He was also a diplomat. On Dr. Miki's rare visits the qualified Tokyo doctor addressed the coal-merchant as though the latter was a world-famous surgeon and the former a medical student.

Dr. Miki was affable and pleasant enough, though he made no secret of the fact that he did not like the officers. Perhaps he knew that we realised he was not a doctor. He was far more interested in the rates of pay of officers in H.M. Forces than he was in their complaints.

Luke knew perfectly well what the outcome of the war would be for Japan, as he admitted to me in many subsequent conversations. For the moment he took it upon himself to interview every P.o.W. and record on a card the serious illnesses which he had had. He also managed to obtain some vitamin pills which he dispensed to the worst cases.

Luke said that if I would give him a signed chit asking him to buy me a bottle of cod-liver oil he would do so and debit my account in the camp office. I did; and he did too.

We had a nasty scare. One of our Sergeants, a 'Java' man, went to hospital with suspected diphtheria. He would probably never have been sent to the cottage hospital without Luke's good offices. It was only then that we learnt that diphtheria had been rife in the Hong Kong P.o.W. camp and that many of the Hong Kong arrivals were barely out of quarantine.

The 'Java' Sergeant was given 45,000 units of diphtheria serum at the hospital and returned to the camp, with an escort, on foot. Luke regarded this as most inappropriate but there was nothing he could do about it. All in the Sergeant's barrack room were excused work in the dockyard for seven days; they regarded this as most appropriate.

The Japanese were now working themselves up into a frenzy to celebrate the birthday of the first Japanese Emperor, Jimmu, who was born in the year 2690 (Japanese Calendar). Several days prior to this we were all given a Japanese song to learn, with the order that we were to sing it on the great day, the 11th February.

I found myself devoting time to this task on February the 6th, 1943. At midnight I would have been one year in the R.A.F. I wondered what, if anything, the Air Council were thinking about us.

The 11th February came. We had wonderful meals and accessories; soup and rice for lunch; fish, beans and rice in the evening; and to round it all off, ten cigarettes and a roll of toilet paper. Our only disappointment was the Japanese never asked us to sing the song we had so assiduously learnt. I now knew how the young lady who took her harp to the party felt.

One morning at about half past eight Nakano, the interpreter, came slithering into the officer's room like the snake he was. He knew he would find me there. Nomoto had recently agreed that only three of the officers need go to the dockyard each day and Nakano knew it was my day off. 'Cukie,' he said, sneering at me insolently, 'I look for you, Cukie. You are no goodo. Roosebelto no goodo. Churchillu no goodo. You are no goodo. Bad, very bad.'

He paused and looked out of the window. I wondered what was passing through his twisted mind. He was, I knew, furious that I was making progress with my Japanese. On a number of occasions recently, Nomoto had summoned me to his office and had asked me to pass on messages to the prisoners. Nakano clearly resented this. He knew that Nomoto and the rest of the camp staff did not like him. Perhaps he feared that Nomoto would get rid of him and that he would be posted to a less congenial environment, where he would have less influence. Perhaps the fact that he had been excluded from our discussions with Nomoto about the Red Cross parcels was the last straw. He had frequently been seen emerging from the guard-house munching a titbit and it was evident that he had a direct personal interest in the fate of the parcels. It was all I could do to refrain from knocking him down to the floor there and then, but that would have been stupid, very stupid. I waited for his next move.

When he had finished his leisurely survey of the view from our window, he produced from his pocket a grubby piece of paper on which he had scribbled something in pencil. He had also, I saw, affixed to the bottom of the page the imprint of his little rubber stamp reproducing his name in Japanese characters. All Japanese carry with them similar little rubber stamps.

He handed me the paper. 'Taku,' he said, 'this is last warningu.'

Then he turned and shambled off down the stairs.

I perused the 'last warningu' and managed to decipher the following words:

'Cukie. I watch you carefully. You bad man. You not work hardly enough. You make trouble. Commander very angry. If you do not work more hardly Commander send you to far island from where you will never return. Beware. Last warningu. T. Nakano.'

As I was already on an island from which, at times, I thought I would never return, the threat did not impress me much. I thought that it would do no harm to have a show-down with Nomoto.

I went to see him in his office. For once he was there. He smiled as I entered and saluted. I addressed him in my faltering Japanese and shoved the note in front of him. Of course he could not read it but he spotted the mark of Nakano's seal on the bottom.

'What is this?' he said gently.

I explained the contents.

'I know nothing about this,' he replied, which was quite probably true.

I then pointed out that, in accordance with the international law to which he had referred in his 'excellent' speech a few days before, officers were not required to work.

'Officers do not do hard work,' he retorted.

'We don't do anything at all in the dockyard,' I replied, and added, 'All the orders are given directly to the men by the superintendents and foremen. Half the time we do not even know where the men are or what they are doing. All we officers do is to stand about for ten hours in the cold.'

'But you have your overcoats now,' he argued, and then suddenly he bit his lip, recalling his orders forbidding officers to wear overcoats in the yard. Shifting his ground he went on, 'Officers must go to the dockyard to control the men.'

By now a pent-up anger, engendered by all the hours of cold, of boredom and of futility in the dockyard, was suffusing my mind. If we had ever been of any use to the men in the yard there might have been some point in it all. In Java it had been otherwise. There we had sometimes been able to protect the men from the worst excesses of the Korean guards. Now it was all so different. Most of the other ranks had learnt over a period of nearly a year how to manage the Japanese. Many of them handled the Japanese much better than the officers did. At the dockyard the P.o.W.s were working for, and with, civilians with whom, fundamentally, they had much more in common than we had. They frequently seemed to get on much better when we were not around.

'The officers are only there as show-pieces,' I almost shouted, 'as show-pieces to be shown off to "very rank officers".'

By now Nomoto's anger was matching mine. I thought I could lose nothing by adding, 'All officer P.o.W.s should be in officers' camps.'

Nomoto then played his trump card. Without saying a word he left his office. I had no alternative but to return to my room. It was only then that I realised I had left the 'last warningu' on his desk.

Nomoto was quite agreeable at our next encounter. Nakano never gave me any further trouble. Perhaps Nomoto had given him a dressing down for taking his name in vain.

During the next few weeks it became clear that the whole question of working parties was exercising our captors. There were several interesting developments on this front. The first was an ultimatum from Nomoto that at least fifty 'Java' men and eighty 'Hong Kong' men were to go to work each day. If these quotas were not maintained all heating appliances and blankets would be removed forthwith. The effect of this was to establish quotas for the sick. However ill a man might be, he would not be permitted to remain in camp if this meant that the 'acceptable' number of sick was exceeded.

A few days later two officers, Ricky Wright and Tim Hallam, were returned to camp under armed guard at about 8.30 a.m. A superintendent in the dockyard had ordered them to participate fully in the work of their gangs and they had refused point-blank.

Working parties in the yard reported that the composition of the Japanese labour force was changing. Many of the able-bodied men had disappeared, presumably called to the colours, and their places were being taken by Japanese youths who were said to be military rejects.

When we had arrived at Habu and when, as a result of sickness and deaths, the number of 'Java' men capable of going to work was down to thirty-five or forty, we had marvelled at the economics of this arrangement. There must have been very nearly that number of Japanese dockyard officials whose sole task was to organise and supervise the work of this handful of P.o.W.s. In addition, special arrangements had to be made for our meals, and for our safe custody, until the guards arrived to escort us back to camp. We had assumed that the company was willing to bear these economic burdens for our propaganda value.

Now it looked as though all this was changing and as though the company was insisting on having a real accretion to its labour force.

Credence was lent to this view when we were suddenly informed that officers would no longer go to work in the dockyard. Perhaps we had made too great a nuisance of ourselves. Instead, we were to work on a half-acre plot of land on the hillside, about 150 yards up the road outside the camp. It was hoped that the results of our labours would increase the camp's food supply.

Thus it was that the four of us started work as vegetable gardeners on Wednesday the 17th February 1943. We set off with the necessary impedimenta and erected notices in Japanese, informing all and sundry to keep out, around the perimeter. On our first day various dispossessed Japanese vegetable gardeners were permitted to enter to lift their crops.

Our first day as gardeners was most agreeable. A weak sun in a relatively clear sky provided appropriate gardening weather. The hours were not very long; there were plenty of rest periods; and the mild digging and hoeing did us no harm. Ricky Wright and I embarked on the construction of a dry retaining wall and steps. An audience of small Japanese children, with running noses, watched us intently.

Then a snake entered our Garden of Eden. This took the form of half a dozen sick P.o.W.s coiling up the winding road from the camp, bearing buckets of human excreta on bamboo poles. Our garden was never quite the same again.

Nomoto appeared before we downed tools for the day. He was a bit frosty at first, but he soon unbent, dibbling in some of the seedling onions, and paddling merrily about in the filth.

It was not until after the manure had been spread that we noticed about half a dozen potatoes and carrots which had escaped the keen eyes of the Japanese who had lifted their crops in the morning. Hungry men are not unduly fastidious and they made a welcome addition to our evening meal.

Nippy Knight was still very ill in the sick-bay. On our return to camp we visited him and told him of our doings. He seemed to be barely conscious. Luke had been pumping him full of drugs. Tim Hallam, who had the kindest of hearts, but the roughest of tongues, said to me as we left the sick bay:

'Poor bastard, he looks just like a consumptive sheep.'

One day I had a most unpleasant shock.

During journeys my diaries were concealed inside the stiff walls of my Dutch Army pack. This required 'splitting' the fabric of the walls, inserting the note books and papers and re-sewing the seams, a difficult task for someone who had never been much good with his fingers. In camps I adopted a different technique. I had made a little cloth bag with a looped tape at the top. I would then look around for a loose board, in a wall rather than a floor, behind which there were protruding nails. I had to choose this carefully. The place selected had to be in a part of the camp which was reasonably near my bed-space, but not too near. Equally well it had to be sufficiently far from the bed-spaces of any of my companions, so that if the cache was, by any mischance, discovered, they would not fall under suspicion.

When we moved from the old barrack block to the new one I had found a place of concealment which met all my requirements. I had occasion to visit this, to put a recently filled notebook in the bag. It was not there. I was petrified. What could have happened? Had it been found by a Japanese guard or by one of the Japanese workmen who were still engaged in putting the finishing touches to the buildings? Was Nomoto, aided by Nakano, even now trying to make head or tail of the contents?

I was desperately worried. I suddenly felt that someone was watching me and that I had better move off. As I turned, I saw a Japanese guard slowly patrolling the area. I engaged him in conversation, making some remarks about the weather. He responded agreeably enough and I decided he had seen nothing.

By now it was time to fall in for work in the garden and I still had my notebook with me. I raced back to my bed-space, concealed the book among various harmless papers I had, and just made the parade.

For me it was a miserable day in the garden.

When the day's work was over, I returned and, making doubly sure that I was unobserved, pried the board open wider. Then I saw what had happened. The loop of my little bag must have slipped off the nail and there the bag was, nestling on the ground, about a foot beyond my reach.

I left it there for the night. I took an early opportunity of recovering the bag, putting two loops on it and hanging each of these over a separate nail. I was only to have one more problem with my little bag, but that lay two and a half years in the future.

The Japanese P.o.W. organisation showed signs of life. On Sunday the 14th February 1943 two Japanese Intelligence Officers visited the camp and demanded to see Ricky Wright. The latter reported that they had discussed generalities and that they had asked him a few questions about aircraft, to which they already knew the answers.

On the same day all the officers and thirty-five men, selected by the Japanese, were asked to fill in a questionnaire.*

In conversations with my friends from Hong Kong I had learnt something of conditions there. Most of the camp guards were a very rough lot who had been fighting in China. They were very trigger-

* I made a copy of the questions, and of my answers, which is reproduced in Appendix I.

happy and loosed off at the slightest provocation. A light, left burning for a few seconds after 'lights-out', was extinguished by rifle-fire through the windows. Chinese women and children collecting shell-fish on the shore outside the camp were picked off, one by one, and their bodies left on the beach for days.

Our own problems were less dramatic but none the less real. The cement round the new rice-boilers had disintegrated; too much sand had been put in it. All the new boilers were out of action for several days. Not only did this diminish the already minute rice rations, but, far worse, the supply of drinking water, all of which had to be boiled, was severely cut. It seemed as though we were back on the *Dai Nichi Maru*.

Luke diagnosed that MacKinnon, a Lance-Corporal in the Hong Kong Volunteers, and senior partner of MacKinnon MacKenzie, importers and exporters in Hong Kong, had got T.B. This grieved us all. MacKinnon must have been by far the oldest man in the camp. A man of great wisdom and experience, he was always cheerful and never complained. As a result of his patriotism, destiny had brought him into the camp as an 'other rank'; and he had to do heavy manual labour in the dockyard, of which he would have been well qualified to have been a director.

MacKinnon was put in a room by himself in the old barrack block. I visited him frequently and learnt much from his deep and extensive knowledge of the Far East and its problems. I was glad to be able to ask Luke to buy him a few trifles, and to debit my account in the Commandant's office.

It was about this time that we had our first official punishment. One of the P.o.W.s refused to go to work, complaining that he was sick. It may well have been that he was malingering. Even the sympathetic Luke could find nothing wrong with him. In any event, the quota of allowable sick was already filled.

He was deprived of food for a whole day, which he was forced to spend on his knees. He went to work the following day.

I found myself in a much more cheerful frame of mind. There were many reasons for this.

Our hours of work in the garden were far shorter than the long hours we had spent doing nothing in the dockyard. This afforded me much more time to apply myself to my study of Japanese. Although, like the rest of the prisoners, the officers had to get up at 5 a.m. for breakfast and the early-morning roll-call, we could retire to bed again until we paraded for work in the garden at 9 or 9.30 a.m., according to the weather and the whim of the guard-in-charge. My companions were amused, and slightly scornful, that I should prefer to sit in the cold room, with my gloves on, working away at my Japanese, rather than return to bed for another two or three hours' sleep. Tim Hallam, in particular, teased me unmercifully.

'Local boy, trying to make good,' he would say, as he turned over in his blankets.

Nature, too, was making a great contribution to my higher spirits. It was getting appreciably warmer. All heating had been stopped on the 28th February. Although it was still cold, the sun, which was now more often present than absent, increased in warmth every passing day.

I found the work in the garden most agreeable and interesting. 'Hedging and ditching' has always been that element of gardening which has appealed to me most; and our plot provided us with many problems of this nature.

We had unearthed an enormous block of concrete, which appeared to have formed part of the bed of some pumping engine in the past. The disposal of this created problems. There were three schools of thought. Len Cooper and Tim Hallam were all for cracking it up with a sledge-hammer. The Japanese guard insisted that it should be dragged away. Ricky Wright and I thought it would be easier to bury it.

As usual, we started by following Tim Hallam's lead, for he was the nearest thing we had to a professional agriculturalist. When Len Cooper had smashed two sledge-hammers, the Japanese guard called a halt to this approach and we considered the other possibilities.

It was now the Japanese guard's turn; and we helped him to attach ropes to the block. We then applied our joint efforts to hauling on the ropes, all of which broke. In due course the block was buried.

In excavating a grave for the concrete block, I unearthed some treasure trove—two china bowls and a tea-cup. To the great amusement of the guard I took these back to camp and washed them.

Of course we had our differences of opinion in the garden. I was collecting stones and building a dry retaining wall, but it never seemed to get any bigger. When I was off collecting stones, Ricky Wright would be plundering my wall to build a drain in another part of the plot.

There were some matters about which we had no differences of opinion. One of these was that we would take back to camp half of all the seed potatoes we were given for planting and eat them.

It was never dull in the garden. One day a large party of school-boys marched by to the sounds of martial music emanating from half a dozen buglers. The older boys, who were about fourteen or fifteen, were carrying rifles and bayonets; the younger ones, aged about four or five, were carrying wooden rifles with pads on the ends for bayonet practice.

On another occasion we heard a band coming down the winding road before we could see it. The music was gayer and less martial. A colourful procession soon came into view. It was led by a Japanese carrying a large banner. Behind him were costumed drummers and geisha girls, in their gaily coloured kimonos, strumming mandolines. When they saw us on the hillside they halted and gave us a little concert in the bright sunshine. The guard told us they were adver-tising a forthcoming variety show to be held in Habu. It was the first bit of colour we had seen for many months.

By now Nature was painting not only the days but also the nights. On one of my innumerable nocturnal excursions to the latrines, I heard the sound of a pipe. As I turned the corner of the barrack block, I saw him. He had laid down his rifle on the parapet over-looking the sea. His squat uniformed figure was bathed in the light of the enormous moon which had just risen from behind the hill across the water. He was playing a most plaintive chant on his pipe; and the notes fell on the quiet night air with an indescribable purity of tone. He was playing for himself; he had no known audience. I could not know what thoughts were passing through his head. Perhaps he, too, was far from home; perhaps he was a shepherd, thinking of his flocks in the northern island of Hokkaido. I was content to enjoy, for a few minutes, the beauty and enchantment of this natural scene, to which the only other human being present was contributing so gracefully. I only regretted that L. was not there to share the experience with me.

When we returned on the eve of a rest day, from our morning's work in the garden, we found another notice in our room. It read as follows:

NOTICE

'Examination of clean will be held at 10.30 tomorrow morning by the Commander. And so you must clean in the room and tidy your kit from when you get up in morning. If you do not success that examination you must clean once more, therefore you will not be able to have your play times or rest times.'

It was all so reminiscent of my first kindergarten, as indeed was the day of the 'examination of clean' itself. We passed the test the first time. Our reward was a large quantity of highly coloured Japanese cultural propaganda. We were told to spend the day reading this, and this only. I don't think Tim Hallam had much use for it, though he found one before the day was over.

As much of it was in both English and romanised Japanese I studied it avidly. Later the same evening, Nakano, the interpreter, came round with a large form which he had had duplicated in the camp office. By means of this form, we were permitted to 'apply' for a Japanese work of art. I cannot recall whether this was to be a gift from His Imperial Majesty or whether we were expected to pay for it.

The form requested three things: the applicant's name and number; a description of the work of art required; and a list of the reasons which had led the applicant to the conclusion that the object requested was a work of art. There was a very large space provided for this latter dissertation. The whole was rounded off by the words 'T. Nakano', and, inevitably, the imprint of his little rubberstamp.

As I still have the form in its virgin state, and as I have no Japanese work of art, I can only conclude that I must have failed to apply. Tim Hallam, I know, did not apply. The following day he put the form to the same use as he had put most of the advertising literature.

It was only later that I learnt that Nakano's uncle owned an art shop, the profitability of which had, no doubt, been seriously impaired by the outbreak of war.

This rather unusual day was rounded off by a visit from a number of puppies. That is the only word I can find to describe the four young and beaming Japanese guards who had suddenly been drafted for service overseas and who came bounding into the barrack rooms to say 'Sayonara'. Heads were patted and tails were wagged. Photographs were shared and cigarettes exchanged. We wished them luck and they wished us luck. It was all rather like the prefects leaving at the end of the summer term.

Only one of them could not be described as a puppy, and that was 'Dim Joe'. Of very limited intelligence, as his sobriquet implied, he was a harmless creature. The general impression he gave was of a hollow, very hollow, mangel-wurzel, with a lighted candle inside, perched on top of a large sack, stuffed with straw. His arms hung down on either side like monstrous bananas. His enormous eyes, bulging behind even larger glasses, completed this grotesque apparition. It seemed a pity, I reflected, that soon, no doubt, he would be lying dead, in a pool of blood, in a fox-hole in some remote Pacific island. He had certainly done nothing to us to deserve such a fate.

The Hong Kong party had brought a number of books into the camp. Among those which passed through my hands was a Penguin anthology of verse containing a poem by Thomas Hood about the Willow Pattern which I found rather fun. In a volume of short stories by 'Sapper', the first one was about a man who had been away from his wife for four years. When he returned he found that she was estranged. That was not so much fun.

Arthur Koestler's *Scum of the Earth* also came my way. It was interesting to compare his account of conditions in an internment camp at Le Vernet in France in the autumn of 1939 with our own. There seemed to be two main differences.

Despite the appalling conditions at Le Vernet, there seemed to be no restrictions on the writing and receiving of letters. We had still neither written nor received any. We began to believe that the rumours about Innoshima being a 'prohibited area' were perhaps correct. This unhappy thought was reinforced when we were informed by Nomoto that the records of our so-called 'wages' for the month of October 1942, the first and only month for which we were paid for work in Java, had been received, and had been duly credited in our pass-books. This at least showed that the Japanese authorities now knew where every P.o.W. was and that their communications with South-East Asia were reasonably effective. But this knowledge disturbed rather than consoled us. If the Japanese knew where we were, why were we not receiving any letters? It could only be, we thought, because Innoshima was a 'prohibited area'.

Another point that Koestler had made was the difference between the standards of living of those internees who had money and those who did not. This was equally inapplicable in our case. Among us no one could spend more than a few cents; and every P.o.W. could do that.

Apart from these differences, so much was the same: the cold, the latrines, the obsessive thinking about the date of release.

Koestler's book was stimulating for other reasons. Having been out of Europe when war broke out there in September 1939, I had never understood quite why France had collapsed so rapidly. Koestler, for me at least, provided a possible answer to this question; and his views were very similar to those put forward by the author of *Les Verités sur la France*, which also came my way. Books such as these helped to stimulate our intellectual activity; and we discussed them at great length. When the stomach is empty, food for thought is better than no food at all.

It was on the 11th March 1943, twelve months to the day after I had formally become a P.o.W. in the tea estate in Western Java, that we were allowed to send our first postcard.

This was a pro-forma card and read as follows:

'IMPERIAL JAPANESE ARMY

'I am interned at FUKUOKA, JAPAN.
My health is usual. I am not working.
Please, see that........... are taken care of.
My love to you.
'(signature)'

Of course our health was far from being 'usual'; and of course we were 'working'. But at least our signatures would show that we were still alive.

We were puzzled by the reference to Fukuoka which is a large town on the southernmost island of Kyushu, not far from Moji, our landfall in Japan. Fukuoka must have been nearly 250 miles away from our forgotten island.

I enquired of Nomoto what all this meant. He replied that Habu was among the P.o.W. camps which were controlled from Fukuoka and that it was known as Fukuoka Camp No. 12. To confuse matters further, control of Habu was soon to be transferred to Zentsuji on the island of Shikoku, when it would be re-designated as Zentsuji Camp No. 2. Zentsuji was only fifty miles or so away by ferry; and this made much more sense. We could not, however, help feeling that perhaps all these organisational complexities explained why we had received no letters.

Another inspection was announced. Clearly 'an extremely rank' officer was expected on this occasion. The camp staff were beside themselves with anxiety and activity. Instead of going to our garden, we were detailed to make sacks from the gunny in which the Red Cross parcels had arrived, fill them with sand and distribute them throughout the barrack blocks as evidence of fire precautions.

One of the rooms in the old barrack block was turned into a cobbler's shop. A work-bench and a cobbler's last and tools were 'borrowed' from the dockyard with some difficulty; a pile of worn-out boots was assembled with no difficulty at all; and an appropriate sign was put up over the door.

The adjoining room was similarly decked out as the 'Tailor's Shop', complete with a borrowed sewing machine.

We had been in the camp for four months and, despite repeated requests, we had never been able to get any boots or clothing repaired. We knew that we never would. As we foresaw, all this paraphernalia was taken down and removed immediately after the inspection.

It was the same with the dozen or more shining new kettles which were distributed throughout the barrack rooms for the great day; they were all removed on the morrow.

On their visits to Habu the one thing that all these distinguished visitors had never seen was the P.o.W. population. We were always kept well out of the way and, if necessary, taken for a walk under guard. We thought that we would try to arrange things otherwise on this occasion. The camp staff might be terrified at the thought of a Japanese General; we were not.

We were all up very early on the great day, Wednesday the 17th March 1943. Before the working parties were allowed to leave for the dockyard the camp looked resplendent.

The General, it was rumoured, was due to arrive at 10 a.m. A last-minute 'flash' suggested that a representative of the International Red Cross might be accompanying him. We agreed that it was vital that we should see him.

Nothing had been said as to whether we would, or would not, be going to work in the garden that day. To make our own position clear, we put on our own uniforms instead of the Japanese worksuits.

As nine o'clock came and went, and as there was no sign of one-armed George, who now normally escorted us to the garden, we decided that we had won our point. We were wrong. At five minutes to ten the normally lethargic George came bounding up the stairs and told us angrily to follow him to the garden. He then saw that we had on our uniforms and not our work-suits. This enfuriated him still further. After much shouting and glaring, he dashed down the stairs.

A minute or two later the interpreter appeared and said: 'The Commander orders you to go to the garden quick.'

We explained that we wished to see the General. The interpreter replied that the General would come up to the garden and talk with us.

It was here that we made our mistake. If we had stood our ground, Nomoto would never have dared to do anything, with the General breathing fire down his neck. In all good faith we changed into our work-suits. But we still had some doubts. Before we set off for the garden, Ricky Wright had a quick work with Pritchard, who was still very sick, and gave him some directions as to what to say to the representative of the International Red Cross, if he turned up.

Once we had arrived at the garden, George was content to leave us alone. He curled up under a bush and dozed. The General never came to the garden.

Without a word of explanation, George took us back to the camp by a very round-about route. This manœuvre, so patently designed to prevent us seeing the visitors, nevertheless had its compensations. Instead of descending the hill, and walking the 150 yards back to the camp, George set off over the hill, and led us down into a concealed and peaceful little valley. It reminded me of the countryside round Lake Garda in northern Italy. The sea, a beautiful translucent blue, was still visible. The surrounding hills and the valley itself were bathed in warm sunshine. There was no sound to break the stillness and peace.

We stopped and, sitting on some warm rocks, smoked a cigarette. The valley was filled with vivid green rice-plots, all neatly terraced. In two places, right across the valley, walls had been built to conserve the water for irrigation.

It was the first change of scene we had had during the four months we had been at Habu and yet it was less than a quarter of a mile from the camp.

A bird broke the silence and so did George, but only to explain that we should soon be hearing the nightingales. The peasant in him was reacting to this pastoral scene.

'In many places the peach blossom has already appeared,' he said to me in Japanese.

We noticed that the barley which had been planted along the sides of the valley was coming on well.

Finally, George made a move and we returned to the camp, traversing a number of peasants' back gardens.

Outside the camp there was an impressive-looking car. It looked as though the visitors were still there. George hustled us up to our room and told us to stay there.

As soon as he had gone, we slipped down the stairs to see the ailing Pritchard in the W.O.s' room. The latter told us that the General had been accompanied by a Swiss, representing the International Red Cross, and by a Japanese, representing a Japanese Relief Fund. Pritchard himself, Harry Radford, the P.o.W. Sergeant in charge of the cook-house, and a P.o.W. medical orderly had each been allowed to talk to the Swiss.

'What was discussed?' Ricky Wright asked.

'Well,' replied Pritchard, 'I told him that we had received no mail at all and that we had only been allowed to send one postcard each, and that was only a few days ago.'

'What was his reply?' I enquired.

'That shipping communications were difficult,' said Pritchard.

'Did you tell him about the Red Cross parcels?' someone enquired.

'Yes—I said that we'd had one between two and that that was all we'd had,' replied Pritchard.

'What did the Swiss say to that?' the questioner retorted.

Wearily Pritchard replied, 'That shipping communications were difficult.'

'Was anything said about medical matters?' Tim Hallam asked.

'I gave him a list of the drugs we need and he said he would do what he could,' replied Pritchard; and then he added, 'I also asked whether a P.o.W. doctor could be sent to the camp, to which the Swiss replied that he would look into this.'

'Was the question of more, and more appropriate, food raised?' Len Cooper enquired.

'I gave him a long list of our food requirements, stressing in particular fats and sugar,' came Pritchard's reply, 'but the Swiss said that shipping communications were difficult.'

'What a lot of balls!' interpolated Tim Hallam. 'What the hell do the Swiss know about ships, anyhow?'

Pritchard then went on to say that the Swiss had commented not unfavourably on the accommodation and facilities. No doubt he had been persuaded to spend a minute or two in the 'Cobbler's Shop' and in the 'Tailor's Shop'.

'I told him he should have been here three months ago,' Pritchard said. 'I also told him to come back, unannounced, next week.'

We all laughed at this. We then returned to our room.

Discussing all this among ourselves, we agreed that Pritchard, who was still very ill, had done well, but that there were several points we would have liked to have made to the Swiss ourselves.

Why had all the officers been prevented from talking to him? Why were the officers not in an officers' camp? Had he got a record of every P.o.W. in the camp? Why had no clothing been sent in for the winter months?

We had missed a golden opportunity. We should never have followed George to the garden.

8

Bushido

Innoshima—April–December 1943

During the whole of my time as a P.o.W. I had taken every possible opportunity of talking to Japanese about the progress of the war. This became easier as my Japanese improved and many in the dockyard had spoken quite freely.

By the middle of 1943 I had detected a number of shifts in the views expressed to me.

Originally, in 1942, the Japanese had, I think, convinced themselves that it would all be over within a few months. The Americans were written off as a people whose vitality had been debilitated by sex, sport, strong liquor, ice-creams, and the cinema. The Japanese aim was to conquer Australia and to consolidate their control over the raw materials of South-East Asia. Faced with this, the Japanese argued, the Americans, by now fully committed to the war in Europe, would be only too willing to do a deal with the Japanese in the Far East.

When the outposts of Australia stood firm, when the Americans started fighting back, and, particularly, when the Americans had retaken Attu in the Aleutian Islands, Tojo's propaganda machine shifted into a different gear. The Americans were no longer described as soft and impotent but as strong and merciless. Hospitals, and hospital ships, schools, shrines and irreplaceable buildings of artistic value were the prime targets of their bombers. The war would, of course, still be won by the Japanese but it might take a little longer. It might take eight or ten years to effect the full exploitation of the riches of South-East Asia, but, long before this, the Americans would have wearied of the war. A settlement would be arranged whereby Japan would retain most, if not all, of her conquests.

The Japanese to whom I spoke believed this almost to a man. But there was one word which terrified them all, 'Russia'. They feared that even if the Russians did not participate actively in the Far Eastern War they might offer the Americans bases from which to bomb Japan. But the thought at which they trembled was that the Russians would mount an attack on the mainland of Japan; that would be the end of Japan. Later, when it became abundantly clear that the Americans planned to push their northward thrust to the limit and to mount an attack on the Japanese mainland, the Japanese would laugh this off.

As one of them was to say to me, in 1945: 'If the Americans land on the sacred soil of Nippon we will make them pay in their hundreds of thousands for their desecration. We will kill all the prisoners of war. We will never give up. Even if the Americans overwhelm us we shall not be afraid. We know the Americans. They will give us money; they will re-construct us; and ultimately the United States Senate will demand that the "boys be brought home". We are an ancient people; we can afford to wait before we take the next step in our national destiny. Did you not, in England, have a Hundred Years War against the French?'

When I nodded he went on: 'But the Russians—that is the danger. If the Russians land in Nippon they will never leave. We shall be a Russian colony for ever. I almost hope that the Americans get here first. If they do, then we shall all be allies—Nippon, England and America—all against the great enemy, Russia.'

I recorded in my diary, in March 1943, that those of us who survived might hope to be released in about two years. I underestimated the time it would take by six months.

The weather was getting much warmer. One or two hearties plunged into the sea on return from work but were hauled out by the guards. After a day or so we were told that we could plunge naked into a small and filthy disused concrete basin, adjoining the camp on the beach. It had once been a very small dry dock, long since abandoned. It was most unappetising and there were patches of oil and other rubbish floating on the surface. As hot baths were now cut down to one or two a week, it was the only method of washing off the grime of the dockyard or the earth of the garden.

One hot afternoon, following a stint in the garden, Tim Hallam and I decided to have a go. We plunged in very reluctantly.

F

I thought Tim was in the throes of a seizure of some sort. As he surfaced, he was threshing about and uttering the most peculiar noises. I swam over to see what was wrong.

'What's the matter, Tim,' I said, 'don't you feel well?'

"Nve 'ost 'y oody 'appers,' he replied, looking like death.

It took me some time to realise what had happened. The silly fellow had plunged in with his mouth wide open, and the water, and oil, had washed his false teeth away. The loss of his snappers, top and bottom, was serious. It didn't matter much as far as eating was concerned, for there was not much to eat. But the loss would clearly impede his powers of self-expression, and for Tim, who had acquired a very rich vocabulary since he had emigrated to Australia twenty years previously, this would be a disaster of the first magnitude.

We quickly assembled half a dozen volunteers, who have by now, no doubt, engendered large families of 'goggle divers'. These worthies plunged time and time again into the murky depths, and although they surfaced with many objects which they put to good use in the camp, there was no sign of Tim's dentures.

What could be done? An approach through official channels would certainly be useless. Nomoto and his staff would, no doubt, split their sides at this misadventure; and when they had brought their mirth under control they would explain that there were no dental facilities available for P.o.W.s, which we knew was, at that time, true.

I thought of Luke; and I also recalled that workmen, still finishing off the second two-storey block, had left a quantity of putty lying about.

As soon as Tim was dressed, I took him to an empty barrack room in the unfinished block, where I had seen some putty wrapped in paper. His mouth was filled with this loathsome stuff; and amid his protestations, fortunately limited in scope, though I knew him well enough to know what he was trying to say, two very rough impressions of his upper and lower jaws were taken. These I took to Luke and explained the problem. Within a few days he returned with two sets of teeth which would have done credit to a shark. They couldn't have been at all comfortable, and in due course Tim complained of lumps developing. These, I believe, were treated, and his dentures replaced, in the next camp to which we were sent. For the moment, they were better than nothing.

As spring became summer, the daily battle with our environment eased a little. Nomoto had invested in a beautiful white Angora rabbit. I visited her daily and watched with interest as she started to pluck the white silken hairs away from her throat and breast to make a nest for her young. The camp which had seen so many deaths in the winter was soon to have new life.

I suddenly recalled the lines from Wordsworth's 'Nutting':

> 'A little while I stood
> Breathing with such suppression of the heart
> As joy delights in . . .
> A temper known to those who, after long
> And weary expectations have been blest
> With sudden happiness beyond all hope.'

Now we were all downcast again. The postcards which we had sent off a month or so earlier were all returned to the camp from Fukuoka. Nomoto had not read the instructions properly. He had told us to copy out the pro-forma card in long-hand. The authorities required that all cards should be typed. This would mean another long delay. The cards would have to be taken up to the dockyard and typed out separately there. I was also told that only cards addressed to the United Kingdom would be accepted. So I had to send mine to my mother, instead of to L. in India.*

I learnt, too, that the cards would be sent to Shanghai and thence, by train, across Russia to Switzerland. From Switzerland they would go to London via Lisbon.

I was summoned to Nomoto's office. He addressed me in Japanese:

'Cukie, *Chui*, you have been appointed Japanese instructor in this camp.'

I thought to myself, 'He probably thinks that I know much more Japanese than in fact I do.' I had been talking Japanese to as many of the camp staff as I could but I always chose the subject-matter. I found it very difficult to follow when a Japanese spoke to me about a subject of his choice.

I replied to Nomoto, 'I am very willing to start on these duties

* This, my first postcard, reached its destination in January 1944, more than ten months after it was signed, and two years after I had said good-bye to L. in Singapore.

but not until the additional books, which I have ordered through your office, arrive.'

Nomoto beamed and said the books would soon be coming. They had still not arrived when I left the camp at the end of 1943 and I never did take up my duties as camp instructor in Japanese.

In the garden one-armed George regaled me with a detailed and highly colourful account of his nights with a geisha girl, or rather with three geisha girls, aged between nineteen and twenty-two. He had been 'living it up' for some time past and had been paying each of them twenty yen a night for their company between 8 p.m. and 11 p.m. One night he had got so carried away, and so drunk, that he had given each of them one hundred yen. He was now broke, and these delights would have to stop until he was in funds again.

We never discussed sex among ourselves. It had no interest for us whatever. We had an obsession with food. We exchanged recipes; we discussed wines; and we gave each other the names of good restaurants in various parts of the world. I made up several recipes which my listeners solemnly took down on the back of empty cigarette packets. I have often wondered how many happy homes were broken up by well-meaning attempts to follow these fantasies after the war.

We were learning to accept the minor irritations of life. The glorious weather painted the surrounding hills and the tranquil sea with an ever-changing palette of colours. Then, unexpectedly, we were brought face to face with reality again.

One of the Hong Kong Volunteers, a naturalised British subject, of Russian birth, by name Holster, played the leading role in this unpleasant incident. A Japanese in the shop in which Holster was working in the dockyard apparently wished to attract the latter's attention. The Japanese bombarded Holster with nuts and bolts, causing the latter some injury. Holster, not unnaturally, objected to this treatment and asked him to desist. The Japanese continued to pelt Holster. The latter, infuriated, attacked the Japanese and beat him up severely. The sympathies of all the other Japanese workers in the shop were with Holster, and after the superintendent had been summoned it appeared that the matter had been satisfactorily settled.

The next morning, however, the Japanese aggressor was unfit for work. The matter was then brought to the notice of higher authorities in the dockyard and Holster was marched off to an office and asked for an explanation. There he lost his temper, using very bad language and referring to the Japanese in most uncomplimentary terms. He was then savagely set upon by the Japanese guards, dragged back to the camp and put in the solitary confinement cell. Holster was the first occupant of this cell, which was so small that he could neither stand up nor lie down. He was given a handful of rice and a little salt once a day.

Although the days were warm it was still bitterly cold at nights. Holster was allowed no coat or blanket and he remained there, without access to any facilities, for several days.

The atmosphere in the camp and in the dockyard changed immediately. In the camp the N.C.O. of the day would deliberately arrive early for roll-call and beat up all those who, although on time, arrived after he did.

On one such occasion, while this expression of Japanese spite was in full swing, Tim Hallam muttered to me, inconsequentially, out of the corner of his mouth, 'I remember that at Charterhouse the roll used to go, "Briggs, White, Balls, Gawne, Green",' an observation which, for a moment, distracted my attention from the pogrom all round me.

Even Luke, at this time, declined to buy me some toothpaste in the village.

More important still, an unfortunate precedent had been set. The solitary confinement cell, which for six months had been but a mute threat, had actually been used.

Our descending morale was lowered still further when W.O. Fabel was seriously injured by a falling thirty-metre girder in the dockyard, which all but killed him.

A separate block had been built for, and was now occupied by, all the camp guards. Hitherto only those on duty came to the camp and their leisure hours were spent elsewhere. Now the barrack rooms were constantly visited by both on-duty and off-duty guards.

One of the off-duty guards came into our room one day and stayed for about an hour. He had taken part in the Malayan campaign and had been severely wounded by a fragment of a mortar shell. The action in which he was wounded had taken place at Gopeng, not far from Cameron Highlands. He proudly showed us the livid scars on his stomach and back.

He told us that he had been in the Army since 1937, but was still only a Private Second Class. Like many others, he spoke bitterly about the Japanese officers who took no interest whatever in the welfare of their men. A Japanese soldier addressing an officer had not only to salute but also to bow and scrape until the officer felt disposed to tell him to desist. When serving Japanese officers at meal-times, all food had to be carried above the level of the server's mouth, which in effect meant above his head.

As he told us all this, the guard was chain-smoking the while. This was a serious offence, as no Japanese, whether on or off duty, was permitted to smoke in the prisoners' barrack rooms. I suddenly heard the Corporal of the guard calling out our visitor's name downstairs. I dashed down the stairs and told the Corporal that he had left the building. I had made a friend for life.

One of our greatest problems was to keep the latrines clean. The users of the latrines appeared to have no sense of responsibility at all. Not only were the seats and floors fouled but even the walls and doors. Everyone agreed that it was disgusting but conditions never improved.

As all fit men went to work in the dockyard, it was impossible for us to make effective provision for latrine fatigues.

The admirable Pritchard then came up with an excellent idea. Four specific latrines were allocated to each barrack room of thirty-two men. From that time on, and once the latrines had been cleaned up, they remained as clean as could be expected in the circumstances. Was this an argument in favour of private property? we wondered.

One morning the camp interpreter came in to ask me if I would translate some German documents into English for him. This was so important, he said, that I would not be allowed to go to the garden that day.

He handed me a sheaf of documents which turned out to be the sentence sheets of German P.o.W.s, mainly sailors, in Japanese hands, during World War I. I gathered that they had been captured at Tsingtao.

These documents were most interesting. Some related to deceiving the canteen manager about the amount of beer consumed; some to being too drunk to attend roll-call; and some to drinking wine in a place other than that appointed for the purpose. The highlights, and there were dozens of these, were the proceedings of the 'courts' in cases in which P.o.W.s, who had been given permission to go out of camp to have sexual intercourse with a woman, had overstayed their 'leave'.

While the translation of these documents was not without interest, it seemed to be wholly irrelevant to our own circumstances. When the interpreter had read my translations he observed in Japanese:

'You are a well-behaved lot here.'

To this I replied, 'We don't get a chance to be anything else.'

I then asked him what this particular exercise was in aid of.

'Well,' he replied in Japanese, 'yesterday at the dockyard one of the prisoners, working on a ship and wishing to attract the attention of a Nippon man working below him, gently put his foot on the head of the Nippon man. In my country that is a great insult. The head is a member of great importance.' He paused and then added: 'It is worse even than touching his *chimpo-champo*.'

This was a Japanese slang word which I had not come across previously but the context made its meaning clear and I stored it away for future reference.

The interpreter went on: 'The Commander has put the man, who is a "Java" man, in the solitary confinement cell but he does not know what to do with him. He hoped that these papers would help him.'

By this time I was nearly in convulsions but did my best to keep a straight face.

The interpreter went on, 'You must not laugh. It is very serious. When the Commander asked the "Java" man if he would have done the same thing to another "Java" man he replied "No", but that he had done it to many Indians when he was working in Ceylon and that they had not minded.'

The interpreter collected the papers. The 'Java' man remained in the solitary confinement cell for a few days. And I had had a change from the garden.

I found the company of two of the Hong Kong Volunteers particularly congenial.

Hew Bruce was a Wykehamist who had emigrated to New Zealand in the early twenties. His father had at one time been British Minister in Peking. In 1941 Hew had been New Zealand Trade Commissioner in Shanghai and he had been visiting Hong Kong when the Japanese attacked. He had joined the H.K.V.D.C. and thus it was that he had come to Habu.

A widower, he had lost his wife at the birth of his only daughter. He was a very large man, and large-hearted too. It was difficult enough for those of more modest build to maintain themselves on the scanty rations provided, for Hew it was well-nigh impossible. As the days passed he became more and more gaunt, and the bones of his huge frame protruded in every direction. I spent many hours walking and talking with him but never expected him to survive the war.*

My other companion was an equally refreshing cup of tea, of a completely different flavour.

Norman Mackenzie, a South African, was a Reader in English at the University of Hong Kong. He had done a considerable amount of research in the India Office Library, the Public Records Office, the British Museum and the Bodleian, which had earned him a London University doctorate.

Mackenzie was a very precise and most amusing little man. As he frequently said, 'A research-worker is the only person who is really interested in the subject-matter of his research.' This may be true, but his knowledge and personality were such that he opened many windows for me in the field of English literature.

He was particularly interested in 'de-bunking' those writers of travel books who had never visited the countries they so vividly described. He had, at his delicate finger-tips, innumerable examples of those who, since the Elizabethan age, had repeated errors of fact, in culling from others without any acknowledgement the material with which they constructed their travel fantasies. He would have made an admirable detective.

After a lapse of three months another lot of Red Cross parcels arrived in the camp. Once again there was not enough for one per man. In any event, Nomoto and the camp staff insisted on opening every parcel and, as they put it, 'searching' for illicit items.

When the pilfering was over, and after much discussion, it was decided to adopt a different method of distribution on this occasion. Equal quantities of what was left were distributed to each barrack room of thirty-two men, who were then to distribute this among themselves in accordance with personal preferences. A

* As I learnt after the war, he had been at death's door for many months subsequent to my departure from Habu. But his indomitable spirit kept him alive and I re-established contact with him in New Zealand after his release. He sent me most welcome food parcels from New Zealand in the early post-war years and in 1953 he agreed to be the godfather of my daughter Gillian. Although they correspond, they have never met. I, too, have never seen Hew Bruce since 1943.

complete parcel was set aside for the 'Java' man who was still in the solitary confinement cell for putting his foot on a Japanese head.

It was interesting to observe Mr. Justice Williams sitting on his bed-space, counting his tins and endeavouring to effect exchanges with his neighbours, in furtherance of their, and his, personal preferences.

Harry Radford observed that the arrival of these Red Cross parcels, and a limited quantity of good-quality boots and clothing, had done more for the Allied cause than the P.o.W.s had ever been enabled to do, even as free men. The Japanese were flabbergasted that 'starving' Britain should be able, and willing, to send such things, which were quite unobtainable by anyone in Japan, half-way round the world for a group of P.o.W.s, who, in Japanese eyes, were beneath contempt.

It was a fact that, fundamentally, the Japanese were frightened of the P.o.W.s they had taken. The Japanese had killed many of them in circumstances of indescribable brutality; they had permitted many, many more to die by neglect; they were continually degrading, in every possible way, those who were still alive. But none of this could conceal the fact that they had an indefinable fear of us. They had never begun to understand us and it is natural, I suppose, to fear what one cannot understand. They seemed obsessed by the idea that, somehow or other, we were always about to produce trump-cards from our tattered sleeves.

Perhaps the very existence, and even more the endurance, of the P.o.W.s was making some small contribution to the Allied cause of which we were wholly unaware.

I have always been a bit of a fresh-air fiend and have found it impossible to sleep in a room with closed windows. In the old barrack block this did not matter much because the gaps in the roof and the walls let in all the fresh air that even I could take.

The new block was much better finished and I could no longer rely on natural ventilation at nights. With the advent of summer I felt I had to do something about it.

I had two adversaries in my struggle. The Commandant's orders were that all barrack-room windows were to be kept tightly shut all night, and if any were found open by a patrolling guard, all the occupants of the room were woken and their attention drawn to the serious nature of this offence.

More specifically, my four companions were unanimously

opposed to having any windows open at night; they preferred a good 'consumptive fug'.

I had two advantages of terrain in my unremitting campaign. I slept next to the window at the end of our room on the landward side, and the building was so constructed that if I opened that window it was unlikely to be observed by a patrolling guard below.

My tactics were simple. I was nearly always last into bed and, as soon as I was satisfied that my companions were asleep, I would slide the window back a few psychological inches. The success of this procedure required that I should wake up before any of my companions and silently close the window. I trained myself to do this with unfailing regularity.

If by any chance one of my companions, on a nocturnal prowl, noticed the open window I would apologise for having forgotten to close it.

I like to think that this subterfuge made a substantial, if unappreciated, contribution to the health of my colleagues.

May the 1st, 1943, was a day to remember. It started with my thoughts, which were three in number. 'Would Joe Stalin declare war on Japan this Labour Day?' I wondered. I came to the conclusion, alas!, that he would not.

Then I recalled that my mother's birthday would fall on the following day and that, for only the second time in my life, I would not be able to send her greetings. I had to content myself with a little note for her in my diary.

My third mental enquiry reflected a nostalgia for Oxford which had been tearing at my heart for many months past. 'Would the choristers be singing from the top of Magdalen Tower this fine May morning?' I could find no answer to this, as I had no idea what was happening in England.

So I turned to make the most of a beautiful day at Habu.

At 8.30 a.m. George arrived to tell us that a special task lay ahead of us that day. It had all started with the cook-house. The warmer weather, and the adjacent latrines, had filled the cook-house with flies and other insects. The answer to this problem was to be a series of pendant bamboo curtains and door-screens. The string was at hand; it had come off the Red Cross packages. The bamboos, which had to be of a very special kind, were far away. George and another agreeable guard were to accompany us on this excursion.

We wandered through the village where the local inhabitants

smiled and waved to us. The bright sunshine set off to perfection the abundant peach and cherry blossoms which were to be found in every garden. Red maple and a rhododendron-like flower provided a bass accompaniment to the more delicate treble blossoms.

We passed a local hall which, judging from the posters, was offering a tantalising programme of varieties.

'Rebew—very goodo,' said George, waving his artificial arm. A few days earlier he had shown me photographs of the Empress herself handing him this at some Limbless Ex-Servicemen's ceremony in Tokyo.

George and his companion spent some time examining the posters in detail, and projecting their thoughts with a wealth of obscene gestures, interlarded with appropriate Japanese and English terms which they had picked up somewhere. They seemed a little disappointed that we did not exhibit a great interest in their attempts at titillation.

We took a path up a wide valley, lush with flowering shrubs and grasses. We must have been walking for an hour or two before we found the first clumps of bamboo. George studied them carefully.

'No goodo,' he said, though they looked 'quite goodo' to us.

We didn't care. We were enjoying the excursion and drinking in the accompanying beauty.

Eventually we found another clump. George pronounced that they were suitable; and we cut down about twenty-five. For a moment we thought that this meant the accomplishment of our task. But no!—these were male bamboos and it was also necessary to collect twenty-five female bamboos. These were, apparently, harder to run to earth and more difficult to cut.

We continued our search which was, in due course, rewarded. Personally I could see no difference whatever between the two sexes. George and his companion, however, found in this situation another opportunity for much bawdy talk and banter. As we started off for home we might have been a group of Chaucer's Pilgrims on their way to Canterbury.

On the way back we all laid down in a field and abandoned ourselves to the sun and fresh air.

Eventually we moved on again *botsu-botsu* which, as George explained, meant 'slowly slowly'. Ricky and I carried the female bamboos; at a decent distance the others carried the male bamboos.

George then imparted an interesting piece of information.

'No more prisoners will be coming to Habu,' he said, and added,

'Nippon people find it is too difficult to bring food and other supplies from the mainland to this, and other, islands.'

We ambled on in the heat. We stopped in the village, where George bought Ricky a pair of dark glasses.

As we approached the camp, we passed Nakano, the interpreter.

'Do you know his nickname?' George enquired.

'No,' I replied.

'It's Quarter-past-six,' he said, shrieking with laughter.

'Why?' I asked.

'Haven't you noticed? He always has his right hand on his *chimpo-champo* and his left hand on the middle button of his tunic.'

This recollection sent both our guards off into uncontrollable guffaws. We all returned to camp in very high spirits.

In the evening I gave a lecture to the sick on the workings of the Colonial Office. They did not seem to be any the worse afterwards.

The following day I had an interesting talk with George about financial matters. He had a pension for life of one hundred yen per month for the loss of his arm. On his death, his widow would get fifty yen per month for life. By volunteering to be a P.o.W. guard he drew an additional one hundred and five yen per month. He was also the owner of a small fancy-goods shop, which was being run for him by his sister in his absence. He visited the shop frequently, and it produced a further four hundred yen a month. In all, George, a Private Second Class, was getting over six hundred yen a month which was more than twice as much as a Japanese Major was paid.

Captain Nomoto, the Camp Commandant, drew ninety yen a month as salary and thirty yen a month allowances. An unskilled worker in the dockyard was getting at least ninety yen a month; skilled workers got considerably more.

A day or two later I had a major personal disaster.

Two or three of us had gone up to the garden to work. I had got into conversation with a friendly old 'Annie' who was hanging up her washing on a neighbouring plot. I managed to borrow a few tools from her for the weeding operation. During the course of our conversation she expressed the hope that we would all be friends after the war, but, more important still, she gave me a cigarette which she lit for me.

It was very hot and I took off my shirt, vest and cap and hung them on her clothes-line. This intrigued me. It consisted of two cords wound round each other very tightly. By this device, clothes pegs were rendered unnecessary. The loose ends of clothes could be slipped between the twisted cords and thus held in place.

I weeded away among the potatoes for some time until my attention was drawn by a sharp cry from Ricky.

I turned and saw that my precious clothes were a mass of flames. When I took off my shirt a part of the lighted ash of my cigarette must have got caught in the shirt.

My shirt, vest and R.A.F. cap, all by courtesy of Corporal Shrivenham at Garoet, were burnt beyond repair. I was lucky to save my battle-dress tunic and I was glad that 'Annie's' undies were unscathed. I thought I ought to apologise to 'Annie' for any inconvenience caused. I entered her hovel where she was chopping wood. I offered to do it for her. She was pathetically grateful.

As clothes were irreplaceable at Habu, this was a severe blow. Hew Bruce very kindly gave me an enormous white shirt, but it was so large that I felt like a petrol-pump attendant whenever I ventured to put it on.

On the way back to the camp, George told me that our postcards were still in Habu Post Office as the postmaster did not know what to do with them. What an organisation! What a day!

The working parties in the dockyard were reporting a general tightening up of regulations and restrictions. The midday break had been cut down to ten minutes. The P.o.W.s' response was indicative of their resourcefulness. They refrained from taking their spoons from the camp to the yard. When the midday rice was served they demanded chopsticks. The Japanese could hardly refuse this request which indicated that the P.o.W.s, as the Japanese had hoped, were adjusting themselves to the superior Japanese way of life. Unfortunately, and as the prisoners well knew, there were not enough chopsticks to go round. There was only one chopstick per man. The lunch break continued to last as long as it had done previously.

Searches of the working parties, returning from the dockyard, were now more frequent, and more thorough. A Japanese worker had reported to his superiors that he had 'incontrovertible' evidence that the prisoners were taking photographs in the dockyard. He had seen a P.o.W. taking a photograph out of a latrine window; and, by contriving to brush against the prisoner as he emerged, he had felt the camera in the prisoner's pocket.

Despite the rigorous strippings and searchings no cameras were found, for there was none to find. The 'incontrovertible' evidence of the eager Japanese worker proved to be illusory. He had observed a P.o.W. vainly trying to light a cigarette in a latrine by focussing the sun's rays on it through a magnifying glass. He had mistaken an empty tobacco tin in the prisoner's pocket for a camera.

I went as Ricky's representative to a meeting of barrack-room leaders held in the Commandant's office to explain the position as regards air raids, which were now regarded as imminent. Nakano, the interpreter, was in the chair; Nomoto himself was in an adjoining room weighing out toilet paper!

Nakano's English had an old-fashioned flavour about it that day.

'We are here,' he said, 'to discuss uncommon times,' meaning 'emergencies'. He went rambling on about the need to move 'heavy sick men' out of the buildings. 'If the fire becomes too grand, you may leave the rooms,' he added.

Having painted a lurid picture of the devastating effect of incendiary bombs on the wooden buildings of Japan, referring to notes and photographs in front of him, he admitted to his own personal fears by saying, 'I must confess that I am very terrible.'

A bugler was then introduced, who demonstrated the calls for air-raid practice and for an air raid; also for fire practice and for a fire.

We had a genuine air-raid alarm a few nights later but unfortunately nothing came of it.

The camp and dockyard authorities suddenly became convinced that we were all spies. Following the 'camera' incident, another P.o.W. was observed making a sketch in the dockyard. In fact he was drawing a small yacht he had noticed, a replica of which he had set his heart on building for himself after the war.

The result was that all pens, pencils and paper, except toilet paper, were declared to be 'prohibited objects' and were confiscated forthwith. In addition, all books and other reading material were also confiscated. Nakano informed me that Nomoto wished to satisfy himself personally that they contained nothing 'unsuitable', before he would release them again. As George was always telling me that we should be P.o.W.s for fifty years, Nomoto would no doubt take his time about censoring the books, most of which had been read by the prisoners anyway.

Another sign of the general disquiet among the Japanese authorities was the promulgation of a new set of camp rules which included the following:

'At the sounding of the breakfast bugle call, all men must take their meal in a silent and polite manner; the room leader must give the order to commence.
'Before the evening roll-call, open the inspection of the duty N.C.O. [*sic*]
'Everyone must order, report and number in Nipponese.
'Personal kit that is not in use will be made into one bundle and labelled with owner's name and will be kept in the Commandant.' [*sic*]
(This particular rule was greeted with coarse cries of 'Stuff it up his arse'.)
'Label bearing owner's name in Nippon and measuring 10 x 2 millimetres [*sic*] will be placed at foot of bed.
'All pens, pencils and stationery forbidden.
'Night guards shall be fully dressed but not in possession of fire-arms. [*sic*]
'The staple diet is rice and barley.'
(We hardly needed to be reminded of this.)
'In case of uncommon occurrence all personnel must sit on them and keep silent.' [*sic*]

Severe punishments were prescribed for breaking camp rules, disobedience, refusal to work, attempted escape or open defiance, revolt or instigation of revolt, and taking up organised action. A footnote in large letters read: '*Anyone SUSPECTED of any of the above will also be punished*'.

The promulgation of these rules caused more mirth than gloom, except for the loss of writing materials. This was a severe blow to those who had not foreseen that this might happen and who had not taken the necessary precautions.

I found a tiny black and white kitten near the latrines and consulted George as to what should be done about it. We took it to the rabbit-hutch where the Angora had just produced another litter. 'Black and White' was added to the bar without difficulty.

This sight of fecundity reminded me of the news item in the latest issue of the *Nippon Times*, by now our only permitted reading matter. It recorded that, as the British birth-rate was falling so fast, the British Government had, in desperation, recalled all British troops from overseas!

Two days later George told me that a number of young guards off duty, for want of something better to do, had removed the kitten from its foster-mother and had poured scalding water over it 'to see what would happen'. George had remonstrated with them, but it was too late to prevent another unnecessary camp death.

A solitary figure, wrapped in melancholy, was fishing from the camp pier. It was Nomoto. The previous day he had been ticked off for his shortcomings by an inspecting Japanese General in front of the whole camp, including the P.o.W.s and Japanese staff. Quite which of these shortcomings the General had in mind was by no means clear. It might have been the lack of ferocity in the exhibition of bayonet-fighting put on by the guards, shouting like wild animals, to entertain him; though this seemed ferocious enough to us. It might have been the inadequacy of Nomoto's air-raid precautions; these certainly seemed perfectly futile to us. It might even have been that George, who did not care for Generals, had deliberately put on his oldest and most disreputable uniform, to which the General had taken a marked exception.

Whatever it was, Nomoto was a broken man for the next few days. At one time we feared that he might be replaced. We hoped not; we might be landed with someone much worse. That evening Nomoto consoled himself by pinching a pair of Red Cross boots which he wore on every possible occasion thereafter.

On the same day another solitary figure was at work, heating the bath-water for the now resident Japanese guards. Sweating profusely, and clad only in a *hundoshi*, probably the smallest item of clothing in the world, he shovelled and stoked for an hour or more. In response to a query from a passing P.o.W., he indicated that he had consumed all but three of his twenty-one Red Cross dried raisins. The stoker was Mr. Justice Williams, formerly one of His Majesty's Puisne judges in Hong Kong.

With the advent of summer, we now had mosquitoes to contend with. The Japanese produced some little green coil burners but they did not seem to do much good.

Harry Radford visited us to announce that all rice rations were to be reduced, particularly for the officers, who were now deemed

1 Habu Camp, Aug: 1969. 'We welcomed our sick at the little pier to which they had been brought in a small boat . . . ' (page 75)

2 Zentsuji, Aug: 1969. 'I recalled . . . the two-storey building in which we had been herded like cattle . . . and the open exercise space on which we had walked for hours . . . ' (page 292) The building facing the camera did not exist in 1944.

3 Illuminated scroll containing the names (and signatures) of all those who were present at the Oxford and Cambridge Gathering held at Zentsuji War Prison Camp on Tuesday, the 12th December 1944.

4 Author in Lahore, 11th Nov: 1945, the day before emergency admission to the British Military Hospital. (page 284)

5 Habu Dockyard, Aug: 1969. '. . . a passing Japanese work-man was forcibly deprived of his safety helmet which was firmly placed on my head. Stressing the fact that the Japanese had never been so solicitous about my safety when I was actually working there, . . . I reluctantly agreed thus to be photographed.' (page 295)

6 Habu Village, Aug: 1969. '. . . the pharmacist . . . reluctantly agreed to be photographed outside his shop . . . ' (pages 77 and 293)

7   Habu Ferry, Aug: 1969. 'On the ferry I noticed a handsome
Buddhist priest . . . and with the help of a young Japanese mother . . .
I indicated my objective.' (page 292)

8   Matsuyama, Aug: 1969. 'We withdrew to a room furnished in
the Japanese style where I had ordered a traditional dinner. This
was served by attractive young Japanese girls in *kimonos* and *obis*.'
(page 290) Nagano nearest camera.

to be 'non-workers'. During the previous winter 600 kilos of rice had disappeared, no doubt pinched by the guards who were then living out. To remedy this we were to have a series of rice-less days, and a new scale of rations which provided 786 grams for a Japanese soldier, 550 grams for an 'other rank' P.o.W. and 420 grams for an 'officer' P.o.W. per day.

At the following weighing I had dropped a further seven pounds which brought me down to a hundred and twenty.

George must have thought I looked a bit under the weather, for when I accompanied him alone to the garden to work, all the others being sick, he produced a bottle of *biru* from under his tunic, which he shared with me.

Perhaps as a result of the General's visit, Nomoto had instituted a scheme whereby each of the officers, in turn, should be P.o.W. Duty Officer of the week. This involved wearing a red and white arm-band, taking all roll-calls with the Japanese N.C.O. of the day, and making out the working-party rosters. Both the officers and the other ranks welcomed this; the officers because it brought them into closer contact with the men and the other ranks because they had never had any wish to see their officers ignored and degraded by the Japanese.

By now the Japanese must have been beginning to realise that their world 'image' as the custodians of a large number of P.o.W.s was not a good one. In an issue of the *Nippon Times* there was a report, dated the 1st June 1943, of a statement by Attlee in the House of Commons that, among the more than half a million casualties since the outbreak of war, 226,706 were still reported as 'missing'. This suggested to us, which was in fact the case, that the British Government had not yet had any official intimation from the Japanese that we were P.o.W.s.

To improve their image the Japanese authorities decided to indulge in some propaganda. One Sunday, towards the end of the summer of 1943, some seventy P.o.W.s, including Ricky and myself, were marched to a school at Mitzonoshi, in another part of the island. There the Japanese selected thirty to make up a number of volley-ball teams. The rest of us were posed around as happy volley-ball fans. Innumerable photographs were then taken for propaganda purposes. One of the players had taken off his shirt when his team took the field. He was told to put it on again and the photographing was suspended until he had. P.o.W.s look better fully clothed.

As soon as the photographers were satisfied, the volley-ball games were abandoned. Two P.o.W.s were then selected to play ping-pong, with the rest grouped round, in eager anticipation of a needle match. A Japanese thought it would look better if the officers and N.C.O.s were seated. So the match was held up until adequate chairs and benches had been produced. After a few interchanges had been photographed, the ping-pong was, in turn, abandoned, and we all marched back to camp.

I was detailed to go with George to a garden the other side of the dockyard to take cuttings of sweet potatoes to be planted in our plot, the ordinary potato crop having been lifted the day before. For this excursion I was provided with a dwarf's bicycle.

George was in an expansive mood and as we rode along in the warm sunshine he told me the story of the loss of his arm.

George had been in the Japanese cavalry in China. Perhaps this explained, in part at least, the bond between us. His troop was attacking a Chinese strong point. A shell burst and killed his horse; his left arm was completely severed above the elbow; and fragments of the bursting shell pierced his calf, his right elbow and the side of his head.

Despite these severe wounds, he was still conscious and he managed to bind up the stump of his left arm with his towel, and to apply a tourniquet. He saw the blood pouring out from his severed forearm on the ground. With shells still bursting all round him, two stretcher-bearers arrived and carried him off to a Casualty Clearing Station, situated in a Chinese farmhouse. There were two Japanese army doctors there, a Captain and a Lieutenant. At this stage George wished ardently that he had been killed outright; he had no desire to face life in his mutilated condition.

For a moment he thought that his wish would be fulfilled. Having stripped him, the doctors agreed that he was so badly wounded that nothing could be done for him.

Meanwhile, his great friend had been brought into the C.C.S. with most of his stomach blasted away. George insisted, in view of the doctors' prognosis about himself, that his friend should be attended to first. While this was being done, his friend died. With his last words the friend begged the doctors to do their best for George.

George's wounds were then dressed and he remained in the

C.C.S. for thirty-six hours without water. He subsequently spent eighteen months in hospital, recovering from his wounds.

On his discharge from hospital, he returned to his village to look for a wife. None of the mothers would permit their daughters to have anything to do with him.

George became very morose and depressed. He became a constant *habitué* of brothels; and there, one day, he found a girl who took pity on him. They married and had a child. She was now expecting their second child.

It was clear, from all his references to his wife, from his constant production of her photograph and from the fact that he had, with considerable difficulty, found a little house for her near the camp, that George loved his wife and child dearly.

But he was still sad. He told me that most adult Japanese and all children, except his own, jeered at him for being one-armed. He dared not go to the public bath-house. He was terrified that his own child would be taunted and mocked at school.

I knew now why George found pleasure in my company. We were both, in a sense, odd men out.

We brought the sweet-potato cuttings back on our bicycles and in the afternoon planted them.

The following day we went up into the hills, on foot, to get some more cuttings. I picked three flowers; I gave two to George, one for his wife and one for his child. The other I pressed in my diary for L.

The food situation was becoming serious. For weeks we had had nothing but the reduced rice rations, supplemented from time to time by boiled cucumbers or *daigong*. This latter was an obscene-looking giant radish, appropriately described as the only known example in the world of water standing on end.

Our weights were going down rapidly and I lost another fifteen pounds in six weeks. Even the camp authorities were becoming a little alarmed at this. A quantity of rotting horse meat was brought into the camp. The P.o.W. cooks, realising that it was infected, refused to put it in the stew. The Japanese N.C.O.-in-charge of the cook-house overruled them. As a result, virtually the whole camp came down with food-poisoning.

Dr. Miki refused to accept that this was caused by the infected meat. He had another and much more ingenious theory. The prisoners' hair was too long; they were cutting it off surreptitiously and eating it, like cats. The order went out that all heads were to be shaved and kept shaved.

The officers found this particularly degrading. We had succeeded in securing from the Japanese some small signs of recognition that we were officers and now it seemed that we were about to slip back a bit. As the four of us were discussing how best we could make our protest, Tim Hallam came into our room with a head like a billiard ball.

'Much more hygienic,' he said, as he ran his hand over his crenellated skull. We did not pursue our protest.

Dr. Miki, who had caused this crisis, had now taken up residence in the camp. He used one of the P.o.W. medical orderlies as a batman. He had also been improving his English.

'Bring me my boots,' Miki would bellow to the unfortunate orderly; and those who heard this clarion call would respond:

'And saddle.'

'Bring me my sword,' Miki would continue; and the response would come:

'Of burnished gold.'

During the preceding months a number of the Japanese guards had brought stray puppies into the camp. These had been looked after by the sick, for whom they provided some companionship while the rest of us were at work.

Whether it was Nomoto or Miki who took the decision, I do not know. One day the Japanese guards bayoneted all the dogs and puppies to death 'for practice'; and it was said that the remains went into a stew.

George had been away from the camp for about ten days, on paternity leave. He returned one afternoon to inform us with disgust that his wife had presented him with, of all things, a daughter. We were bathing in the sea at the time. When I saw him on the beach waving to us, I emerged and displayed to him the much-admired swimming trunks which I had made out of an old Japanese flour sack, found on the camp refuse heap.

'Do you know what the Japanese characters on the sack mean?' he enquired.

I shook my head.

'Virility flour,' he replied with a coarse laugh. 'That's no good to you; you had better give them to me.'

We sat on the beach for a few minutes, looking at the enormous Japanese aircraft carrier anchored off the cape and awaiting its turn to go into the dockyard for a re-fit.

George then informed me that Habu camp had now become 'Zentsuji Camp No. 2'; and that we had severed our connections with Fukuoka. He went on to tell me about Zentsuji, on the island of Shikoku.

Zentsuji, he said, was a large garrison town and the headquarters of a Japanese military command. All arms of the Service were represented and he had done some of his cavalry training there. A large P.o.W. camp, in permanent buildings, with many British P.o.W. officers, had been established in Zentsuji. The P.o.W.s worked on allotments in the surrounding hills. George added that some of us might be going there in the near future.

I thought to myself, 'I would welcome a change, I am tired of my companions here and I'm sure they're tired of me.'

George picked himself up from the beach and went back to his paternal duties. As he left he said he would be returning to duty the following day.

A few days later a pleasant-looking, slim and immaculately dressed young Japanese civilian came bounding up the stairs and addressed us a number of questions in impeccable English.

'Do you know Pilot Officer Kenny?'

'Do you keep chickens here?'

'Was the fighting fierce in Java?'

'How are things?'

We noticed that he had a camera with him and, taking him for a journalist, our replies were rather curt.

He looked a little crestfallen when he left.

It all came out later. His name was Shiro Asabuki. He was a graduate of Trinity College, Cambridge, where he had been from 1935 to 1938. He was the chief interpreter at the main Zentsuji camp and an avowed Anglophile.

A delegation from the main Zentsuji camp, led by a Colonel, had come to inspect their new 'ward'. They had arrived unannounced so we had been spared the usual pre-inspection flummery. We did not see any of the delegation except Asabuki. The latter had also had a word with Harry Radford and had told him that the British officers at Habu seemed to be 'a frosty lot'.

As soon as the delegation had left, a rumour went round the

camp that the officers were going to be moved to Zentsuji main camp in the near future.

The following day, which was a rest day, Nomoto, wearing his purloined Red Cross boots, clambered up on to a rostrum and addressed us at some length. He might well have saved his breath, and allowed us time to get on with our chores. All the essential points he made were repeated in a 'hand-out' duplicated in English, which was subsequently distributed.

These were that Colonel Sugiyama was in command of all Zentsuji War Prisoners' Camps, of which Habu was now one; that the Colonel hoped to see more signs of improved 'labour efficiency'; that 'comfort bags', now kept by the Colonel, 'would soon be presented for services rendered'; and that henceforth all other rank P.o.W.s would salute all Japanese soldiers and not, as heretofore, only N.C.O.s and officers.

The camp was about to become the setting for a dramatic interlude of which, hitherto, we had not seen the like.

A distinction must be made between the permanent camp staff and the guards. The former were responsible for the administration of the camp; the latter for security. The respective areas of responsibility of these two emanations of Japanese power were never wholly clear to us. As far as the P.o.W.s were concerned, they were all 'bloody Nips', some of whom were 'bloodier' than others.

Nomoto, as the only Japanese officer in the camp, was theoretically in command of the guards as he was of the camp staff. But Nomoto was a weak man. This had some advantages, as far as we were concerned; it also had considerable disadvantages. His control of the guards was most erratic. If the guard detachment posted to the camp was composed of new recruits who had never been overseas, he usually managed to keep them in some sort of order. If a detachment of more experienced guards, with a good record of active service overseas behind them, arrived, Nomoto was quite out of his depth. This became particularly marked if the Sergeants, that is to say the Guard Commanders, were tough characters who had served with their guards overseas. These latter would make no secret of their scorn for the camp staff in general, and for Nomoto in particular.

The bulk of the P.o.W.s came into much closer and more continuous contact with the guards than they did with the camp staff. The guards were responsible for all roll-calls, for patrols within the camp and for escorts outside the camp.

The 'complexion' of these transient guards was a matter of great concern to all P.o.W.s.

In Boei Glodok we had become accustomed to the indiscriminate and purposeless beatings of the Korean guards. The mental strain engendered by such an environment has to be experienced to be appreciated. Anything could happen round any corner and there was nothing we could do about it.

There had been plenty of beatings at Habu, but at least there had been apparent reasons for these. A prisoner might have left a button undone; he might have omitted to salute a Japanese whom he had not noticed; he might have been a fraction of a second late for a roll-call; there were a hundred and one things that might go wrong, however hard one tried.

But, so far, we had been spared, at Habu, a repetition of the continuous nervous tensions which was such a marked feature o life in Java.

It was with considerable dismay and many forebodings that we, and no doubt Nomoto too, witnessed the arrival of some new guards. They were all well-built veterans of the campaign in the Solomon Islands. As genuine *samurai* warriors, they were bursting with the spirit of *Bushido*. They would be looking for means of demonstrating this in the comparatively placid atmosphere of Habu.

The two Sergeants in command were terrifying characters. One, with a large scar running down the side of his face and bull-neck, was immediately dubbed 'Scarface'. The other, slighter in build, looked a little more intelligent. He proved to be even more dangerous and was referred to as 'the Snake'.

From the very outset it was clear that these two, and their henchmen, were determined to beat up the prisoners; and that they were not going to bother about looking for excuses.

They started on the working parties as they escorted them to and from the dockyard. Then came two ugly incidents within twenty-four hours.

One of the P.o.W.s whose turn it was to do night fire-watch guard in the old barrack block had to pass the guard-house to take up his post. He was a Scotsman and he was wearing his glengarry. As he passed the guard-house he was called inside.

Scarface concluded that he was trying to be funny by wearing this unusual headgear on duty. His glengarry was snatched from his head. Scarface pulled off the badge, the pom-pom and the tapes and throwing the whole lot on the floor, trampled them triumphantly underfoot. Meanwhile the other guards were beating up the P.o.W.

When the beating was over, what was left of the glengarry was restored to its owner. The latter, unfortunately, coughed inadvertently as he was leaving the guard-house. He was promptly set upon again and beaten savagely.

The following day Scarface decided that one of the P.o.W.s was not looking straight ahead of him during roll-call. He was pulled from the ranks and badly beaten with a three-inch-thick pick-helve, as a result of which his arm was seriously injured.

We knew the officers' turn would come: and it did.

The first onslaught took the form of a minatory harangue from the Snake during a roll-call.

He bellowed that the officers were deliberately defying all the regulations. We were saluting Japanese N.C.O.s 'reluctantly and with insolence'; this was true. We were improperly shod at roll-calls; this was partly true, as some hoped that their clogs or sandals would not be noticed in the darkness. Finally, Ricky Wright did not bring us to attention and salute every time one of the Sergeants passed along the corridor downstairs; this was impossible.

After this brush we knew the Sergeants were gunning for us, and I turned out to be the hapless victim.

Ever since we had moved into our upstairs room in the new barrack block, some eight months earlier, we had always switched off our lights at night; and it normally fell to me to do this. Nomoto and others, who frequently prowled around the barracks at nights without warning, were fully aware of this practice, and they had never raised any objections.

On my return from a visit to the latrines in the middle of the night, I found that the light had been switched on during my absence. I turned it off before getting into bed.

I did not know then that Scarface had deliberately turned it on while I was away, and that he was lurking in the shadows below to see what would happen. I had fallen into his trap and this was his chance.

He roared up the stairs, shouting and shrieking as though he was attacking some strong-point in the Solomons. He demanded to know who had turned the light off. I admitted that I had. He ordered me to follow him to the guard-house. My heart disappeared into my gym-shoes.

As I followed him along the corridor, I snatched off the wall a notice, signed by Nomoto, to the effect that every possible effort should be made to save electricity.

By the time I got to the guard-house, Scarface had alerted his guards, who all set upon me as I entered. During a pause in their attack Scarface asked me why I had insulted him by turning off the light which he had just switched on.

During the mêlée I had managed to hang on to the notice and, although his desk seemed to be where I would have expected to find the ceiling, I succeeded in putting the bedraggled paper on his desk, the right way up.

He could not, of course, read it, as it was in English, but he did notice the imprint of Nomoto's little rubber-stamp, and that of the interpreter, Nakano, on the bottom. I think that this must have infuriated him even more than my participation in the events of the preceding quarter of an hour.

He let out a roar for 'Quarter-past-six', and the wretched Nakano stumbled to his feet from a pile of blankets, on which he had been trying to get some sleep in a corner of the guard-room.

What followed exceeded my highest expectations—an acrimonious altercation between Scarface and Nakano.

It could best be described as a 'Gentlemen versus Players' fixture.

Scarface, as opening bowler for the 'Players', referred professionally to the orders which, he claimed, bound him as Guard Commander. He produced an enormous tome and practically rubbed 'Gentleman' Nakano's nose in the relevant paragraph. The paragraph apparently stated that all lights in all barrack rooms were to be kept burning all night.

Nakano, for once a worthy upholder of the amateur traditions which had characterised the administration of Habu camp from its inception, produced an even larger tome, which apparently contained the correspondence leading up to the issue of Nomoto's notice.

Mercifully I was forgotten and I made myself as inconspicuous as possible in the shadows, while bat parried ball, over after over.

Eventually stumps were drawn.

I myself who, in all the circumstances, had got off comparatively lightly was ordered to return to bed; from now on, whatever Nomoto said, all lights in all barrack rooms would be kept burning all night; Nomoto's 'misleading' notices were to be taken down and destroyed the following day.

As Scarface gave these orders, I suppose it could be said that the 'Players' had achieved a first-innings lead.

Before returning to bed, I thought it wise to wake up the leader of every barrack room and tell him to switch on any lights which had been switched off.

The following day, Scarface, flushed with his apparent victory, was on the war-path again.

I had made him lose a little 'face' at least, and he wanted his revenge.

I was writing my diary as he bounded up the stairs unexpectedly. I dropped it on the floor and stood on it all the time he was in the room. He left, but the nervous tension remained.

A few days later his side-kick, the Snake, who was a much smoother character than his colleague, paid me a visit. I noticed that he had brought with him the P.o.W.s' Records Book.

Referring to the entry relating to myself, he started asking me questions. I suddenly thought to myself, 'This is the second prong of an attack which these two bastards have cooked up together!'

'What were you doing in Malaya?' he asked me in Japanese.

'I was the District Officer at Cameron Highlands before I joined the Royal Air Force,' I replied.

'You know the Cathay building in Singapore,' he enquired.

'Yes—I have been to the cinema there. It was quite a good film,' I answered.

This obviously irritated him, as it was meant to. He went on, 'I don't mean the cinema. I mean Room 36, the Secret Room.'

'I have never heard of it,' I said, which was true.

'You are lying,' he retorted, 'I have seen it. I have seen the papers. I know that you had some connection with Room 36.'

I thought to myself, 'Here we go again. If only I hadn't turned that bloody light off, these two bastards would never have known that I existed. Now they are determined to make my life here hell.'

The conversation continued for some time. He persisted with his questions. He clearly fancied himself as an interrogator.

At that moment the bugle went for the nine o'clock changing of the guard—and he was late!

I was to have one more brush with these 'heavenly twins'.

The following Sunday, which was a rest day, Scarface summoned me to the guard-house at 9.30 a.m. I was P.o.W. Duty Officer of the week and I knew that he had gone off duty at 9 a.m. and had handed over to the Snake, who was also in the guard-house, still poring over the P.o.W.s' Records Book.

Addressing me in Japanese, Scarface said: 'Cukie, I order all men to come and watch my guards fighting with the bayonet. You will go and tell them—now.'

'None of the men has finished washing or cleaning yet,' I replied, and added, 'they cannot come.'

He glared at me. I could see that he loathed me as much as I loathed him.

'Alas!' I thought, 'he is slightly better placed to give expression to his feelings than I am to mine.'

'You are defying me. You will tell three men in each room to do the washing and cleaning. The rest will come immediately,' he said.

'They cannot; they must clean the rooms. It is the Commander's order,' I retorted. As I hoped, the reference to Nomoto got under his skin.

'I give orders here,' he said. 'Who is the Commander? He is not a soldier. He has never seen the enemy—except you.' To emphasise his point, he spat on the ground. 'I am a soldier,' he went on, 'I, and my men, have fought the imperialists all over the Pacific. We are the true Nipponese warriors. Nomoto is a clerk who sits on his arse all day long. I spit on Nomoto too'—and he was as good as his word.

He had worked himself up into such a rage that he left the guard-house and started chivying the men out of their rooms, telling them to assemble on the space reserved for the guards' bayonet-practice.

I went in search of Sergeant Hirano, who, I knew, was the camp staff N.C.O. on duty. When I told him what was afoot, he was furious.

No doubt Scarface would also have described Hirano as 'a clerk who sits on his arse', but he showed great courage on the occasion. He ordered all the P.o.W.s he could see back to their rooms; and then he went down to the bayonet-practice ground and, in front of Scarface and his guards, repeated his order to the P.o.W.s who had begun to assemble there.

Scarface seized a rifle and bayonet from one of his guards and I thought for a moment that he was going to dispose of Hirano on the spot.

Hirano withdrew, beckoning me to follow him. As I looked over my shoulder, I saw Scarface working off his frustrations, and his *Bushido*, in bayonet practice with one of his guards. Judging by the noises that Scarface was making, his adversary must have appeared to him as an amalgam of Nomoto, Hirano, Nakano and myself.

Despite their first-innings lead the 'Players' had clearly lost the match.

Shortly afterwards Scarface left the camp under an armed escort. He had attacked one of his own guards with a bayonet. This was too much even for Nomoto, who had sent in a report to higher authority.

Habu had had enough of *Bushido*.

We were working in the garden picking the last of the tomatoes and lifting the onions. I had just disturbed a vicious-looking and highly coloured snake fighting with a crab, in a crevice of the retaining wall I had built. Of course I had left my snake-knife in the camp.

Then George said quietly, 'This is your last day in the garden. The dockyard authorities require the plot for a new building.'

'Who said,' I wondered to myself, 'one is nearer to God in a garden than anywhere else on earth?'

Before he was taken prisoner in Java, Ricky Wright had bought a magnificent pair of brown boots which he had intended to wear while flying. As all our boots and shoes were rapidly disintegrating, he had decided to have these cut down so that he could wear them. He had entrusted these boots to one of the P.o.W.s, who was doing his best at boot repairing, to have the tops cut off.

Nomoto had spotted them and paid us an unofficial visit, in the hope of persuading Ricky to sell them to him. Unfortunately Ricky had to tell him that the boots had already been decapitated. Nomoto was as heart-broken as a child who had lost its favourite teddy-bear.

Nomoto was a lonely man and he took this opportunity of staying with us and talking to us for an hour or more.

It was evident from various remarks he made that we five officers would soon be going to the main Officers' Camp at Zentsuji and that he was awaiting a final movement order for this. The clearest pointer was that the officers were no longer required to have their hair cropped. The untimely end of the officers' garden was another straw in the wind.

'How is your baby?' I said, for we had heard that his child had been sick.

'Much better,' Nomoto replied, 'and thank you for asking.'

Having got him in a good mood, I thought I would press home my advantage.

'We have had no letters since we became P.o.W.s a year and a half ago,' I said. 'What is happening?'

'I have written to Zentsuji and Tokyo about this but have had no reply,' he answered.

It seemed clear that he wanted to forget the camp and its problems and the conversation took a more general turn.

He asked harmless questions about the organisation of H.M. Forces and about badges of rank, and about the badges of various regiments and other units. Like all Japanese he was particularly interested in the special uniforms worn by Scottish and Irish regiments, by Paratroopers and so on. He exhibited some interest in naval matters and Len replied to his questions in this field.

We might have been a group of retired officers discussing Service matters over a whisky and soda in some club in Cheltenham or Bath, only there was no whisky and soda!

When he left we felt we had learnt more about this strange character in an hour than we had in the previous year.

The second batch of postcards, which we had so hopefully written some months previously, were returned to the camp. On that occasion we had been permitted to write not more than a hundred words. It appeared that they had not been censored, as they should have been by Nakano.

Nakano, when he felt like it, was now engaged on this task. The P.o.W. officers were required to re-type the cards after Nakano had finished with them. If there was anything that he did not understand—and that included a great deal—Nakano would strike it out. The contents of some of the cards, now being re-typed by our stiff and suppurating fingers, were thus reduced to little more than 'Love Tom'.

Nakano was particularly interested in one card which he showed to me. It contained the following passage:

'I am sleeping next to a man who has a girl from Chesterfield. We often discuss the old familiar spots.'

'Prisoners not allowed to have girls in camp,' said Nakano. 'Where is this girl from Chesterfield? I would like to have her.'

I tried to explain the context of the sentence and to assure Nakano that there was no girl from Chesterfield, or indeed from anywhere else, in the camp.

'But he says so. She must be here. How can they be discussing her "familiar spots", if she is not here?' he retorted.

It was no good. He cut it all out as he also cut out such passages as, 'I look forward to resuming our interrupted honeymoon', and 'I am getting ready for tennis, dances and you know what'.

The confusion was beyond description and we amateur one-finger typists did not help much. One man writing to his father requested the latter to 'give my love to Edith'. By the time Nakano had finished censoring the card, and one of us had finished re-typing it for the P.o.W.'s signature, it read, 'give my love to Edna'.

It fell to me to take the card round for the sender's signature. His remarks still ring in my ears.

'Fuck Edna,' he said. 'I finished with that bitch years ago. I want my love to be given to Edith.'

The summer was over. Torrential storms and gales pounded and flooded the camp and sent the high seas crashing over the parapet wall, right up to the barrack blocks.

A plague of rats, driven from their summer quarters by the rain, infested the camp and were visible and audible both by day and by night.

It was a time of melancholy. George contributed to this by announcing that he was leaving us. We never went outside the camp, now that the site of the officers' garden had been taken over by the dockyard. George, who had become accustomed to us, did not fancy any of the other jobs Nomoto had offered him and had decided to return to the management of his fancy-goods shop.

My own melancholy was somewhat lightened by Norman Mackenzie, the Hong Kong Professor of English. He took me through all the poems of Byron, Shelley and both the Brownings. He could have made a fortune as a reader of poetry—or as a Shakespearian actor.

His penetration and fascinating commentaries on all that we read together, especially on Browning's 'Rabbi ben Ezra', led me to wonder why schoolboys are ever made 'to do poetry'. Puberty should precede poetry—and by several years to get the most out of the latter.

Norman Mackenzie introduced me to a poem which might well be sewn into the tunic lining of anyone likely to become a P.o.W. in he future.

It runs as follows:

'PRESENT IN ABSENCE*

Absence, hear thou my protestation
Against thy strength,
Distance, and length;
Do what thou canst for alteration:
For hearts of truest mettle
Absence doth join, and Time doth settle.
Who loves a mistress of such quality,
He soon hath found
Affection's ground
Beyond time, place, and all mortality.
To hearts that cannot vary
Absence is Present, Time doth tarry.
By absence this good means I gain,
That I can catch her,
Where none can watch her,
In some close corner of my brain:
There I embrace and kiss her;
And so I both enjoy and miss her.
                              Anon.'

Nomoto informed us that the first anniversary of the establishment of Habu P.o.W. Camp would be celebrated on the 23rd November. It was on the 23rd November 1942 that he and the camp staff had formally 'opened' the camp. We had not arrived until a few days later. We were informed that the day would be marked by special treats. We wondered what our masters had in store for us.

About ten days prior to the 23rd some twenty-five musical instruments were borrowed from the dockyard school and delivered to the camp. The strings consisted of violins, ukeleles and banjos; the wind instruments included mouth-organs, a clarinet, two cornets, two trombones, a euphonium and a tuba; and in support there was an assortment of drums and a xylophone.

It was then that the Bandmaster of the Middlesex Regiment took over. He called for volunteers and a not inconsiderable amount of talent was forthcoming. My hesitant offer to play the euphonium

* Poem No. 9 in Palgrave's *Golden Treasury.*

was accepted. At Malvern I had played the French horn—the second French horn—in the college orchestra.

It was all very rag-time but we had great fun practising for two hours a day. I suppose I must have disposed of most of my surplus liquid into the euphonium. For the next ten days my nocturnal visits to the latrines were very substantially reduced.

Nomoto was determined that its first birthday should be a memorable one in the annals of Habu Camp and so it was.

An enormous stage was built on the open space between the two large barrack blocks; the wood for this was brought by boat from the dockyard. Large Nippon flags and banners were suspended from every window. The island was scoured by working parties for small fir-trees, no doubt to give a 'palm court' atmosphere. Although the band produced a very large volume of noise, this was not enough for Nomoto, and powerful amplifying equipment was also installed.

It seemed strange that all these things could be obtained at the drop of Nomoto's hat, while the things we really needed were never forthcoming.

The band was, of course, the central feature of these festivities. Among the numbers rendered were three Japanese military marches, all played in minor keys, 'Anchors Aweigh', and 'Officer of the Day', a British regimental march. In a more sentimental vein, we did our best with 'Here we are again', 'Pack up your troubles', and 'Auld Lang Syne'. We also played a very attractive, if somewhat plaintive, Japanese piece. The name escapes me; the tune still haunts me.

It was not only the Bandmaster who came into his own on this occasion but *mirabile dictu* Warrant Officer W.

He had an agreeable voice himself and for some time past had been rehearsing a choir which he had formed. This was quite first-class. If his other contributions to our life at Habu during the past year had appeared to be minimal, he had, on this occasion, fully redeemed himself. At last I was glad he was with us.

There were several other individual and group turns of varying degrees of merit. One of these, quite unrehearsed, had not been provided for. A very drunken Nakano staggered on to the stage and tried to make a speech. He had to be forcibly removed by other members of the camp staff.

A large number of guests, mainly dockyard officials and their wives and daughters, had been invited. They proved to be a most appreciative audience. Their movements throughout the decorated camp were controlled by notices, roped-off paths and P.o.W. ushers.

We ourselves had had two good meals that day. The visitors were offered a magnificent spread. We looked forward to sharing out the 'left-overs'. Alas! What the visitors could not eat on the premises they wrapped up and took home with them.

As we tidied up afterwards it all seemed highly reminiscent of 'Parents' Day'. It was certainly the most enjoyable day we had ever spent at Habu.

The latest issues of the *Nippon Times*, dated September 1943, which had just come in, contained one or two interesting items.

An editorial contained the following passage:

'At least if we limit our scope of observation to the present stage of fighting in the South Pacific area we cannot necessarily say that we are not permitting the development of the foe's island to island operation. Therein lies the gravity of the situation'.

Another item read:

'Many English prisoners of war have told us that the inhabitants of London outstayed the "blitz" only because the British Government gave them unlimited quantities of whisky, because jazz-bands beat the drums on the ruins and because the authorities did not interfere when morals broke down and free love was rampant. It seems that the Germans have better nerves than the English because they are facing the Anglo-American terror raids without these things.'

The Japanese Minister of Commerce was quoted as saying:

'The Efficiency Association, following a painstaking survey, has reported that most plants carry too many men, or much more than they legitimately require. The Association officials, upon timing the work of some plants with stop-watches, have found out that, out of ten hours the operatives are supposed to work, they really put in three hours of actual work. This means that they waste the other seven hours by smoking, chatting or simply idling.'

The officers' days at Habu were now numbered. We did not know this until the 17th December, when we were suddenly informed that we were to leave for Zentsuji the following day. But, as we subsequently learnt, the movement order had been received in the camp office on the 1st December. This no doubt accounted for Nomoto's extraordinary behaviour on the 6th December. By then he knew, though we did not, that we would soon be in direct contact with his immediate superiors at Zentsuji. He was, it would appear, somewhat fearful as to what account we might give of his stewardship at Habu.

Nomoto summoned Ricky Wright and myself into his inner sanctum. There were only the three of us present. Nomoto referred to the further consignment of Red Cross parcels, which we knew had recently arrived, and told us that a count revealed that there were about twenty more parcels than there were P.o.W.s. He asked whether one of these extra parcels could be given to Katouka, the Japanese Sergeant-in-charge of the cook-house, who would shortly be leaving the camp.

I was flabbergasted at the cheek of this request. I put Nomoto's question, in English, to Ricky Wright, who indicated to me that he could see no objection. I whispered to Ricky that, as the parcels were not ours to give away, I thought the whole camp should be consulted. To this he quickly agreed. I informed Nomoto that we would like time to consider his request and he gave us leave to withdraw.

It seemed strange to me that the Japanese, who claimed to be winning the war hands down, should be coming cap-in-hand, to the prisoners, to beg for a single Red Cross parcel, particularly as we knew that they had pilfered a large number from the previous consignment.

Camp democracy was then called into play and all the P.o.W.s were assembled in one of the large barrack rooms.

The discussion ranged widely.

Len Cooper argued that, although we were supposed to have the same food as Japanese soldiers, we never did. They had eggs, fish, meat, and bread and butter, regularly. We saw these things perhaps once in two months, and then only in very small quantities. The Japanese wolfed what was destined for us. There was no question of sharing on their side. Why should we share with them?

I myself took the line that money had been contributed at home, in very difficult times, to provide these parcels and that it was certainly not the intention of the subscribers that they should go to the enemy. We could not, of course, prevent the Japanese staff from stealing them, as they had done previously, but I thought that we should consider very carefully before agreeing that they should be given any.

Some took a more pragmatic attitude. If we gave them one parcel that might, perhaps, 'sweeten' them and result in a general improvement in the rations. We knew that the camp pig was due for slaughtering and we hoped to see something of it. If we did not give them a parcel they could always take it and, out of pique, cut down our rations to boot.

Others argued that if we agreed to the request we might secure an immediate issue of the parcels. If the parcels were left under Japanese control until Christmas, as was Nomoto's intention, anything might happen. Apart from the certainty of Japanese pilfering, there was a serious probability that the rats would have a go at them too. In any event, rations had been so bad during the past two months that the psychological fillip of an immediate issue was highly desirable.

Suddenly someone made a brilliant suggestion. They had asked for one; let us give them three. In this way we would put ourselves in a position of superiority. Moreover, this would mean that Smiler, the not disagreeable Camp Sergeant, who had never been suspected of pilfering the previous parcels and who had never come round to barrack rooms trying to cadge, as others had, could have one too.

It was then agreed, by acclamation, that I should make the following points to Nomoto. First, he should be forcefully reminded of the facts adduced by Len Cooper and myself during the course of the discussion; and secondly it should be made clear to him that in no circumstances should any of the three boxes, or their contents, be taken out of the camp. We had no wish to see an article in the *Nippon Times* to the effect that grateful P.o.W.s at Habu had given three Red Cross parcels to Nomoto and his staff in recognition of their kind and sympathetic treatment. Finally, from as lofty a position of superiority as could be achieved, I should explain that the P.o.W.s had decided to give a parcel each to Nomoto, Smiler and Katouka, as a Christmas present. This was to be conditional upon the immediate release of the parcels to the prisoners.

Nomoto was waiting for our reply outside his office. As I struggled to explain, in my faltering Japanese, the philosophical background to our decision, Nomoto looked more and more crestfallen. Harry Radford, who, unobserved himself, was observing Nomoto from the cook-house, reported later that he was clasping and unclasping his hands behind his back in a dreadful state of nervousness. He feared a complete rejection of his request.

When I came to the end of my address Nomoto expressed his thanks and then asked, timidly, for permission to show a fourth parcel to the dockyard police, who required to see it for security reasons. Almost cringing, he undertook that it would be returned intact and in due course it was.

Within an hour every man in the camp had his parcel and the contents of the balance were being split up for a draw.

We had, it was generally agreed, gained a great moral victory. What was more important, we had recovered some of our self-respect.

9

Officers' Camp

*Zentsuji, Shikoku—December 1943–August 1944**

It was 9 a.m. on Saturday the 18th December 1943. There were seven of us sitting on the quay-side at Onomichi, my four fellow-officers from Habu and myself and our two escorts, the Habu Camp Sergeant, Smiler, and a Japanese Warrant Officer, who had come from Zentsuji to collect us.

Suddenly two other P.o.W.s appeared. They were from another camp near Onomichi and had come down to the docks to collect stores. We managed to have a quick word with them.

They had been on the *Dai Nichi Maru* and on the same train which had brought us from Shimonoseki to Onomichi, just over a year previously. It was quite fortuitous, like so much else in the life of a P.o.W., that they had been hauled out of the train just before it arrived at Onomichi. It might well have been us.

They told us that, out of a hundred P.o.W.s, twenty-two, some of whom we knew, had died during the past twelve months. Despite this, they seemed to have enjoyed better conditions than we had. They described their Camp Commandant as being very under-standing and most sympathetic; and they made our mouths water with their descriptions of the food and the canteen facilities available. No doubt the fact that they were on the mainland had helped considerably.

Smiler thought the conversation had gone on long enough. He came over, genially enough, and told our two informants to get on with their work. We continued to wait for the ferry that was to take us to Tadatsu on the island of Shikoku.

*See map 3, page 318.

Our last twenty-four hours at Habu had been hectic. I had persuaded the P.o.W. 'cobbler' to patch up my shoes. We had handed in the kit which had been issued to us by the Habu authorities during the previous year. In return, Nomoto had handed back our personal belongings; for me this amounted to a gold watch, now broken, which an aunt had given to me, many years previously.

Nomoto summoned us to the sick-bay, where he favoured us with his last, and mercifully brief, speech. Addressing us in Japanese, which I had to interpret, he said that he had done his best for us and that he wished us luck in our new camp. Ricky Wright replied that, although we had not always seen eye to eye with him, particularly at the start—a masterly understatement—relations had improved, and we realised that he had done what he could for us. Nomoto gave us a tin of salmon, to be shared with our escort on the journey to Zentsuji; and the next morning he came down to Habu jetty to see us off on the ferry at 7 a.m.

It was sadder to say good-bye to our fellow P.o.W.s with whom we had been through so much. An impromptu concert was arranged; and Warrant Officer W.'s choir sang even better, or so it seemed, than at the camp 'open house' a month earlier.

The senior P.o.W. would now be W.O. Pritchard. We could not have left our charges in better hands.

We were up at 5.30 a.m. the following morning. We warmed up in the bake-house, with Harry Radford's gay banter and general helpfulness forming our final memories of Habu.

Ricky Wright and I had pinched a bamboo fire-beater on which to sling our kit, in case we had to carry it any distance. For the moment we did not need it. 'Porterage' to the Habu jetty was provided by the off-duty P.o.W. cooks, pushing two barrows.

We marched down, through the awakening dockyard and village, to the jetty.

On the ferry, Smiler and the Zentsuji W.O. herded us down into what appeared to be the crew's sleeping-quarters. We were to pass through a 'prohibited area' and, with our well-known reputations as spies, we were not to be allowed to see anything. We were told to take off our boots. We went to sleep.

The Onomichi-Tadatsu ferry arrived and we said farewell to Smiler. We were glad that Smiler had been given a Red Cross parcel. He had always been scrupulously honest and fair. He was a much stronger character than Nomoto and he was tough enough to stand up to anybody for what he believed to be just.

The ferry journey to Tadatsu took about three and a half hours. We shared the tin of salmon with the Zentsuji W.O. and he bought us cups of tea. After a spell on deck, which permitted us to enjoy a magnificent view of the Inland Sea, and its myriad islands in all their morning glory, we repaired below, once more to sleep.

We were met at Tadatsu by four American enlisted men with a lorry. Ricky Wright and I left the stolen bamboo pole on the ferry; it was clear that it would not be needed.

During the eight-mile drive to Zentsuji Camp the American P.o.W.s told us that it was a good spot. One of them had received seventy letters and many parcels from home.

On arrival, the lorry turned through a narrow entrance into a large compound. There were a number of P.o.W.s standing about and we noticed many friends.

The Japanese Duty Officer, who met us, told us that we were now P.o.W.s in Zentsuji Camp and that we would have to go into quarantine for some time. We had no chance to talk to our friends.

Still in the compound, we had to open up all our kit for inspection. All (visible) books, notebooks and papers were removed. We were told that all books would go into the library after being censored. Notebooks and papers might, or might not, be returned. All knives, including table knives and cut-throat razors, were confiscated.

We were then herded into the sick-bay by a back entrance. There were two other occupants, a Dutch naval Lieutenant, Arps, who had been seriously ill with beri-beri for some months, and an American army Captain, Quist, who had damaged his ankle.

Virtually our only contact with the outside world was one of the few saints I met in the course of my captivity. A regular U.S. Navy Pharmacist's Mate, First Class, Albertazzi, known to all as 'Al', was handsome, amusing and professionally most competent. In addition, he was thoughtful and one of the most unselfish men I have ever met.*

We had visits, from time to time, from another Pharmacist's Mate, Johnny, who had been captured in Guam. He was a typically good-natured and loud-mouthed American. Before enlisting he had

* I was told after the war that on his return to San Francisco from captivity, Albertazzi was being driven home to meet his wife, whom he had not seen for five years. The car was involved in a serious accident, as a result of which Al broke his back and was paralysed for life.

been an embalmer. Until I had become used to his accent I thought he had said 'bomber'. He regaled us with some of the secrets of his trade, interlarded with much professional patter.

'Take the human cadaver,' he said, pronouncing the word as though it rhymed with Kay Laver, and rolling the final 'r', round and round his tongue, 'you must always remember, gentlemen, that the human cadaver is full of death-dealing germs. Of course, the Egyptians were the boys. Never a cut or an incision; just an injection in the nostrils.'

We listened spell-bound as he went on:

'My speciality has always been T.B. cases and babies. It's wonderful how beautiful you can make them. Wax cosmetics, and flesh-coloured gut to sew up the incisions, and they look as pretty as the day they were born. Of course,' he continued, dropping his voice a little, 'there are difficult cases. Take a truck-driver who's been incinerated when his truck caught fire. There's not much to work on there. But give me a couple of coat-hangers and a photograph or two and I can build up, as good as new, all that his folks will want to see of him before he's buried or cremated again!'

He had got a captive audience and nothing would stop him. He told us that all U.S. Service personnel who died overseas in peacetime were embalmed and sent home. Most people who died in accidents or on the street in the U.S.A. were embalmed and kept 'frozen' for six months or so, in case there were identification problems.

'A good embalmer who gets the body early can preserve it for a year,' he went on, and added, 'and then you can always "top up" with fresh injections. It's a risky business, of course. Take me,' he said proudly. 'When I started, I caught diphtheria twice and blood-poisoning three times. But I know better now. You must first pump out all the blood and other liquids. Then you fill the veins and arteries with formaldehyde. That fixes it. Of course, if the cadaver is to be used for demonstration purposes you must hang it up for six months in a vat full of disinfectant.'

Al announced that our meal was ready and that, as we were clearly very interested in what Johnny was saying, he had taken the liberty of inviting Johnny to stay and eat with us. We looked at each other's raised eyebrows, but there was nothing we could do about it. Johnny continued:

'I remember once I was embalming an old girl of sixty-two. I was hurrying a bit. I had a date with a pretty young blonde popsie and I did not want to keep her waiting, or myself. Well, while I was sewing up the old girl, I ran the needle into my finger. This set up blood poisoning. I wasn't much good that night, I can tell you.'

We glanced at each other again, but here was a man who took a pride in his profession and nothing was going to divert him.

'Mind you,' Johnny went on, 'I know what I'm talking about. I've got a Master's degree as a "Mortician" from the University of Chicago; and I did post-graduate work at the University of Nebraska. That was a rum business too. I chose Nebraska for my research because several girls in that State were slowly turning into stone. We were trying to find out why. It was something to do with their liver juices. Anyhow, we didn't have to embalm them. When they died they were absolutely, and literally, petrified.'

At last there was a pause. Johnny got up from the table, wiped a huge fist across his mouth and said, 'You seem a nice lot of guys.'

We had, in fact, had no opportunity of showing how beastly we could be.

'I'll come back and tell you some more soon. I'll be seeing you.'

For an hour or more we had lived in another world. We had forgotten we were P.o.W.s. We were grateful for that.

Our introduction to life at Zentsuji was a leisurely one. The 'reveille' bugle went at 6.30 a.m. and roll-call was at 6.40. As we were technically 'sick' we did not have to move and Al answered for us. The *Nippon Times* appeared early every morning.

In the afternoon we walked for thirty minutes in the yard, escorted by the Japanese Duty Officer, but we were not allowed to talk to anyone. We paid a 'courtesy' call on the Japanese Colonel Commanding and, once again, signed the 'no escaping' declaration.

A few days later, Smiler visited Zentsuji on some official business from Habu. He came in to see us and was most affable. He took back notes which we wrote to Pritchard.

Al told us about the camp. There were concerts, and lectures; and carols were being practised for Christmas. A mammoth production of *Ali Baba and the Forty Thieves* was in rehearsal for the New Year. The barrack rooms were being decorated. It all sounded too good to be true, but we had still not had any letters.

In addition to their constant flow of letters and parcels, the Americans had been broadcasting messages to their families in the United States. The Senior British Officers, wisely, would not permit the British P.o.W.s to participate in this scheme.

The camp was situated in flat fertile ground on the southern outskirts of Zentsuji, near a temple compound and wooded hills. The P.o.W.s were accommodated in two main two-storey permanent buildings, formerly, I believe, Japanese army barracks. Ample space for walking was available in a large compound. A number of out-buildings and temporary structures completed the picture.*

There was no heating during the winters of 1942–43 and 1943–44. To some extent this was compensated for by the fact that the camp was grossly overcrowded. Five P.o.W.s had died during 1942 and 1943, a remarkably low figure compared with the death rate in many other camps, including Habu.

There were just under 700 P.o.W.s, made up of 300 American officers, 110 British officers, 80 Australian officers and 70 Dutch officers. In addition, there were about 130 American enlisted men working in the cook-house and in various ancillary services. Al told us, with unconcealed disgust, that these latter spent most of their time organising 'rackets'.

'They have built up an extensive "black market" network,' he said. 'You can buy anything—or practically anything,' he added with a wink, '—at a price!'

During a visit to the latrines I encountered an American Major wearing a life-like donkey's head made of cardboard. He seemed to be completely unconcerned by his unusual appearance.

'Obviously a performer in the pantomime,' I thought.

'Oh! no,' said Al, when I asked him about this, 'the Nips don't allow any dressing up for these shows. They all have to be done in ordinary clothes.'

'Well, why was he wearing a donkey's head?' I enquired.

'There are a lot of nut-cases here,' Al replied, 'nothing serious, you know, but people get funny ideas in their heads.'

As I was soon to learn, almost anything was possible at Zentsuji. I assumed that the American Major was an adherent of some obscure nature cult which gathered together for worship in private.

Al also told us that Asabuki, the intelligent young interpreter who had visited us at Habu and had found us 'frosty', had to attend every public show and concert, and, indeed, all permitted religious services as well.

The Japanese waited until the last possible moment. Then during the afternoon of Friday, the 24th December, Christmas Eve, 1943, we

* See also Epilogue.

were summoned to see the Japanese doctor. All he did was to look at
our throats and ask us if we felt well. Len Cooper was still suffering
considerably from his endemic dysentery but nothing would have
induced him to mention it at that stage.

We were formally discharged from the sick-bay.

Ricky Wright and Len Cooper were whisked off to the Majors'
quarters—twelve to a room—upstairs; Nippy Knight was, appropriately enough, led off into the darkness to join the Captains
in the second building; and Tim Hallam and I, as *Chui*, found
ourselves in one of the grossly overcrowded junior officers' rooms.

There we found a horde of U.S. Air Corps pilots, aged, apparently, between fourteen and sixteen. The row was unbelievable.
They spent most of their time gambling. They gambled for everything, food, cigarettes and money; gambling debts in the latter
were to be paid after release.

There were twenty-eight bed-spaces in the room but the arrival
of Tim and myself brought the complement up to thirty-two. We
started our lives as 'sardines'.

As new-comers Tim and I were next on the list as room orderlies,
a chore which we had been spared in Habu. This involved walking
many miles every day to fetch tea-water at all hours, and food at the
appointed hours. We also had to do the washing-up and sweeping.
We were naturally given the worst times to perform our duties as
night fire-watch guards.

We learnt, too, that there were no hot baths such as we had
enjoyed at Habu. Once a week we were allowed five minutes to
sponge ourselves down with hot water from a bucket in a bitterly
cold shed.

After we had 'settled in', Tim and I decided to go for a walk
in the exercise yard, if only to get away from the noise, the horse-
play and fooling about. We both wished we were back at Habu. It
was a good thing that Tim still had his 'sharks' teeth'; he could at
least give proper vent to his feelings.

Gradually we fell into the rhythm of life at Zentsuji. Tim and I
attended a number of the Christmas and New Year concerts and
shows. It was remarkable what a high standard was achieved in view
of the Japanese ban on costumes.

I made a formal call on Captain Oliver Gordon, R.N., who was
the Senior British P.o.W. Officer. He had been Captain of H.M.S.
Exeter which had been sunk during the Battle of the Java Sea. His

father had been Colonial Secretary, Trinidad, and I had a most agreeable and interesting talk with him. I felt a little better when he told me that he, too, had not yet received any letters.

One of the most agreeable features of life at Zentsuji at that time was the round of 'parties'. Every conceivable occasion was 'celebrated', even when there was nothing with which to celebrate it; birthdays, wedding anniversaries, wives' birthdays, all these were appropriately marked.

This party system soon brought us into contact with the many friends who had been with us in Boei Glodok and with others whom we had not seen since we had been captured.

Immense trouble was taken by the organisers of these occasions. Whenever possible, rice and bread were hoarded and, somehow or other, made into cakes with cocoa powder, condensed milk and prunes, saved from the occasional Red Cross parcel. Menus, name-cards and table decorations were fashioned out of scraps of all kinds. Invited guests, if they could, contributed raw materials for these occasions; in any event they were expected to provide some form of entertainment by singing, telling a story or devising a charade.

The working parties at Zentsuji were not too onerous. My first excursion was to collect food for the camp rabbits. Twenty of us had volunteered and we marched for about two miles to the bank of a river, where we scrounged around to find some suitable greenery.

One of the working party was Graham Hill, a history scholar of Christchurch, who had been engaged in research when the war broke out. He had then joined the Middlesex Regiment and had been captured in Hong Kong. We agreed to co-operate in giving a series of history lectures.

Another member of the working party told me an amusing tale. He had been marching up and down the exercise yard with his head down. He had not seen, and he had therefore failed to salute, the English-speaking Japanese officer, Lieutenant Nakajima, known as 'Sake Pete' who was second-in-command of the camp. Sake Pete had tapped him on the shoulder and had said gently:

'Remember where you are; the war is not over yet.'

I recalled Scarface and his *Bushido* antics at Habu.

I was finding it very difficult to concentrate on my Japanese studies. The din in the 'kindergarten' was intolerable and it was, as yet, far too cold to try and work out of doors. There was, however, one compensation—there always is.

Among the P.o.W.s at Zentsuji was a Lieutenant in the United
States Navy, Wilson, who had been Assistant Naval Attaché at the
U.S. Embassy in Tokyo before the war. He was a qualified Japanese
translator and interpreter. He very kindly offered to help me. After
a few sessions with him I realised how little Japanese I knew, but
under his guidance I suppose I made some progress.

It was Ian Graham who, quite unconsciously, made me aware of
one aspect of our captivity. Ian was the finest type of British
army officer. He was at the Royal Military College, Sandhurst, from
1931 to 1933. At that time we were living in Camberley and,
although I did not meet Ian while he was at the R.M.C., I knew a
number of the Camberley residents whom he had known too.

He was commissioned into the Seaforth Highlanders and
subsequently seconded, with the rank of Major, to the Malay
Regiment, where he was highly successful.

His sole concern seemed to be for the welfare of others, for
his men, for junior officers and, at Zentsuji, for his fellow P.o.W.s.
He was a tower of strength to many, including myself. He would, and
did, give the shirt away off his back if he felt that someone had a
greater need of it than himself. I have seen him give a portion of
his food away to someone recovering from a bout of fever, lying hard
that he was not, himself, particularly hungry that day.

Here was a man who had chosen the profession of arms and who,
in normal circumstances, would have risen very high in that profession. Now he was a P.o.W. like the rest of us; and he was demonstrating, day in and day out, the same qualities that he would
have demonstrated on the field of battle or in a peace-time appointment.

Another thought occurred to me as I brooded on this one night.
It was difficult enough for all of us to avoid the cardinal sin of
self-pity. Sometimes I thought to myself, 'How much more difficult
it must be for the professional soldiers, sailors and airmen than
it is for me.' They had given years of their lives, they had undergone
unremitting training, they had endured what, in peace-time, would
be regarded as hardships—and separations—to prepare themselves
professionally for the defence of their country. Then, when war
came, thousands of them became P.o.W.s through no fault of
their own, many without hearing a shot fired.

For them, as for the rest of us, the years were slipping by. It
was worse for them. In Britain's hour of need their professional

skills and experiences were being wasted. Others, they knew, would be making their names in the various theatres of war around the world. At this crucial moment in Britain's history they were, like us, 'forgotten' men.

There were other regular British officers at Zentsuji who must have thought this too. Many of the naval officers from H.M.S. *Exeter* were among our number. Like Ian, they never complained, though for some of them captivity in Japanese hands was to lead to the premature ending of their service careers.*

There were other things that puzzled me in captivity.

Among my fellow P.o.W.s, at various times, were young pilots in the R.A.F. and in the United States Air Corps. One of the latter, who had been shot down somewhere in the Pacific, had managed to get all his personal kit sent to him at Zentsuji from the United States. On the face of it they were 'hand-picked' young men, in the pink of physical condition. Many of them turned their faces to the wall and died. 'Why?' I asked myself.

They received the same treatment as the rest of us; they had youth on their side. Why did so many of them fold up and die?

From the very beginning they had kicked against the pricks. 'Why should this happen to me?' they had asked. 'If I had not been taken prisoner, I would by now have been a Squadron-Leader or, with luck, a Wing Commander. I'd have a chance of getting some "gongs". I could have had any girl I wanted.'

These were brave young men, who had risked their lives every time they had gone up in the air. But they found it more difficult than most to adjust themselves to their fate. Their sense of frustration grew; they burnt themselves out; and many of them died.

At the other end of the scale were the older men. Some of these were sixty-five and more, skippers of little cargo-boats plying up and down the China coast. One, at least, of these was a diabetic, and the Japanese had taken away his syringe and the pathetically small supply of insulin he had with him when he was captured.

* After the war Ian Graham was invalided out of the Army. I myself firmly believe that his many acts of unselfishness during captivity contributed, in large measure, to the state of health which occasioned this. I knew him well enough to appreciate what a blow this must have been to him. It was wholly in character that he should have volunteered to act as the Secretary of the Zentsuji Association which arranged annual gatherings in London after the war. On one such occasion he told me, with joy in his eyes, that his son had just been appointed to command one of the battalions of his old regiment. God moves in a mysterious way.

But most of them, including, I believe, the diabetic, survived captivity. They had had much experience. They knew that life was full of 'ups and downs'. This was a 'down'—a 'down' to be faced up to and accepted with patient resignation.

They could be seen washing their 'smalls'; they could be seen darning their clothes. Some whittled little bits of wood; some attended every lecture they could manage. They adjusted to their circumstances, although these were not of their own choosing.

I was sitting on the beach, about five miles away from the camp, talking to Lipscombe, who had been the Torpedo Officer in H.M.S. *Exeter*. About twenty of us had gone down to the sea-shore to collect sand and shells for the camp's chicken population. We had two barrows, each pulled by five of us at a time for a quarter of an hour; and then our reliefs took over. Fortunately it was flat all the way.

We had taken with us, as our midday meal, a small roll of bread and a minute piece of fish. Even the Japanese guard who accompanied us thought this was inadequate and he tried to buy us something extra, but he was unsuccessful.

It was good to get out of the camp. On the way down, we had seen some Japanese Horse Artillery practising limbering up and unlimbering.

As I sat with 'Torps' on the beach, munching our frugal meal, we watched four Japanese sea-planes practising landing and taking off on the deep blue sea. Just behind us, in some trees, there was an old pagoda. We strolled over and inspected it. The pagoda, which was beautifully constructed, hadn't a nail in it.

The now heavily laden barrows put a strain on our limited strength on the way back. But it had been worth it.

The rations at Zentsuji, though a little more varied, were even more limited in quantity than those provided at Habu. I had not believed that this could be possible. The P.o.W. doctors were becoming very worried and had satisfied themselves that life could not be maintained on the minute quantities of rice and other food-stuffs provided. Protests were made to the Japanese Commandant but there was no improvement. I suspected that some of the rice provided by the Japanese never left the cook-house. The American enlisted men, who worked there, looked extremely well nourished; and Al's words about the 'black market' were still ringing in my ears.

Tension was building up in other directions too. The Japanese

Colonel commanding the Camp informed the Committee of Senior P.o.W. Officers that he had managed to obtain a new plot of agricultural land just outside the camp; and he asked for officer P.o.W.s to volunteer to work it.

The Committee considered the matter carefully and then replied to the Colonel's approach. While officers could not be forced to work, they were very willing to volunteer but only in return for certain undertakings by the Japanese authorities. The first was that everything produced, whether inside or outside the camp, by the officers' voluntary efforts, should go to supplementing the ordinary rations and not replacing them. Evidence was submitted to the Commandant that rabbits, chickens and eggs produced in the camp, and vegetables produced on plots outside, were being sent out of the camp; and that even the few 'home-grown' foodstuffs which were consumed in the camp were used to replace, rather than supplement, the prescribed rations. Furthermore, the Committee added, the very small amount of Red Cross supplies were not being properly handled and there was evidence that many of these were on sale in the town.

The Colonel was furious. The whole camp was mustered in the exercise yard and he repeated his call for volunteers to work the new plot. No officer volunteered. The Colonel, by now even more furious, dismissed the parade.

Later the same day he saw the Committee again and told them that work by the officers was not voluntary and that he had issued an order that all officers should work. We were then divided up into three main groups. The Majors would work inside the camp; the junior officers would work outside the camp, one party on the old plot and one on the new.

To emphasise his point, the Colonel had added that supplies of tea-water would be cut down from five a day to one a day. Shortage of fuel was given as the reason.

For the first time in over two years I learnt to distinguish between being hungry and actually starving. Like others, I was forced to tie a piece of string very tightly round my stomach at nights in order to minimise the gripes and cramps of an empty void. Without this, sleep was impossible.

The halcyon days of Habu were things of the past.

We tried to forget our misery by throwing ourselves into intellectual pursuits. I found myself lecturing on subjects about which I knew something and on subjects about which I knew nothing. As lecture

audiences were not permitted to exceed ten in number, lectures
had to be repeated *ad infinitum*. When I could lecture no more, I
went to lectures given by others. It was thus that many of us tried
to anaesthetise ourselves against starvation. Now, we no longer even
looked forward to the next meal, for we knew that we would be just
as hungry after it as before. 'It was never as bad as this at Habu,' I
thought. But perhaps it had been. We no longer had any yardsticks
by which to measure anything; facts and fancies became inextricably
mixed.

Oh! for oblivion. Perhaps the young pilots had been right after
all.

Despite the Colonel Commandant's oral indications to the Committee that work was not voluntary and that he was ordering all
officers to work, we still, following the Committee's lead, refused to
go to work, until and unless a written order, signed by the Colonel,
was issued and posted.

On the 1st March 1944 the following order, with the imprint
of the Japanese Colonel's inevitable little rubber stamp at the bottom,
was posted:

'ZENTSUJI CAMP—ORDER

'Based upon the plan shown on the separate sheet, Officer
Prisoners shall engage themselves in agricultural work (cultivation).'

I found myself, with many of the Majors and Colonels (for,
of course, the original plans had all been changed), in a working
party of about ninety—allocated to the clearing of the new plot.
It took us about twenty minutes to climb very slowly up the hill
where, on a precipitous slope, we found the site. Our task was to dig
out and remove the enormous tree-stumps. It seemed to be a ludicrous project. The tools which we had carried with us were of very
poor quality and were always breaking; and the slope was so steep
that it was difficult to see how the top soil could ever remain there
when we had removed the monstrous roots.

Once again it seemed to me that it was a propaganda exercise
rather than an economic undertaking. 'These arrogant officers say
they will not work; they shall work, even if it is wholly futile and
unproductive. We will show them who are the masters.'

It did not last long. A few weeks later a senior Japanese naval
officer, from the Tokyo department dealing with prisoners of war,

inspected the camp. He must have told the Commandant that officers could not be forced to work. Another notice was posted to the effect that the project had now been completed. Our compulsory labours ceased.

It was not, however, the end of the matter. We continued clearing the plot, even though 'the project had been completed'. But now we were working as volunteers and subject to certain conditions laid down by the Committee, which the Commandant had accepted. Moreover, to encourage our voluntary efforts, the Japanese officers themselves started digging up ground within the perimeter of the camp.

The truth was that the Japanese authorities had convinced the Committee that the food situation was becoming very bad, and was likely to get worse.

We were now digging, voluntarily, to survive.

St. Patrick's Day, the 17th March 1944, came and went. It marked the abortive attempt by J.F. and myself to escape from Java. I wondered where J.F. was now. 'Would we, could we, have done any more to achieve success, if we had known what lay ahead of us?' I did not think so.

I joined the Choral Society to sing in the Easter Concert. The programme included 'The Tangle of the Isles', 'The Soldiers' Chorus' from *Faust* and the 'Hallelujah Chorus'. Community singing was a great morale builder.

I had still not had any letters. Another P.o.W., similarly placed, was told that 138 letters had arrived for him in the camp office but that it would be a little time before they were released, as they all had to be censored. Not all letters received brought good news. Many told of the deaths of fathers, mothers and wives. One P.o.W. had a letter to the effect that, as a court had given leave to presume his death, his estate had been wound up and his wife had re-married. Perhaps it was better not to receive letters after all.

My weight in April 1943 was down to 115 lbs. I had nearly reached the fifty-kilo danger mark. As a late-comer to Zentsuji I had not been issued with a mattress and I had none of my own. The bare boards on which we slept were scraping away at my protruding bones and my body was a mass of sores.

Perhaps it was fortunate that, at this time, I was taken off the outside agricultural party and put in the chicken squad which worked inside the camp. This was led by Frank Twiss,* who had been Gunnery Officer in H.M.S. *Exeter*. I was appointed 'Keeper of the Records' and had to keep a record of each bird, showing the amount of food it was given and the number of eggs it laid. I would have preferred a job which had less direct contact with forbidden food. My dreams were now nightmares of chickens as large as ostriches, consuming mountains of corn and laying eggs the size of cannon-balls.

It was 2 a.m. in the morning. I was doing my one and a half hours' night fire-watch guard. I was felled to the ground by the blow of a rifle-butt between my protruding shoulder blades. There he was glaring down at me, the Japanese Sergeant-in-charge of the Japanese night patrol.

I was too weak to get to my feet unaided, so he hauled me up and boxed my ears for good measure.

'What were you doing prowling around outside?' he said to me in Japanese.

'I have not been outside,' I replied.

'You are lying,' he went on.

I shook my head which was aching severely. The Sergeant turned to speak to one of the attendant guards.

'Was this the man?' he said.

'I think so,' replied the Japanese Private, 'but he looked bigger outside.'

The Sergeant turned to me again: 'Whom did you relieve?' he asked. 'Come—we will go and find him.'

I had relieved Tommy Thompson, a young R.A.F. pilot who was, in fact, much taller than I was.

We returned to the barrack room and Tommy was unceremoniously hauled off his bed-space.

The Sergeant shouted at him, waking up another thirty men, 'Why did you leave your post and go prowling around outside?'

'I went out to look at the stars,' replied Tommy innocently. 'I am interested in the stars. And it's a lovely night, you know.'

'Come with me—and you too,' the Sergeant said, jerking my arm.

I was dropped off at my duty-post and Tommy was taken on to the guard-house. I thought he would be beaten up and thrown into the solitary confinement cell.

* Later Admiral Sir Frank Twiss, K.C.B., D.S.C., Second Sea Lord and Chief of Naval Personnel (1967–70), and subsequently Black Rod.

I was still awake when he returned.

'What happened?' I whispered.

'Well, it took me an awful long time to make them believe that I was just looking at the stars. They beat me about a bit but eventually they believed me, I think. And here I am,' he replied softly.

His face was so fresh and innocent. 'Even the Japanese had had to believe him,' I thought.

The next morning the Sergeant came round and was quite friendly. He even apologised for knocking me down!

It was 9 a.m. on Friday the 28th April 1944. Captain 'Stew' Nottage, an Australian on the P.o.W. Camp Committee, came in to tell me that at least two letters had arrived for me in the camp office. I rushed off to see my four Habu companions. Nippy Knight had been told that there was one for him; the other three had heard nothing, which grieved me as much as it grieved them.

After a separation of two and a quarter years I could not believe it. I found it impossible to concentrate on anything that day. I could not wait to get my hands on the letters. Until I had them in my possession I could not, I would not, believe it.

I did not get them that day. The Commandant and his staff were far too preoccupied with arrangements for the arrival of Monsieur Pestalozzi, a Delegate of the International Red Cross who had chosen the 28th April to visit Zentsuji.

One of these 'arrangements' was that we had beef and eggs in our midday soup, the first time that we had ever had these at Zentsuji.

Another 'arrangement' was that, although I had been at Zentsuji for over four months, I was given my camp number—958, burnt on to a bamboo tag.

The Colonel inspected the camp himself at 11.30 a.m. At 1.30 p.m. Monsieur Pestalozzi strode through the barrack rooms, looking neither to the right nor to the left. He spoke to no one. We had a glimpse of a well-fed and well-dressed European walking freely—a strange sight. His ruddy complexion made me realise how pale all prisoners, including presumably No. 958, were.

The Red Cross Delegate was not in a good mood when he left. The Japanese staff car which was to take him away would not start.

For half an hour the Japanese guards and a number of impressed P.o.W.s, of whom I was one, pushed the car up and down the driveway in a vain attempt to get it self-propelled. In the middle of this exercise the bugle went for the P.o.W.s' evening meal. Following a reflex action, induced by Japanese insistence over the years that bugle calls were to be obeyed immediately, the P.o.W.s scattered like a flock of pigeons at the crack of a gun. We left our captors to wrestle with the reluctant vehicle.

We relished the loss of 'face' by the Commandant and his staff.

It was later reported that the dour Delegate had had a brief talk with the Senior British P.o.W. Officer, Captain Oliver Gordon, R.N., and the Senior American P.o.W. Officer, Captain W. T. Lineberry, U.S.N.* The latter were informed that there were no more Red Cross supplies in Japan and that certain complaints, which they had previously submitted in writing to the Red Cross, had been forwarded, via Geneva, to their respective governments. There was not much consolation for us in this, but at least I still had my letters to look forward to.

Self-interest is a motivating force in most men. It was very marked among almost all the P.o.W.s.

There were three Roman Catholics in my barrack room and during Lent they had been going to Mass every morning, just at the moment the hot water for tea was brought in. No one seemed particularly anxious to keep their tea warm for them and it was usually stone cold by the time they returned.

A working party, doing a job in the Japanese Officers' Club, had stolen some eggs, which they had managed to smuggle back into camp. Several of the young officers in my barrack room had three or four eggs apiece. The 'thieves' nearly came to blows for the privilege of keeping the Roman Catholics' tea hot in their screw-top milk-powder tins. This would provide them with a means of cooking their eggs while their colleagues were at their devotions.

It was nearly a week before I received my letters, of which there were seven. The delay in censoring, occasioned by Pestalozzi's visit, was prolonged to enable the camp staff, including Asabuki, the interpreter, to celebrate the anniversary of yet another Japanese Emperor's birthday.

One of the letters was from my mother. It had been posted over two years earlier, just before J.F. and myself had taken to the jungle

* 'Bill' Lineberry was a U.S. Navy Medical Officer. He was subsequently promoted to the rank of Rear-Admiral and after the war became President of the American Zentsujians Association.

in Java. The most recent of the letters from L. was over a year old
and the rest had been posted in the middle of 1942, when I was at
Boei Glodok in Java. One or two of the envelopes looked as though
they had been in the water and the earlier ones had clearly been to
Java. Stamped on the back of one of the envelopes was the injunction;
'Use the telephone—it makes life easier and saves time'!

Reading, and re-reading, these letters brought me weeks of joy.
I wrote long commentaries on them in my journal. They did more
for my morale than all the food in the world would have done. The
only shadow was that three of my Habu companions had received
nothing. I knew only too well how they felt.

With my battery re-charged, I threw myself into a variety of
activities. I sang in a quartet of R.A.F. officers who presented, to
an appreciative audience, 'Room 504' and 'A Nightingale sang in
Berkeley Square'. I lectured to the American Colonels on European
Art and to the British Colonels on the American Monetary System.
I also lectured to various mixed groups on life and work in the
pre-war Colonial Office.

In the course of this latter lecture I retailed a number of stories
I had heard from Sir Cosmo Parkinson, the Permanent Under-
Secretary of State, whose Private Secretary I had been before going
to Malaya. Among other amusing tales, Sir Cosmo had told me of
the following incident.

Shortly after the Duke of Devonshire had taken up office as
Secretary of State for the Colonies, arrangements were made for His
Grace to receive a deputation headed by the Bishop of Melanesia
regarding the New Hebrides. At that time Sir Cosmo was a junior
member of the department which handled the affairs of the New
Hebrides and he was asked by his Head of Department to prepare
a note to guide the Secretary of State during the interview.

Five minutes before the deputation was due to arrive, Sir Cosmo
and his Head of Department had gone to the Secretary of State's room
to make sure that the latter had all the information he needed. Sir
Cosmo was due to keep a record of the interview.

As the two officials entered the room His Grace shook hands
with them, warmly welcomed them and motioned to them to sit
down in the chairs reserved for important visitors. His Grace then
addressed them, in accordance with the draft they had prepared
for his use.

Ten minutes later the main door of the Secretary of State's

room was thrown open and the Bishop, his Chaplain and others were ushered in by the Private Secretary. The two officials took post at the Secretary of State's side and the latter, completely unruffled, started his address all over again.

When, finally, the deputation had withdrawn the Duke apologised profusely to Sir Cosmo and his Head of Department. The latter, Sir Cosmo had told me, was heard to mutter as he left the room, '*Nolo episcopari*, even in the New Hebrides'.*

I also told my audience another story about the resourcefulness of a certain senior administrative officer in the Colonial Office. The pre-war leave provisions in the Colonial Office were very generous, so generous in fact that few senior officers could ever take their full entitlement. But they were not, apparently, generous enough for one officer who had a passion for fishing. If the latter felt like having a few extra days' fishing he would lay in a stock of cigarettes, much cheaper in those days, and arrange with a complacent messenger to ensure that the ashtray on his desk was never without a lighted cigarette during working hours. A hat and coat were left hanging on the wall to add to the verisimilitude. The leisurely progress of files in the Colonial Office of the thirties did not appear to have been unduly dislocated by this subterfuge.

My lecture was, I hope, enlivened by these and many other stories of human idiosyncrasies. It seemed to go down well and it was much in demand.

But on one occasion, when I had been invited to give it to a mixed group of senior British and American officers, I was firmly put in my place by a very stuffy British Major, who took me aside after the lecture was over and the group had dispersed.

'Fletcher-Cooke,' he said, 'I enjoyed that very much. I found your talk most interesting and amusing. But I don't think you should have told all those stories in front of the Yanks. Ever since 1776 they have convinced themselves that the British don't know how to handle their colonies. And I felt that some of your stories were rather letting the side down. That one about the Duke of Devonshire, for example. I mean we all know these things happen but there's no need to tell the Yanks about them.'

I wondered, for a moment, whether I had made a mistake and whether it was, in fact, this British Major, and not an American Major,

* An account of this incident will be found on pages 14 and 15 of *The Colonial Office from Within, 1909–1945*, by Sir Cosmo Parkinson, G.C.M.G., K.C.B., O.B.E., published in 1947 by Faber and Faber Ltd.

whom I had encountered in the latrines, wearing a life-like donkey's head made of cardboard, on my arrival at Zentsuji.

Irritations and discomforts which would have loomed large ten days earlier passed over my head now that I had received some letters. I thought nothing of it when a large rat bit me on the arm while I was asleep. 'It was only a playful nip,' I thought. I counted myself lucky not to have been as badly bitten as many of my bed-mates had been. I hardly noticed when two of my American teen-age companions had a stand-up fight about food, even though, as room orderly, I had to clean up all the blood. One of the contestants was, indeed, so badly knocked about that he had to have several stitches put in. Even the chore of doing my laundry in cold water, under an outside tap and without soap, seemed less disagreeable; at least I could sing to myself, which was not encouraged in the crowded barrack room.

Of course, this euphoria could not last and it did not. As more mail and cables came in and there was none for me, my spirits sank again. At the next weighing I had dropped another five pounds. The food became worse. The flies and mosquitoes were intolerable. We were all getting so weak that we began to lose interest in lec-turing, concerts, and shows, which diminished in number consider-ably. Now we spent most of our spare time lying down.

Tim Hallam was in trouble. During an inspection of kit the Japanese Camp Authorities accused him of losing a cup which had been issued to him on arrival. He contended, quite rightly, that we five had not been issued with any eating utensils when we had come into Zentsuji. In the course of his interrogation in the camp office he had mentioned my name and I was sent for.

The civilian interpreter, Kobyashi, who was conducting the proceedings on this occasion, for the Supply Officer, Lieutenant Nakanishi, was a comical little Japanese known as 'Donald Duck'.

When I entered the office Donald Duck addressed me in English.

'Do you know this oddu manu, Hallamu?' he said.

I replied that I did and that we had come together to Zentsuji from Habu, the previous December.

'Where is your campu cupu?' he went on.

'None of the five men in the Habu party was issued with camp cups,' I replied. 'We are still using our own metal mugs.'

'You are insulting me,' he retorted. 'I know English. Now you are referring to me as a "mugu". And I know that is an insult word in English.'

He gave me a box on the ears to emphasise his point.

I tried to explain that no offence was intended. He would not listen. He jumped about, quacking away, and then he said:

'You are lying. You all lie. Hallamu is lying. You are lying. I will have no lies.'

It seemed useless to intervene, so I let him go on. Suddenly he burst out shouting:

'You may think you can cheat a small potato but I am a big potato.'

'You're more like a potato crisp,' I thought to myself.

'You said something?' he shouted.

'No,' I replied. 'I was just thinking.'

'What were you thinking?' he said. 'Evil thoughts?'

This charade had already gone on for an hour and a half. He had clearly forgotten how it had all started and, indeed, why we were there at all.

By then I had learnt that this frequently happened. One would be called in for an interrogation about something trivial, and the exchanges would go on so long that, eventually, one's tormentors would forget why one was there. By a few skilful moves and asides, one could sometimes accelerate this process. It was clear that Donald Duck was getting bored.

'You are badu menu. Go away. I will watch you.'

We saluted the Supply Officer who had remained silent throughout the whole proceedings. Donald Duck, who was standing between us and the Supply Officer, thought the salute was for him and smiled genially as he opened the door for us.

The Colonels occupied small rooms upstairs—six or eight to a room. A short passage ran along outside their rooms and they were required to keep this swept. The Colonels, taking turns, had apparently accepted this minor chore without demur for many months. When the turn of a Colonel in the U.S. Marine Corps came round he ordered, or persuaded, his junior officers to do this for him. This put ideas into the head of a certain R.A.F. Wing Commander who had already performed this task, without complaint, in the past. He sent an emissary to enquire of the junior R.A.F. officers whether they would like to undertake this sweeping when his turn came round again. The emissary retired with his tail between his legs and with a magnificent flow of invective from Tim Hallam's now re-furbished mouth ringing in his ears.

It was on Wednesday the 7th June 1944 that we learnt about the Allied landings in France. The original rumours had started, as rumours always do, in the cook-house. They seemed highly plausible, but so many false rumours had been spread around during the preceding two and a half years, that we waited for at least some measure of confirmation. It was not long in coming.

The Japanese Colonel Commandant decided to visit one of the outside working parties during the morning. While he was watching the P.o.W.s at work he spotted Colonel Scanlon, the Senior Australian P.o.W. Officer, planting pumpkin, and said to him quietly in English:

'When do you think the Allies will land in France and open up a second front?'

Scanlon replied, 'Any time now. I am surprised it has not happened already, sir.'

The Colonel whispered to him: 'It has. We have heard that the Allies have landed in France.' Colonel Sugiyama turned and walked off dejectedly.

As I lay awake on my bed-space turning over this news in my mind, I resolved to re-double my efforts to make more rapid progress with my Japanese. I felt that I wanted to react positively and personally to this news. This was clearly the beginning of the end for the Axis Powers. Quite when, and in what circumstances, the end would come for us in Japan we could not know. But I felt that when that time arrived a reasonable fluency in Japanese might be a useful asset for my companions and myself.

Nature was moved to mark the occasion too. In the evening of the same day we had the severest earthquake we had experienced in Japan. The barrack rooms swayed and creaked, the electric lights were transformed into golden pendulums and hundreds of tiles crashed down from the high barrack roof and shattered into fragments in the exercise yard.

Morale among the P.o.W.s bounded upwards and my own, in particular, soared with the arrival of more mail from my mother and my brother Charles, the latter telling me of family deaths and marriages. All but one of these communications had taken nearly a year to reach me, but the latest, a postcard from my mother, had only taken five months.

The food situation, however, was becoming extremely critical. At one stage there was no food in the camp for the next meal. All of us were moving about very slowly and listlessly. Several of my companions collapsed into unconsciousness from weakness and with distressing regularity. Even their buoyant morale was not enough to aid some of the senior, and more elderly, officers up the steep stairs where the casualty rate from 'fainting' became alarmingly high. The presence in the soup, on one occasion, of fifty rabbits for 700 men did little to remedy this situation.

My brother's interesting and most welcome letter had been written on the notepaper of his London club where he had clearly had an excellent dinner. He had enquired whether I was bored and had kindly offered, not knowing the impossibility of this, to send me some books. At Zentsuji, where books were not hard to come by, I would have exchanged any book in the world for half a bowl of soup. I would never have done that at Habu where the food was never as inadequate as it was in the Officers' Camp; and the five of us had asked to be sent to Zentsuji!

The air-raid siren went at 6.15 one evening. Those Japanese officers who were temporarily absent from the camp in the nearby village returned at top speed. All Japanese guards were doubled. They fixed bayonets and were issued with live ammunition. The interpreters and other Japanese civilian staff were issued with swords. The Cambridge graduate, Asabuki, wore his with great elegance and dignity, but with a certain air of revulsion at being required to play such stupid games. Donald Duck, however, the self-styled 'big potato', had acquired an enormous *Samurai* sword commensurate with his personal estimate of his own importance rather than with his build. Having tripped over this unaccustomed encumbrance, he was observed struggling on his back, unable to rise to his feet, like some carapaced beetle.

Japanese guards with drawn swords in one hand and binoculars in the other were positioned on the roof of the cook-house. All P.o.W. fire-squads took post. All cooks' and butchers' knives were removed by the Japanese from the cook-house, as were the toy-like sickles used to cut greenery for the camp rabbits.

After an early roll-call all P.o.W.s, other than those in the fire-squads, were ordered to bed in complete darkness, all lights having been extinguished and all black-out curtains drawn.

The American 'teen-agers'' barrack room, of which Tim Hallam and I were still reluctant inmates, was the scene of great excitement, It had been chosen by the Camp Authorities as one of the Japanese air raid precautions command posts. The siren went off again at 1.30 a.m. There was much coming and going of Japanese soldiery throughout the night. All were uttering ferocious cries, no doubt to scare off the raiders. Those who did not have fire-arms brandished their swords continuously. Whether this was to frighten us or to give themselves courage it was impossible to say.

As I lay watching these swordsmen practising their skills, I recalled a conversation I had had in the *Dai Nichi Maru* with a Japanese Sergeant, who could speak a little English. He had asked me whether British pilots wore their swords while flying.

'Of course not,' I had replied, 'they'd only get in the way of their flying.'

With the hiss of a quick intake of breath, the Sergeant had observed, 'Now I know why Nippon pilot beat British pilot in Singapore. You see, Nippon officer always have sword with him. When he have no more bullets he fly his plane close to British man's plane. Nippon man lean out of window and chop off head of British man with his sword.'

I had laughed and the Sergeant had clouted me.

'Do not laugh at *Samurai* warrior,' he had said. 'Many British planes crash because of brave Nippon man's swords. I know. I have seen pictures. You British not use swords. You are silly people—you are afraid of swords.'

I had let it pass. Certainly Tojo's propaganda machine had been doing its stuff.

Alas! there were no air raids that night; at least there was no air raid in the vicinity of the camp. It was rumoured the following day that Allied aircraft had dropped bombs on Nagasaki and Moji. The only casualty at the camp was our breakfast, as the authorities would not allow the cook-house fires to be lit until it was broad daylight.

We had all had a disturbed and sleepless night, but it made a change.

A few nights later all was quiet as it could be in a room where thirty-two men were sleeping. Suddenly about 2 a.m. one of the young American pilots started shrieking and moaning. He was obviously in great pain. I went along with the barrack-room leader to the guard-house to report this. We were told to go away and tell our companion to stop his 'yelling'. He could go to the sick-parade in the morning.

We comforted him as best we could and carried him to the sick-parade as early as possible the following morning. He was then examined, if that is the right word, by a Japanese Warrant Officer in the Medical Corps. What the Japanese was in civilian life I do not know. The young pilot, who was still in great pain, was told that there was nothing wrong with him and that he could remain on his bed-space for the rest of the day.

We didn't like the look of the patient and we asked an American P.o.W. doctor, a Commander Van Pienan in the United States Navy Medical Corps, to come and look at him. He diagnosed an acute appendicitis and went off to the Camp Authorities to recommend that the patient be taken immediately to hospital and operated on. The Camp Authorities refused.

Van Pienan then decided to operate himself. He had virtually no equipment or facilities at his disposal. It was said that his scalpel was made out of a strip cut from a tin; it was said that he had only a small local injection to give the patient. Van Pienan operated in the middle of the night; the appendix had already burst; but the patient, whose name was Fisher, survived.

It was in July 1944 that the rumours started that Zentsuji camp was to be broken up. The most persistent of these rumours was that 130 American enlisted men would be leaving first, taking with them, we hoped, their Mafia black-market. But by then rumours had ceased to have any value, except as new subjects of conversation.

As if to disprove the rumour, a solitary new P.o.W. arrived, the first addition to the P.o.W. population since we five had arrived from Habu seven long months earlier. He was a U.S. Air Force Colonel who had been shot down over Rabaul in January 1944. He had been very badly beaten up on many occasions since his capture and he refused to talk about anything.

In a sense, I suppose, the newcomer could have been regarded as a replacement for an American Major who died in agony shortly after the Colonel's arrival. The Major had been suffering for some time from untreated duodenal ulcers. The senior P.o.W. officers had begged the Japanese authorities to remove him to hospital for an operation, but, as always, they had refused.

The Major's corpse was put in the bath-house pending arrangements for the funeral. We all fell-in in six ranks on the exercise yard for the funeral service, which was taken by one of the British Army chaplains. We then lined the long driveway to the guard-house at the entrance to the camp, and saluted as six bearers bore the coffin out of the gate. A choir of P.o.W.s, standing in a coal-dump, sang 'Abide with me'.

Behind the coffin walked the three Senior P.o.W. Officers in variegated uniforms. Captain Lineberry, the American, was magnificently apparelled in his white tropical uniform, with plenty of gold braid. He was wearing white shoes which suffered grievously as he marched through the coal-dump. Colonel Scanlon added a splash of colour with his red tabs and cap band. I supposed that Captain Gordon must have lost most of his kit in H.M.S. *Exeter*; he was more drably dressed.

The three senior officers seemed to be unable to make up their minds whether or not to do a 'slow march' behind the coffin. Captain Lineberry did not try; Colonel Scanlon's thoughts were clearly miles away; and Captain Gordon, though trying, was hesitant. The result was very ragged. It would have been better if the drill had been settled, and, if necessary, rehearsed in advance.

No Japanese, except the interpreter Donald Duck, attended the service or participated in the procession; and his comical appearance and behaviour inevitably detracted from such attempts as others were making to lend some dignity to the occasion.

'What a contrast with the first few funerals on the *Dai Nichi Maru*,' I thought to myself.

By the second half of 1944, significant defeatist articles were appearing in the English language newspapers distributed to us by the Japanese authorities. One complained that everything had gone wrong with the Japanese war plans since the Battle of Guadalcanal. Another indicated that many would like to stop the war there and then, if only an honourable way could be found. There were hysterical cries for action to turn the tide but no suggestions as to how this could be done.

Shortly after this, the newspapers reported that the Tojo Cabinet had resigned. From then on no more English language papers were distributed at Zentsuji.

10

The Threat of Starvation

Zentsuji, Shikoku—August 1944–June 1945

'We are starving to death,' shouted a naval officer, half-crazed with hunger, and his bold lead was taken up by dozens of others.

The occasion for this outburst was a visit to the camp by a member of the staff of the Swedish Embassy in Tokyo. Sweden was the Protecting Power for Dutch interests in Japan and the Swedish diplomat had come to Zentsuji primarily to see the seventy Dutch officers. He told them about the efforts being made by the Dutch Government to try to provide adequate maintenance for the thousands of Dutch women and children still in Java.

The Swede left, no doubt, to return to his nourishing diplomatic fare. Some of the starving men who had shouted at him were beaten by the Japanese for causing a disturbance.

The deterioration in the fortunes of Japan and her allies, a series of air raid warnings and the genuine shortage of food, which was undoubtedly causing the Camp Authorities concern, even though their end of the stick was not as rough as ours, engendered a tetchy and irritable attitude among the captors. Many P.o.W. officers were thrown into the solitary confinement cells for minor offences. The atmosphere in the camp took a marked turn for the worse.

One Dutch officer was put in a solitary confinement cell for a week because he had cut off the sleeves of a Japanese issue shirt. He was not allowed to wear long trousers, which ensured that the mosquitoes devoured him; he was not allowed to have any water to drink between meals, although the small cell was stifling hot; and he was woken up by the Japanese guard every quarter of an hour during the night. There was some doubt whether he would live at all after his release. But a few days on his bed-space restored him to the feeble state in which he had been when he was incarcerated.

One of the inside working parties was suddenly ordered by the Japanese to make a number of crosses, to be kept for emergencies.

A group of us were engaged on some domestic job in a part of the camp. A number of American enlisted men were working with us. The Japanese guard in charge of the working party told us we could have a break. He lit a cigarette and so did some of the P.o.W.s who were lucky enough to have any. We sat down on the ground where we were and enjoyed the warm sun.

Suddenly there was a scuffle and I saw two of the officer P.o.W.s fighting like animals. One was a British Regular Army officer and the other an American. I gathered that the Japanese guard had thrown away his half-smoked cigarette and that the two contestants had pounced on it at the same time.

A very young American sailor who was squatting next to me was watching the officers fighting with fascinated eyes. He was a pleasant, fresh-faced lad. I guessed that he came from some rural community in the Middle-West and that he'd probably left school at fourteen or fifteen. Suddenly he nudged me and said:

'You know, sir, my mom would have told me that that was all wrong.'

As always, it was the unexpected that happened. Having half-accustomed ourselves to the idea that Zentsuji Camp was going to be broken up and its occupants dispersed to other camps, we were surprised to learn that a large number of new officer P.o.W.s was expected at any moment, to add to our overcrowding.

As the intake was likely to be anything up to a hundred, it would be quite impossible for them to go into the sick-bay for their quarantine. Three large rooms near the sick-bay were therefore cleared for their reception. One of these was the American 'kinder-garten' which Tim Hallam and I had now endured for nine months.

Following this re-shuffle. Tim and I were allocated to a smaller room in the second building, where we found most congenial company, more appropriate to our advancing years.

We were glad, too, that the only other P.o.W. in the 'kinder-garten', with whom we had anything in common, was able to come with us. Pete Kenny was flying a Catalina over the Indian Ocean when he spotted the Japanese Task Force on its way to bombard

Ceylon. He had managed to get off a warning radio message before he had been shot down.

Among our new bed-fellows was one of the army padres, Harper-Holcroft, and an Australian, David Hutchinson-Smith, one of the most likeable men in the camp. Another of our new companions had had a bit of bad luck. Woodward, an officer in the Royal Army Service Corps, had been on duty in Australia when war broke out in the Far East. He was posted from Australia to India and the ship in which he was travelling was captured by the Germans who made him a P.o.W. Then they handed him over to their gallant allies, the Japanese, for safe-keeping. An American, Lou Besbek, was room leader. In civil life he had been a film producer in Hollywood. The U.S. Navy Lieutenant Wilson who had helped me with my Japanese was another occupant; a couple of pleasant Australians and a young R.N.V.R. Lieutenant completed the room's complement.

Our new quarters were quiet, restful and more airy. Tim and I were delighted with this stroke of luck.

Fifty officers arrived from Tokyo and thirty from Hokkaido. We found a number of friends among them. They told us that their rice ration had been 700 grammes of wet rice a day; we told them that they would now be getting 390 grammes a day, if they were lucky. They told us they had had fish, oysters, milk, strawberries and sweet buns. We asked them what those words meant. They told us that they had been putting on weight; I told them that I had weighed 182 pounds on the outbreak of war and that I now weighed under 100 pounds.

On the night of their arrival the new-comers rejected one of our better soups as inedible. This rejected nectar was solemnly distributed among the other barrack rooms and sufficient reached our new room to fill six bowls. We drew cards for these and I drew the Queen of Clubs which entitled me to a bowl. My cup of good fortune, if not exactly overflowing, was certainly as full that day as was my extra bowl of soup, which had contributed so much to it.

I wondered whether the new arrivals had come to Zentsuji with the same high hopes we had had and how long it would take them to adjust to the harsh realities.

Donald Duck suddenly became very friendly. He invited Commander H. du Pré Richardson, D.S.O., R.N., of H.M.S. *Exeter* and myself into the camp office for a smoke and a chat. He suggested helping me with my Japanese if I would engage in French conver-

H

sation with him. He was clearly concerned to 'mend his fences' before the inevitable Japanese collapse.

On another occasion Donald Duck showed me the manuscript of the book he was writing called *The Story of Zentsuji*. It was interesting to read his description of the camp, the staff and the P.o.W.s, as seen through his eyes.

A few days later he asked me to help him with the English translation of a critical appreciation of some Japanese poetry which he had written. A strange and unpredictable man, like so many Japanese.

On Sunday the 3rd September 1944 we had a church service to commemorate the fifth anniversary of the outbreak of war. Padre Godfrey, the younger of the two British Army chaplains, as usual preached an excellent sermon. He dealt with the criticism that religion was an opiate. He put forward the point of view that in circumstances of great strain such as we were enduring there was a place for the opiate of religion, as a balm to frayed nerves and to temperaments out of gear. As always during these church services we thought of our families; L. was very close to me that night.

Hitherto I had not had any fainting fits. But starvation now began to take its toll of me as it had already of many others. Three times in one week I had collapsed and after a brief spell of unconsciousness had been helped to my feet by passers-by. On one occasion I thought the end had come for me.

In the middle of one night I had occasion to go to the *benjo*. This involved dressing, that is pulling on my uniform over the rags in which I was sleeping, and making my way very slowly down the corridor and down the stairs to the entrance of the second barrack block in which I was now housed.

The *benjos* were about seventy-five yards away from this second barrack block. After I had covered about half the distance my legs gave way and I collapsed in the middle of the yard. I do not know how long I lay there, but eventually I regained consciousness and managed to get to my feet.

I continued for about another twenty yards and then my legs gave way again. I did not lose consciousness this time and I decided to complete my journey on all fours.

On arrival at the row of evil-smelling *benjos*, I hauled myself to my feet by hanging on to the doorpost. I still felt very shaky and the stench was intolerable. Before proceeding to lower my trousers I tried to compose myself and to collect my strength. Quite what happened thereafter I do not know. When I came to, I had my right leg, from which all the skin had been scraped off, in the *benjo*. I had also lacerated my right arm. I had crushed my testicles on the edge of the *benjo* as I had fallen and they ached intolerably. I was violently sick into the pitch darkness all around me.

I must have remained in that awkward and painful position for some time. I recalled all the bawdy songs I had ever heard in the past about lavatories and about people being locked in lavatories. I found myself smiling. Suddenly the thought struck me, 'My companions will have a good laugh when they learn that poor old No. 958 was found dead in the *benjo*!'

All kinds of thoughts passed through my mind. Gradually the will to live reasserted itself. I said to myself, 'You haven't come all this way to die in these ludicrous circumstances. You may be bayoneted by a drunken guard tomorrow. You may be killed in an American air raid the day after tomorrow. You may be unlucky enough to get some complaint for which no treatment is available, when you will die, lying down, as many others have. But to die in these ridiculous surroundings is just not to be contemplated.'

I must have remained there, spreadeagled, for an hour or more, hoping against hope that someone would come who could help me out of the stinking trap into which I had fallen. No one came. The *benjos* appeared to be singularly ill-patronised that night.

Finally, I decided to make a move. How I managed to extricate myself, I shall never know. Some outside source gave me the strength which I could not find within myself.

I crawled on hands and knees to the nearest tap and, for my own sake as well as that of my room-mates, I washed off as much of the filth as I could. It was getting light now and by the time I had made the long journey back to my bed-space the sun was up and it was nearly time for roll-call.

After roll-call, during which I found it peculiarly difficult to remain upright, I made my way to the admirable American doctor, Van Pienan. He had nothing with which to dress my lacerated arm and leg. He had nothing to give me which might obviate another collapse. But he gave me something which was more valuable, a reassurance that I had not irreparably damaged my prospects of paternity. He also told me to attend the Japanese sick-parade.

'They won't do anything for you, I'm afraid,' he said, 'but

the more names I can get on to the Nip sick-lists, the more ammunition I shall have to get something out of them for the treatment of the sick and injured.'

I duly staggered to the Japanese sick-parade. I sat waiting for one and a half hours. The so-called medical officer, Lieutenant Saito, then read my name off a slip of paper. I rose unsteadily to my feet and saluted him, pointing to my lacerated arm and leg. Without asking me any questions he waved me aside, dismissed me and that was that. I had never expected anything more; and in any event to have had the opportunity of sitting down for one and a half hours was itself a great solace. Many of the others who had waited with me were in much worse shape than I was. I only hoped that he would do something for them.

This chapter was not, however, closed. When I had returned at dawn to my bed-space I had discovered that the wallet in which I kept the photographs which L. had sent me was missing from my trouser pocket.

I retraced my steps to the *benjo*. Fortunately the 'night soil' party had not emptied the enormous bucket which had nearly been my tomb. After half an hour's search I recovered my wallet. Neither the wallet nor the photographs were ever quite the same again but I was glad to have them back.

The Camp Authorities suddenly decided on a complete re-organisation of the accommodation, by nationalities, with Majors as room leaders. Although this meant that I returned, as a junior officer, to one of the large rooms in the main barrack block containing thirty-two men, there were certain advantages. Ian Graham, for whom I had acquired the greatest affection and respect, was our room leader. I was back on the ground floor, and much nearer the *benjos*. We were all British and among my companions were many pre-war friends from Malaya.

Tim Hallam, as an Australian, although serving in the R.A.F., was whisked away upstairs to one of the rooms allocated to his compatriots. I had shared sleeping accommodation with Tim ever since we had left Java some two years previously. We had been through much together and I was sorry to lose touch with him. The ill-fitting teeth with which we had furnished him in Habu had caused a number of large and painful growths in his mouth. Donald Duck referred to him as 'Cheek-Ball'. The fact that he now had the steep stairs to contend with did not help matters.

But Tim had not changed. He never belly-ached about his personal problems, about the intolerable pain in his mouth or about his difficulties in negotiating the stairs. He never ceased complaining about our conditions generally. His rich vocabulary put him at a distinct advantage in this respect. None could articulate as well as he could the unspoken thoughts and frustrations of so many of us. I was to miss his acid wit and his dry commentaries on the unpredictabilities of our captors' behaviour.

The re-shuffle was marked by an issue of Red Cross parcels, one parcel between four men. These were the first parcels we had seen for over six months when we had had one parcel between three men. Each man's share lasted him for about twenty-four hours and then we were back to rock bottom again.

A few days later the Japanese Camp Authorities issued a formal notice to the effect that the food situation throughout Japan was very serious and that nothing could be done about increasing our rations. This was the first official statement that Japan was suffering from a general food shortage. It gave little consolation to starving men, but we derived what comfort we could from the admission that the Allied noose was tightening around Japan's neck. The only additions we were getting at that time to the minute quantities of rice were the stalks of the common dock-leaf and the vine tops off sweet potatoes, which the Japanese normally burnt as rubbish.

The Japanese statement added that we were now formally permitted to lie on our bed-spaces during any 'free' time we might have.

While I was availing myself of this 'concession' a postcard arrived from my brother Charles, who was serving in the R.N.V.R., giving a glowing account of a holiday he was spending with my mother in Merionethshire. 'Plenty of good golf here', he wrote. 'Ye Gods!' I thought, 'no wonder the war is dragging on and that we are still P.o.W.s.'

One of my new room companions, a British subject of Greek extraction, was an epileptic and the poor chap suffered from distressing fits almost daily. Others brought trouble on their own heads by purchasing from the so-called canteen, and consuming, bottle after bottle of so-called vitamin tablets, to allay the pangs of hunger. This invariably resulted in vomiting or diarrhoea. I avoided these vitamin tablets like the plague but took a chance with a small snake I had killed on a working party. I managed to skin it and then ate the raw flesh, munching it off the vertebra. It didn't seem to do me any harm.

Early in November 1944 a cook-house rumour cast us all into deep dejection. One of the Japanese interpreters was said to have translated an item from a Japanese newspaper to a group of American enlisted men. This was a reported speech, alleged to have been made by Churchill in the House of Commons, during the debate on extending the life of Parliament for one year.

Churchill was reported as saying that the war in Europe might continue for a further nine months and that it might take a further eighteen months after that before Japan was defeated. This gloomy news suggested that we might have to endure our incarceration until the end of 1946.

It was strange how we now tended to believe in bad rumours rather than good ones, and how the very mention of Churchill's name would lend even greater credence to such rumours.

Whether the cause was this gloomy prophecy or whether it was conditions generally, I do not know. But for the first time, to my knowledge, during two and three quarter years' captivity two P.o.W.s became mentally deranged and had to be put under restraint in the sick-bay.

It must have been about 11.30 p.m. We had been asleep, or sleepless, for a couple of hours or more. As the sharp and strident notes of the bugle pierced my unconsciousness, I thought for a moment that it was the 'Last Trump'. 'Perhaps,' I thought, 'this is the end of all my woes, or perhaps it is just the beginning!'

The bugler was standing outside the window, near which I was sleeping. I recognised the call for 'muster', but the impatient urgency of the notes, beating on the cool night air, indicated that this was to be no usual roll-call.

Our forebodings were increased when Japanese N.C.O.s and guards came pounding into the barrack room, ordering everyone to dress and stand by their bed-spaces. No one was allowed to leave the room for any purpose and, as it was bitterly cold, many urinated where they stood.

We were kept standing about, under the watchful eyes of armed guards, for an hour or more and then ordered to get back on to our bed-spaces. We were too cold to sleep and we spent what was left of the night having whispered discussions with our neighbours as to what was behind this midnight floor-show.

The next day started normally enough. I went to the library to change a book and returned by way of the rubbish heap, near the rabbit hutches. I was hoping to find a few radish tops which had been deemed unsuitable for the rabbits. There were none; either someone had been there before me or the rabbits, too, were now eating anything they were given.

I then decided to take a cold shower. Hot baths were now a thing of the past. There were a few hardy fools like myself in the bitterly cold bath-house when the bugle for an abnormal muster went again. We dressed hurriedly and dashed to our allotted places in the exercise yard.

We were kept standing about for a very long time while the Japanese conducted a thorough search of the barrack rooms. Then the story filtered down the ranks.

For some time past a number of the P.o.W.s had been breaking out of the camp by night and pinching tobacco, food, etc., from shops and bakeries in the nearby village. A bakery immediately beyond one of the walls surrounding the camp compound had proved to be an irresistible target. It was said that some of the P.o.W.s had been caught going over the wall the previous night, which accounted for the midnight alarms and excursions.

When the Japanese had finished their searches of the barrack rooms they came out on to the exercise yard and searched a number of those on parade.

Eventually we were dismissed and returned to our rooms. The search had been a very thorough one and it took us some time to sort out the chaos which marked the wake of the Japanese searchers. Later I checked unobtrusively on my diaries. They were quite safe.

It was reported that half a dozen P.o.W.s, some officers and some enlisted men but none of them British, had been thrown into the solitary confinement cells pending further investigation. Some pilfered biscuits had been found soaking in a tin on one man's bed-space; and much illicit tobacco and other incriminating evidence had also been found.

A day or two later the camp was swarming with Japanese Military Police taking photographs of the scene of the 'break-out'.

It was easy, and it was true, for the majority to say that all would suffer for the thoughtless and selfish actions of a few. It was also easy, and it was also true, to conclude that the task of the Committee of the Senior P.o.W. Officers, in their unremitting battle with the Japanese Authorities for improved treatment for all, would be made infinitely more difficult. But these judgements had to be tempered by the realisation that starving men are desperate men.

Some had found escape from the pangs of starvation in going out of their minds; others had gone over the wall. If this critical state of affairs continued, which of us could be sure how we would react *in extremis?*

In the light of the official statement of the Japanese Authorities that the food situation throughout Japan was so serious that there was now no prospect of any increase in our rations from Japanese sources, the Committee, wisely, concentrated their efforts on attempting to secure an increase in Red Cross supplies. The Camp, which was grossly overcrowded when we had arrived there from Habu nearly a year previously, was now bursting at the seams with a P.o.W. population of some 800.

Colonel Sugiyama had no wish to be faced with a complete break-down of discipline in the camp. He knew that he could get no more food for us from Japanese sources. He, too, was willing to press his higher authorities for Red Cross supplies—to the extent that these were available in Japan.

For weeks the camp buzzed with rumours about the impending arrival of large quantities of Red Cross parcels. Meanwhile the rice ration was cut again to 230 grammes of wet rice. The position was desperate.

Finally, the parcels arrived, after many delays. First, there was no shipping to bring them from the mainland to Takamatsu, the large port on the north-west coast of Shikoku. Then there were no lorries to bring them from Takamatsu to Zentsuji. There was, however, no shortage of volunteers among the starving P.o.W.s, who stood by for days ready and eager to go to the docks at Takamatsu, load the parcels on to the lorries and unload them on arrival at the camp.

For some this succour arrived too late. There were several deaths from malnutrition during the waiting period. One of those who died was an R.A.F. officer, Flight-Lieutenant Moulden, who had been with us at Boei Giodok in Java. It seemed hard that he should die having survived so much, but none of us knew how much more we who were still alive would have to endure.

Those in the R.A.F. who were with him in Boei Glodok took it in turns, two at a time, to stand vigil by his body in the sick-bay during the twenty four hours that preceded his cremation.

Another for whom help came too late was one of the P.o.W.s who had lost his reason. He had become so violent that it was no longer safe to keep him in the sick-bay. The Japanese insisted on putting him into a solitary confinement cell.

It was at this time, mid-November 1944, that Smiler visited Zentsuji from Habu for a meeting and paid us a call. He told us that there had been three further deaths at Habu since we had left: Mackinnon, Asheton Hill, Professor of Chemistry at Hong Kong University and Stirling Lee, Hong Kong and Shanghai Bank. He added that most of the 'Java' men had now had mail and that W.O. Pritchard was coping well.

Smiler commented favourably on my beard, an 'Imperial', which I had been forced to grow because I had no soap of any kind left. I kept it trimmed by 'dry shaving' twice a week but I was determined to have it off the moment I could lay my hands on any soap.

Smiler commented unfavourably on my 'puffy' appearance, which, he said, meant that I had wet beri-beri; this I knew only too well.

Although the Red Cross parcels were now in the camp the Japanese administrative machine was taking its time before releasing them. Eventually one parcel per man was issued. This was accompanied by a very sensible chit, bearing the signature of the Senior P.o.W. Officer, Captain Lineberry, the U.S. Navy doctor. Lineberry advised all those who, like myself, were suffering from beri-beri to eat the proteins first, leaving the carbohydrates for more leisurely consumption later. He also added that he had made it clear to the Japanese that anything less than one parcel per man each fortnight would do nothing to improve the P.o.W.s' rapidly deteriorating health. As there was now a considerable number of parcels in the camp, the Japanese would be held personally responsible for any further deaths from malnutrition.

I did my best to follow Lineberry's guidance but all my proteins were consumed within forty-eight hours.

I managed, however, to hang on to my carbohydrates for a bit and I decided that I would try to organise an Oxford and Cambridge gathering, which would provide a suitable occasion to consume these goodies in congenial company. But first I shaved off my beard, using the small piece of soap in my parcel.

I consulted Graham Hill, with whom I had co-operated in giving a joint series of history lectures to various camp audiences before the food situation had become so desperate. He was strongly in favour of such a gathering. I then consulted the most senior of the Oxbridge men. This was Commander Richardson who, as a serving naval officer, had spent a year at Gonville and Caius College,

Cambridge, in 1920-1. He too gave his full support and we decided that the 12th December would be an appropriate date. In 1944 the 12th December was the second Tuesday in the month and we were mindful of the fact that the Oxford and Cambridge rugger match was normally played at Twickenham on the second Tuesday in December.

Among the other Oxonians were the two army chaplains, the Reverend R. N. Harper-Holdcroft and the Reverend R. C. R. Godfrey, and an agreeable American, Thomas Magee.

We decided that we would make it a coffee-party during the afternoon and that we would invite Asabuki.

For the next few days we were all engaged in making cakes and titbits from the carbohydrates in our parcels, using hoarded rice as a base. While I was making my cake, we had another earthquake which, alas! upset a bowl of chocolate sauce I was mixing.

The gathering itself was a great success. A kind soul lent me an R.A.F. blue uniform. We all wore light or dark blue rosettes. Asabuki contributed cigars and tangerines. In conversation with him I discovered that he had read architecture at Cambridge and that he had heard my brother Charles speak at the Union. After the party had been going for ten minutes, Asabuki was summoned to the camp office by the Commandant, who urgently required his services. He returned shortly afterwards.

Pete Kenny had made for me a beautifully decorated illuminated scroll and I managed to get all those present to sign it.

The party only broke up when an order came round that every P.o.W. was to return immediately to his bed-space to receive another Red Cross parcel. We did not linger over our farewells.

It was our third Christmas as P.o.W.s. There were the inevitable attempts to create the right spirit. Efforts were made to decorate the barrack rooms, an undertaking which was frequently interrupted by innumerable inspections. Just before Christmas Colonel Sugiyama had been replaced as the Colonel commanding the camp and his successor wished to make his presence known.

There were carols and a pantomine, *Babes in the Wood*, in which Frank Twiss† excelled himself as one of the robbers. I modestly entertained to coffee, and the remnants of the cake I had made for the Oxford and Cambridge party, Al Albertazzi and Johnny, the

† See footnote on page 177.

sick-bay Pharmacist's Mates who had been so kind to us on our arrival from Habu just a year previously.

But we were all weak, listless and depressed, and somewhat fearful as to the future. During Christmas some American enlisted men from the cook-house came round and offered Red Cross parcels for 500 dollars, payable after the war. This was the first time I had had any personal knowledge of the 'black-market' about which Al had warned us. Whether the parcels offered for sale had been pilfered from the store, which we all suspected, or whether the cook-house boys had had so much to eat that they were selling their own parcels, I did not know. So far as I was aware there were 'no takers'.

Snow fell early in the New Year and it turned bitterly cold. Air-raid alarms became more and more frequent, sometimes as many as three or four a night.

The new Colonel showed his teeth. As the Americans had bombed the Ise Shrine, all entertainment and lectures were henceforth prohibited. 'What will happen,' we thought, 'when the bombing really starts?'

The Colonel also issued an order that all P.o.W.s would hand in any aluminium cups, bowls, plates, or other utensils which they had in their possession in exchange for earthenware crockery. I had an aluminium bowl which I had acquired at Boei Glodok and which I had hoped to have appropriately inscribed after the war. This was spotted and removed from me, as my compulsory contribution to the Japanese war effort.

We had been without any news of the outside world for well over six months. Then on the 14th February 1945 the new Colonel Commandant sent for the senior P.o.W. officers and told them that there were 150,000 Americans in the Philippines and that they had entered Manila which was in flames. He added for good measure that the Japanese forces had retired to the hills and that they would be retaking the whole of the Philippines in the very near future.

Things were not so good for the Axis powers in Europe, he said. The Russians had made substantial advances towards the west and in his view Germany might be forced to capitulate at any time.

Whatever happened in Europe, the Colonel went on, Japan would never give up. The Japanese were prepared to endure any amount of bombing from the air. Hadn't the British and the German peoples stood up to the unbelievable aerial bombardments? he asked, and added: 'The Japanese people, too, can if necessary take any amount of bombing. The Americans will never, never be able to land on the sacred soil of Nippon until every Nipponese has been killed.'

The Colonel went on to re-emphasise that the food situation in Japan was extremely serious and that he was contemplating moving a number of the P.o.W. officers from Zentsuji to a camp where they could grow their own foodstuffs and look after their own cattle. The site of this new camp would be so remote that there would be no chance of any Japanese civilians trying to take the P.o.W.s' food.

This remarkable statement formed the subject of much speculation among the P.o.W.s. It seemed clear to most of us that it foreshadowed a certain amount of movement out of Zentsuji in the not too distant future.

In the succeeding weeks rumours of the break-up of the camp and the dispersion of its occupants multiplied. 'I must make time,' I thought, 'to sort out my kit so as to be ready for a move at short notice.'

A Japanese General, the Head of the P.o.W. organisation in Tokyo, arrived to inspect the camp. His visit didn't do us any good. When he left the camp he took with him two of the camp chickens and four Red Cross boxes full of charcoal to cook his own meal in the local inn.

The Colonel Commandant told Captain Lineberry that one more Red Cross parcel would be issued at Easter and that unless any more parcels arrived there would be no further issues. Camp morale dropped to below zero. By now it had become quite impossible to sustain life on the Japanese issue of rations and without Red Cross parcels it could only be a question of time for all of us.

On the same day I was issued with a new number. I became No. 688 instead of No. 958. The significance of this change escaped me, though it might have accounted for the fact that I had had no mail for several months.

With the complete cessation of Red Cross supplies and with further cuts in the rations, the Committee of Senior P.o.W. Officers made further protests to the Japanese Authorities. The Committee stressed the facts that P.o.W.s were collapsing in dozens during roll-calls and, indeed, at all other times, and that beri-beri was now the lot of every P.o.W.

They pointed out that it would soon be impossible for the prisoners to be dispersed, since they would be incapable of moving at all.

In reply the Camp Superintendent said that all Japanese efforts were now being devoted to strengthening Shikoku's fortifications to ward off the threatened American invasion of the island. As regards food, the only positive step being taken was the fencing-in of a pond inside the camp, near the *benjos*, where bull-frogs were being encouraged to breed. Our P.o.W. experts informed us that, as it took at least twelve months for a bull-frog to be 'fattened up', we would all be dead long before this delicacy was available.

The bull-frogs did not care for Zentsuji any more than we did. They soon died off at an even more rapid rate than the prisoners. The project was cancelled almost before it had started. We found a few corpses in the soup one night.

American planes were not infrequently observed over the camp. On one occasion well over a hundred American air-craft passed over at a great height. One U.S. Air Force Colonel commented that there were, on occasions, more 'free' Americans in the air over Zentsuji than American P.o.W.s in the camp. A nice thought for one's head, but it did nothing to fill one's belly.

I got up shortly after 5 a.m. on the 12th April 1945. It was a glorious spring morning. It was also L.'s birthday and I wanted a few minutes alone with her before the camp came to life. I slipped off my bed-space, leaving my thirty-one companions still apparently fast asleep.

It was very fresh outside the barrack block. I studied the buds on the trees, with their promise of new life. The sun was coming up, blood-red over the cook-house at the eastern end of the camp. The chorus of birds had started, birds which one could rarely see, and never hear, once the din of the camp had started. A family of rats appeared from under the barrack block and romped about in a patch of pale sunlight.

I went over to the wash-rack and rinsed my face in cold water. I had brought my blankets with me and hung them up to air.

As if to help prolong my moments of silent communion, the bugler was ten minutes late that morning and the bugle did not go for roll-call until ten minutes past six. This gave me time to perform another chore.

I had hoarded a little rice overnight and I formed this into four little cakes with some fish-powder. I then found a spot on a window-sill which the rising sun would soon touch and thus dry out my cakes.

I smiled as I put the cakes on the window-sill. This action recalled to my mind an incident which had occurred nearly a quarter of a century earlier.

At my preparatory school I was, like most of my companions, a keen photographer with my Brownie box camera. Half the fun of this was the daylight printing of sepia prints. I could never get the timing of this operation quite right. My prints always came out either a bilious yellow or a dark brown burnt-toast colour. Then one day I made a discovery.

Morning prayers were in three parts: standing for a hymn, sitting while the captain of the school read a lesson and then turning round and kneeling down for the final prayers.

I was strategically placed near an open window, where the morning sun caught the window-sill. By a process of trial and error, I had learnt how to get my timing right. If I prepared my frame with the negative and printing beforehand, I could slip it out of my pocket and put it on the window sill, as I turned round for prayers. The time taken by the headmaster to read the final prayers was exactly right. I made many perfect prints in this way before I was discovered. I hoped my cakes would be as successful.

In the evening a letter from L. arrived. It had been posted sixteen months earlier, but it was nice to receive a letter from her on her birthday.

On the 10th May 1945, two days after the war in Europe had formally ended, the Camp Authorities announced that the bulk of the P.o.W.s would be leaving Zentsuji within a month. No further details were given except that prisoners would be permitted to take with them only such kit as they could carry. In our enfeebled state this meant virtually nothing. We were so weak that we could not even contemplate trying to take any warm clothing with us. We knew well enough that if we were still in Japan for the winter of 1945–6 we would be long past having a need for any clothing at all.

We were all, the Japanese guards included, living on a knife-edge. There was an ugly incident one evening at the roll-call held in our barrack room.

When the Sergeant of the guard came round we all numbered off in Japanese as usual. The Guard Commander, who spoke a little

English, said that the 'dressing' was bad and ordered Ian Graham
to get us properly 'dressed'.

'Right dress, gentlemen, please,' said Ian quietly.

'Not so much of the "gentlemen",' bellowed the Sergeant.

Ian then yelled a real parade-ground command and turning to
the Sergeant said, 'Perhaps that will suit you.'

The enfuriated Sergeant felled Ian with a blow and the latter
fell back on to a bed-space. Struggling to his feet, Ian spat at the
Sergeant, 'You bastard,' and made as if to floor his assailant but
just managed to control himself.

The Sergeant then launched into a tirade contending that Ian
had insulted him and had threatened him with violence. By now
Ian's dander was up and he challenged the Sergeant to a fight outside the barrack block, taking off his jacket as he issued the challenge.
The Sergeant drew his sword and was about to follow Ian out.

At that moment the Japanese Duty Officer arrived and pulled
both Ian and the Sergeant back into the room. There followed,
inevitably, the interminable argument which lasted for half an hour.

Subsequently Ian was taken under armed guard to the camp
office and then flung into a solitary confinement cell without blankets and without any protection against the swarms of mosquitoes.

It was clear that tempers were becoming frayed on both sides,
an evil omen for the months that lay ahead.

During the second half of May there was considerable activity in
anticipation of the impending and, as we were then informed,
complete break-up of the camp. Library books were called in, all
kit issued by the Camp Authorities was collected, bed mats were
removed and much Japanese equipment and many stores were
removed from the camp in lorries. Some of these were destined for
the hundreds of Japanese civilian refugees, victims of bombing, who
had been pouring into Zentsuji and given temporary shelter in
schools.

On the 1st June the Japanese conducted a thorough search of the
kit of the first American party, due to leave on the 5th June. When
this had been searched and stored under guard, the Americans'
departure was postponed. They had to make do for three weeks in
what they stood up in.

Like the Americans, we had already been issued with 'iron
rations' for our journeys; but the longer we remained in this state
of suspended animation the more inroads we made into these. The

rice rations had again been severely cut, probably because the Camp Authorities had assumed that the American party would have left on the due date and what had been left for half the camp now had to provide for the whole.

The cheerful rumour went round that we were moving to the centres of targets most likely to attract the attention of the U.S. Air Force. Some new Japanese guards told us that movement in Japan was now very difficult as many railways had been completely destroyed by American bombing. One party of P.o.W.s whom the new guards had been escorting to another camp had to walk for ten miles along the side of a destroyed railway track. Many had died on the way.

Zentsuji was clearly disintegrating more rapidly than the Japanese Authorities had planned. Several parties of famished Japanese civilians had broken into the camp in search for food and fights had occurred, both between these rival predatory gangs and with the camp guards. Japanese girls from the nearby bakery, which had earlier been the scene of a raid by a number of American P.o.W.s, were now coming over the wall, into the camp by the same route, and offering sweet buns, and other more personal favours, in return for soap!

Confusion still reigned in the Japanese administration and parties of P.o.W.s were assembled for departures which were immediately cancelled.

As there had been no air-raid alarms for some days the optimists contended that the war was over and that the Japanese authorities were faced with the task of revising our movement orders so that we could all be transported to waiting American ships which would convey us to freedom. These optimistic hopes were short-lived. On the 10th June we had the longest air-raid alert to date.

On the 18th June I learnt that I was in an all-British party which would be going to one of the Fukuoka camps on the southernmost island of Kyushu, the island on which the Americans were most likely to make their first landing.

Most of my friends were in the larger British party destined for Tokyo, but Ian Graham, Tim Hallam and Peter William-Powlett, with whom I was to share an adventure in the, as yet unknown, future, were in the Fukuoka party.

The Japanese issued instructions about discipline during our forthcoming journeys. Among these was a reassuring intimation that if we passed through any areas which were being, or had been, subjected to Allied bombing, our Japanese military escorts could accept no responsibility for our safety, 'should the Japanese civilian population decide to take matters into their own hands'. Another was an expression of hope that if circumstances permitted food would be supplied en route.

The Fukuoka party's kit was assembled and searched, and then stored under guard. Having discarded a large number of items including books and lecture notes, I had packed the remainder into two bundles, one of which I would hang on to at all costs and the other which I would dump, if I found myself too weak to carry it. We then joined the ranks of those who had had to wait for their moves in what they were wearing.

During this 'waiting' period several of the P.o.W.s developed chicken pox; and several, for a variety of minor offences, were put into the solitary confinement cells. All the wooden ceilings in the barrack rooms were pulled down as a precaution against incendiary bombs.

The first two parties left on Saturday the 23rd June—350 Americans for an unknown destination and forty Dutch for Nagoya. The American group was rigorously drilled, carrying all their kit on their backs, for some time before they were marched out of the camp. They were also told that they would be made to walk, carrying all their kit, through extensive bomb-damaged areas in Kobe en route to their new camp.

When the British party, bound for Tokyo, was paraded on Sunday the 24th, prior to departure, they were ordered to cut down drastically on their kit. The reason for this was that the heavily laden American party, which had left the previous day, had jettisoned most of their kit on the way to the railway station. This had led to disturbances among the local Japanese civilians who had come to blows over this pathetic flotsam and jetsam, deposited by the tide of war, on their doorsteps.

The kit of those in the Tokyo party was severely pruned by the Japanese before they left.

The Fukuoka party paraded with kit at 10.15 a.m. on Monday the 25th June. The Japanese guards who formed our escort, and in particular the interpreter, were not unfriendly. I was too weak to get my kit-bag on to my shoulders but if someone helped me to get it in position I could just stagger with it. Somehow we managed to reach the station. Several P.o.W.s collapsed but we succeeded in getting them on their feet again. The escort permitted us to have three or four stops on the way.

We had a long wait in the broiling sun outside the station. There were many boxes, containing the ashes of Japanese soldiers killed in action, under a ceremonial guard on the platform. We entrained for Takamatsu where we were to take the ferry to Tamano on the mainland. It was the first time I had been in a train for nearly three years.

On the ferry I had a violent attack of diarrhoea and spent most of my time on board queueing up for the *benjo*. The moment I emerged, I took my place again at the end of the queue. The Japanese interpreter, becoming aware of my predicament, gave me a yellow powder to take. I just had time, before we landed, to pop up on deck and watch a number of Japanese fishing craft sweeping for mines.

I felt very weak as we disembarked and half fell into the water but was hauled on to dry land by the Japanese guards. We then got into a train for Okoyama. On the train we were given six small buns, each about the size of a digestive biscuit, but without the flavour, or indeed any flavour.

At Okoyama we were herded into a waiting room where crowds of Japanese civilians gaped at us through the windows. Visits to the *benjo*, of which I required many, were under armed guard. There was no water at the station and we were marched, again under armed guard, to a public bath about a quarter of a mile away to fill our water-bottles.

After a long wait we were hustled into a train which carried us through the night to Moji, on the island of Kyushu, which we reached at 6.30 a.m. For the short journey across the Straits of Shimonoseki the train was shunted on to a train ferry.

It had been a most uncomfortable journey. We had been packed into the carriage, six of us to a little bay designed for four Japanese. Sleep was impossible for all, and for me in particular, as the interpreter's little yellow powder did not seem to be very efficacious. The black-out curtains had to be kept tightly drawn, but we caught glimpses of burnt-out rolling stock, of rows of wooden houses cleared as 'fire-breaks' and of a few sunken ships in Moji harbour.

Apart from our six little biscuits we had had no food for twenty-four hours.

It was strange to be back at Moji, where we had landed from the *Dai Nichi Maru* two and a half years earlier. 'To what future,' I wondered, 'will Moji be the gateway on this occasion?'

11

The Coal-mine

Miyata—Kyushu—June–August 1945[*]

We still did not know exactly where we were going, although we knew that the official description of our new home was Fukuoka War Prisoners Camp No. 9. It seemed to be very remote. Having left the train, in which we had spent such an uncomfortable night, at Moji, we changed trains twice more on to ever smaller branch lines. We arrived at Miyata, the back of beyond.

At the 'halt', for the squalid pause in the neglected railway track, as it snaked through the hills, hardly merited description as a 'station', we were met by our new Camp Commandant and a couple of Dutch P.o.W.s with a small hand-cart. Even though we had to leave much of our kit behind, the two Dutchmen blenched a bit at the amount our party of some forty-five had managed to tote from Zentsuji. Only a few of the belongings of our halt and sick could be squeezed into the small cart which could hold little more than a wheelbarrow.

The rest of us shouldered our burdens once again and stumbled up hill and down dale through mean little mining settlements, perched among the hills. The whole area smelt of decay. Later we were to learn that the mines had been abandoned in 1937 as uneconomical and unsafe. But Japan's desperate shortage of fuel, once battle had been joined, brought about their reopening. The economics of war had overcome the first reason for their original closure; the availability of P.o.W. slave labour permitted the second to be ignored.

It seemed a very long walk, and then, turning an abrupt corner on a mountain path, we saw the camp, desperately trying to main-

[*] See map 3, page 318.

tain its precarious foothold on the side of a steep hill. The buildings looked very temporary. We hoped they would be.

The camp was surrounded by a high wooden fence, with guard posts mounted on stilts, commanding the perimeter. I imagined that the salt-mine camps in the frozen wastes of Siberia must have looked much the same. The only difference was that July in Japan can be oppressively hot and July 1945 was no exception.

As the camp gates were closed behind us, we were marched to the slope which served as a parade ground. The Commandant, a slovenly man, addressed us with the help of an even more slovenly and illiterate interpreter, whom we came to know as 'Charlie McArthy'.

The Commandant did not mince his words. By then I knew enough Japanese to recognise that Charlie McArthy's translation was fair enough, even though not couched in very elegant English.

Charlie McArthy said: 'This my speech of welcome. Let me speak you that any man who tries to escape outwards or who disobeys what I will speak will be immediately shot or stabbed to death. You will now hold up your hands to show you comprehend and that you swear to obey all I speak.'

We had all become very stiff during our long train journey, and as a result of humping our kit up and down hill. It was quite a relief to stretch out our arms and many put up both for good measure.

The Commandant, according to Charlie, continued, 'Miyata is a working camp. I make it a very hard-working camp. I mean to keep it so.'

During both the original delivery and the translation of this passage the Commandant was drawing and sheathing his sword and indulging in a few practice swipes the while.

Charlie went on: 'Officers and soldiers all same here. No differences. All work hard. But officers must work hardest because officers most arrogant.'

It was clear that there would be even less chance of finding a copy of the Geneva Convention on the Treatment of Prisoners of War at Miyata than there had been at Zentsuji.

'Look these men well,' Charlie went on, pointing to what appeared to be a group of hirsute gorillas dressed up in Japanese uniforms at one side of the parade ground.

I myself had not hitherto noticed them. They did not look particularly reassuring to me as they flexed their bulging muscles and slashed the air with enormous pick-helves, in response to the 'spot-light' which Charlie had focussed on them.

Surprisingly enough, Charlie continued, 'These men are your friends.' But before we had got over this shock he went on: 'As friends, they can be good and kind but as enemies . . .', and then breaking into Welsh he concluded the Commandant's speech with the two words, 'Look you.'

Our new-found 'friends', beaming through their ferocious beards and moustaches, then ushered us to our quarters. It was 'service with a smile', of a sort—but not for long.

The ten or more flimsy barrack huts, ranged above each other on the steep slope like two rows of steps, contained six rooms each, with an open verandah along one side. There were twelve men to a room and I was lucky to get a space in a corner. The flea-ridden huts reminded me of the rest-houses at Port Dickson and elsewhere on the sandy beaches of Malaya. In the prevailing hot weather, and provided it did not rain, they were airy and not inappropriate; in winter—but we dared not think about winter.

Having been allocated our bed-spaces, we went down the mountain to collect our kit at the guard-house. This had been searched, and pilfered, during the Commandant's harangue; I had lost quite a bit.

Many collapsed as they carried their kit up the precipitous slopes. As we were soon to learn, the configuration of the terrain made movement inside the camp both difficult and exhausting.

The arrival of the Zentsuji party had brought the total P.o.W. population up to about 750, of whom about 100 were officers. Miyata had started as a camp for Dutch P.o.W.s and most of the other ranks were Dutch who had been captured in various parts of the Netherlands East Indies. There were a few American enlisted men and some British and Australian other ranks.

We were struck by the rags which many of the older inhabitants were wearing. We gathered that virtually no kit had been issued in this remote place.

The Senior P.o.W. Officer on our arrival in the camp was a Dutch Medical Officer. He handed over his 'command' to Wing Commander G. Matthews, a regular R.A.F. Equipment Officer who had led our party from Zentsuji.

As befitted a 'working camp', we were to take our meals in a communal dining-hall, in shifts, as we came off work. We learnt that there were different scales of rations according to the type of work done; underground workers, surface workers and workers on the farms attached to the mine all got different scales and none of these was adequate.

Our meal on arrival at Miyata, the first food we had had for thirty-six hours, except for our six small biscuits apiece, consisted of a very small quantity of rice and potatoes. It was welcome but not encouraging. We hoped that this meant that there was a fourth scale of rations—for new arrivals.

The following morning we had a cup of weak coffee for breakfast to celebrate the birthday of Prince Bernhard of the Netherlands.

As we settled in on our first night, we were glad to meet a number of old friends among the British officers. I was particularly pleased to come across Robin Black* again.

Robin told me that he and another officer, Eric Wotton, who had also been with us in Java, had worked for some time at the P.o.W. Mail Sorting Office in Fukuoka. They had come across many letters for me, but, as there was no indication of my whereabouts and as they had never heard of Habu Camp, the letters were all filed, as they could not be forwarded. I never did receive them.

Whether the Camp Commandant was acting under instructions or whether he was merely giving expression to his own personal prejudices, I did not know. But, as we were soon to learn, officer P.o.W.s, and particularly those from Zentsuji, were to be picked out for beatings on every possible occasion.

Our first day at work was Wednesday the 27th June 1945, the day after our arrival. We thought we had been let off lightly when we were paraded and ordered to weed the area round the Japanese guards' quarters and to clear the undergrowth from the side of the adjacent hill. Then it all started when Peter William-Powlett failed to notice, and therefore to salute, an approaching Japanese guard. Peter was made to stand with his hands above his head and then received half a dozen heavy blows with a rifle-butt across his back. Wing Commander Matthews protested and was knocked to the ground and kicked violently in the stomach by the guard commander. Foolishly I intervened, explaining to the guard commander, in Japanese, that Peter had not seen the approaching guard. I found myself on the ground with a splitting headache. We all felt very sorry for ourselves as we climbed the hill to our respective huts when our labours were over.

* See footnote on page 56.

One redeeming feature was the prospect of a hot bath. But this meant going down the hill again, returning and then descending again for our evening meal. Even then our mountaineering was not at an end. After the meal we returned to our rooms but had to go down again to the parade ground, brightly lit by arc-lights, for the evening roll-call, which could take anything up to an hour. The final climb up the hill to bed seemed well-nigh impossible. We were, by now, so exhausted that neither the fleas nor the constant air-raid sirens could prevent us from sleeping.

It was clear that a climax was approaching. I speculated on this in terms of both the temporal and spatial contexts.

We had learnt enough, before we had left Zentsuji, to know that the Allies were now gathering their forces for an all-out attack on the Japanese mainland. We assumed that first there would be heavy air raids; indeed our eyes and ears bore daily witness to the fact that the introductory bars of this 'overture' were already being played under the baton of General Douglas MacArthur.

Then the Allied landings would come. Presumably Kyushu, the island on which we now were, would be among the first of the Americans' objectives. Everything we had seen and heard confirmed our view that any Allied attempts to land would be resisted by the Japanese to the last man. 'Would the landings come during the summer of 1945?' I wondered, 'or would they be deferred until the spring of 1946?'

Then I focussed the lens a little more closely on our own position. At Habu and Zentsuji we had been in the middle of somewhere, even if that somewhere had only been the Inland Sea. Now we were on the extreme edge of nowhere. At Zentsuji itself there had been Japanese Army Command, capable, presumably, of enforcing a measure of discipline on the camp staff and on the neighbouring civilian population in an emergency. Miyata seemed infinitely remote from any Japanese governmental authority. We could be massacred by the Japanese guards or lynched by the Japanese miners before anyone in authority became aware of what had occurred. It was not a cheerful prospect.

We started our work outside the camp. My first few days were spent on one of the farms associated with the mine. This was several miles away and we made the journey on the mine railway. Our first chore was to carry heavy boxes of camp refuse to the 'station'.

We were rigorously searched at the guard-house and we were not permitted to take anything with us except our rations. The search was conducted, and we were escorted to the railway, by young Japanese boys, members of some Youth Corps, who chivied us about in emulation of their elders. We dubbed these auxiliary guards 'goons'.

About eighty of us piled into two damaged goods wagons, of which one was a closed wagon and the other an open 'flat-top'. I managed to get a place on the flat-top but fell off before we started, dropping the contents of my precious refuse box on the ground. It was a messy business replacing the contents with my bare hands.

The railway line went through the mine and eventually deposited us at the farm. The goons with much shouting and many gesticulations divided us up into squads for different assignments. It was thus that I started my career as a rice-planter. Wading about in the filthy paddy-fields, infested with water-snakes, and with invisible but more dangerous parasites, was not a very congenial pursuit.

At a later stage I found myself planting rice seedlings. Naked, save for a *hundoshi*, and with a little bag of seedlings tied round my waist, I felt like some character out of the Bible. But the sowers of the Bible were free men; we were not. A dozen of us would be lined up about a yard apart, facing the 'bund' at one end of the paddy-field to be planted. Two Japanese soldiers, each of whom would be standing on one of the side bunds, would peg in a string to give us a line. When the command was given we would each plant half a dozen seedlings to our right and left. One of the guards had a long whip. He was extremely skilful at flicking the back of any man whose seedlings showed signs of falling over, as mine only too frequently did. When the seedlings were 'dressed' like Guardsmen, one of the guards would give the order and we would all take a step to the rear in unison. The pegged string was then moved towards us and planting was resumed.

All this, and the various other agricultural pursuits allotted to other squads, took place in a huge, open and treeless valley. The heat was intense, and many suffered severely from sunburn. The hills at either side of the valley were pitted with quarries and caves. Out of the corner of my eyes I could see large numbers of Japanese guns and large quantities of military stores being concealed in these quarries and caves. The Japanese were digging in for their siege.

Our eleven-hour working day was divided only by the lunch-break, when we consumed the, by then, cold rice which we had drawn from the P.o.W. cook-house at seven in the morning. Sometimes I was sent off to a neighbouring peasant's hut to fetch boiling water for the guards' tea. Occasionally the peasant's wife would ask me in and offer me a cup of tea and a cigarette. Invariably, if the cover was good enough, I would steal a pumpkin or vegetable marrow from the peasant's plot and gobble it down raw on the spot. It hardly seemed a very ethical response to an act of courtesy, but I overcame my scruples more quickly than the indigestion which inevitably followed.

The twelve- to fifteen-year-old goons could have been more profitably employed carrying out the agricultural tasks entrusted to us; and no doubt they would have made a better job of them. As it was, they delighted in tormenting us, beating with heavy sticks P.o.W.s old enough to be their grandfathers. All P.o.W.s were required to salute any goon wearing an armband. All goons, except new recruits, wore armbands.

The Japanese soldiers, who also accompanied us, did nothing to stop the goons' activities. It was intolerably hot and oppressive and, no doubt, the guards were only too glad to conserve their energies and let others perform the ritual beatings without which no day was complete.

We marched back, day after day, to the train which would take us home. Unlike metropolitan commuters we knew we would never miss it.

On arrival at the camp we were searched again and after a bath, a meal and roll-call we were in bed asleep. There was no time for reading; and there were no books to read.

All buttons had to be done up, and caps worn, at all times in the camp. Returning from my bath after my first day at work outside the camp, I had wrapped my towel, with gay nonchalance, around my neck. A twelve-year-old goon—with an armband—spotted me and I had to stand to attention where I was caught, for two hours, thus missing my evening meal.

A few days later we had been breaking up new ground on the farm in the valley. It had been pouring with rain when we left the camp and a bitterly cold wind had been blowing all day. We had eaten our midday meal, huddled together like sheep under an enormous unserviceable earth excavator. There had been a couple of incidents, to which I had been summoned to interpret, naked except for a pair of dripping shorts. We were, indeed, glad when the senior guard gave the signal for the roll-call and the march back to the railway. We piled into the wagons as though they were first-class Pullman cars.

Then suddenly we were all pulled out of the wagons. Two of the goons had reported to the senior guard, who had been asleep in a nearby peasant's hut for most of the day, that we had not worked hard enough. We were made to walk the four or five miles back to the camp in the still torrential rain. Many of the P.o.W.s had festering feet and bad blisters. We missed our baths and half our evening meal.

Later I went to the camp office to interpret for the Wing Commander. He protested that the Japanese guards, and especially the goons, were molesting us unnecessarily. He also requested an extra hour's sleep the following day, which was a rest day. The request was rejected out of hand; and, as there was no subsequent change—for the better—in the behaviour of either the guards or the goons, we had to assume that the protest had been similarly ignored.

The events of the following day, our first rest day, were of greater significance than was apparent at the time.

We had all settled down, after roll-call, to the normal chores of a rest day, laundering, mending and thinking, when the goons came rushing through the huts announcing that we were to parade for air-raid precautions drill.

We assembled on the precipitous parade ground with two blankets apiece. We were then marched up a very steep path to a patch of the hillside where it was even more difficult to keep one's foothold. The goons, armed with sticks, then drove us down a deep and dark incline into a disused mine-shaft. It was dripping wet and there were pools of water in the mud underfoot. We were crammed in so tightly that if a P.o.W. fell, and some did, it was almost impossible to get him on his feet again. I observed that, at the entrance to the tunnel down which we had slithered, two Japanese were posted with machine-guns—pointing inwards.

Eventually we were released from our cavern and marched back to the parade ground. There we were told of the Commandant's displeasure that the exercise had taken too long. We were warned that there would be frequent practice drills of this operation in the future and then every rabbit would have to be in the burrow within fifteen minutes of the alarm. It had taken us, in our enfeebled state, at least half an hour to get up the hill; and the whole exercise had taken forty-five minutes. We undertook, to ourselves, to bear the Commandant's counsel of perfection in mind.

Many, like myself, had cleaned our boots before this unforeseen excursion. Now we had to clean them all over again.

Most of the Zentsuji party were suffering from severe shock. Miyata had clearly been a tough camp from the time it had been opened. The older inhabitants, particularly the Dutch other ranks, had become inured to the hardships of the rough life there; though even they admitted that the previous Commandant had been less draconian. Moreover, the rations for those who worked in the mine were substantially larger than any we had ever seen in Zentsuji.

We had become soft at Zentsuji and seriously weakened by grossly inadequate rations. It would take time before the somewhat larger quantities of rice we were now getting could build up our strength adequately enough to meet the demands of the hard work now expected of us.

The guards were much thicker on the ground at Miyata than they had been at Zentsuji; and there were the goons in addition. The layout of the camp, with its tortuous steep paths and its complex of irregularly sited buildings, and with the dining-hall, the bath-house and the parade ground at some considerable distance from our sleeping quarters, inevitably brought us into closer and more continuous contact with our captors. The nervous strain of always being properly dressed for these casual and unforeseeable encounters and of being instantly ready to salute unseen, as well as seen, guards preyed upon us.

During the long working day, including the journeys to and from the valley, the irrepressible and energetic goons never ceased to play their role as picadors. Months of malnutrition at Zentsuji had taken its toll of our physical condition. To this was now added an unrelenting battering of our frayed nerve-ends.

At Zentsuji it had at least been acknowledged by the Japanese that we were officers. It was, in fact, an officers' camp. At Miyata no such distinction was made. We had had our heads shaved shortly after we had arrived and we had been told that moustaches were not allowed—except, of course, for the Japanese gorillas!

In compliance with this order I had clipped my moustache as closely as I could with scissors. As I had worn this embellishment since I was seventeen, I was very loath to part with it, especially at the bidding of the Japanese. I tried to maintain my self-respect by persuading myself that I had it still, even though it was barely visible.

It was, however, more visible than I thought. One evening I had occasion to go to the camp office on an errand for the Wing Commander. There was a particularly unpleasant Japanese Sergeant on duty, the proud possessor of a magnificent moustache.

When I had finished my official business the Sergeant said to me in Japanese:

'Come over here, nearer the light. I want to look at you.'

I approached him.

'As I thought,' he said, 'you still have your moustache. Why have you not complied with Commander's order?'

'But I have,' I replied. 'I have cut my moustache off.'

'Not enough,' he said, rising from his desk. He called to one of his guards who was squatting in the corner. The two of them lifted me up and laid me on the table with my head in the light. Then the Sergeant took a pair of hair-pluckers from his desk drawer. I had noticed that many Japanese possessed these implements and spent hours plucking hairs from their ears and nostrils, but never from moles or warts, whenever they had nothing better to do.

'I must teach you to obey Commander's orders. All you Zent-suji officers are too arrogant,' he said.

He then proceeded to pluck out a number of my moustache hairs, laughing the while.

From the appearance of my distorted upper lip, he must have thought that I was laughing too.

'Do not laugh,' he said clouting me on the side of the head, 'you are too arrogant.'

I could see he was getting angry. He then turned his attention to my lower eyelids and pulled out a number of my eyelashes.* When he found his task impeded by the flow of tears I could not control, he lost interest and hauled me to my feet.

'Now go. Perhaps that will teach you to obey Commander's orders in future.'

I did not shave off, or even trim, my moustache again at Miyata, and I got away with it. The Commandant and the guards had more important things on their minds in the weeks which lay ahead.

* The loss of my lower eyelashes has caused me considerable trouble with cysts on my eyelids ever since this unrequested treatment.

As I lay on my bed-space nursing my sore eyes, I brooded. We had a few small mercies for which to be thankful. Unless our return from work was inordinately delayed, we could always look forward to a hot bath. Fuel was no problem here. The camp was so high up in the hills that mosquitoes and flies were less of a problem than they had been at either Habu or Zentsuji. The inveterate pessimists could, however, argue that the plentiful fleas had taken their places.

We were spared the curse of night fire-watch guard. I relished the thought that at Miyata this task fell to be performed by the goons.

We continued to go to bed ravenously hungry and I still tied a piece of string tightly round my stomach before retiring. But the gaunt spectre of starvation, which had stalked the corridors of Zentsuji, was less frequently visible.

My own particular worry was that the long working day made it impossible for me to devote any time to improving my knowledge of Japanese. Yet I was convinced that the time was rapidly approaching when my investment, such as it was, would pay off.

Our second precious rest day in the camp was rudely interrupted by an order from the camp office that we were all to turn out to make a path up the hillside to the Japanese Sergeants' quarters. Wing Commander Matthews, who was always willing to take up the cudgels with the Japanese, summoned me to interpret his protest in the camp office. The Japanese Corporal on duty was not unsympathetic but said that, as it was the Commandant's order, there was nothing he could do about it.

The ever resourceful Wing Commander then tried another tack.

'If we must work on our rest day we should at least have a working day's rations for three meals and not two,' he said.

On rest days we were only allowed two meals.

The Japanese Corporal took the point but again said he could do nothing about it. The reduced rations for a rest day had already been issued from the store.

Of course, we got no satisfaction. Neither of us had ever thought we would. Indeed, we were fortunate that it was the mild little Japanese Corporal who was on duty. Protests always carried with them the risk of being beaten up. But such protests by the Senior P.o.W. Officer were essential if the morale of the P.o.W.s was to be maintained. The Wing Commander never shirked this unpleasant duty. His persistence helped greatly to maintain his authority over the men when, in due course, this was most needed.

So we toiled up the hill and spent most of the day constructing a path to make life easier for the Japanese Sergeants. When the work was complete we were famished. There were, however, 'ways and means'.

The 'black market' at Miyata was under the control of the Dutch other ranks who worked underground in the mine. Over the years they had established many contacts there and they smuggled into the camp various delicacies, for the most part concealed in little bags slung in their grimy crotches.

Unlike the 'black market' at Zentsuji where the American enlisted men withheld, or stole, for re-sale foodstuffs which should have been distributed among their fellow P.o.W.s, the Miyata 'black market' was respectable. Everything the Dutch miners smuggled into camp was the subject of a barter or a purchase by them; and they took a great personal risk every time they brought such contraband into the camp.

Many dwindling stocks of yen were further diminished to 'celebrate' the completion of the Sergeants' 'cat-walk'. I bought three hard biscuits, each the size of the palm of my hand. They were absolutely tasteless; they chipped off two bits of teeth; but they were worth it. The string around my stomach was not tied so tightly that night.

Another order was promulgated by the Camp Commandant. We were to write letters describing the horrors of the Americans' indiscriminate bombing of the civilian population, the zeal and determination with which the Japanese Armed Forces were waging the war, and would continue to wage it to the bitter end, and the excellent state of our health. Our future treatment in the camp would depend upon the accuracy with which we described these three things.

From time to time the camp staff came round to see what progress we were making with these essays.

They were never despatched. Events were to move too quickly.

I was looking out of the window at the superb and well-wooded hills with which the camp was surrounded. The beauty of this otherwise breath-taking scene was sadly marred by the ugly mine shafts and exposed outcrops of coal deposits.

An Australian other rank entered the room and disturbed my reverie.

'Can I have a word with you, sir?' he enquired.

'By all means,' I replied. At Zentsuji I might have been able to have offered him a cigarette or one of my home-made fish-powder cakes. At Miyata I could only invite him to sit down on my bed-space.

'You were at Zentsuji, sir?' he asked.

When I nodded my assent, he went on:

'Can you tell me about some of the Australian officers there? I was captured with Colonel Scanlon at Rabaul. A fine officer, sir. How is he? And how are the others?'

I gave him all the news I could.

He told me that to start with he had been in captivity with most of the other Australians in his unit, who had been taken prisoner with him. When they had been sent to another camp he had been too ill to move. After he had recovered he had been sent to Miyata, the only Australian among a large Dutch party. A few individual Australians had subsequently arrived at Miyata, but none of them was from his unit and he had not known any of them. He had been very lonely during the past couple of years, cut off from his 'cobbers'.

There was no doubt that members of the same unit who had got to know each other well, either in peacetime or, even more so, in action, before they were taken prisoner, could do much to sustain each other's morale in captivity. This was even more markedly so where officers shared captivity with their own men.

It had struck me very forcibly that, at Zentsuji, Colonel Scanlon and his Australian officers had formed a very closely knit group. Similarly, the officers of H.M.S. *Exeter* mutually supported each other in adversity in a way which just never seemed to happen as between members of the same service, or even between fellow-nationals, who had not been in intimate contact with each other before they were taken prisoner.

Throughout my captivity I had felt that this was particularly so among the R.A.F. P.o.W.s. They rarely seemed to have been members of the same units as other R.A.F. prisoners in the same camp.

I knew just how my Australian visitor felt. I hoped I had cheered him up a bit.

I was suddenly switched to another working party. We laboured on a farm much closer to the mine and under the direct control of the Mine Manager. There I found quite a different atmosphere. The Farm Superintendent, Honda, employed by the mining company, was quite agreeable. We found ourselves working side by side with aged Japanese, who had many years as underground mineworkers behind them. They were the salt of the earth, kindly, thoughtful and, despite their obvious poverty, hospitable. They would share their own meagre rations with us, giving us tea, titbits and cigarettes.

Although we were usually accompanied by a sleepy guard or two, it was Honda who was responsible for seeing that we worked. We were spared the attentions of the irrepressible goons who were conspicuous by their absence. Someone, I hoped, must have noticed how much more effective work the P.o.W.s did in such circumstances.

This agreeable interlude did not last long and we were soon back in the valley. There, days marked by heat and glare alternated with days marked by rain and wind. The only constant was the ever-present tribe of goons, with their searchings, beatings and attempts at degradation.

After one such particularly wearing day I had just dropped off to sleep when I was woken up by a goon who demanded my immediate presence in the camp office. I was required to interpret for the Wing Commander who himself had been summoned to the office from his bed in connection with a protest he had made.

The Japanese guards and goons had been making a practice of entering the huts after work and demanding that all kit should be put on the floor. They would then go through this. They were particularly interested in soap and cigarettes, of which they themselves were desperately short. If they found any, they would point to themselves and, threatening the owner with their rifles, say 'Presento?' Whatever the owner replied he had seen the last of his soap or cigarettes.

These 'hold-ups' were becoming so common that a protest had to be, and was, made.

When the Wing Commander and I had staggered down the hill to the camp office we found that one of the less pleasant Sergeants was dealing with this protest. No doubt he had hoped to keep it from the notice of the Camp Commandant.

The Wing Commander repeated his complaint and the Sergeant listened unconcernedly to my translation.

Suddenly the Commandant came into the office on an obviously unexpected visit. The change in the atmosphere nearly destroyed my 'antennae'.

The Sergeant immediately launched into a discussion of the kit inspection which was due to be held the following day. We made an effort to raise the question of the 'hold-ups' but were unceremoniously pushed out of the office before we could get the point across. We returned to our beds.

About three hours later, at midnight, the guards rushed into the huts, turning on all the lights and jumping all over the recumbent forms with their heavy muddy boots, brandishing their rifles to which they had affixed their bayonets.

'This is it,' I thought, 'the American invasion has started and we are all to be bayoneted in our beds.'

But no! All officers were to assemble on the parade ground immediately. 'Perhaps that is where we are going to be bayoneted to death,' I thought.

The guards waited while we 'dressed' and then, amid the usual cuffings and cloutings they marched us down, in pitch darkness, to the parade ground.

There we saw a couple of lorries. Another thought ran through my mind, 'The Americans have landed and we are to be taken off in the lorries to another camp—or to be shot in the hills.'

We fell in, propping up the sick and dying, as was customary on such occasions. Then the order was given that all the sick were to return to their beds. The sigh of relief was almost audible.

Another order followed. All officer P.o.W.s were now to unload nails and sweet potatoes—an unusual assortment—from the lorries.

Wing Commander Matthews and I were spared this chore. We were summoned, once again, although it was now 12.30 a.m., to resume our discussion of the Wing Commander's protest with the Sergeant. We were a little disappointed to see that the Camp Commandant was no longer visible. The Sergeant was not afraid of us but he was afraid of the Commandant.

After several hours of inconclusive discussion we were dismissed to return to bed. The protest appeared to have been rejected on the unassailable grounds that there was nothing to protest about.

But the officers had been pulled out of bed in the middle of the night to teach them that protests did not pay.

The following day we were weighed. I was now under ninety pounds—less than half my normal weight.

I

It looked as though our weights would continue to decline. On the same day a more rigorous search than usual revealed that five returning Dutch miners were wearing their little 'crotch-bags' full of pancakes, biscuits, etc. They were put in the solitary confinement cells for twenty-four hours and beaten up every quarter of an hour by the Japanese gorillas. What was left of the Dutch was then slung into the hut which served as a 'sick-bay'.

By mid-July 1945 we were living like animals—very close to the earth. The Commandant took a delight in degrading the officers. I was a member of an inside working party whose coolie task was to carry heavy buckets of 'night-soil' from the *benjos* to a plot just outside the camp perimeter, on which *taroh* was growing. The paths and terraces were a morass of slippery mud from the torrential summer rainstorms. The slopes were so steep that the heavy bucket, slung on a pole between us, seemed to be permanently stuck to the back of the man in front. If, as frequently happened, we slipped and fell, the contents of the overturned bucket had to be replaced with our bare hands. As it was easier to wash our emaciated bodies than our ragged clothes, this loathsome task was performed in the minimum of clothing—a *hundoshi*.

The Commandant, who could never be found whenever we had occasion to lodge protests in the camp office, took an undisguised delight in personally supervising our performance of this menial task.

Suddenly he ordered us to stop. The relief to our aching backs and sensitive nostrils was premature. He had another, and seemingly more revolting, task for us to perform.

The heavy rains had brought down a mass of slime and mud from the hillside, which had choked the paddy-fields below. We were ordered to take off our boots and socks and to wade barefooted into this quagmire. There we were to remove the filth with our bare hands and put it into baskets, taking care not to damage the by now invisible paddy-plants. The mud was knee-deep. Then the rain came down in sheets. Like a hail of pitchforks, it pierced the raw patches on our bare bodies, burnt by weeks of work at the valley farm under the pitiless sun.

At that moment I felt more miserable and dejected than I had ever felt in my life.

Our next working assignment led to a further protest to the Camp Commandant. An officers' working party, of which I was a member, was detailed for surface work at the mine. This involved very exhausting manual work moving heavy balks of timber from one part of the mine to another.

Since we had arrived at Miyata it seemed to have been tacitly agreed between the Camp Commandant and the senior P.o.W. officers that while officers would work on the farms or in the camp— we had no option about this anyway—they would not be required to work at the mine.

The detailing of officers to work at the mine created a precedent which the Wing Commander was determined to challenge at the earliest possible opportunity. I accompanied him to the camp office to interpret.

As always, the most senior representative of His Imperial Majesty that we could find was a Corporal. We lodged our protest. The Corporal's reply was clear and to the point:

'Officer P.o.W.s are required to do any type of work for which they may be detailed by the Commander.'

When the Wing Commander boldly questioned this, a Sergeant was sent for who confirmed his subordinate's ruling, adding that no distinction was made between officers and other ranks at Miyata. This was not wholly true, as officers were discriminated against on all possible occasions.

The Sergeant took the opportunity of favouring us with a lengthy, and very menacing, address in which he listed the shortcomings of the British and Americans generally and our own wickednesses in particular.

The officers continued to work at the mine. Particular care was taken by the Commandant to ensure that all senior P.o.W. officers were away working at the mine when the Japanese Colonel commanding all the Fukuoka War Prisoners Camps visited Miyata.

When our next rest day came round on Wednesday the 25th July 1945 the officer P.o.W.s were required to fall-in three times on the parade ground, and were then, after standing at attention on each occasion for half an hour, dismissed. As previously, the object of this exercise was to show that protests did not pay.*

---

* An outline of the main developments which occurred in Japan between the 28th July and the 15th August 1945 will be found in Appendix II. The P.o.W.s at Miyata knew nothing about these momentous events at the time. The reader, however, may find this outline interesting as a backdrop to the scenes to be played on our little stage at Miyata.

On Monday the 6th August 1945, although we did not know it then, the first atomic bomb fell on Hiroshima, about 150 miles away from Miyata. My thirty-fourth birthday fell on the 8th, two days later.

Before attempting to describe the 'indescribable' events which marked my thirty-fourth birthday and which are for ever indelibly imprinted on my memory, it is necessary to go back a bit.

During the first few days of August I found myself once again a member of the valley farm working party. For most of this time the Wing Commander had remained in camp in a gallant effort to see the Commandant. He was determined to get some satisfaction about his many outstanding protests, all of which had been brushed aside by subordinate members of the camp staff.

I had had several conversations with the Sergeant-in-charge of the guard which was escorting us on these excursions. He was one of the less disagreeable of our captors and I wanted, if I could, to find out exactly what was going on in the minds of the Camp Authorities and, more important still, what was going on in the outside world.

During the first of these talks the Sergeant repeated what we had already heard *ad nauseam*, namely that the British officers from Zentsuji were an arrogant lot and that it was time we realised that we were P.o.W.s. He then went on to elaborate about the impertinence of the Wing Commander in trying to secure access to the Camp Commandant over the heads of the Japanese N.C.O.s.

'Matthews,' he said, 'has remained in the camp today to try and see the Nipponese Commander. He will be thrown out of the office every time he appears. Those are my Commander's orders. And if he goes on there will be trouble for all of you.'

'But Wing Commander Matthews has a right, and a duty, to protest to the Camp Commandant,' I replied. 'He has plenty of courage and we respect him for it.'

'You are as arrogant as he is,' he retorted. 'Why do you interpret his protests for him?'

'It is my duty to obey my senior officers,' I replied, 'and I am glad to be able to help him.'

'You will all be in trouble soon if this protesting does not stop,' he said.

Despite the unsatisfactory tenor of this conversation, the Sergeant remained in a good mood. I asked whether we might light a fire to warm up our midday rice. He agreed. Later, as the afternoon heat beat down upon us, I asked if we might have a break. He agreed again.

We returned to the camp as weary and hungry as ever but not as despondent as we had been on some previous occasions. The Sergeant had kept the goons under control and it was not raining.

On Monday the 6th August I engaged the same Sergeant in conversation again. He told me that there had been many heavy bombing raids at Moji and Fukuoka. This was hardly news as we were now used to the sounds of ever-increasing aerial activity. We had grown accustomed, too, to hearing the thud of heavy bombs falling in the distance. He added, however, that in parts of Japan many P.o.W.s had been killed in these American raids.

It must have been about four o'clock in the afternoon, just before we were due to pack up for the day, when the Japanese equivalent of a Land Rover was seen approaching in a cloud of dust along one of the tracks. The vehicle stopped and a member of the Japanese Military Police beckoned to the Sergeant to approach. There was a hurried conversation and the Sergeant returned, looking grim-faced and angry. It was clearly not the moment to engage him in conversation and in any event he gave me no chance.

He barked out orders that we were to pack up and return to the camp immediately.

I had succeeded in getting myself allocated to an inside working party on Wednesday the 8th August, my birthday. Three of my fellow P.o.W.s had each given me a cigarette to mark the occasion. I had never expected to spend four birthdays in captivity.

The Japanese guards had been irritable and in a bad humour all day. In the morning all work had been stopped to enable them to hold a ceremonial parade. It was the eighth day of the eighth month and one of the days on which the Divine Imperial Rescript had to be read to all members of the Japanese Armed Forces, wherever they were serving.

I had learnt over the years that the reading of this Rescript, which was designed to re-kindle the spirit of *Bushido*, nearly always did. In particular, the words 'death is lighter than a feather, but duty is higher than a mountain' seemed to fan the flames of Japanese fanaticism into a roar of hate. Trouble of some sort usually followed hard on the heels of such a reading. It had not been an auspicious beginning to my birthday.

After my bath and evening meal I had to go down to the camp office to ask for the return of a violin which had been 'borrowed' or stolen by a Japanese guard from one of the Dutch other ranks.

Kurihara, the normally pleasant camp Sergeant who had escorted us from Zentsuji, was on duty. I hardly recognised him. He launched into a tirade against the Wing Commander, who, he told me with relish, had been thrown out of the office several times recently. Kurihara then attacked me for interpreting for the Wing Commander. Finally, he said that he was going to beat up all the Zentsuji officers and reduce them to such a state of pulp that they would wish they had never been born.

I left the office without the violin and without much hope of a quiet night.

After the evening roll-call the officer P.o.W.s were ordered to remain behind on the parade ground, in one corner of which was the bath-house.

Kurihara arrived with a large thick bamboo pole. He was joined by a number of the gorillas with their deadly pick-helves. The guard commander on duty turned up with a large stave pulled off a broken hand-cart.

Sergeant Kurihara, who was the senior Japanese present, called us to attention. He then ordered all 'Fukuoka' officers, that meant all officers who had come to Miyata from other camps in the Fukuoka War Prisoners Command, to fall out and return to their huts.

The Fukuoka officers had previously told us that mass beatings had been organised by the Japanese N.C.O.s in other Fukuoka camps commanded by our present Commandant, and with his knowledge and approval.

The noose was now tightening round Zentsuji necks.

We were ordered to form two ranks, about twelve feet apart, from the lower to the upper end of the sloping ground. All lights, except one very bright arc-light which was focussed on a wooden platform, were extinguished.

Kurihara then mounted the platform and started his speech. He was interpreted by the camp's P.o.W. Japanese expert, a Dutch naval Lieutenant, who had been Assistant Naval Attaché at the Dutch Embassy in Tokyo before the war. Like his counterpart, the American Naval Lieutenant, Wilson, at Zentsuji, he was a qualified Japanese interpreter and translator.

The Zentsuji officers had been complaining and protesting far too much, Kurihara said. Wing Commander Matthews had actually dared to try to see the Commandant without going through the camp office. The Zentsuji officers were always grumbling about the work. They did not conduct themselves like soldiers, least of all like soldiers in disgrace for having allowed themselves to be taken prisoner. Soldiers must learn to obey and the arrogant British officer war prisoners must learn to obey, without question, the orders of their captors, the brave sons of Nippon.

'You wear your hair too long,' he shouted, 'you wear moustaches. Only brave soldiers may wear moustaches, not contemptible prisoners who should be dead.'

Kurihara, who had obviously learnt much from Tojo's propaganda machine during the previous few years, then treated us to a *tour d'horizon* of South-East Asia. He lingered on British oppression in India, Burma, Malaya and the Pacific Islands. Indeed, he told us much about British actions in Malaya of which I was quite unaware.

'You think,' he yelled, 'that the British are superior to the peoples of Asia. I tell you, you are wrong. You are soft. You are decadent. You believe in material things. We believe in the things of the spirit.'

At times his voice reached such a pitch of frenzy that I thought he was going to have a seizure and fall off the platform. He nearly floored the Dutch interpreter, standing at his side, on a number of occasions as he gesticulated wildly with his flailing arms.

Eventually he was exhausted.

The Dutch interpreter had wisely limited himself to translating only about half of what Kurihara had said, but that was far too much. We had heard it all before but never quite at such length. Any one of us could have delivered the same speech in his sleep.

The silence was electric as Kurihara studied his victims with a sneering smile.

Suddenly he shouted: 'All those who want to protest about their treatment here will take a pace forward.'

Not a man moved.

'All those who agree with what I have said and who agree to obey orders will lift their right arms.'

Every man raised his arm. Then the gorillas went to work beating all those who had, in error, raised their left arms or whose arms were not raised high enough. Some, when the aching became too intense, tried to change arms.

Kurihara observed this and promptly ordered everyone to raise both arms. The beatings continued and Kurihara resumed his speech to the forest of imploring arms in front of him.

'For your behaviour,' he yelled, 'you shall be punished and punished severely. You will wish you had never been born.'

At this stage Wing Commander Matthews most gallantly took a pace forward and, addressing Kurihara through the Dutch interpreter, said:

'If I have done wrong, though I do not think I have, then I, and I alone, should be punished. It was I who made the protests and I take full responsibility for them. The others have done nothing. They should not be punished. They should not suffer.'

But Kurihara and the others were not now prepared to deny themselves the pleasure of the meal to which they had been looking forward all day. The *hors-d'œuvres* had already been served; the main dishes would have to follow.

Dropping his voice Kurihara said quietly, 'In Nippon we have a principle. All must suffer for the sins of a few, or even of one.'

There was another silence as the courageous Wing Commander resumed his place.

'Now you will all be punished,' said Kurihara, resuming his high-pitched scream. 'You will all get down on the ground—on your hands and feet but without your knees touching the ground.'

By now the full team of gorillas was in attendance. Springing out of the darkness with their heavy pick-helves, they lammed into the arched backs of those who had managed to retain this position for a few seconds and belaboured indiscriminately those who had not. Many of the P.o.W.s collapsed into crumpled bleeding masses. Several with sore backs and bad boils, screaming with agony, were dragged by the now maddened guards into the bath-house, revived with cold water and hauled out again for a further bout of clubbings. The most fortunate were those who lost consciousness at the first blow.

Quite apart from the physical pain, which was more intense than anything I had ever had to endure personally, the whole episode was so sadistic and obscene that, like many others, I was physically sick where I lay.

The beatings went on for a quarter of an hour or more. Then, penetrating the miasma which surrounded us, the echoes of Kurihara's voice ordering us to our feet reached out towards our bleeding ears. Some would never get on their feet again that night, however loudly he shouted. Few could stand without support from their neighbours on both sides. Some forty men, each one of them holding

His Majesty's Commission, swayed from side to side in a congealed mass, like some huge indecent jelly flecked with red.

Kurihara had not finished with us yet. He looked around for the Dutch interpreter. The latter, perhaps assuming that his services would no longer be required once the pogrom was under way, had wisely slipped off into the darkness. To my horror, Kurihara spotted me and beckoned to me to mount the platform beside him.

'You are always ready to interpret for Matthews when he makes his impudent protests. This time you can interpret for me,' he said.

Kurihara embarked upon the second part of his address. This was largely a re-hash of the first part. As most of his audience was only semi-conscious, it mattered little what I said. I was, myself, shaking like the huge jelly which was wobbling before my eyes and I could not think very clearly.

At one stage Kurihara required all those who believed that Europeans were superior to Japanese to raise their right arms. I thought he had said, and I had so interpreted, that all those who did not believe that Europeans were superior to Japanese should raise their arms.

I could see in the darkness, as I had expected, some feebly waving arms. Kurihara let out a bellow and turned to order the executioners to get to work again. It was then that I realised my mistake and I apologised for misinterpreting him. The last thing I heard was Kurihara's grunt to one of his strong-arm 'boys' nearby.

Someone must have carried me back to bed, as they carried the others who were unconscious. I had two long scalp wounds on my head, which was aching uncommonly when I woke up the next morning, the 9th August. I had also lost three teeth.

When I could manage it I stumbled round to the Dutch doctor's 'consulting room', which was on the verandah of the hut in which he slept. He dressed my cuts and said that he did not think my skull was fractured.

I took the opportunity of this visit to ask the doctor about my ribs which had been hurting me a lot. He examined them and said that they were disintegrating as a result of a deficiency of calcium phosphate. One of them was broken in two places and another in one.

'They will soon mend when you get some decent food,' he said cheerfully.

'And when will that be?' I wondered.

He gave me a biscuit with butter on it. We sat chatting for a few minutes. I asked him the time. He replied that it was eleven o'clock.

Neither of us was conscious of the fact that just at that moment the second atomic bomb was bursting over Nagasaki, about sixty miles away.

12

The Moment of Risk

Miyata, Kyushu—August–September 1945

Life resumed its uneven tenor at Miyata.

I went to the mines with a small working party of five, which included Tim Hallam.

It was Tim's first time out since he had arrived back from Kobe a few days earlier. There he had been subjected to several severe, but apparently successful, operations for cancer of the mouth. He had told us that Kobe and Osaka had been 'flattened' by American bombing. In the Kobe P.o.W. camp in which he was accommodated pending his operations, four prisoners had been killed and many wounded during an American air raid.

Our task of moving heavy pit-props was frequently interrupted by the air-raid sirens. Someone counted 174 U.S. aircraft in the bright blue sky above us. 'Dog-fights' were going on all around and we could see both Allied and Japanese planes plunging to the ground.

The five of us had to move and stack 500 of the ponderous balks of wood before we could return to the camp. Four of us would carry and the fifth would count the props to ensure that the pile was neatly stacked.

I could see that Tim was in a poor way. Not only was his mouth still very sore but I knew that he suffered from two serious hernias. When my turn came to be 'counter and stacker' I suggested to the goon that Tim should do this and that I would go on carrying. The goon refused. Tim could easily have been his grandfather.

Eventually the task was completed and we returned to camp. There we learnt from the Dutch, who had been so informed by

Japanese at the mines, that Russia had entered the war and was occupying Manchuria.

After I had had my bath and meal Kurihara came round to my hut with two pretty little Japanese girls whom he described as his 'sisters'.

He asked me to arrange a concert to be held in the Sergeants' quarters after the evening roll-call. The Wing Commander and myself were to be present.

I dashed off to sign up such talent as was available. After the roll-call we repaired to the Sergeants' quarters. They were all there. Kurihara, the gorillas, the guard commander and others, including, of course, the two 'sisters'.

These were the Japanese who had beaten us up forty-eight hours earlier. 'Were they anxious to make amends?' I wondered. 'Had they some idea that the end of the war was near?'

They beamed and cracked jokes, they handed round beer, sweets and cigarettes. What was more surprising still, in view of Kurihara's recent diatribes against Western decadence, was their insistence that the Dutch P.o.W. quartet should sing over and over again such numbers as 'Dinah', 'My Blue Heaven', and so on. Tangos, in particular, seemed to appeal to our 'hosts'.

I could see that the performers, mostly Dutch other ranks who worked underground in the mine, were desperately tired. They frequently asked me to seek permission for them to leave and go to bed, but Kurihara would not hear of it.

Eventually it became clear that the time was approaching for the 'sisters' to play their parts and for us to withdraw. I was glad to observe that Kurihara gave the Dutch lads a little extra food to take away as a reward for all their exertions.

We returned wearily to our respective huts. It was rather like going back to our respective colleges after a party in someone's room at Oxford.

I lay awake for some time, trying to fathom what made these incomprehensible people tick. As my eyes closed, a nursery rhyme of my childhood passed through my mind:

> 'There was a little girl,
> Who had a little curl,
> Right in the middle of her forehead.
> And when she was good

She was very, very good.
But when she was bad, she was horrid.'

It must have been on the 11th August that copies of an 'open letter'* to the British Government were brought round by the Japanese to be signed by every P.o.W. in the camp. We played for time which, by now, we felt was on our side, saying that we would have to read and consider it carefully before signing it. It was never signed.

August the 15th was a lovely day. There had been no air raids for twenty-four hours. We were out working in the valley farm. About 4 p.m. a goon arrived from the camp on a bicycle and spoke to the Sergeant. The latter then told us that His Imperial Majesty had broadcast a message to the people of Nippon at midday. We were to pack up immediately and return to camp.

As usual, I went into the camp office, as soon as the working party was dismissed, to find out how many men would be required for the valley farm the following day. I was informed by the Camp Sergeant that there would be no officers' working parties on the 16th. One of the Corporals in the office, no doubt in a vain attempt to save some 'face', added that there was an epidemic of small-pox in the neighbourhood and that, as always, the Japanese did not want us to run any risks.

The camp was alive with rumours. A party returning from the mine said that they had been told by some Japanese mine-workers that the Emperor had graciously agreed to the frantic appeals of the Allies for an armistice. Another group had been inform-ed that the Emperor's broadcast was a personal appeal to His Majesty, King George VI, to join him in persuading the Americans to bring the war to an end. Another report suggested that the war had ended at twelve noon and that since that time talks between the Japanese and the Americans, to settle certain details, had been proceeding on board a United States battleship in Tokyo Bay. It was also bruited around that the Russians had conquered the whole of Manchuria.

Later in the evening of the 15th I was sent down to the camp office by the Wing Commander to ask whether, as the following day was to be a special rest day, officers could be excused from attending the morning roll-call. The request was refused.

* The full text of this document is reproduced as Appendix III.

I was interested to observe that goons had been posted all round the camp office to prevent any P.o.W.s from entering. Inside the wireless was going at full blast. I was not allowed to enter the camp office and the Sergeant himself came outside to convey the refusal of our request.

In the middle of the night I was woken up by a Dutch other rank, a member of the underground night shift at the mine. He whispered to me that when his shift had reported for work at 1 a.m. they had been sent back to camp and informed that they would not be going to the mine again.

Our unexpected rest day on the 16th was a day of speculation. Most of us were now only prepared to accept facts. Rumours had disappointed us far too often in the past. But the facts themselves were sensational enough. The Emperor had undoubtedly made a broadcast; all work, except for a few minor camp fatigues, had ceased and there had been no air raids for forty-eight hours.

On the 17th there was another welcome change. As there were now no working parties, with differing scales of rations, every P.o.W. would receive the same amount. For the officers this meant a modest increase.

The same day the Japanese Sergeant-Major, Hayashi, made the strange announcement at roll-call that smoking was not permitted while prisoners were dancing.

There had still been no official word from the Camp Commandant, who was as elusive as ever. Padre Godfrey must have had a greater measure of faith than most of us, as he arranged, at short notice, a Service of Thanksgiving which was attended by virtually every prisoner who was able to stand. Some of us subsequently wondered if the Padre had not been a bit premature. Prisoners continued to be beaten up for not saluting guards and goons and for other minor offences.

There was an issue of all that was left of the Red Cross supplies in the store. This amounted to three small tins of butter, a tin of dried milk and a tin of jam per man.

At the evening roll-call on the 17th Sergeant Kurihara made the surprising, and disturbing, announcement that we should all be ready for another air-raid precautions exercise. When the alarm went we should take with us down the disused mine-shaft not only two blankets but also all our personal possessions.

'What did this mean?' we wondered. It was only later that we discovered its sinister import.

No one slept much during the night of the 18th/19th, expecting to be woken up for the forecasted A.R.P. practice.

During the morning of Sunday the 19th the Camp Commandant sent for the Dutch interpreter and told him that the war was over. In a jovial mood the Commandant added that P.o.W.s could now smoke when they liked, that the two camp pigs would have to be killed and consumed before we left the camp and that he would entertain any requests which the senior P.o.W. officers might wish to put to him.

At midday a Japanese aircraft was observed dropping leaflets over the mine area outside the camp.

While we were resting after our midday meal the Wing Commander was summoned to the camp office. We all assumed that the Camp Commandant wished to discuss with him various matters which would have to be settled for the duration of this 'twilight' existence.

We were dumbfounded when the Wing Commander returned with the order that all officers were to parade immediately in working clothes. He added that an English-speaking Japanese guard had told him that hostilities had broken out again, and that when the Japanese guards had heard this they had exclaimed: 'Thanks be to His Imperial Majesty. Now we can all fight to the end and die as soldiers should.'

By now the strain of all these uncertainties was beginning to tell on every one of us. Some of the officers, convinced that there must be some misunderstanding, took their time to get off their bed-spaces and to put on their working clothes; and further time was lost in heated discussions.

Those who were late down on the parade ground, including myself, were beaten on the head or across the shoulders by the guards. One officer had his eye split open.

We were formed into squads under the direction of Sergeant Kurihara who was in his most evil mood. Our task now, it seemed, was to strengthen all air-raid shelters.

Eventually the Commandant arrived and took charge. We gathered that the leaflets which we had observed being dropped on the mine area had been issued by a General in the Kyushu command, possibly even by the Kyushu Area Army Commander, and were to the effect that, whatever the Emperor might have said in his broadcast, all Japanese soldiers in Kyushu at least were going to do their duty and fight to the last man.

We spent the afternoon, in a most despondent mood, strengthening the camp's air-raid shelters. Some of the old hands, who were well acquainted with the mine, assured us that they could hear the coal-washing and other machinery, which had been silent for several days, being started up again.

At the evening roll-call Sergeant Kurihara informed us that, owing to the small-pox epidemic, we would not be resuming work for a day or two but that we should do all our laundry and other chores so as to be ready for work in three or four days' time.

During the night of 19th/20th those sleeping in the hut nearest the camp office saw many Japanese despatch-riders coming into the camp with orders, over which the camp staff pored throughout the night.

On the 20th I had occasion to go to the camp office and found Kurihara there.

'Why were the officers late for the parade yesterday?' he asked. 'I was sorry that I had to beat them for being late. But they should not have been late.'

'Well, we never expected a parade,' I replied, 'and the officers were all over the place. Some were trying to get some sleep in the dining-hall and it took time to let them know.'

'War prisoners must always be ready for parades at all times,' Kurihara retorted sharply.

'But we are not P.o.W.s now,' I said, 'or at least, we are P.o.W.s awaiting repatriation.'

'Why do you say that?' he asked. 'You are war prisoners and you will be until you die.'

'But the Commandant told the Dutch interpreter only yesterday morning that the war was over,' I said.

'The Camp Commander never said that,' Kurihara shouted. 'You are lying—or dreaming. The war is not over. And even if it was, you would still be P.o.W.s—as you will be for ever, until you die.'

As was usual with Kurihara it was an inconclusive discussion. But I noticed that heavy baggage belonging to the guards had been packed and was now stacked in a corner of the camp office.

As I returned to my hut, I passed by the cook-house and had a word with one of the cooks. He told me an amusing tale. When the Camp Commandant had told the Dutch interpreter, on the 19th, that the war was over and that the two pigs would have to be slaughtered, the P.o.W. butcher promptly went off and killed one of the pigs. The carcass was hung up in the cook-house.

During the afternoon and evening of the same day the Camp Commandant, and the camp staff, had become convinced that some 'fire-eating' General was making a last-ditch stand on Kyushu and that hostilities had broken out again. Thereupon the Japanese cooks and butchers left their own cook-house and descended *en masse* on the P.o.W. cook-house. They demanded the carcass of the pig which, they claimed, had been prematurely killed by the over-eager P.o.W. butcher. Hostilities broke out between the staffs of the rival cook-houses and in the struggle the pig's head came off. The Japanese, however, obtained the greater part of the carcass.

When on the 20th it appeared that the rumours of a last-ditch stand in Kyushu were not based on fact the P.o.W. cooks and butchers mounted a raid on the Japanese cook-house.

After a bitter struggle, during which the pig's legs were pulled off, the P.o.W.s succeeded in recovering the greater part of this meat.

A number of Japanese civilians who worked in the P.o.W. cook-house as clerks and storekeepers now entered the lists. Believing that the war was over and thinking of their famished families and the probability of unemployment ahead, they took the opportunity of the P.o.W. cooks' rest period to reduce the remnants of the pig into even smaller pieces, which they concealed about their persons. When the P.o.W. cooks returned, after the Japanese civilians had left, there was nothing of the pig left except the severed head.

The Japanese civilians did not, however, get very far with their loot. When they were searched by the Japanese guards at the camp gate the remnants of the pig were found and removed from them. The Japanese guards on duty wasted no time. They grilled the remains there and then and consumed them on the spot.

On learning of this, the P.o.W. butcher went out and slaughtered the second pig. It was reported that he slept with the carcass until it was ready for the stew.

On the 21st August a Japanese Major and two Lieutenants were observed going round the camp escorted by the Sergeant-Major, Hayashi. We thought it strange that no opportunity was afforded either to Wing Commander Matthews or to the Senior Dutch Officer to meet them.

One of the Japanese Corporals told me the same day that apart from reproducing the text of the Emperor's broadcast, the Japanese press had disclosed nothing whatever about what was going on.

I recorded my views in my diary, later that evening, as follows: 'I am inclined to the view that the terms of the Armistice will not be made public in this country until we prisoners have been handed over; and that whatever Japanese power, be it the Emperor or the Government, which has signed the peace, will need Allied support and all kinds of co-operation, if a revolution is to be avoided when the terms are known.'

It was not until 10 a.m. on Wednesday the 22nd August 1945 that we heard, officially, the news for which we had been waiting for three and a half long years.

The whole camp was paraded, the inevitable table was produced, and the Camp Commandant addressed us. He first read out a message in Japanese from the Colonel Commanding all the P.o.W. Camps in the Fukuoka group. This was translated by a Japanese interpreter, whom we had not seen before, into an English reminiscent of the first Elizabethan era.

The gist was as follows: hostilities formally ceased on Saturday the 18th August, thus confirming the *de facto* cessation of hostilities which had started on the 15th; we would soon be returning to our families; we would be handed over to the Allies at ports to be designated later; and meanwhile the camp staff would do their best for us for as long as we had to remain at Miyata.

Regrets were expressed for the deaths of those of our comrades who had not lived to witness this great day; the camp staff had always done their best for us; if they had not done more, it was because of circumstances beyond their control.

The interpreter then referred to one presumably 'mythical' camp where the P.o.W.s had been so grateful for all that their compassionate guards had done for them that they had made them 'liberal grants' from their Red Cross parcels. At this a Dutch officer standing nearby whispered to me:

'I've been here three years. These bloody Nips have stolen most of the small quantities of Red Cross supplies which have ever reached this God-forsaken dump. What a lot of two-faced bastards!'

'Moreover,' the interpreter added, 'the kind and deeply grateful war prisoners in that camp, considering that Red Cross nourishment was inadequate to pay their great debt to the kind and gentle guards, have never ceased to press upon them presents from their own valuable personal belongings.'

It went on in this vein for half an hour or more. It was a little reminiscent, I thought, of the sales-talk accompanying a 'whip-round', at the end of the summer term, to buy a wedding-present for a popular games master who was getting married during the holidays.

I suppose that if we had been really courageous we would have shouted out, 'How can you dare to say such things on this very ground on which, just two weeks ago, some fifty British officers were all but beaten to death?' But we were still anxious; there were many unchartered rocks and eddies ahead and this was not the time to rock the boat.

The camp staff subsequently told the Wing Commander that it would probably be another ten days before we were moved. In the meantime morning roll-call would be at 6.30 a.m. instead of 5.30 and there would be no more beatings, 'provided we obeyed the rules'.

As we discussed these matters among ourselves later, Ricky Wright Tim Hallam and I tried to picture the final ceremony at Habu.

It was at Habu, our first camp in Japan, and particularly during that first terrible Japanese winter of 1942–3, that we had really learnt all that we would ever learn about what it meant to be a P.o.W. in Japan. It was at Habu that the constant irritations had formed the nacre into pearls around the grains of sand, which were all that was left, after the *Dai Nichi Maru*, of our battered personalities.

What had happened at Zentsuji and what had happened at Miyata had prised the oysters open on many occasions. But nothing, nothing could touch those Habu pearls, of whatever quality they might be, which would be embedded in us for ever.

We wished that we could have been at Habu for the final ceremony.

Few slept soundly at Miyata on the night of Wednesday the 22nd August. Was it my imagination or did I really hear brave men weeping, men who had never permitted themselves a cry or a whimper, however hard they had been beaten.

Further relaxations of discipline were announced on the 23rd. There would be no more roll-calls and only the Japanese Camp Commandant would rate a salute in the future. Sergeant-Major Hayashi went to the War Prisoners Administration Headquarters in Fukuoka. We hoped this meant that things were moving.

When Hayashi returned early on the 24th we were told that the letters 'P.W.' were to be painted in yellow on the roofs of the main buildings in the camp. There was no lack of volunteers for this task.

In the evening of that day Sergeant Kurihara took to task some of the Dutch P.o.W.s who had been working all day painting the roofs. They had added to the letters 'P.W.' the word 'FOOD', to which Kurihara took exception.

'You must not ask for food,' he said. 'We give you much food here. You must change that.'

'O.K.,' replied the Dutch, 'we will change it early tomorrow morning.'

The Japanese were not, therefore, surprised to see Dutch P.o.W.s up on the roofs at first light the following day, the 25th. It was not until it was too late that the Japanese noticed that the Dutch had painted the word 'NO' in even larger letters in front of the word 'FOOD'.

With somewhat more justification than on the previous occasion, a second General Thanksgiving Service was held on the 24th. This Service was conducted partly in English and partly in Dutch. The Service was concluded by the singing of the American, Dutch and British National Anthems, in that order. As practically everyone, irrespective of nationality, knew the British National Anthem, this was sung last as the finale.

It was the first time I had sung it, or even heard it sung, for over three years.

By now we were beginning to discipline ourselves. P.o.W.s were strutting around the camp in pairs, wearing 'M.P.' armbands. Everyone was smartening up, to the fullest extent of his resources, for the final march out of the camp gates. In our innocence we still believed that this might come on the morrow, or, at the latest, the day after.

Late in the evening of the 24th we were told that American aircraft would be flying over the camp very early the next morning, to drop food and messages. They might be expected at any time after 6.30 a.m.

Kurihara, who confirmed this information to me, added, rather ominously, that the reason we had had to paint the letters 'P.W.' on the roofs was that the name and exact whereabouts of Miyata camp, as indeed of all other P.o.W. camps on the island of Kyushu, had not yet been disclosed to the Americans. I was to learn the reason for this later.

Kurihara also told me that there were 200 Japanese troops

'ringing' the camp, some distance away from the perimeter fence. If any food or supplies fell outside the camp the troops had strict orders to bring the errant 'drops' into the camp immediately. We wondered if they ever would.

The excitement was intense as we went to bed on the 24th. This was enhanced for me by the delivery, just before I went to sleep, of two postcards, one from my mother and one from my brother Charles. They had been posted early in March, nearly six months before. It was the first mail to reach Miyata since we had arrived there.

To say that Saturday the 25th August was a bitter disappointment would be an understatement. It was a breaking of many hearts. We stood for hours in the scorching sun, waiting for the planes which never came. It was not just that we were famished and wanted food. It was also that our nerves, frayed by the uncertainties of the past ten days, desperately needed the balm which only the sight of friends, flying freely in the sky not too far above us, could give.

It is true that in the far distance we saw three fighters which we presumed were American. It is true that we subsequently saw a formation of eighteen bombers, flying at a great height, which again we presumed were American. But we saw none of the waving pilots about whom we had all dreamed the night before.

This grievous blow led to a ground-swell of discontent throughout the camp. 'Who can be trusted to tell us the truth?' the P.o.W.s began to mutter. 'Can we believe the Camp Commandant? Can we believe the Wing Commander? Do the Allies know we are here? What is really happening?'

These were dangerous thoughts, for, if pursued too far, they would lead to a breakdown of discipline throughout the camp and, ultimately, to chaos.

The senior P.o.W. officers were now responsible for controlling the pitifully small trickle of food that was still coming into the camp. There were growls of unwarranted criticism about the way these matters were being handled.

The P.o.W. 'Military Police' met with little success in their attempts to prevent their fellows from stealing pumpkins and sweet potatoes from various plots in and around the camp. The goons had all disappeared and many of the Japanese guards failed to turn up for duty. Those who did now wore armbands with 'P.o.W.' in English letters on them, as well as the Japanese character resembling a '7', which stood for *hurioh*, 'prisoner of war'.

The Japanese Camp Authorities issued some clothing. My share was a tunic and pair of slacks which I badly needed. Many of the P.o.W.s immediately exchanged what had been issued to them for scraps of food from the remaining Japanese guards.

Sunday the 26th and Monday the 27th came and went without any supply drops and without any news.

Many P.o.W.s complained that, far from receiving the treatment due to free men, they were not even being treated as P.o.W.s should be treated. This terse assessment of the situation, however accurate, did not do anything to improve our circumstances which appeared to be beyond anyone's control.

The tension in the camp continued to build up. Some Dutch desperadoes broke out of the camp and raided a Japanese farm in an attempt to steal some chickens. Two were killed and others injured by the irate farmer. Another Dutch party broke out at night and raided a liquor store, of which they knew the whereabouts from their days in the mine. Some were said to have died as a result of drinking 'doctored' methylated spirits.

During the morning of the 27th I went down to the camp office to see if I could get any news out of Sergeant-Major Hayashi. He and Kurihara were busy packing up. They were both wearing clothing which I recognised as being part of the issue made on the 25th. Whether they had stolen it or obtained it in exchange for food or cigarettes I did not know, nor did I enquire.

The Sergeant-Major said that we could go for a walk or have a bathe in a nearby lake during the afternoon.

'I will tell two Nippon soldiers to show you the way and to protect you, if you want to go,' he said to me in Japanese.

It had been pouring with rain since midnight and the gale-force winds had broken several of the hut windows during the night. We had had all the bathing we needed for the present and I declined his offer.

He had nothing else to suggest but he could not refrain from mentioning, with a guffaw, that as the electric oven in the cookhouse had broken down, we would not have any bread that night but would have to eat the uncooked mixture which had already been prepared. Kurihara joined in the laughter at this, in their eyes, well-merited misfortune. Then the two of them returned to the task of packing up their loot.

It was Tuesday the 28th that the planes came. Three or four American B.29s were circling round the camp for half an hour or more during the early afternoon. When I enquired of someone whether there were in fact three or four, he replied that it was impossible to tell.

As they turned in their huge sweeps, they disappeared among the neighbouring hills and not more than one, or at the most two, of them were ever visible at the same time.

This observation reminded me of the reply given by a Private newly arrived in Hong Kong, who had found himself doing his first spell of sentry duty. In reply to a question from the Sergeant commanding the guard as to whether he had seen anything, he said: 'Well, Sergeant, I have either seen twenty Chinese or the same Chinese twenty times!'

My companion added that however many aircraft there were they all had large 'V' for Victory signs painted on their tails.

By now all the prisoners were rushing about shouting and waving blankets, towels and home-made flags.

'They must have seen us by now,' we thought as each sweep appeared to bring them lower and lower.

As the planes finally wheeled away without dropping anything, we felt ourselves slipping deeper and deeper into the 'slough of Despond'. Our hopes, which had been raised so high, were once again cruelly dashed to the ground.

One wag suggested that the pilots had mistaken the significances of the letters 'P.W.' and had taken them to mean 'Patiently Waiting'.

'What has happened?' we asked each other. 'What does it all mean?' No one could find an answer.

An answer of a sort came a little later the same afternoon when a Red Cross Delegation appeared in the camp, accompanied by the Colonel Commandant from Fukuoka and various Japanese hangers-on. They started by having an enormous meal of steaks, eggs, pancakes and so on in the Camp Commandant's office. This did not endear them to us. If we had known that these things existed in the Japanese cook-house the visitors would certainly have never enjoyed this spread.

Thus refreshed, the well-fed Delegates, who consisted of a Swiss businessman, Monsieur R. C. Angst, two Swiss diplomats, Messieurs G. B. Blayler and Miasaki (a Swiss though bearing a

Japanese name), and one Swedish diplomat, Monsieur C. E. Necker, summoned for a discussion the senior officers of each nationality represented in the camp. Tim Hallam attended as the senior and, only, Australian officer.

The Delegation then made the following points. They confirmed that the Emperor had broadcast to the world on the 15th August, indicating Japan's willingness to surrender. Subsequently two Japanese plenipotentiaries had gone to Manila. Japan's unconditional surrender had been accepted by the Allies, who had agreed that the Emperor should remain on the throne. Hostilities had ceased in Japan on the 15th and elsewhere on the 18th August. A formal Armistice would be signed on board a U.S. battleship in Tokyo harbour on the 1st September. Allied troops, mainly air-borne and including some British, were due to land in the Tokyo area almost at the same moment as the Delegation was visiting Miyata. U.S. forces were planning to occupy Kagoshima aerodrome, on the southernmost tip of Kyushu, on the 3rd September.

Japan's transport system was in a state of complete chaos. The aircraft which had been dropping supplies on certain P.o.W. camps in Japan were believed to have come from Okinawa.

The Delegation undertook to get in touch with the American forces as soon as the latter had landed and to arrange for relief supplies to be sent to Miyata.

The Delegation expressed the belief that it might be another two or three weeks before any P.o.W.s were moved from Miyata. They would probably go to Nagasaki, a journey which might take ten to twelve hours.

Nagasaki had been completely destroyed by bombing and there would be no accommodation for P.o.W.s in transit there. Another reason for the delay was that Nagasaki harbour was thick with mines which would have to be 'swept' before any relief ships could enter.

It was planned that P.o.W.s would be transported by ship from Nagasaki to Manila. There was just a possibility that the sick might be flown out earlier. A list of the Miyata P.o.W.s still alive would be broadcast from Tokyo as soon as possible.

The Japanese Camp Authorities had given the Delegation an assurance, our representatives were informed, that the rice ration would be increased immediately to 710 grammes per man—and, to cap it all, that a final issue of 25 Japanese cigarettes per man would be distributed on the 31st August.

Our representatives smiled as these observations were made—as well they might.

The Delegation added that Wing Commander Matthews might telephone the Red Cross Office in Tokyo—presumably transferring the charges—if he could get through! The Delegation finally said that the Allied Governments had offered to redeem any yen in the hands of P.o.W.s on arrival in Manila at the rate of ten yen to one United States dollar.

This latter item of information caused an uproar in the camp 'Stock Exchange' as soon as it became public. For months, if not years, P.o.W.s had been disposing of their small quantities of, as they thought, worthless yen at a discount. Fabulous prices had been paid in this 'useless' currency for spoonfuls of rice and cigarettes. Now, apparently each yen was worth ten U.S. cents. The money-lenders and traders had a night of anguished calculations ahead of them.

No P.o.W. could complain, after all this information had been disseminated throughout the camp, that he had been kept in the dark—though much of the information proved to be erroneous and most of the undertakings were never honoured.

While the national representatives had been having their meeting with the Red Cross Delegation, during the afternoon of the 28th August I had been engaged in a rather more distressing task.

I had been asked to compile a list, with various particulars, of all those who had died at Miyata Camp. This required the reconciliation of the records in the camp office with those which had been kept by the Dutch doctor. There were many discrepancies, particularly as regards the recorded cause of death. When in doubt I followed the doctor.

In the course of this task I had occasion to enquire about any valuables left by the dead. Although the records were there, there was no trace of these valuables. Further enquiries established that the valuables of the living had also 'gone astray'. Each living P.o.W. had, unless he had lost it, a receipt from the Camp Commandant for all the valuables removed from him on entering the camp. When we had moved from Habu to Zentsuji, and then from Zentsuji to Miyata, meticulous care had been taken by the Japanese Authorities to return our valuables and to obtain a receipt from us. These things, and many others, were done differently at Miyata.

The Miyata Camp Authorities were filled with alarm when they realised that this state of affairs had come to our notice. The camp staff went round to various P.o.W.s begging them not to press their claims or, in lieu, to accept a settlement in yen.

This Japanese approach had more chance of success, now that the Allies had apparently 'pegged' the value of the yen in P.o.W. hands, than it would have had twenty-four hours earlier. But there were a large number who doubted these assurances. Many hard bargains were struck during the night of the 28th August.

This matter had not been finally resolved when I left the camp. Fortunately I was not directly concerned, as I had parted with my only valuable, a broken gold watch, for food much earlier.

When I left the camp office, having completed my labours, I found a couple of Japanese civilians wandering about the camp selling curios. These were of very poor quality, plaster of Paris dolls and women's heads. I did not believe that much business was done.

The night of the 28th was marked by a severe gale. Several of the inside walls of one hut collapsed and the verandah corridor was six inches deep in water.

We all agreed that we had occupied this uncomfortable accommodation long enough and that it was time we were moving. Someone suggested that we might profitably spend the following day scanning the advertisements in the local press for something more suitable.

When the laughter which this sally had evoked had died down we decided to turn in.

I suppose I must have been asleep for about ten minutes when someone woke me up. It was a guard from the camp office who said to me politely in Japanese that Sergeant-Major Hayashi 'presented his compliments and would be obliged if I could make it convenient to go to the camp office'.

With this acknowledgement that circumstances had changed, I could hardly refuse. I dressed quickly and followed the guard down the path.

I found Hayashi in the camp office, wrestling with the statements of particulars about the dead which I had prepared earlier that evening.

'These are not quite what Fukuoka requires,' he said.

'Why not?' I retorted, speaking rather more curtly than I would have dared to do a fortnight earlier.

'All names must be in alphabetical order and five copies are necessary. Please help me. You know I do not understand how to write these European names,' he replied.

'Is there anything else wrong?' I asked, relishing the feeling that I now had the whip hand.

'Yes, there are dates under the column marked D which are the dates of death. But there are no dates under the column marked N. What does the N mean anyhow?' he enquired plaintively.

'I don't know. You should know. They are your forms.' I was rather enjoying myself by now.

We both pondered this knotty problem for a few minutes. To encourage my musings he offered me a cigarette. I took it, saying to myself, 'When the planes do come back and drop something, I'll give you that one back.' I was rapidly recovering my self-respect.

Then suddenly I saw it.

'Could the column marked N be for the dates the dead officers or other ranks'—I deliberately avoided the word 'prisoner of war'—'first came to Nippon?' I enquired.

'Yes that's it,' he replied, as happy as a child who had just put the last piece of a jigsaw puzzle into place.

I got down to work. It was a fiddling job.

Like an office boy, Hayashi furnished me with fresh forms on ridiculously thin and rotten paper. Only two carbon copies could be made at a time owing to the quality of the paper. As five copies were required this meant that the whole exercise had to be done twice. The sharp-pointed pen was for ever piercing the flimsy bundle of three forms and two carbons.

Hayashi could see I was irritated with the whole footling business.

'I am not doing this for you, you know,' I said. 'I am doing this for the dead men and their families.'

He nodded. After a few moments he said: 'Would you like some tea and some bread and butter?'

'Yes, I would, thank you,' I replied brusquely.

He went off to get it.

When he returned I was faced with another problem.

'Do you think the N column refers to the date of the dead man's arrival in Nippon proper or in Taiwan?' I enquired. Several of the dead men had been P.o.W.s in Taiwan camps before being moved to Japan.

'Taiwan of course,' he replied. 'Taiwan is part of Nippon.'

'Well it won't be for long,' I answered. 'I shall put down the date of arrival in Nippon. In any case if they had meant Taiwan or

Nippon they would have put a T and an N at the top of the column.'

This was too much for him. He replied weakly, 'As you think best.'

Transcribing the Dutch names was causing me a lot of difficulty and it took a long time to get the list in alphabetical order. It was already 3 a.m. and I could see I would be there for hours.

'I'm hungry. Would you be good enough to get me some food? I'm not particularly fussy but I'm feeling hungry,' I said.

He shuffled off and returned a few minutes later with some rice and a stew which had clearly come out of the Japanese cook-house.

'Thank you,' I said, adding to myself under my breath, 'that will be all for now, Hayashi.'

Thus reinforced I made more rapid progress, but I could see that it would be 7.30 a.m. before I would be finished. I thought that a good breakfast from the Japanese cook-house would not be amiss. I asked for it at 6.15 a.m. and I got it.

I assembled the forms, five copies of each and thrust them into the hands of the representative of the Japanese military bureaucracy. He hadn't noticed that I had made a sixth copy which I took away with me and subsequently gave to the Dutch doctor, as most of the dead were Dutch.

As I left the camp office I said to myself, 'I wonder how many of the individuals whose names were on those long lists of dead would have been alive today if you, Hayashi, and your ilk, had done everything within your power to save them. Many would have died anyway, I know. But many could have been saved, even with the limited resources available to the War Prisoners' Organisation, if the will to save them had been there.'

It was not until the morning of Wednesday the 29th that I learnt of an incident which had occurred while I had been labouring in Hayashi's office.

A message had been received in the camp during the night that a single canister, apparently dropped by one of the American planes, had been found near the valley farm. The garbled report indicated that the parachute had failed to open and that the canister was smashed to pieces.

Hungry men are desperate men and although it was pitch dark, a fatigue party was immediately sent out. By then no nationality represented in the camp trusted any other nationality. The fatigue party therefore consisted of two British, two Dutch, two Americans, two Canadians, two Australians, etc. As someone was said to have observed: 'It looked like Noah's Ark all over again, except that all the couples were of the same sex!'

Eventually the party returned. They had lost a night's sleep, as I had, and they had found practically nothing. Every tin and packet in the canister had been broken and all the contents spilt. The meat and the fruit salad, the butter and the chewing gum, all had been scooped up in buckets and churns borrowed from the farm and brought back to camp. It was put, lock, stock and barrel, into the breakfast soup. It was my second unusual breakfast that day.

The fact that a canister had been dropped and found was in itself enough to raise our drooping spirits a little.

Some swore, now, that they had seen it, and many other canisters falling in the direction of the valley farm. There was also some evidence, brought back by the search party, that the canister was never intended for Miyata Camp at all but for another P.o.W. camp, the existence of which we were quite unaware but which was said to be situated some distance the other side of the farm.

Such speculations helped to pass the time which was hanging heavily on our hands but did nothing to improve our conditions.

Suddenly about midday on the 29th, the B.29s returned again. This time it was 'the real thing'. For two hours the camp was in an uproar as the three huge aircraft swooped down in turns to drop their loads. They first made a number of 'dummy runs' at a fairly low level. The actual 'drops' were made from a somewhat higher altitude. The first drop consisted of eighteen canisters attached to gaily coloured parachutes. Two of the parachutes did not open and one of the canisters fell into the compound of the Japanese guards' quarters. The P.o.W.s had all the scattered contents collected and out within thirty seconds.

Most of the canisters landed just outside the camp. The P.o.W.s, brushing aside the remaining Japanese guards on the gate, were out in a flash.

One P.o.W. officer was very seriously injured when a heavy iron release bar, accidentally dropped from one of the planes, struck him on the head, splitting his skull open.

One canister crashed through the roof of the Camp Commandant's office. He was standing in the doorway at the time. He thus missed the fate which we felt sure would be his when, as we hoped, he came up before the post-war Japanese War Crimes Commission. Another canister demolished the roof of the dining-hall; yet another brought down an electric cable which electrocuted one of the Dutch prisoners.

In all some sixty canisters and cartons were dropped. The parachutes of about ten failed to open.

Each of the aircraft crews of eleven men dropped a signed message. One, which came my way, read: 'Hullo, fellows. Hope you get home soon. Good luck. We are glad to be of some help to you. So long.' The message was signed by the captain of the aircraft, Lieutenant R. V. Burdick of Rochester, Minnesota, by four other U.S. Air Corps Lieutenants and by six U.S. Air Corps Sergeants.

At last we had seen our 'waving pilots' and, what was more, we knew all their names and addresses.

Bundles of newspapers and magazines were also dropped. From these we learnt much that we did not know about the events of the last few hectic weeks.

We gathered that hostilities had, indeed, broken out again on the 18th August when Japanese aircraft had attacked a formation of American planes flying over Japan to photograph Japanese aerodromes. On the same day Japanese naval and air forces had attacked Allied naval vessels and troopships off the island of Shikoku. The Japanese-controlled radio stations in Singapore and Batavia had announced that all Japanese forces in Malaya and Java would continue to fight, despite the Emperor's broadcast. Although all Japanese troops in Manchuria had surrendered, the Russians were continuing their advance.

For the first time we learnt that Hiroshima and Nagasaki had been obliterated by atomic bombs, of which we had never heard. It was strange, we thought, that the Red Cross Delegation had made no reference to such bombs.

The events of the 29th August had restored our morale and had removed much of our bewilderment.

The Japanese were stunned beyond belief. Their grandstand view of the roaring B.29s had been too much for them. They slunk around the camp with faltering steps, like men who had suddenly been deprived of their sight. They were making no attempt to rebuild the camp fence, the whole of which had blown down in a recent gale.

The Red Cross Delegation had brought with them a wireless receiving set for the use of the P.o.W.s. For some twenty-four hours the Japanese Authorities had retained this in the camp office. The arrival of the B.29s had changed their minds. On the 30th August they released the set.

From this we learnt that evening that General Douglas Mac-Arthur had landed in Tokyo earlier during the day and that Admiral Nimitz had arrived in Yokohama.

The Japanese had surrendered in Java, the British had landed at Penang and those of the P.o.W.s working on the Burma–Siam railway who were still alive were being flown out from Rangoon and Bangkok.

Not all the news was good. One of the aircraft dropping relief supplies on P.o.W. camps had crashed. Ten of the eleven crew had been killed and the eleventh had been badly burnt.

Friday the 31st August was the birthday of Queen Wilhelmina of the Netherlands. We were now in a position to celebrate this in appropriate style with the Dutch, who were strutting round the camp as proud as turkey-cocks. Most of them were sporting their national colours and wearing orange flowers which had been pilfered from some Japanese peasant's garden.

During the evening of the 31st I had occasion to go to the camp office to get a bright electric-light bulb in exchange for one of our dim ones. The camp staff said that they had no bright bulbs left. I therefore mounted the office table and removed the bright bulb hanging there, replacing it with our dim one. Several guards and members of the camp staff were in the office but no one had protested.

They then crowded round and asked me what the P.o.W. national representatives had said to the Red Cross Delegation about the treatment of P.o.W.s in Miyata. I replied, without knowing whether it was true, that detailed reports on the behaviour of every guard and every member of the camp staff had been given to the Delegates and that similar reports would be made to the first representatives of the Allied Forces with whom we came in contact. I then left them to draw their own conclusions.

At the Camp Commandant's meeting with the P.o.W. national representatives later, he announced that the Mine Authorities had decided to give each P.o.W. a cotton *kimono*. He added that his own personal gift would be a fan. Tim Hallam's comments on this news were unprintable.

The radio brought us news on Saturday the 1st September that the first 500 P.o.W.s had left Tokyo. The announcement added that the Americans were horrified at their condition. Advance

Allied parties landing in Singapore had found 30,000 prisoners of whom about twenty-five per cent were hospital cases.

We were a little alarmed at the continuous flow of atrocity stories being pumped out by the American-controlled radio station in Tokyo. Not only would this worry our families, until they had definite news of our circumstances from Allied sources, but it might also goad fanatical Japanese into acts of despair. By now many of the Japanese knew that their necks were in danger. It would be quite in character if some of them ran amok and then committed *hara-kiri*.

The more reports that came in to the effect that P.o.W.s were on their way home, the more unsettled and anxious we became about our own fate. We were still living on a knife-edge and Kurihara's abrupt removal of the radio set did nothing to allay our apprehensions.

During the late afternoon of the 1st September Colonel Petrie, who was the second senior British P.o.W. officer after the Wing Commander, asked me to go down to the camp office and get the radio set back from Kurihara. I must confess that I did not relish this task and my heart was in my mouth as I entered the camp office. I knew how unpredictable Kurihara was and what he was capable of.

I found Kurihara packing up the radio set with the rest of his baggage. I asked him what he was doing with it and reminded him that the set had been provided for the use of the P.o.W.s by the Red Cross Delegation.

He turned and glared at me, fingering his sword.

'War prisoners have no rights,' he shouted. 'The war may be over but you are still war prisoners and so long as I am here'—which did not appear likely to be very long, in view of his packing—'you will be treated as war prisoners.'

We argued for some time and then I told him to unpack the set. I said I would send the Dutch wireless operator down to collect it within ten minutes. This I did and a few minutes later the Dutch P.o.W. delivered the set to the Wing Commander's hut.

We listened to the news again that night. We picked up a broadcast from New Delhi during which messages for P.o.W.s in Japanese hands from their wives in India were being read. I hoped to hear a message from L. but I was unlucky.

A subsequent broadcast from Tokyo indicated that the Japanese Government was attempting to postpone the formal signing of the Armistice but that General MacArthur would brook no delay.

During the afternoon of Sunday the 2nd September we were summoned to the parade ground to be addressed by the Camp Commandant. He told us, through the good offices of Charlie McArthy, that the Armistice had been signed on board U.S.S. *Missouri* in Tokyo Bay at 9 a.m. that morning and that we were no longer P.o.W.s.

That was the last we saw of the Camp Commandant, who disappeared into thin air. Most of the Japanese followed suit, but Sergeant-Major Hayashi and Sergeant Kurihara returned to the camp occasionally. They still had certain administrative chores to perform.

The P.o.W.s took over the guard-house and rifles and bayonets were issued to those P.o.W.s detailed for guard duty. Some of the P.o.W. guards managed to acquire, and wear, Japanese swords. The camp was now ours.

On our return to the huts, I noticed, pegged out with coloured parachutes on the hillside, the word 'THANKS'. We were all hoping for another early visit from the relief planes. The supplies in the first 'drop' were now virtually finished. If more supplies were not dropped within forty-eight hours food would again become a worry. The inhabitants of the neighbourhood would be neither able, nor willing, to meet our needs. There were still many problems ahead but at least we were beginning to feel 'free' for the first time.

The Wing Commander took over the Camp Commandant's office. Three Japanese police, who were to act as liaison officers with our Japanese civilian neighbours, were allocated a small room. It began to look as though we might remain at Miyata for ever.

The radio set would not work. There was some evidence that a disgruntled Japanese, possibly Kurihara, had sabotaged it before leaving.

This was a severe blow, but there were others to come. Monday, September the 3rd, produced another gale. It was clear that relief planes would not come that day.

The P.o.W. officers whose rags, in many instances, made them indistinguishable from the other ranks, were issued with coloured strips of cloth to be worn on their right breast, red for the senior officers and light blue for the junior.

In the evening of the 3rd three wireless sets were sent into the camp by unknown Japanese Authorities. They brought us the news that half a million Japanese were now P.o.W.s of the Russians in Manchuria. We did not envy them their fate. The Russians had also occupied the Kurile Islands and the southern half of Sakhalin Island, hitherto part of the Japanese Empire. I recalled the words of those Japanese who had said to me, 'If the Russians land in Nippon they will never leave.'

On Tuesday the 4th September some more American relief supplies came into the camp. The weather had been so bad during the preceding forty-eight hours that the U.S. Air Force had decided that it would be safer to drop supplies in bulk in some central place than to risk flights over all the camps in the hills. These supplies reached us in a Japanese lorry. Judging by the amount received, which was about a quarter of what had been dropped on the camp, the Japanese must have been helping themselves liberally en route.

A party of Japanese soldiers came into the camp to repair the perimeter fence. They were rigorously searched by the Dutch guards on the gate when they left the camp!

Wednesday the 5th September was marked by visits to Miyata of P.o.W.s from other camps. Three Dutch officers drove over in a car from a camp nearby, the existence of which we had been quite unaware. Some Dutch and American other ranks came from Fukuoka by hitching a lift in a Japanese truck. They spent the night in the camp and returned to Fukuoka in the same truck the following day.

This latter group had a most unsettling effect on the P.o.W.s at Miyata. They told us that Fukuoka was packed with relief stores. Fifty tins of meat, a huge carton of chocolate and a thousand cigarettes had been issued to each man and there was more of everything for the asking. British P.o.W.s were patrolling the streets as Military Police and the prisoners were patronising cinemas, dance-halls and cafés.

They also told us that many P.o.W.s had been killed during the 'drops'. One American had died later of injuries received when the parachute attached to a huge carton of chewing-gum had failed to open.

The Miyata prisoners began to get very restive again. It was now nearly three weeks since hostilities had ceased and we were still rotting at Miyata while those in Fukuoka were 'beating it up'.

Following upon this visit, six Americans and four Australians made off from Miyata on their own.

On Thursday the 6th September I was one of a party of four officers who went out to the *bokuyo* near the valley farm. This was

a large cattle ranch and our object was to purchase milk and vegetables for the camp. While we were engaged in this task we persuaded
the farmer to give us an excellent meal, in exchange for which we
gave him some soap and a blanket.

The outing had been both fruitful and pleasant. We all agreed
to repeat it on the following day. By now officer P.o.W.s were
permitted to leave the camp for such excursions, provided they
notified the Camp Adjutant where and when they were going.

With the morrow in mind, I entered into negotiations with an
aged Japanese crone who was to prepare our midday meal. In
return for some old clothes, a blanket and some soap she would
obtain and cook for us two chickens and a rabbit. The chickens would
be cooked 'à la casserole' and would, with rice, form our lunch. The
rabbit we would take back to the camp to be eaten cold with our
evening meal.

Our second day at the *bokuyo*, the 7th September, was even more
delightful than the first. We chatted, we dozed under the trees,
and we all made plans for the future. We walked back to the camp
in the cool of the evening, replete, and without a care in the world.

Sergeant-Major Hayashi and Sergeant Kurihara still had a mass
of paperwork to do, winding up the camp's affairs. Even if the
war was over the bureaucratic behemoth still required its quota
of forms and returns. Hayashi and Kurihara had established a
small office in a school just outside the entrance to the camp,
from where they maintained a tenuous contact with the Wing
Commander and his staff, who now worked in the camp office.

After returning from my second excursion to the *bokuyo*, I
had a bath and evening meal. I then heard that Kurihara had been
looking all over the camp for me and that he wanted to see me
urgently.

I walked down, out of the camp gates, to Kurihara's office.
I found him desperately worried about the six American enlisted
men who had left Miyata after the Fukuoka visitors had regaled
us with their accounts of the 'high jinks' going on there.

'I am personally responsible to His Imperial Majesty for their
safety,' Kurihara said, 'I would never forgive myself if they were
killed by angry Japanese or if any other misfortune should overtake
them.'

I felt it was much more likely that their sudden departure had
thrown his nominal rolls out of gear and that the wrath which

he feared was not that of the Emperor but that of some fiery Fukuoka functionary.

'Well, there's nothing I can do about it, is there?' I said. 'They've gone and that's all there is to it. We don't even know where they've gone.'

'Oh! but I do,' Kurihara replied. 'They've gone to Kagoshima. You must go after them and bring them back, or at least bring back a receipt from the American authorities acknowledging that they are there. I must have that for my books.'

I began to roar with laughter. It all seemed so ludicrous.

Kurihara looked at me with incipient tears in his eyes.

'How different you look now,' I thought. 'You don't look a bit the same as you did a month ago when you signalled to one of the gorillas to crack my head open for misinterpreting you!'

'You must go to Kagoshima and bring them back,' Kurihara pleaded.

'How could I get to Kagoshima, even if I wanted to?' I replied.

'With the Dutch officers who are going down there by car tomorrow. Why not?' Kurihara enquired.

This was the first I had heard about any Dutch officers leaving. I couldn't believe it was possible. I pricked up my ears.

I questioned Kurihara further and satisfied myself that he was telling the truth.

'I'll come back,' I said, as I rushed out of his office in search of the Wing Commander. The latter was nowhere to be found, but eventually I found Peter William-Powlett, a Major in the 7th Hussars, who appeared to be the Senior British Officer in the camp. He too knew nothing about Dutch officers leaving.

We went to beard the Dutch doctor in his 'consulting room'.

After a great deal of dissimulation and prevarication, he admitted that he was sending a party of Dutch officers off the following day and that he had not informed the Wing Commander.

'It is a matter of national pride,' he said, 'that the Dutch should be taking an initiative in this matter—and it must be an all-Dutch party.'

Eventually we ran the Wing Commander to earth. He was as astounded as we had been. He gave orders that it should be a joint party consisting of two Dutch officers, Horsthuis and Schrinkel and two British officers, Peter William-Powlett and myself.

Peter had been a stockbroker before the war. I had seen quite a bit of him at Zentsuji. He and his wife were staunch Christian

Scientists. She had frequently exchanged letters with my mother, who was also a Christian Scientist, when it became known that Peter and I were both at Zentsuji. I was glad that he was to be my companion on this adventure into the unknown.

By now it was getting late and the party was due to leave Miyata by car for Fukuoka at 5.30 a.m. the next morning, Saturday the 8th September.

The Wing Commander had our authorisations typed out. Mine read as follows:

TO WHOM IT MAY CONCERN

The Bearer Flying Officer Fletcher-Cooke is AUTHORISED to represent me in his visit to the ALLIED OCCUPATION FORCES Headquarters at KAGASHIMA'

Fukuoka 9   (signed) G. Matthews W/Cmdr.
(Miyata)   Officer O/C Troops, Miyata.
7/9/45.

When all this had been settled I returned to Kurihara's office and told him what had happened. I asked him to write out for me a Japanese version of the Wing Commander's authorisation, which he did. I asked him for the names of the six 'missing' American enlisted men and told him that I would explain what had happened to the Allied Occupation Forces at Kagoshima. Although this gave Kurihara some comfort it did not give him his receipt about which he was still muttering. I told him, as I said good-bye, that there was no time to bother about that now.

He saluted me as I left his office.

I was up very early the next morning and Peter and I walked down to the gate together. I was horrified to see that he had brought all his kit with him. I had assumed that we would be returning with a relief column of Allied Forces which we would guide through the hills to Miyata. I had only brought an 'overnight change' which for me meant little more than a self-laundered clean *hundoshi*. Although I had not left much of value behind, there were certain things that I would have liked to have brought with me.

There was no time to think about these matters now. The two Dutch officers, bursting with 'national pride' and anxious 'to take an initiative', were waiting impatiently by the car. If we had been any later they would certainly have left without us.

We piled in and were off immediately. We had soon left behind any of those landmarks within the vicinity of the camp which I could recognise.

As we bowled along in the sunshine I thought to myself, 'Well, you'll miss your cotton kimono from the Mine Authorities and the Camp Commandant's fan too.'

Then suddenly the awful truth struck me.

In all the haste and confusion I had left my little bag with all my diaries in its secret hiding-place. I had deliberately never told anyone else where I had hidden them. I had not wished to put anyone else at risk. Indeed, I doubted whether any of my companions even knew that I had been keeping a diary. They had become so accustomed to see me scribbling away that they had probably thought I was writing letters or preparing notes for a lecture.

'How could you have been such a bloody fool to have left them behind?' I said to myself.

— 13 —

The Long Road Home

September–December 1945*

I had never thought that it would be like this. Sometimes I had been convinced that we would never leave Miyata at all. In my more pessimistic moments I had had visions of the Japanese guards shooting or bayoneting us to the last man. When hope had overcome despair I had assumed that we would all travel by train or lorry to Moji or Nagasaki, where we would be warmly welcomed by the Americans and then shipped off south.

Now the four of us were going off into the unknown to find the Allied Occupation Forces and to acquaint them with the plight and whereabouts of our fellow-P.o.W.s. It was well over three weeks since hostilities had ceased and it seemed strange that we had had no visit from any officers of the Allied Forces, nor even a message indicating what arrangements were contemplated for our evacuation.

I was puzzled, too, by the fact that if Kurihara had not told me we would never have known that the Dutch were contemplating 'taking the initiative' until after they had left.

The Dutch at Miyata had always been 'difficult' and 'prickly'. They had regarded it, with some justification, as primarily a Dutch P.o.W. camp. They had not taken kindly to the arrival of the Zentsuji party of British officers, some of whom, in addition to the Wing Commander, were senior to the Dutch doctor who had hitherto run the camp his way and, not unnaturally, in the interests of the Dutch.

After the 15th August, and as the P.o.W.s gradually became responsible for administering their own affairs, these underlying differences of opinion and approach had become even more marked.

*See map 3, page 318.

The arrival and distribution of the American relief supplies had exacerbated these differences. I knew that the Wing Commander had not had an easy time.

There were other factors in this complex equation. The Netherlands East Indies had been by far the richest part of the whole area which had fallen under Japanese control in 1942 and early 1943. The loss of the Netherlands East Indies, coupled with the German invasion and occupation of Holland itself, had perhaps represented greater affronts to 'the soul of the Netherlands' than anything which Britain had had to endure, including even the loss of Malaya and Singapore.

There was also a general awareness, shared by British and Dutch alike, that the British had fought hard, if in vain, during the whole of the Malayan campaign. Every possible step had been taken, during the retreat down the peninsula, to deny the resources of Malaya to the advancing Japanese.

In Java, and elsewhere in the Netherlands East Indies, it had been different. With a few very gallant exceptions, resistance to the Japanese invaders had been limited. Again, with a few exceptions, the 'scorched-earth policy' had not been prosecuted with the same vigour in the Netherlands East Indies as it had been in Malaya.

To crown it all, British Forces had been fighting with an ever-increasing measure of success in Burma and elsewhere, as part of the Allied efforts to defeat Japan, during much of our time in captivity. The participation of Dutch Forces in this task had, of necessity, been less significant, having regard to the earlier loss of virtually the whole of their empire and the destruction and disruption wreaked on their homeland by the Nazi invaders.

Now that the war was over, the proud Dutch, as representatives of one of the victorious Allied Powers, were determined to make their presence felt again.

I could understand the Dutch doctor's feelings and his desires to take some action. I could not excuse his failure to consult the Wing Commander who was the Senior P.o.W. Officer in command of all Allied P.o.W.s in the camp.

I felt, however, that it would not be long before our two Dutch companions found some excuse to continue their search for the Allied Occupation Forces on their own. I recalled the Dutch doctor's words, 'It must be an all-Dutch party'.

For the moment, however, we were an 'Allied' party. Perhaps to underline this Peter was sitting next to the senior of the two

Dutch officers in the back and I found myself next to the junior, who was driving.

I decided to engage my Dutch companion in conversation. This was difficult, as the somewhat decrepit car was making a lot of noise. Our conversation was conducted partly in English and partly in Malay. My companion was far more fluent in Malay than he was in English and I could remember enough of my Malay to understand him without too much difficulty.

He gave me one startling piece of information which made a lot of things clear.

He told me that at some stage after the 15th August the Dutch interpreter had had the chance of a brief look at a document in Japanese characters in the camp office. This appeared to be an order from the Ministry of Defence in Tokyo to the Camp Commandant. It was to the effect that if and when the Allies 'polluted the sacred soil of Nippon' by landing on Kyushu, all prisoners at Miyata were to be taken down a disused mine-shaft and killed. The Dutch interpreter gathered that this was to be done, once the P.o.W.s were down the shaft, by spraying them with petrol, throwing in grenades and then, as a *coup de grâce*, opening up with machine-guns.

Suddenly all the pieces of the jigsaw puzzle fell into place.

I had always thought it strange that, although we had had a number of air-raid precautions drills, no doubt to accustom us to going down the disused mine-shaft on the side of the hill, we had never been ordered to go down the shaft during an actual air-raid alert.

I recalled now the two Japanese with machine-guns posted at the entrance to the tunnel on the first occasion we had been required to practise this drill.

I also recalled Kurihara's strange announcement at evening roll-call on the 17th August that we should hold ourselves in readiness for another such air-raid precautions drill and that on that occasion we should take with us not only two blankets but also all our personal possessions.

This announcement had been made, I recalled, at a time when the camp was buzzing with rumours that hostilities had broken out again and, in particular, that a Japanese General in Kyushu had decided, despite the Emperor's broadcast, to fight to the bitter end. Indeed, as we had subsequently learnt from the newspapers dropped by the relief planes on the 29th August, hostilities had broken out again in various parts of Japan on the 18th August.

I remembered, too, my conversation with Kurihara on the evening of the 24th August when he told me that the exact whereabouts of Miyata Camp, as indeed of all other P.o.W. camps on the island of Kyushu, had not yet been disclosed to the Americans.

'Why had our whereabouts not been disclosed to the Americans by the 24th August?' I wondered. 'Was it because the Japanese authorities in Tokyo did not know whether the Camp Commandant had, or had not, put their plan into effect?'

This seemed the most likely explanation to me. By the 15th August communications in Japan had been so disrupted that Tokyo could not have been sure what had happened, or what was happening, elsewhere. Kyushu's abortive and short-lived 'Unilateral Declaration of Independence' might have had results of which Tokyo was unaware and which Tokyo would not wish to advertise to the Americans unnecessarily. It would be better to play safe.

The fact that relief planes had visited us on the 28th and the 29th August was not in itself of any significance. By then, American relief planes were flying all over Kyushu and the large letters 'P.W.' on roofs would be quite enough to attract their attention.

Again, the fact that the Red Cross Delegation had also visited us on the 28th August meant no more than that the Red Cross was aware of the existence of Miyata Camp. There was no possibility of us knowing whether, or when, the Red Cross, with all its many preoccupations, would be able to pass this information on to the proper Allied occupation authorities.

Perhaps all this explained why we at Miyata had had no visits nor even messages from the Allied Occupation Forces, even though we had heard on the wireless on the 1st September, a week previously, that the first batch of 500 P.o.W.s had left Tokyo.

Of one thing I was certain. If the Japanese had decided to oppose an Allied landing on Kyushu the plan to dispose of the P.o.W.s would undoubtedly have been carried out.

I hoped all this would become clearer if and when we established contact with the Americans at Kagoshima. It did.

It was at this moment that the car broke down. I supposed that we were about half-way to Fukuoka. When we failed to get the car started again we abandoned it and walked towards a village we could see in the distance. It was very hot and I was almost glad that I had not brought my kit.

The village had a railway station, though there were few signs that it was ever visited by a train. Enquiries elucidated that no trains were expected, so we returned to the car. Again I was glad I had not brought my kit. Eventually we got it started. It was clear that we would be lucky if we could coax it as far as Fukuoka.

As we approached Fukuoka we saw masses of military equipment —tanks, guns, lorries, ammunition and rifles. We passed the main Fukuoka War Prisoners Camp No. 1, which was agreeably situated, and very well marked, beside a river. The camp was festooned with flags made from hundreds of parachutes and we could see masses of relief supplies, in unopened cartons, stacked all over the camp. If we had dared to, we would have stopped the car and asked that some of these supplies should be sent to Miyata.

On arrival in Fukuoka we made for the station. The Dutch took the car to a garage to be repaired. They said they would need it for 'their' return journey to Miyata.

Peter and I went into the station where we each purchased, and consumed, the contents of three lunch-boxes.

To my surprise the Dutch rejoined us and we went in a body to a Japanese Military Police post in the station. I was the only one who could speak Japanese and, waving Kurihara's translation of my 'authorisation', I put on a great show in an attempt to impress upon the evil-looking *Kempetei* the vital importance of our mission. A *Kempetei* cadet got us seats on a train. We noticed that he made four Japanese soldiers get up for us, which restored our self-respect a little.

It was intolerably hot and the train was packed with stunned Japanese. Some of them told me that they had already been standing for more than twelve hours without food or water.

The train passed slowly through very hilly country which even to my untutored eyes would have been easier to defend than to capture. We noticed whole villages, and even isolated buildings, which had been razed to the ground. I had never seen such complete and utter destruction.

We stopped at every station and at every station one of us got out and filled out empty water-bottles, the contents of which we shared with some of our thirsty Japanese travelling companions.

The coaches, of which the train was composed, had clearly been damaged in earlier bombing raids. There were many signs of burning and scorching; several of the seats had been burnt or otherwise damaged; the luggage racks hung down at grotesque angles and all the windows had been shattered. The heat was such that we particularly welcomed this latter piece of destruction—until our faces were blackened, like those of the Dutch underground miners at Miyata, by the soot and grime of the poor-quality coal.

As the train took us further and further south, we could see that the countryside was thick with Japanese troops moving in all directions. Every house and hovel left standing was being used as a billet. Most of the civilian population seemed to have been evacuated.

We arrived at a station where the train came to a complete halt and everyone got out. I leant out of the window and hailed a passing Japanese.

'Is this Kagoshima?' I asked in all innocence.

'Oh! no,' he replied, 'this is only Kumamoto. Kagoshima is another hundred and fifty miles.'

'How far is this from Fukuoka?' I asked.

'About a hundred miles,' he answered.

'Why have we stopped?' I enquired.

'Because there is no railway line,' he replied, laughing. 'It's all been blown up.'

We alighted from the train.

A Japanese naval Commander who had recognised that we were P.o.W.s was very helpful. He paid no attention to the Dutch, but told me with pride that he had been on a naval officers' course in England when he was a young officer. He then explained that the railway line had been destroyed by American bombing and that we would have to walk for some distance until we could pick up the line again.

By now it was dark, though there was enough moonlight to show us all we needed to see of the eerie desolation which lay ahead. We humped our kit through the remains of what must have once been a large and flourishing city. There was nothing, absolutely nothing, of it left, except acres and acres of twisted steel and ashes. 'Was it worse than this at Hiroshima and Nagasaki?' I wondered. I doubted whether it could have been.

By now the Japanese, who had been on the train with us, were several hundred yards ahead, delicately picking their way, as we were, over the debris.

'We shan't lose sight of them,' I thought. 'There's nothing high enough left to block our view.'

When we reached the 'rail-head' there was no train. So we found a space among the rubble and settled down for some sleep.

Just as it was getting light, the train arrived, disgorging hundreds of termites who were now faced with the long crawl across the 'desert' in the opposite direction.

We took their places in the train. Two other sections of the line had been destroyed by bombing further south. It was dark when we finally reached Kagoshima on the evening of the 9th. Kagoshima, like Kumamoto, seemed now to be little more than the name of a city which had once existed.

We made contact with the Japanese Military Police post in what was left of the station at Kagoshima. There we learnt that there were no Americans in Kagoshima and that they were all confined to the aerodrome at Kanoya which was some distance away.

'Any chance of getting there tonight?' I asked in Japanese.

'I don't think so,' replied the Japanese Military Policeman. 'There might be a lorry going out tonight, but I doubt it.'

Having extracted a promise from the Japanese M.P. that he would wake us if a lorry turned up, we retired to sleep in a damaged railway coach in a siding.

At 4 a.m. the Japanese M.P. brought us tea and biscuits. They tasted better than any tea and biscuits I had ever had. After this early-morning 'service' they gave us some rice balls for breakfast in their hut.

We left on foot about 4.30 a.m. as the Kagoshima–Kanoya line had also been cut. We had to walk along the destroyed track until we reached a place where there was a large crowd waiting for the train to Kanoya. It was impossible to say whether it had once been a station; it certainly wasn't then.

Peter and I managed to get in a quick shave as the dawn came and before the train arrived. The Dutch did not bother.

There were innumerable tunnels and some very steep gradients on the journey to Kanoya and we had to change trains on several occasions.

At each 'change' I made a bee-line for the Japanese Military Police who always gave us something good to eat. At the last 'change' before Kanoya we had the best meal we had ever had in Japan, omelette 'aux fines herbes', slivers of delicious meat, a salad and as much perfectly cooked rice as we could eat. I decided to volunteer for the Military Police if the need for my services should ever occur again.

The station at Kanoya was a bedlam. A rabble of undisciplined American and Australian other ranks P.o.W.s were milling around

and making a bit of a nuisance of themselves as they waited for
lorries to take them to the aerodrome.

One huge American, who had clearly been drinking heavily,
lurched up to Peter and, putting out a hand the size of a ham—'He
must have worked in a cook-house,' I thought—said:

'Saay, Lewtenant, am I glad to seeze yer.'

Peter replied with all the dignity he could muster:

'I happen to be a Major and in the British Forces it is customary
to salute officers.'

Perhaps our Japanese guards had not beaten the 'arrogance'
out of us, after all!

It looked as though the Japanese detachment of soldiers on
duty at the station were going to herd us in with the rabble of
stragglers, when the lorries from Kanoya arrived.

'Come on, Peter,' I said, 'let's go and find the Japanese Military
Police. They've never let us down yet.'

We found the police post. I asked a Japanese M.P. on duty
if he would be good enough to ring up the Americans and say that we
had arrived and that we had urgent and important business with
their Commanding Officer. He did so and gave us a snack to boot.

When the Kanoya lorries arrived we noticed that there was
a Jeep as well. Peter and I jumped into the Jeep. As we drove off,
we saw our two Dutch companions being herded into one of the
lorries with all the 'ragtag and bobtail'.

It looked as though the 'initiative' I had taken, some three
years previously, to learn Japanese was paying some modest divi-
dends after all.

Peter and I were driven straight to the Kanoya Allied Occupation Forces H.Q.

We had last seen our Dutch companions, whose 'initiative'
had hardly matched up to the worthy Dutch doctor's hopes, almost
invisible in the middle of a tightly packed scrum of Australians
and Americans. We hoped they would survive the ride to the
aerodrome. We never saw them again.

We had gathered quite a lot of information as we drove in the Jeep
to the aerodrome, partly by conversation with the three American
Servicemen who had come to fetch us and partly from observation.

No Americans were allowed outside the perimeter of the camp,
except for specific duties as authorised by the Commanding Officer,
Colonel Sillin. Each authorised 'sortie' from the camp was carried

out by three men—no more and no less. As we could see from our own observations of our companions, each of the three Americans in each party was armed to the teeth. They carried automatic weapons, grenades and 'walkie-talkies'. Parties of similarly armed men were constantly patrolling the outside of the perimeter. They were taking no chances, even though hostilities had ceased three weeks previously.

At Kanoya there was a force of some 2,000 Americans in all and their sole task was to hold and protect the aerodrome. It was no part of their assignment to make contact with P.o.W. camps; and, indeed, the task of transporting to the aerodrome those P.o.W.s who had found their way individually to Kanoya station was, strictly speaking, outside the scope of their duties.

My visions of guiding a Task Force from Kanoya to Miyata had evaporated before we had even passed through the aerodrome gates.

We had a warm American welcome from the guard on the main aerodrome gate and we were then driven immediately to see Colonel McGowan, Executive Officer to the Commanding Officer.

The latter wasted no time but escorted us immediately to Colonel Sillin's office. As soon as we were all seated, we told them about the conditions at Miyata and stressed the urgent need for food, for medical supplies and, above all, for early evacuation.

Colonel Sillin expressed astonishment at our message. The Americans had been categorically assured by the Japanese that there were no P.o.W.s on the island of Kyushu, though he had begun to doubt this when dozens of stragglers had begun arriving at Kanoya. These P.o.W.s, we learnt, were being flown off to Okinawa as soon as possible.

I told them about the order to kill all the prisoners which the Dutch interpreter had seen in the camp office at Miyata. The last piece of that particular puzzle had fallen into place.

Colonel Sillin undertook to try to arrange with Okinawa or Saipan for medical personnel, medical supplies and food to be parachuted into Miyata.

Peter and I were given a room in the Infantry Officers' Mess as there was no accommodation available in the 5th Air Task Force Mess.

After dinner in the Mess—our first Western food, and what a spread it was, for nearly four years—we went to the camp cinema to see a film.

Later that evening, and to our great surprise, Colonel Petrie arrived from Fukuoka. He had come with an urgent request for

carbon-dioxide which was required for the treatment of many
P.o.W.s in the Fukuoka Group of War Prisoners Camps who were
suffering from liquor poisoning.

Some fifty prisoners from various camps had celebrated V-J
Day not wisely but too well. Six had already died and a further
thirty were not expected to live.

The following morning, which must have been the 11th September, Peter and I were 'grilled', separately, by American Intelligence
Officers.

Among many other things, they wanted the names or descriptions of all Japanese guards and camp staff with whom we had
come into contact during our captivity, with an indication of their
degree of culpability for our misfortunes.

We had another long session with Colonel McGowan. While we
were there a Red Cross Delegation arrived to discuss arrangements
for the evacuation of the some 16,000 P.o.W.s on the island of
Kyushu, whose existence was known to the Red Cross. Colonel
Petrie flew back to Fukuoka with the Delegation.

I spent the rest of the day on the air-strip, taking down the
names and other particulars, including the names and numbers of
the P.o.W. camps from which they had come, of all the prisoners
who were being flown out to Okinawa in B.24s.

A number of American and Dutch P.o.W.s had huge sacks of
unused Red Cross boots and other stores with which, no doubt, they
proposed to set themselves up in business on their return to civil
life. Many of these sacks weighed twice as much as a P.o.W. In
view of the pressure on the accommodation in the planes, this loot
was removed from them, but in many cases not without a struggle.

The departing aircraft were being packed to capacity. Many
of the P.o.W.s were accommodated in the empty bomb-bays. A
report was received during the late afternoon that a 'slap-happy'
pilot, forgetting that he had P.o.W.s in his bomb-bay, had inadvertently opened his 'bay'. All the P.o.W.s in the 'bay' had fallen into
the sea and were drowned.

When I returned to the Mess after my labours I found a note
from Peter awaiting me. This somewhat confusing message read as
follows:

11.30 hours

Dear John,

I am off to Okinawa immediately. Since this plane has not
come in I shall go to their base (I hope)—come up tomorrow—and

ask them to drop me here on the way home to get any messages Petrie may have.

You stay here and if a B.29 drops in tomorrow morning, which will mean I have not got to their base and that we have by-passed each other—Pilot it up yourself and come back here.

Yours
Peter

I spent some time trying to decide what all this meant. I took it to mean that Peter was waiting for a plane, probably from Tokyo, which would be touching down at Kanoya en route for Okinawa. He proposed to take passage in it, and to spend the night at Okinawa. He then planned to return in the same plane the following morning, which would again touch down at Kanoya, this time on its way to Tokyo.

This seemed to make sense of the first paragraph. We had learnt at Kanoya that all food and medical supplies were coming up from Okinawa and I knew that Peter had it in mind to go there in an attempt to stimulate some action for Miyata.

The second paragraph I found more difficult and I spent some hours trying to decipher what it meant. It was clear that I was to stay where I was, that is in Kanoya, but what the rest meant I did not know.

I decided to sleep on the problem.

It all became crystal clear early next morning when I learnt that Peter had apparently been put into the wrong aircraft. He had been taken to Saipan in the Marianna Islands, which was almost 1,500 miles away from both Kanoya and Okinawa!

With Peter in Saipan and Colonel Petrie, I presumed, back in Fukuoka with, I hoped, his carbon-dioxide, I was on my own.

The same day, with some officers of the 5th Air Task Force, I was invited out to lunch on board U.S.S. *Clifton*, a navy tanker anchored in Kanoya cove. There were plenty of refrigerating facilities on board and once again I was treated to a wonderful meal.

On my return to the aerodrome I was shown two messages. One was to the effect that Peter 'had proceeded further south'; the other indicated that the evacuation of the Miyata P.o.W.s was planned to take place by ship from Nagasaki on the 13th and 14th September. It was now the 12th September.

I desperately hoped that I would be in time. Ever since I had left

Miyata on the 8th September I had been worrying about my diaries. I wrote out two notes—one to Colonel Petrie and one to Tim Hallam.

In my note to Colonel Petrie I gave him the names of all the Fukuoka Group P.o.W.s whom I knew had passed through Kanoya on their way to Okinawa. I also told him about Peter's movements, in so far as I was aware of them, and added that I proposed to fly out to Okinawa that afternoon.

My note to Tim was more difficult. I had to describe exactly where, and how, I had hidden my diaries and beg him, whatever else he did before leaving Miyata, to retrieve them and bring them with him.

I then took my notes to Colonel McGowan and asked him whether it would be possible for one of his pilots to drop them by parachute over Miyata Camp that afternoon. He said that he thought that it could be arranged. Subsequent events were to prove that it was.

Later that afternoon I got a seat in a B.25 which was flying to Okinawa. Although I had been in the R.A.F. for nearly four years it was the first time I had ever flown in an aircraft. Kyushu looked beautiful from the air and the Americans at Kanoya had been extremely kind and helpful, but I could not say that I was sorry to be leaving.

We had an excellent flight from Kanoya to Motobu air-strip in the northern part of Okinawa. The B.25 in which I was travelling was the mail-carrier. There was only one other passenger, an agreeable, but fortunately taciturn, American Colonel. I was glad to be alone with my thoughts.

We saw a number of American ships steaming northwards towards Japan. As we approached Okinawa, I could see the brightly coloured coral-reefs just under the surface of the sea.

On arrival at Motobu airstrip the American Colonel, whose kindness exceeded even his taciturnity, took me to the 5th Air Task Force Officers' Mess. There I was surprised to learn, though it proved, apparently, to be a false rumour, that Peter had passed through during the morning of the same day I was told that I would probably find him at the P.o.W. Transit Camp at Kadena, another airstrip at the southern end of Okinawa.

The Colonel took me to an officers' tent to rest. After a shower I was taken to the Mess for a meal. At the table where I was bidden to sit there was an American woman doctor, the first white woman

I had seen for over three years. She was not very pretty, but she was warm and sympathetic; and she was a woman. She threw her arms around me and kissed me repeatedly on my mouth, my emaciated cheeks and my shaven head. I burst into uncontrollable tears. My dinner was spoilt for me.

Later a U.S. Air Force Major, Cox, who had been detailed to fly me down to Kadena, came to collect me. He flew me down in a C.46, passing over the enormous fleet at anchor. All the ships were flashing messages to each other and to the shore, like a swarm of fire-flies.

At Kadena I was taken to a P.o.W. Reception Tent. I enquired for Peter. He was paged continuously over loud-speakers in the P.o.W. Transit Camp, which was some distance away, without result. Eventually I was assured that a search of the records had proved conclusively that he had never been there.

I waited for some time in the P.o.W. Reception Tent on the air-strip for transport to take me to the Transit Camp. There were dozens of American Red Cross girls there who filled me up with coffee, coca-cola, ices and doughnuts. If some of them had offered me a kiss, I don't think I would have cried that time. Many of the girls had come straight out to the Far East from Europe after V.E. Day without a break in the United States.

The P.o.W. Transit Camp was not much better than Miyata. In some ways it was worse. The overcrowded tents had neither floors nor lights. But the complete absence of any food, the rain, the mud and the general confusion were sufficiently reminiscent of Miyata to put me at my ease.

I grabbed a bed in a darkened tent. Then I ploughed through the mud to the camp office. There I learnt that a bottleneck was building up. There were more aircraft available to fly P.o.W.s from Kanoya to Okinawa than there were to fly them on to Manila. Some P.o.W.s had been hanging about in the Transit Camp for two or three days. This prospect did not appeal to me. I persuaded the U.S. Air Corps Lieutenant to put me on a plane leaving for Manila very early the following morning.

I was far too excited to sleep and I was determined not to miss my plane. I wandered round the camp and met an Aircraftsman whom I knew. He told me that Jimmy Addison, a fellow R.A.F. officer who had been with me in Zentsuji, was in the camp. I spent two boxes of matches, and most of the night, looking into darkened tents for Jimmy. I did not find him but I found a number of other friends. Among them was Tommy Thompson, whose interest in astronomy while he was doing night fire-watch guard at Zentsuji had resulted in my being felled to the ground by the Japanese guard commander.

Tommy gave me news about the first British party which had left Zentsuji, for Tokyo, in June. They did not seem to have had quite as bad a time as we had had, though Captain Gordon and Colonel Lindesay, as the senior officers, had been badly knocked about. There had been a few deaths in Tommy's party after they had left Zentsuji.

By now it was time for me to queue up for transport to the Kadena air-strip. I found that I was the only officer in the party. The others were all Dutch, many of them of mixed blood. Once again sacks of loot had to be removed from them forcibly to make room for their comrades. We were all issued with 'K' hard rations.

I persuaded the pilot to let me sit in the co-pilot's seat of the B.24. I was anxious to learn something about flying an aircraft before it was too late.

The pilot was a cheerful customer. He told me quite casually that the B.24s had a very bad record in evacuating P.o.W.s. He confirmed the report of the 'bomb-bay' accident of which I had heard at Kanoya on Kyushu. He added that a couple of days earlier a B.24 taking off from the air-strip on which we were now revving up our engines had crashed in flames at the end of the runway and that the aircraft's crew and all the P.o.W.s aboard had been burnt to death. As we, mercifully, flew over the spot a few minutes later, I could see where the tragedy had occurred.

The pilot was irrepressible. As soon as we were over the sea, he recalled that another B.24, piloted by one of his friends, had crashed into the 'drink' a few days before. All the P.o.W.s had had to jump out with their parachutes. As I learnt later, one of these, Maloney, had been with me at Zentsuji. He was in the water for some hours before he was picked up by a destroyer of the Royal Navy and transferred to a hospital ship bound for Australia.

'Many of the P.o.W.s, learning of these accidents, have flatly refused to fly in a B.24, you know,' he added.

'It's a bit late to tell me all this,' I said to myself, adding aloud to him, 'How do these damned things work?', pointing to the 'Mae West' and the parachute with which I was encumbered.

I think the pilot must have found me a bit fussy, but as the risk of sudden death at the hands of the Americans appeared to be even greater than it had been at the hands of the Japanese, I wanted to be prepared for all eventualities.

It was an agreeable flight. When not in the co-pilot's seat I was lying on my belly in the for'ard gunner's post, enjoying the magnificent view. I also paid a visit—a very brief visit—to the bomb-bay and another to the rear-gunner's post.

I learnt more about flying on this trip than the R.A.F. had ever had time to teach me, but in neither case did it amount to much.

We landed at Clark Field in the Philippines about 2 p.m. We waited about, drinking the inevitable coffee and munching the inevitable doughnuts, for another aircraft to take us on to Manila.*

On arrival, we were transported by lorry to an enormous tented camp, situated on what had previously been the Madrigal Estate. It was some fifteen miles south of Manila and a couple of miles from a large lake, Laguna de Bay.

This was the 5th American Replacement Depot. The 3rd Australian P.W. Reception Group, which formed part of this vast complex, was responsible for dealing with all British P.o.W.s. A number of British Naval, Army and R.A.F. officers were attached to the Australian Reception Group. Some of these had themselves been P.o.W.s in Germany; Flight-Lieutenant Eric Williams, who won an M.C. for his escape from Stalag-Luft III in October 1943, was among them.

The huge Australian other ranks who formed the camp staff of this Reception Group reminded me of London policemen. They had all volunteered to come up from Australia for this task and they were 'wonderful'. Nothing was too much trouble for them. They made up our camp-beds in the tents with 'real' sheets. They brought us morning tea in bed. They waited on us in the mess-hall.

I needed a 'hussif' to do some sewing. There were no 'hussifs' left in the Quartermaster's Store, so the Australian storeman insisted that I should have his.

Their invariable kindness was accompanied by much good-humoured banter which soon revived our spirits.

It was the 13th September 1945. Technically I had been a 'free' man for a month. I was only just beginning to feel like one.

Brigadier H. Wrigley, the Commander of the 3rd Australian P.W. Reception Group, had issued a 'message' to each incoming P.o.W.

The first thing to be done, the message said, was to send off

*See map 2, page 317.

a cable to one's family announcing one's safe arrival in Manila. This I did and the news was reflected in a notice, announcing that I was safe, which appeared, with many other similar notices, in the Personal Column of the *Daily Telegraph* on the 30th September 1945. I had not received any letters from L. for over a year and the last one I had received had been dated May 1944, nearly eighteen months previously.

The second requirement was a series of medical examinations, not only in our own interests but in those of our families too.

Finally, we had to submit to further 'interrogations', designed not only to give information about our own treatment, Japanese atrocities, and so on, but also, and where possible, to give particulars about the fate of individual prisoners whom we had reason to believe were dead.

All this took some time, but the competence, understanding and kindness of the Australians made these tasks as painless as possible.

Within a week one could not recognise the man next to whom one might have slept for months. Most of us were having ten or twelve meals a day. The whole structure of well-remembered faces and bodies changed almost overnight.

We visited the other ranks' camp in another part of the depot. We established contact with our respective Accounts Officers and drew advances of pay.

It was on Sunday the 16th September that I started to make enquiries as to how I could get to India. Most of the P.o.W.s had two options open to them: either to go to Australia or to the west coast of the United States. As L. was, I supposed, still in India, that, I decided, was where I was going, whatever the authorities might think.

With a fellow-P.o.W. I went to Nicoll's Field where we learnt that the Americans had a once weekly flight, over 'the Hump', to Calcutta via Kunming. I knew that there were others similarly placed who wished to go to India, so I 'reserved' a block of fourteen seats on the aircraft due to leave on Wednesday the 19th September.

Several of us went down to Nicoll's Field again on the Wednesday hoping to catch the plane. There we learnt to our amazement that, as 'Lend-Lease' had come to an end with the termination of hostilities, the Americans would only take us if we put down 400 U.S. dollars in gold. Having no gold, we returned disconsolately to our camp.

On Thursday the 20th I went into Manila with an army

officer who had been with me at Boei Glodok in Java. He wanted to visit a particular bank. I accompanied him, not that I had any hope of persuading a bank to let me have 400 gold dollars but because I wanted to see what Manila looked like. The destruction and devastation caused by artillery fire, when the Americans retook the city from the Japanese, came as a shock, even to one who had seen something of the flattened cities and towns of Japan.

The days slipped by and it seemed as though I would never get moving again.

There were concerts, plays and film shows in the camp. I attended sick parade for various minor complaints. I went into Manila several times and on one occasion paid a call on the British Consul who kindly sent off a cable to the Colonial Office for me.

I tried, with Len Cooper, whom I had not seen since we left Zentsuji in different parties, to get on a 'conducted tour', going to Corregidor, where the Americans had made their gallant last stand before General MacArthur slipped away to Australia on the 11th March, 1942. We must have got on the wrong lorry, as we found ourselves dumped in the middle of the city where we wasted time until the American lorry-driver saw fit to take us back to camp.

A cable arrived from L. giving her address in New Delhi.

On Wednesday the 26th I went again, with others, to Nicoll's Field in the hope of getting on the weekly aircraft to Calcutta.

'No dollars? No seats,' said the U.S. Movements Officer.

The plane left with nine empty places!

Two distinguished visitors arrived in the camp. Each in their own inimitable ways cheered us up. One was Gracie Fields and the other was Admiral Sir Bruce Fraser.*

The Admiral was commanding all British Naval Forces in the Far East, and a Brigadier Ballentyne raised with him, and thus our hopes, the question of transport to India.

It was not until the 2nd October that I ran into Ian Graham in the camp.

'Hallo! John,' he said casually. 'I've a funny little bag here which Tim Hallam asked me to give you. He's gone off to hospital, I believe.'

I was, indeed, glad to have recovered my diaries. They had been

* Later Admiral of the Fleet Baron Fraser of North Cape, G.C.B., K.B.E.

my constant companions since the Japanese attacked Malaya on the 8th December 1941. Even during my 'escapade' with J.F. in the Java jungle in March 1942 I had managed to keep them intact, though the bundle was much smaller in those far-off days.

I sent up silent prayers for the admirable Colonel McGowan, for the pilot from Kanoya who had dropped my message over the camp at Miyata, for the unknown P.o.W. who had taken my message to Tim, for Tim himself, now in hospital, who had managed to find them, and for Ian who had brought them to me.

The following day, the 3rd October, I re-read the final entry I had made at Miyata on the 5th September. Then from various notes I had made on scraps of paper I brought the record up to date.

Now that I had recovered my diaries there seemed to be even less reason to hang about in Manila.

A number of us decided to make yet another assault on the American Air Transport Command. At Nicoll's Field we found that the normal weekly plane to Calcutta had left at 4.30 p.m. instead of at its usual departure hour of 11.30 p.m.

Having 'borrowed' a Jeep, we did not relish the idea of returning to camp unless we had to. We asked at the Movements Office where we might find the off-duty pilots of Air Transport Command. We hoped to find one whom we could 'persuade' to take us—or at least take us some of the way in the right direction. We were told that we would find the pilots relaxing in the A.T.C. Officers' Club. We were given directions as to where this was situated, and we set off.

The directions were not very clear and we got lost several times. Eventually we stopped an American Serviceman.

'The A.T.C. Officers' Club?' he said. 'Why, you're right on top of it. It's in the last house up that road on the right.'

We drove up to a large, old and rather dark Filippino house with a painted sign which read 'A.T.C. Officers' Club' outside.

It clearly was an American Officers' Club. On entering we could see nothing but petting couples; one half of each was an American officer and the other half was a pretty Filippino girl. They were all over the place, in the garden, in the passage, on the stairs and in every room. They were evidently 'relaxing', as we had been warned. There were no 'breakaways', nor any un-attached girls, as we strolled around.

Questions directed to the closely knit couples elicited no response whatever. Eventually we found an unentangled officer having a solitary drink in a quiet corner. We supposed that his partner was temporarily absent, as he was as dishevelled as the rest of them.

'Any chance of having a word with some of the pilots here?' I asked.

'Pilots! Pilots!' he shouted, taking another swig of neat whisky. 'There are no pilots here, buddy. This is the Amphibious Truck Companies' Officers' Club.'

We broke off the talks immediately and left as silently, and as unnoticed, as we had entered.

We learnt later that the personnel of the Amphibious Truck Companies had a reputation for getting their claws on such local talent as was available. Being the first to land, they usually managed to corner the market.

Eventually we found the Air Transport Command Officers' Club, but the scene was much the same and we could find no one to take any interest in us.

Fortunately no one had noticed that the Jeep had been temporarily removed from our camp.

The following day, the 4th October, I learnt that there was a British aircraft-carrier, H.M.S. *Colossus*, in Manila Bay and rumour had it that she was bound for Hong Kong.

H.M.S. *Colossus*, 14,000 tons, was one of the largest 'Escort' carriers with a maximum speed of twenty-five knots and a ship's complement of 1,200 officers and men. Her aircraft consisted of one squadron of Corsair fighters and another of Barracuda torpedo-bombers.

I made my way down to the port. Expressing a wish to have a look at *Colossus*, I persuaded the crew of one of her pinnaces to take me out to her. The harbour was full of sunken vessels and it took us some time to arrive.

Once aboard, I asked if I might see the Captain.

Having introduced myself I said that I desperately wanted to get to India to find L. I understood that he would soon be sailing for Hong Kong and I wondered if I might take passage with him there.

'I'm afraid not,' he replied. 'You are presumably under some sort of discipline at your camp and it would be quite inappropriate for me to give any undertakings to individual P.o.W.s. I know that you, and many others, are anxious to get to India and I have a great deal of sympathy with you. But I'm afraid it's just not on, old boy.'

He could see that I was crestfallen.

'Would you care for a pink gin?' he said.

'Thank you, sir,' I replied.

We sipped our gins and chatted about the war.

The time had come for me to take my leave. I thanked him for receiving me and was about to leave his cabin when he suddenly said, with the biggest wink I had ever seen: 'You may care to know that we shall be sailing at noon tomorrow.'

I returned to the camp highly elated and firmly determined to take passage in H.M.S. *Colossus* whatever anybody said.

That night I found a friendly Senior British Officer attached to the Australian P.W. Reception Group and explained my intentions. I believe his name was Scott. I persuaded him to give me a chit authorising my departure. I also changed my Philippine 'Victory' pesos into Indian rupees, as an earnest to myself of my determination to leave at all costs.

I made my way down to the port very early on Friday the 5th October. This time I was careful not to leave my diaries behind.

There seemed to be quite a large number of other P.o.W.s hanging about at the landing stage used by shore-parties from *Colossus*. I realised that I was not the only one with the same objective.

While we were waiting about, an officer of the American Military Police arrived with a small party of American M.P.s. He asked us what we were doing, which should have been obvious. He said that he would not permit us to board H.M.S. *Colossus*, which was not one of the ships 'authorised' to evacuate P.o.W.s from Manila.

The Military Police were 'seen off' by a British Colonel, Bamford, who was among our number.

When at last we came alongside H.M.S. *Colossus* the Royal Marines' Band was playing. The hangar had been cleared and all the aircraft were on deck, the Corsairs with their wings folded upwards, the Barracudas backwards.

The senior officers were allotted cabins; the junior officers, including myself, were given camp beds in a workshop off the hangar; and the other ranks, mainly from the Hong Kong Volunteer Defence Corps, bedded down in the hangar.

It was a relief, after nearly four years of chaos, to find oneself well organised but not pushed around. The ship's company took it all in their stride, as though they did it every day of the week.

Some P.o.W. officers were allocated to the Petty Officers' Mess for meals; others, of whom I was lucky enough to be one, to the Ward Room.

Every P.o.W. was given a 'free' chit on the ship's canteen for five shillings and threepence.

We sailed at noon as the Captain had told me, the day before, that he would.

It was a most agreeable interlude. We read the latest English papers, with news of the recent General Elections. Many of the ship's officers were anxious to have news of their friends in H.M.S. *Exeter* which I was able to give them. We were shown round the ship, we went to concerts, we played bridge and we sat and drank and chatted.

It was very hot on board but the juniors were more fortunate than their seniors, as the hangar was much cooler than the cabins.

On Sunday the 7th October we attended a Church Service. By now we really had something to be thankful for.

At about 1 p.m. the same day we steamed slowly into Hong Kong harbour, which I had never seen before. I was among those invited on to the bridge.

The band of the Royal Marines was playing and the ship's company lined the ship. Few of the P.o.W.s had dry eyes at that moment.

Colossus anchored some distance off shore in the outer harbour. The gallant Colonel Bamford and one or two others went ashore but I was in no hurry. They soon returned saying that Hong Kong, which was still licking its wounds, was not very comfortable.

There was another cinema show that night for officers only. The thirty-two-millimetre machine had broken down and only the sixteen-millimetre machine could be used. Someone in the Ward Room enquired whether we were going to see Betty Grable in *Pin-up Girl*. I observed, almost without thinking, that you couldn't get all of Betty Grable on a sixteen-millimetre film. This remark earned me the unwarranted reputation of being the ship's wit!

We saw *Don't take it to Heart*, a film which passed the time.

The following day, Monday the 8th October, we disembarked at Kowloon. I can only hope that the Captain, the officers and the rest of the ship's company of H.M.S. *Colossus* realised how appreciative we were of all that they had done for us—which was a very great deal.

At Kowloon the senior officers were accommodated in the

Peninsula Hotel. The rest of us were driven up to a P.o.W. Reception Centre at 269 Prince Edward Road.

This was not, alas! a Royal Naval Establishment and the confusion and contrast were unbelievable.

Early contact with the R.A.F. was called for, I thought. I got a lift down to the ferry and crossed the harbour to Hong Kong Island. I found R.A.F. H.Q. and obtained an advance of pay and a promise of a seat in an aircraft to Kunming the following day. Prior to take-off I had to have a medical examination to see whether I was fit to fly over 'the Hump'. The R.A.F. Medical Officer who examined me said, with a sigh, that whisky then cost £18 a bottle in Hong Kong.

I was somewhat ashamed of my appearance. A casual observer would have found it difficult to make up his mind of which branch of the Armed Forces of which country I purported to be a member. I was a proper hybrid—part Red Cross and part American Air Force, with a dash of Japanese.

An application to the R.A.F. stores office for help was not very fruitful. All that the jovial storeman could offer me was a flying suit more appropriate for a trans-polar flight than the sweaty heat of Calcutta, which, I still hoped, would be my ultimate destination. I decided to continue my voyage 'incognito'.

Early the following morning, the 9th October, and after a most uncomfortable night at the Kowloon P.o.W. Reception Centre, I found my way to Kai Tak aerodrome. All passengers and kit for my flight were being most carefully weighed. As I was still grossly underweight and as I had virtually no kit, I did not pose any problems to the authorities on that occasion.

The aircraft, a Halifax, flew high. We were soon above the clouds and I could see little or nothing of the Chinese mainland sprawling below me. We landed at Kunming in the province of Yunnan just before dusk.

We spent the night in a Chinese inn. There was just time for a stroll through the bazaar before we turned in. I was struck by the number of camels and by the acrid smell of the camel-dung, burning on the fires at which the stall-holders were warming themselves.

It was bitterly cold and I almost wished I had accepted the Hong Kong R.A.F. storeman's offer of the 'polar' flying suit.

The following morning, the 10th October, we took off for Calcutta. Fortunately the Halifax engines made conversation

impossible, as we climbed higher and higher over the mountains of
'the Hump'.

By now I was full of apprehensions about my approaching
meeting with L. How could two individuals whose lives had taken
such different paths for nearly four years, and who had had virtually
no communication with each other, begin to pick up the threads
again?

'If only the plane would crash,' I thought. 'I would be lost
for ever in one of those precipitous valleys below. Nothing would
matter any more.'

It was oppressively hot and humid when we landed at Calcutta
in the late afternoon. I was the only P.o.W. on board and I was
easily recognisable as such. As I left the aircraft, someone told me to
go to the P.o.W. Reception Office in the ramshackle airport building.

I was soon on my way to Belvedere. This enormous 'pile',
which dated from the early eighteenth century, had been the
official residence of the Lieutenant-Governor of Bengal from 1854
until the transfer of the Imperial Capital to Delhi. Subsequently
it became the official residence of the Viceroy during his visits to
Calcutta.

By the time I entered its portals, a dark purple camouflage
had concealed the charm which it had undoubtedly possessed in
ampler days.

It was now the 'Recovered Allied Prisoners-of-War and Internees Camp'.

Once again I was subjected to the usual 'processing', medical
examination, interrogation and documentation.

The ladies who looked after my welfare were kindness personi-
fied. It was strange to hear their well-bred and high-pitched English
voices after the Japanese shouts of so many years and the broad
American accents of the past few weeks.

They gave me a watch, they sent off cables, they arranged a
telephone call to L. in New Delhi, and they helped me to get a
uniform. But there was one thing they could not do—they could not
get the hair on my shaven head to grow any faster.

I believe I spent two nights at Belvedere and that I then flew
to Delhi where I met L. on the 12th October.

We had planned a brief holiday in Kashmir and all the arrangements
were made.

During the night of the 11th November, when we were staying with L.'s brother and sister-in-law in Lahore, I was stricken with appalling pains in my back. The acute stabs, as though from a dagger, were intolerable. Nothing I did afforded me any relief. I found myself writhing about on the floor.

A doctor was summoned and in the early hours of the morning of the 12th November I was taken in an ambulance to the British Military Hospital, Lahore.

This was a dark and solidly constructed building, like some medieval castle. I seem to recall flickering oil-lamps among the bare vaulted roofs, as I was wheeled along the huge stone corridors to the dungeon. I expected to be greeted by Florence Nightingale at any moment.

In fact my ministering angel was an Austrian Jew, a refugee doctor from Vienna. Having established that I had stones in the kidneys, he sat up with me night after night in the hope that I would 'pass' these out, thus avoiding the need for an operation.

One night, when I was feeling particularly sorry for myself and, no doubt, letting everyone within earshot know, a pretty English nurse came and held my hand.

'Come on,' she said, 'I know it hurts but you'll soon be all right. You've passed several stones out already and you'll soon get rid of the rest. Then you'll be as fit as a fiddle again.'

She pressed my hand and went on softly: 'You've really nothing to complain about. There's a young Australian P.o.W. in a bed down the ward. You should see what the Japanese did to him. He's no longer a man. What he has got to look forward to?'

She was weeping softly to herself by now and I grasped her hand more firmly in an attempt to comfort my comforter.

'So come on,' she said, pulling herself together, 'stop your whining and think of all you're going to do in the future.'

Somehow or other the pain seemed to get easier and I fell asleep.

Within a few days I was discharged. I counted myself very fortunate that I had not been so afflicted at Miyata three months earlier.

We flew home to England together in a Sunderland flying boat from Karachi early in December. L. was a Major in the Women's Indian Army Auxiliary Corps and it took her a little time to get her release. I frequently wondered whether I should salute her when we were both in uniform.

Our journey to Poole in Hampshire took nearly a week. The weather was very bad in the Mediterranean and we were held up for several days in Augusta in Sicily.

It was good to be back in England in time for Christmas, 1945.

I went to the Colonial Office. By now I had acquired an R.A.F. blue uniform and overcoat. For the first time since February 1942 I felt 'properly dressed'.

My first call was on Sir Arthur Dawe, then Deputy Under-Secretary of State for the Colonies. In 1935-6 I had been an Assistant Principal in the Pacific and Mediterranean Department dealing with Malta and Arthur Dawe had been my Principal.

I had always had a great affection and respect for him and he was the only member of the Colonial Office staff who had sent me a postcard while I was a P.o.W.

'Hallo, John,' he said. 'How are you?' as though I had just been away for a fortnight's leave. 'Come and have lunch,' he went on, 'I have something I want to discuss with you.'

When we had settled down at lunch he asked me: 'When can you get released from the R.A.F.?'

'Well,' I replied, 'I have to go to Cosford Camp in Cheshire to go through all the formalities of getting released but I gather that I should be out by the end of January.'

'Good,' he said, 'that will suit admirably.'

He then explained that Sir Harold MacMichael* was at that moment engaged on a mission as the Special Representative of His Majesty's Government in Malaya.

'When he's finished that,' Dawe said, 'he has agreed to go to Malta as Constitutional Commissioner and we would like you to go with him as Financial Adviser and Secretary.'

He paused and filled up my glass of wine.

'I know, from our pre-war days together, that you have some idea of what makes Malta tick and I would very much like you to go.'

He could see that I was dumbfounded at this proposal and he went on quickly:

'I expect MacMichael will want to spend February and March in the Colonial Office preparing for his task but I imagine that he will be ready to go to Malta in April.'

I hesitated. 'I haven't been in England for nine years,' I said.

* The late Sir Harold MacMichael, G.C.M.G., D.S.O., formerly Civil Secretary in the Sudan, Governor of Tanganyika and High Commissioner for Palestine.

'And I've lost touch with my family and my friends. I have at least a year's leave due to me from my pre-war service in Malaya. And quite frankly I wonder whether, at the present time, I would be capable of doing the job.'

But Dawe was determined that I should go.

'There's another thing,' he said, 'you look very under-weight to me. Food is going to be difficult here for the next couple of years. There's no rationing in Malta and you'll soon pick up in the sunshine there.'

I told him I'd think it over and let him know.

A few months earlier I had been working as a coolie, carrying buckets of 'night-soil' at the direction of the Camp Commandant at Miyata. I had been wading about in paddy-fields or stacking pit-props at the mine, bullied by the goons.

Then there was Dawe's remark about being 'Financial Adviser'. It was true that I had been Secretary, Foreign Exchange Control, in Singapore before I had gone to Cameron Highlands, but that was six years ago. 'How will your limited acquaintance with fluctuations in the value of the yen over the past four years help you in Malta?' I asked myself.

I had practically decided to decline, but my affection and respect for Dawe overcame my hesitations.

I never regretted my decision to go with MacMichael to Malta. To be given a worthwhile job to do imperceptibly restored my self-respect and my self-confidence.

As the months went by, I had contact with many of those who had been in captivity with me and who had not been offered a chance, such as I had been, to get their teeth into something worth while. Many of them were unsettled and brooding about the state of their health or the state of their minds. I had no time for such introspections. I was far too busy with my new task.

For a couple of years after I was released from captivity I did, at times, during the small hours of the night, have qualms about my sanity. It was not until I was posted to the United Kingdom Mission to the United Nations in New York that these qualms disappeared. Three years' experience of the antics that went on at Lake Success and Flushing Meadows soon convinced me that I was at least as balanced as most of those attempting to re-build the shattered post-war world.

Epilogue: Japan Revisited

August 1969

I suppose that it must have been during the flight in the B.25 from Kanoya aerodrome to Okinawa on the 12th September 1945 that the idea first took shape in my sub-conscious mind. 'One day,' I must have said to myself, 'you will come back to Japan as a free man.'

The preoccupations of the following quarter of a century afforded me neither the time nor the money to fulfil this hope, but the hankering grew as the years slipped by.

Then, during the early summer of 1969, I was invited to undertake an Official Mission for the British Government to the Anglo-French Condominium of the New Hebrides in the southern Pacific, —with my return fare paid by the tax-payer. I decided that when I had completed my assignment I would return home via Japan.

I made no plans. If it proved possible I would visit the camps in which I had been a P.o.W. I also hoped to make contact with some of my former gaolers.

This was not achieved without difficulty and it would not have been achieved at all without the great help of a certain Mr. Ken-Ichiro Kondo.

Mr. Kondo, a senior official in the Foreign Ministry, Tokyo, was at that time responsible for the organisation of Expo 70 at Osaka. It was a telephone call to the Ministry, with an enquiry about Expo 70, which first brought me into contact with Mr. Kondo. When he had returned my call, giving me a plethora of information on the point I had put to him, I had ventured to trespass further on his kindness by indicating my desire to revisit the camps. Perhaps it was his innate courtesy; perhaps it was the fact that his own life

L

had been disrupted by the war; but, whatever it was, he decided to take me under his wing.

I subsequently learnt that Mr. Kondo had been in the Japanese Embassy in Washington at the outbreak of war and that it was not until some four years later that he had been able to return to his native land, having spent the war years in Japanese Embassies in various neutral countries. Later he had become Japanese Ambassador in Afghanistan.

A day or two after I had dumped my problem on his already well-filled plate Mr. Kondo called to say that all was arranged. It might be convenient, he ventured to suggest, if I first took the train to Hiroshima. From there I could take the hydrofoil to Matsuyama on the island of Shikoku where two of the Habu Camp staff would be pleased to meet me. There are, of course, quicker ways of getting to Matsuyama from Tokyo than via Hiroshima. Perhaps Mr. Kondo thought that before I began to indulge in too much self-pity it would be good for my soul to feel some pity for others.

The train from Tokyo to Hiroshima passes through Onomichi. I recalled our train ride in pitch darkness from Shimonoseki to Onomichi on a bitterly cold night in November 1942, after we had disembarked from the *Dai Nichi Maru* at Moji. I remembered, too, how we had de-trained at Onomichi prior to taking the tug to an unknown destination, which turned out to be Habu.

Hiroshima came as a surprise in many ways. As a city it appeared, in August 1969, to be much the same as any other Japanese city, teeming, garish, unattractive; but the contrast between the well-kept lawns and the tree-shaded paths of the Peace Park and the gruesome photographs and other relics of the atomic explosion, as displayed in the Peace Museum, came as a shock. A casual visitor to Hiroshima would notice nothing, except for the deliberately preserved skeleton of the former Industrial Exposition Hall, to suggest that the city was completely destroyed on the 6th August 1945. An hour in the Peace Museum is sufficient to put this matter in perspective. I could not, however, refrain from the thought that, but for the bomb, none of the P.o.W.s would ever have returned home.

The following morning I took the hydrofoil to Matsuyama, a city at the western end of Shikoku. Mr. Kondo had booked a room for me in an agreeable Japanese inn at Dogo Spa on the outskirts of the city. A plaque commemorates a visit to the inn by the Emperor. This was to be the meeting place with my former gaolers.

I had given some thought to this encounter. In Hong Kong

I had been told that an American P.o.W., meeting one of his former guards somewhere in Japan, had strangled him on the spot with his bare hands and that the Japanese authorities had taken no action. I was also mindful of the possibility that some Japanese might endeavour to make propaganda out of my visit and to suggest that the very fact that I had returned indicated that the Japanese treatment of P.o.W.s was not so bad as in reality it was. It was also in my thoughts that while one cannot bring back the dead and while one may never forget, one may, perhaps, forgive.

The two Japanese who had accepted my invitation to a Japanese dinner at the inn were Captain Akira Nomoto, the Camp Commandant at Habu, and Sergeant Shigema Nagano, the Camp Sergeant.

Mr. Kondo had previously told me that after the war Nomoto had changed his name to Mizuguchi and that he was now engaged in breeding silkworms. Nagano was also engaged in sericulture, Mr. Kondo had said, adding that the two of them seemed to be good friends.

As I cast my mind back over some twenty-seven years, I tried to imagine how they must have felt when they were first faced with 200 British prisoners in 1942. I also tried to imagine how they would feel when they were faced, in 1969, with a single former British P.o.W.

On my return from a brief visit to a nearby feudal castle, they were there. They did not seem to have aged at all. They were both wearing what appears to be the customary dress of the contemporary Japanese male—black trousers, white shirt, dark tie. I offered them beer, telling them with a wink, which sent Nagano off into loud guffaws, that I had brought with me a bottle of whisky for later!

While the preliminaries were still in progress, English-speaking representatives of the press arrived. They had been given prior warning of the encounter by Mr. Kondo. I was somewhat annoyed at this intrusion; I had visions of being used for propaganda purposes. Not only need I not have worried, but, as matters turned out later, this proved to be a blessing in disguise. We responded in turn to a variety of questions and many photographs were taken.

When a friendly Japanese translated the article for me the following morning I learnt that the journalists had given full weight to my criticisms of Japanese treatment generally and to the brutality of certain individuals. They had also recorded faithfully my observations that my two guests had only carried out their orders and that they had never perpetrated the brutalities of which I had

had experience elsewhere. For their part my guests had said that I had done my best to look after the interests and welfare of the other ranks in the camp; quite what I had been able to do, except to carry the remains of many of them on my shoulders to the crematorium on the rocky promontory, I could not recall.

When the gentlemen of the press had left we withdrew to a room furnished in the Japanese style where I had ordered a traditional dinner. This was served by attractive young Japanese girls in *kimonos* and *obis*. Neither of my guests spoke any English, except for a few words they had picked up in the camp. Nagano, in particular, dredged up some racy words of which I did not myself know the meaning. He also reminded me that his nickname among the P.o.W.s had been 'Smiler'.

I did not eat much; I was too concerned to keep the conversation going with my largely forgotten Japanese and my phrase-book. My guests, however, devoured the raw fish and seaweed with a relish of which I myself would have been more than capable twenty-five years earlier.

Nomoto presented me with a rather attractive wrought-iron bell as a souvenir; Smiler, covered with embarrassment, having forgotten to bring anything, dashed downstairs to the souvenir shop and returned with a beautifully made Japanese doll.

It was I who struck the only discordant note, but I could not resist the temptation.

I told them how, in order to conceal the fact that many Imperial blankets had been cut up and made into suits, we had endeavoured to ensure that camp inspections should start with the upper storey of the barrack block. I reminded them that there they had always found, neatly folded at the foot of each bed-space, three blankets as issued. I went on to disclose that as they had descended the stairs at the end of the block an incident had been contrived to delay them, and that before they had inspected the ground-floor barrack rooms an appropriate number of blankets had been thrown out of the windows of the upper storey, collected and neatly folded in the lower bed-spaces.

My guests were not amused; they had been outwitted and they had lost face. I quickly refilled their glasses of whisky.

The time was fast approaching when they would have to catch the last trains back to their respective villages. I had enjoyed the evening, if not the meal. I was sorry to see them go. We had not discussed anything of moment, though I, and no doubt they, had

had many unexpressed thoughts. They had asked after some of my fellow-prisoners and I had given them such news as I had. I had asked after some of the less agreeable guards and they had shut up like clams, claiming to know nothing about what had happened to them.

Was it all worth it? I think so. Three human beings had passed an innocuous but agreeable evening together.

Very early next morning I set off by train for Zentsuji. I was touched, and surprised, to find Nomoto waiting to see me off. Whether he noticed on the crowded platform, as I did, six Japanese criminals roped together like cattle, with their hands tied behind their backs, I do not know. It hardly seemed appropriate to draw his attention to them. We discussed briefly the article in the *Ehime Shimbun* which, by then, we had both seen. Once again we said good-bye.

The train journey from Matsuyama to Zentsuji, which called for a change at Tadatsu, took several hours. A number of Japanese in the train recognised my photograph in the paper and stared at me. A few spoke to me in a friendly manner and one father insisted on taking my photograph with his wife and children.

On arrival at Tadatsu, I recalled how the five of us officer P.o.W.s from Habu had been met at the ferry station in December 1943 by the American enlisted men who had then driven us in a lorry to Zentsuji Camp.

Alighting at Zentsuji station, I presented myself at the station-master's office brandishing my *Ehime Shimbun*. I asked him where the P.o.W. camp had been. He took me across the village square to the only garage that ran a taxi. The taxi was out on a job.

I waited in the intense heat, pondering on the pile of little boxes, containing the ashes of Japanese soldiers killed in action, which had been stacked on the platform under ceremonial guard when we had left Zentsuji for Miyata in June 1945. I wondered whether this slaughter, of which these boxes had been the mute witnesses, had really changed Japan.

When the taxi returned, the station-master spoke to the driver, who drove me to the obviously flourishing Zentsuji High School.

Although many new buildings had been constructed around the building in which I had lived for eighteen months, I recognised it immediately.

Before I could enter, however, certain formalities had to be

observed. Having perused my newspaper, the porter, with a curt
'Shoes off, please', in Japanese, ushered me into the headmaster's
study.

A few minutes later the Principal, Mr. Tarasaburu Goto,
arrived. He confirmed that the P.o.W.s had indeed been incarcerated
on the premises. Despite my impatience to visit the building, Mr.
Goto insisted on giving me a statistical account of the growth of
his school, plying me with ice-cream and lemonade the while. As
his lecture proceeded, I noticed many smiling Japanese of both
sexes peering through the door and windows of his study, the better
to observe this unexpected freak.

Eventually honour was satisfied and Mr. Goto escorted me
to my former home. I recalled every detail: the two-storey building
in which we had been herded like cattle, sleeping thirty-two to a
room on wooden bed-shelves; the staircase down which we had
pounded for roll-call on cold winter mornings; and the open exercise
space on which we had walked for hours discussing restaurants,
recipes, beer, wines, but never sex. The *benjos* were still there but
were now used to store garden tools.

As the Principal took me into each of the rooms I remembered
so well, I photographed the Japanese girls busy with their knitting
and embroidery. Their smiling faces indicated that they had no
idea of the blood, sweat—aye, and tears—which had drenched the
floors of their classrooms a quarter of a century ago.

We moved out into the exercise yard: I had no need to take
photographs here. The drawn pinched faces of my comrades were all
around me: Oliver Gordon, Frank Twiss, Ian Graham, Kenneth
Scott, 'Pilot' Hudson, Eric Lipscombe, Noel Pace, Ricky Wright,
Len Cooper, Tim Hallam and dozens of others. There were many
American and Australian ghosts, too.

As I took my leave of the Principal, he proudly pressed into
my hands a series of coloured photographs of his school. These were
embellished with such phrases, in both English and Japanese, as
'Our glorious old school', 'Our beautiful fine school' and 'Memories
of our school life'.

I had learnt much at his school while he was still a child.

From Zentsuji I travelled again by train to Imabari where
I caught another hydrofoil to Onomichi. After a night in another
Japanese inn on the hill I was off again, very early, by ferry to
Habu.

On the ferry I noticed a handsome Buddhist priest of about

forty reading a newspaper and staring at me from time to time. He was reading the article which had been reproduced in the local newspaper because of the reference to the Innoshima Dockyard, my destination on this leg of my pilgrimage.

We were soon in conversation and, with the help of a young Japanese mother suckling her baby who surprisingly spoke some English (the mother, not the baby!), I indicated my objective. The priest who was born in Habu, which was also his destination, recalled that as a boy of fifteen he had heard talk of the camp. He promised to help me.

On arrival at Habu, he beckoned me to follow him. An oddly assorted couple, we walked down the narrow streets of the village and those who recognised him paid their respects. We stopped at a coffee-shop; my companion, after ordering orange juices, left me to telephone.

A few minutes later he signalled to me to follow him again. We arrived at a pharmacy; the pharmacist, still wearing his coarse white pyjamas, was squatting on the *tatami* in his shop. Our mutual recognition was instantaneous; he paled and shook like a leaf. He then asked me both in Japanese and English whether I was in good health; he added quickly that he was not and that he suffered from heart trouble, which my sudden appearance from the past had clearly not improved.

He had been the medical orderly at Habu Camp. I remembered how he had passed as 'fit' for work in the dockyard men who were practically unconscious. He was not a person whom I would have invited to dinner and he knew it. It was clear from his agitation that he thought I had arrived to identify him and haul him off before some tribunal.

The priest quickly sized up the situation and his request for information about the camp took on a sharper tone.

When it became clear to the pharmacist that we were seeking information, and not his person, he mellowed a little. He opened three bottles of lemonade; he reluctantly agreed to be photographed outside his shop; and he ordered a taxi, for which I was glad to see he paid.

Soon the priest and I were at the main entrance to the Hitachi Zosen Dockyard, where we were confronted with the inevitable dockyard signs: 'Keep out', 'Positively no admittance', 'No photographs', etc. Two dockyard police, the most hostile faces I had seen anywhere in Japan, glared at us from their booth. Even the priest could make no progress. It looked as though my journey had been in vain but the priest was not to be beaten.

Resuming our seats in the taxi, we drove to the Innoshima City Office, an imposing new building on the waterfront. There the priest patiently explained our mission to dozens of bureaucrats in turn. We were clearly making progress for each temporary set-back was apparently concluded with the words 'Friend, go up higher'. At last we reached the mayoral suite on the top floor; Japanese tea was served in the Council Chamber; photo-copies of my well-thumbed newspaper were made for me; questions were asked and answered; and we waited.

Suddenly there was a move to the lift; and when we arrived at the entrance to the office there was the Mayor's air-conditioned car in all its glory with white lace curtains and fresh flowers in vases. The Mayor's secretary and a number of officials followed me into the car and away we went, with two out-riders, who turned out to be public relations officers, on motor-scooters.

It was then that I noticed that my friend the priest had disappeared. I had had no opportunity to thank him but he must have known how grateful I was.

This time the dockyard gates were thrown open with panache as we roared in; even the evil-looking dockyard police saluted and smiled.

The dockyard had been considerably expanded since the end of the war in 1945. In 1950 a major programme of development had been put in hand. By 1958 Hitachi Zosen had become the second largest shipbuilding company in the world. Since that date even more impressive developments had taken place.

These changes had obliterated most, but not all, of the landmarks I remembered. The expansion of the dockyard to the east appeared to have swallowed up completely the wooden structures on the edge of the beach in which we were frozen in winter and incinerated in summer.

My escort insisted that I should pick out the exact site of the camp. After several false starts I did so with a conviction which I did not feel, but which, I hope, satisfied them.

Photographs were taken of the gates by which the working parties used to leave the camp to shuffle down the winding road to the dockyard.

I was on surer grounds in the yard itself. As we returned, I identified more positively the various shops in which we had worked;

and one or two spots where P.o.W.s had met with serious accidents seemed only too familiar.

The photographing never ceased; at one stage a passing Japanese workman was forcibly deprived of his safety helmet which was firmly placed on my head. Stressing the fact that the Japanese had never been so solicitous about my safety when I was actually working there, an observation which called forth peals of laughter, I reluctantly agreed thus to be photographed.

After all this activity we repaired to a club for municipal workers where the rate-payers in Innoshima unwittingly entertained us to an admirable lunch.

A seat was booked for me on the hydrofoil, and the Mayor's secretary, who insisted on making the journey to Onomichi with me, carried my bags to the station. This seemed, in all the circumstances, to be perfectly appropriate.

I had no time to visit Miyata on Kyushu. I doubt whether I would ever have found it, tucked away, as it was, in the hills 'on the extreme edge of nowhere'.

In the aircraft which took me from Osaka to Hong Kong, and thus home, I reflected on my visit.

I had seen most of the 'sights' in Tokyo and in Kyoto, which my captors had described to me on many occasions between 1942 and 1945. I had seen as much as was permitted of the vast Imperial Palace complex in Tokyo, where the incredible drama of the first fortnight of August 1945 had been staged.*

At Kyoto, the oldest city in Japan, I had visited one shrine which had never been described to me by my captors. It had not been in existence before the war.

The Ryozen-Kwan-On War Memorial had been erected, at the foot of the eastern mountain range of Kyoto, to commemorate the two million Japanese who had died during the war. The memorial takes the form of a colossal stone statue of Buddha, eighty foot high.

A subsidiary monument had subsequently been erected, as part of the same complex, in memory of the more than 48,000 'foreign soldiers' who had perished on Japanese territory or on territory under Japanese military control.

The inscription on this monument reads as follows:

* See Appendix II.

'All honour to him, friend or foe,
Who fought and died for his country!
May the tragedy of his supreme
Sacrifice bring us, the living,
Enlightenment and inspiration;
Fill us with ever-mounting zeal
For the all compelling quest of peace
World peace and universal brotherhood.
                                        June 3, 1958.'

The names of all Allied personnel who died during the war on territory under Japanese occupation are recorded in a small adjoining Memorial Hall.

What were my impressions as a former P.o.W. visiting Japan a quarter of a century later?

Those who were too young to have known the war at first hand, particularly the students, could not have been more kind and helpful. It is true that they appeared to regard me as an archaeologist, concerned with a period of history, so remote in time that it could have little or nothing to do with the contemporary bustle and economic development of present-day Japan. But they were interested and co-operative none the less.

The over-forty-fives were less welcoming—when they learnt that I had been a P.o.W.! Generally speaking they were unhelpful and suspicious. They did not wish to be reminded—particularly by the appearance of a former P.o.W.—that it was they who had started, and they who had lost, the war.

Nomoto and Nagano were different. They can no more forget Habu than I can. They were, I think, touched that I had come half-way round the world to greet them, not as an 'arrogant' victor but as a human being who had shared with them an experience which will remain imprinted on all our memories for as long as we live.

Mr. Kondo, who had made my meeting with my former gaolers and my visits to Habu and Zentsuji possible, was sufficiently wise to know that if one can contribute, in however small a measure, to righting a wrong, one should.

Appendix I

(See footnote on page 115)

COPY OF QUESTIONNAIRE ISSUED BY THE JAPANESE AUTHORITIES AT HABU P.O.W. CAMP, INNOSHIMA ON THE 14TH FEBRUARY 1943, TOGETHER WITH COPY OF MY REPLIES MADE THE SAME DAY.

Questions

1. State your present feeling and future prospect:

My Replies

The Government of Nippon has stated its intention of adhering to the principles embodied in the Prisoner of War Convention. It follows that, as an officer of the Royal Air Force who has been taken prisoner of war, I should:

(a) be sent to an officers' camp (i.e. not kept in a camp with other ranks).

(b) not be required to go to work.

(c) be given facilities for communicating with my wife and family. Although I have now been a prisoner of war for for nearly one year, I have not yet been permitted to write or receive any letters.

(d) be permitted to buy food-stuffs, books, clothing, etc., to enable me to live according to

the standards to which I am
accustomed.
I feel very disappointed that the
authorities have not, so far, been
able to comply with any of the
four points set out above. I am
hoping that it will be possible
for me to be sent to an officers'
camp and that my return to
my own country will not be
long delayed.

2. Give the name of the person
whom you worship or adore:

My wife.

3. What sort of consolation or
relaxation did you want on the
field?

My aim was to keep fit mentally
and physically so as to be able
to undertake any duties which I
might be called upon to perform.

4. State frankly your strong
impressions or mental states such
as, for example, tranquillity or
excitement, pleasure or pain and
sympathy or antipathy on each
occasion as follows:
A. *On hearing of declaration of War
against Japan*
  (i) about your personal matters
(family, occupation and so on)

I was quietly confident.

  (ii) about your comrades

I was sure that they would do
their duty.

  (iii) about your men

I was a civilian at the time and
had no men.

  (iv) about your superiors and
commanding officers

I was not in the service at the
time.

  (v) about the policy of your
Government

My Government had no
alternative but to defend itself
against attack.

B. *During the battle*
  (i) When you encountered the
Japanese land troops for the
first time.

I was concerned with the
welfare of the men under my
command when we were
attacked in a train by night.

  (ii) When you experienced the
first Japanese bombing

I felt that the results would
have been very different if we
had had more fighter opposition
to offer to the Japanese bombers.

C. *At the last stage of the battle*

I realised that, through no fault of my own, my fellow-officers, my men and myself would be taken prisoner; and I was at that time confident that the Nippon Government would treat us according to the principles of the Convention.

5. State the feelings of your comrades during the battle.

I was too busy trying to do my duty to have time to ascertain the feelings or sentiments of my comrades.

6. Did you read any sort of publication on the field? For example, newspapers, magazines, books, pamphlets or leaflets. If you did put the mark O on each of them. And state about the one you found interesting.

I read the newspapers and a few of my own books, Shakespeare.

7. Did you listen to the radio broadcast on the field? If you did state about it.

I did not listen to the radio broadcast on the field.

8. General remarks.

I consider that Nippon made a great mistake in attacking Great Britain, her former ally. The industrial potentiality of Great Britain and the U.S.A. are so great that I do not see how Japan can hope to win this war.

Appendix II

(See footnote on page 225)

(See footnote on page 225)

OUTLINE OF THE MAIN DEVELOPMENTS IN JAPAN BETWEEN
THE 28TH JULY AND THE 15TH AUGUST 1945

AUTHOR'S NOTE

In compiling this outline I have had frequent recourse to the published findings of the Japanese Society for Research on the War in the Pacific.

This fascinating account, with a wealth of detail, of the events which took place in Japan during the three weeks preceding the Emperor's broadcast on the 15th August 1945 was originally published in Japanese in 1965 by Bungei Shounjou Ltd., Tokyo, under the title *Nihon No Ichiban Nagai Hi*.

An English version of this was subsequently published by the Souvenir Press, London, under the title *Japan's Longest Day*. In 1970 a French translation of the English version was published by Trevise, Paris, in association with *Paris-Match*.

For anyone who like myself was a prisoner of war in Japanese hands during this period a perusal of this exciting book will go far to explain the, at the time, almost inexplicable behaviour of our captors.

I would also warmly commend it to those who have a more general interest in this period of contemporary history.

'THE SCENE'

From 1931, when the Japanese military leaders had deliberately provoked the Manchurian incident, the Army had become the most powerful force in Japan and had effectively dictated the policy of the successive Japanese Governments. Since the Meiji Restoration, some half a century earlier, the Army, indeed, had been contending that it, and it alone, understood the true interests of Japan.

In 1940 the Army had pressed hard for a military alliance with Germany and Italy. The then Prime Minister, Admiral Mitsouma **Yonai** (see hereafter), was opposed to this and when the proposal was carried by the Army, against his advice, he resigned as Prime Minister.

From 1941 to 1944 General Hideki **Tojo**, the leader of the militarists favouring the war in South-East Asia, was Prime Minister. His vision was to divide the world with the Germans.

At the **Cairo** Conference in December 1943 the Allied leaders had agreed to insist on the unconditional surrender of Japan. They had also agreed that Japan should be stripped of all the territories seized or occupied by her since the beginning of World War I in 1914; and that Manchuria, Formosa and other territories taken from the Chinese should be restored to the Republic of China.

The Japanese did not know that at the **Yalta** Conference in February 1945 Roosevelt and Churchill had agreed to give the U.S.S.R. certain 'concessions' in the Far East in return for an undertaking that the U.S.S.R. would declare war against Japan as soon as possible after the termination of hostilities in Europe.

As far as the Japanese were concerned, their relations with the U.S.S.R. were still governed by the Russo-Japanese Non-Aggression Pact which was not due to expire until April 1946. The Russians had, however, already indicated that they did not propose to renew this Pact when it expired.

In April 1945 Baron Kantaro **Souzouki**, a former Admiral of the Japanese Imperial Fleet (see hereafter), was invited to form a Cabinet.

At the **Potsdam** Conference in July 1945 the Allied leaders decided to demand the unconditional surrender of all Japanese Armed Forces. This represented a significant change from the 1943 **Cairo** Declaration which had called for the unconditional surrender of Japan.

A radio message was broadcast from San Francisco to Tokyo on the 26th July 1945, conveying this demand for the unconditional surrender of all Japanese Armed Forces and threatening the total annihilation of Japan if this demand was not complied with immediately. The message added that the Allies would require the suppression of the ruling military caste in Japan, the handing over to the Allies of all 'war criminals', including those who had been guilty of cruelty to P.o.W.s, and the 'democratisation and liberalisation' of Japan.

The first reaction of the Japanese Government was, overtly at least, to ignore this message. The ultimatum was not, however, formally rejected.

In the meantime, urgent approaches were made by the Japanese Government to the U.S.S.R., still neutral, pressing the latter to act as a mediator and obtain better terms for the Japanese. These approaches were met by a stony silence in Moscow.

As there was no formal reply, or other reaction, from the Japanese Government, the Allies assumed that the ultimatum had been rejected.

At this stage the following points should be borne in mind:

(a) that the Japanese had never lost a war in the whole of their history;

(b) that it was an integral part of Japanese philosophy that nothing was more disgraceful than to surrender, either as an individual, or as a group, or as a country;

(c) that it was a religious duty, impressed upon every Japanese from birth, to die for Japan and never to surrender, once Japan was engaged in a war;

(d) that every Japanese, whether in the Armed Forces or not, was firmly convinced that surrender would be followed by complete slavery;

(e) that, despite the devastation and the almost complete disruption of communications, which had already been wrought in Japan, and despite the known fact that the 1945 harvest would be the worst since 1931, morale generally was high; and finally;

(f) that the three million members of the Armed Forces in mainland Japan were intact, well equipped and well placed to inflict enormous casualties on any invading Allied Forces. In particular, those stationed in the island of Kyushu were firmly convinced that they could repel the threatened Allied invasion of that island, which was being prepared by the Americans in Okinawa under the code name 'Operation Olympic'.

'DRAMATIS PERSONAE'

His Majesty the Emperor HIROHITO
Forty-four years of age. Ascended the throne in 1928.

Keeper of the Imperial Privy Seal—Marquis Koichi **Kida**
—he had been convinced since February 1942 that Japan would be defeated—he had considerable influence with the Emperor.

Supreme War Council
Prime Minister—Baron Kantaro **Souzouki** (69)
—he favoured capitulation but was apparently incapable of taking a firm decision.

Minister of Foreign Affairs—Shigenori **Togo** (62)
—a former Japanese Ambassador to Moscow—completely convinced that Japan had no alternative but to accept the terms of the **Potsdam** Declaration, provided that the Allies would respect the position and prerogatives of the Emperor.

Minister of War—General Korechika **Anami** (57)

—as the spokesman for the Army, he was the strongest man in the country—he pressed for the continuation of the war to the bitter end —in reply to the Allied ultimatum he proposed four additional provisos which he knew would not be accepted by the Allies, namely:

—that Allied Occupation Forces should be strictly limited;

—that 'war criminals' should be tried by the Japanese and not by the Allies;

—that the demobilisation of the Japanese Armed Forces should be undertaken by Japanese officers and not by the Allies.

—in brief, he could not and would not accept the idea of 'defeat' —for him, as for many others, there would have to be a negotiated settlement to save the Army's 'face'.

Minister of Marine—Admiral Mitsouma **Yonai**

—former Prime Minister—took the same line as the Foreign Minister.

Chief of Military Staff—General Yoshijior **Oumezou**

—took the same line as the Minister of War.

Chief of Naval Staff—Admiral Soemou **Toyoda**

—took the same line as the Minister of War.

It will be observed that three of the members of the Japanese War Council favoured acceptance of the Allies' terms, provided the Emperor could be retained with his position and powers unimpaired. The other three, in effect, wanted to continue the war.

The four senior members of the Supreme War Council were also members of the Cabinet.

The Cabinet was split three ways. Some supported the Foreign Minister's approach; some supported the 'hard-liners' led by the War Minister, General **Anami**; and some, while not going as far as **Anami**, wanted to press for a further amelioration of the terms.

All, in both the Supreme War Council and the Cabinet, were firmly agreed that if the Allies would not commit themselves to respect the Emperor's position and prerogatives, the war should continue to the bitter end. If the quasi-divine Emperor and all that he represented were to be removed from Japan, no Japanese would wish to remain alive.

Japanese public opinion was deliberately kept in the dark as to what was really happening, until the Emperor's broadcast at midday on the 15th August. The truth was that there was nothing definite to tell them as the Japanese Government itself was so deeply divided.

The 'peace' party, led by the Prime Minister and the Foreign Minister, and wholeheartedly supported by the Emperor himself, were concerned to ensure that when the capitulation was announced this would be done in such a way as to obviate the risks of a *coup d'état* by the Army or a civil war.

The drama was played out at two levels—the political and the military.

At the political level the Prime Minister's first task was to secure the unanimous agreement of the Supreme War Council and of the Cabinet to capitulate. If this could not be achieved, it was clear that Japan would be annihilated by the Allies.

But even if this objective was achieved there was always a risk that the Army, with or without the support of the powerful War Minister General **Anami**, would seek to upset such a political decision.

'THE DRAMA'

On *Saturday the 28th July* the Prime Minister held a press conference, to be made public on *Monday the 30th July*, indicating that the Government had decided to ignore the Allies' ultimatum and that the war would be pursued until victory was achieved.

The Foreign Minister was furious. This was not what had been decided by the Supreme War Council or by the Cabinet. All that had been decided was that an urgent approach should be made to the U.S.S.R. to act as 'mediator', and this had already been done.

The Allies, however, on learning of the Prime Minister's press conference, not unnaturally took this as a rejection of their ultimatum and made their plans accordingly.

For the next few days there was complete confusion in governmental circles in Tokyo. All hopes were pinned on an encouraging reply from the U.S.S.R. It never came.

At 8 a.m. on *Monday the 6th August* two B.29s circled high over Hiroshima and its 250,000 inhabitants. One of the planes dropped the first atomic bomb which killed some 64,000 people outright. Many thousands more were to die from the results of this raid in the days to come.

The reply for which the Japanese Government had been waiting had come not from the U.S.S.R. but from the U.S.A. Further broadcasts from Washington later that day confirmed the dropping of this bomb and warned of more to come.

On *Wednesday the 8th August* the Emperor, having been informed by the Foreign Minister of the magnitude of the disaster at Hiroshima, instructed the latter to inform the Prime Minister that arrangements should be put in hand to suspend hostilities without further delay. The tragedy of Hiroshima could not be permitted to occur for a second time, the Emperor had added.

The Prime Minister immediately summoned a meeting of the Supreme War Council but, as one of the members could not attend owing to pressing commitments elsewhere, this had to be deferred.

Meanwhile, the Army, determined not to capitulate, was doing all within its power to 'jam' Allied broadcasts to the Japanese people from Manila, Okinawa and elsewhere. The Army was less successful in its attempt to insulate the Japanese people from the hundreds of thousands of tracts being dropped on Tokyo by Allied aircraft.

During that Wednesday afternoon the Japanese Ambassador in Moscow was informed by Foreign Minister Molotov that the U.S.S.R. would consider itself in a state of war with Japan from the following day. In fact, the Russians did not wait and their attack on the Japanese in Manchuria was launched a couple of hours later.

The postponed meeting of the Supreme Council of War was held at 10 a.m. on *Thursday the 9th August*. Half an hour later the second atomic bomb was dropped on Nagasaki. This news reached the Council before it adjourned, as did also the news that practically the whole of Manchuria was in Russian hands. Neither of these developments induced the three Service Chiefs, **Anami, Oumezou** and **Toyoda**, to shift their ground. They continued to press for 'negotiations' with the Allies.

At this stage the Director of Information Services was received in audience by the Emperor at which His Imperial Majesty agreed to broadcast to the nation, whether the decision of the Government was for peace or war.

At the Cabinet meeting held in the afternoon of that Thursday the deadlock remained unresolved. The War Minister, **Anami**, repeated that in no circumstances would the Armed Forces lay down their arms and that nothing could compel them to do so. No decision had been taken by the time the Cabinet finally broke up at 10 p.m.

The Emperor had always been above politics in Japan. His Imperial Majesty had presided from time to time at meetings of the Supreme War Council and of the Cabinet, formally to ratify agreed decisions already taken. Now a meeting of the Supreme War Council, in which the differences went deep, was to be held with the Emperor presiding.

The meeting was held at midnight in the stuffy air-raid shelter in the Imperial Palace. The only air came from the ventilation of differences of opinion. Finally the Prime Minister invited the Emperor to cut the Gordian knot.

According to tradition, whenever the Emperor of Japan spoke, his words were referred to, as a measure of respect, as 'The Voice of the Crane'.

At 2 a.m. on *Friday the 10th August* the 'Voice of the Crane' declared for peace on the lines proposed by the Foreign Minister.

A Cabinet meeting followed at the Prime Minister's residence. In view of what had happened the Cabinet had only to consider the best method of implementing the Emperor's decision. At 4 a.m. the Cabinet adjourned. Within three hours cables conveying the Japanese Government's decision to capitulate, provided the Emperor's position and prerogatives were respected, were on their way to the Japanese Ambassadors in Switzerland and Sweden for onward transmission to the Allies.

The War Minister, **Anami**, held a meeting of all his senior officers in the air-raid shelter of the War Ministry at 9.30 that morning. He explained to them what had happened. These senior army officers could not believe their ears. **Anami** reminded them that there was no alternative but to obey the Emperor's decision.

Later the same morning Tokyo was subjected to a terrific air raid during which hundreds of B.29s dropped hundreds of thousands of incendiary bombs. Similar raids took place on other Japanese cities.

The people of Japan did not know of the momentous decision taken in the early hours of that fateful Friday. The Japanese Government dared not make a formal announcement until they were certain that the Allies would accept the condition that the Emperor should remain.

An ambiguous 'official' communiqué was drawn up which merely stated that the Government would soon have an important announcement to make.

Meanwhile a group of army officers in the War Ministry were preparing a communiqué designed to inspire all Japanese Armed Forces actively engaged in the war to redouble their efforts. This was never seen by the War Minister, though an attempt was said to have been made to find him and show him the text.

The 'military' communiqué was received at the broadcasting station at the same time that evening as the 'official' communiqué. It was fundamentally in conflict with it, yet both were broadcast. The Japanese people, which had for so long been deceived by official communiqués, saw nothing particularly unusual in such conflicting news.

Aware of the dangers, the Foreign Minister later that Friday evening authorised the Domei Press Agency to relay overseas in Morse a third communiqué which indicated the acceptance by Japan of the terms of the **Potsdam** Declaration. The Foreign Minister apparently had reason to believe that a third atomic bomb was due to be dropped on Tokyo two days later; by his action, he hoped to prevent this.

The struggle between the 'peace' and 'war' parties in Japan had hardly begun.

By the morning of *Saturday the 11th August* the Allies after consultation among themselves had agreed to accept the retention of the Emperor and a message was on its way to the Japanese Government through Switzerland.

During the same day a group of some fifteen army officers, led by Lieutenant-Colonel **Takeshita**, brother-in-law of the War Minister **Anami**, gathered in one of the air-raid shelters of the War Ministry. They decided to assassinate the leaders of the 'peace' party, including the Prime Minister, the Foreign Minister and the Keeper of the Imperial Privy Seal. They also decided, if necessary, to occupy the Imperial Palace and take the Emperor into 'protective custody' even if this meant 'liquidating' Lieutenant-General Takeshi **Mori**, the Commander of the Imperial Guard.

At 12.45 a.m. on *Sunday the 12th August* the Allies' reply was received in the Tokyo Foreign Ministry. A study of the text raised doubts in the minds of some as to whether the passage relating to the retention of the Emperor was satisfactory. The 'peace' party contended that it was; the 'war' party contended that it was not.

At 8 a.m. on that Sunday morning the Foreign Minister formally advised the Emperor that the formula met with Japan's requirements. Others, including, rather surprisingly, the Prime Minister and, quite naturally, the War Minister, took the opposite view.

By the evening the Prime Minister had been persuaded to revert to his original position as a member of the 'peace' party, largely as the result of an assurance by the Keeper of the Imperial Privy Seal that whatever the Allied reply might mean, the Emperor himself was prepared to accept it.

Subsequent meetings of the Supreme War Council and of the Cabinet on *Monday the 13th August* produced no firm decision. The divisions were as deep as ever. Once again the Prime Minister had to have recourse to the Emperor to resolve these.

But the Prime Minister now had another card to play. He knew full well, and let it be known, that the longer this period of indecision continued, the more likely it was that the 'terms' of capitulation would deteriorate. At that time the Americans were in control of the situation among the Allies. If there were further delays the U.S.S.R. would invade the Japanese mainland and the Prime Minister knew that the Russians were not at all in favour of maintaining the Emperor on his throne.

Despite the stand taken by the Prime Minister, delays and procrastinations continued during that afternoon and evening—and they were very nearly fatal to the cause of the 'peace' party.

At about 5 p.m. on that Monday the Japanese Broadcasting Service and various Japanese newspapers received a communiqué from Army Headquarters to the effect that the Emperor had issued fresh orders to the Imperial Armed Forces to resume full-scale operations against the Allies.

Fortunately this was questioned by the recipients and, after reference to the War Minister, **Anami**, this unauthorised communiqué was cancelled. If this communiqué had been broadcast to the outside world, Tokyo would certainly have received its atomic bomb.

During the night of the *13th/14th August* army officers were engaged in putting the finishing touches to their plans for a *coup d'état*.

The Emperor had called a grand Imperial Conference at the Palace at 10.30 a.m. on *Tuesday the 14th August*. This was a gathering of the Supreme War Council, the Cabinet and several other notables.

The Prime Minister invited those who were not in favour of immediate capitulation to expound their views. The War Minister, **Anami**, and the two Chiefs of Staff, **Oumezou** and **Toyoda**, explained their objections, which were the same as they had always been.

Then the Emperor gave his reasons at some length as to why he considered that the surrender terms should be accepted without further delay. For the second time 'the Voice of the Crane' had been heard. The Imperial decision was subsequently 'approved' at a Cabinet meeting held that afternoon.

Thus, by the afternoon of that Tuesday the Japanese Government had formally decided to accept the Allies' peace terms.

There were, however, many problems and uncertainties ahead. It may be convenient to list these and then to trace subsequent developments under each 'head'.

(i) The first task of the Government was to agree the text of the Emperor's broadcast, to make arrangements appropriate to an occasion without precedent for the Emperor to record it, and to ensure that the recording was kept in safe custody until midday on Wednesday the 15th August, when it was due to be broadcast.

(ii) Despite the formal acquiescence of the War Minister **Anami**, in the Emperor's decision to capitulate, it was by no means clear yet whether the General would take vigorous and positive steps to secure the compliance of the Armed Forces with the Emperor's decision or whether, overtly or covertly, he would lend his support to those army officers who were determined to prevent both the Emperor's broadcast and the capitulation.

(iii) Even if **Anami**, with the whole weight of his position and reputation, did call upon the Armed Forces to respect the Emperor's decision there were many who doubted whether even this would be enough to prevent disorders.

From 4 p.m. that Tuesday afternoon the Cabinet was engaged in scrutinising the first draft of the Emperor's broadcast. Engineers of the Japanese Broadcasting Service had been warned to be ready to record the Emperor's words at the Imperial Palace at 6 p.m.

The Cabinet's deliberations proved to be long and difficult; it was not until 7 p.m. that a text, approved after much wrangling, was transmitted to the Palace.

It was then necessary for the Palace scribes to make two copies with brushes on thick Japanese paper, of the 815 Japanese characters, in a form worthy of scrutiny by the Imperial eyes.

About 8 p.m. the Keeper of the Imperial Privy Seal took the text to the Emperor, who, having studied it, requested five small amendments, which had then to be referred to the Cabinet for approval.

Normally more artistic labour would have been required to produce fair copies embodying the amendments. As time was running out this formality was dispensed with. High Palace officials pasted the amendments over the original offending passages.

Later the Prime Minister was summoned to the Palace, formally to present two copies of the text to the Emperor who signed them, after which the Imperial Privy Seal was affixed.

By 11 p.m. every member of the Cabinet had signed the document proclaiming the capitulation, the text of which was immediately cabled to the Allies through the usual network of diplomatic channels.

It was not until all these formalities had been completed that the patient broadcasting engineers were able to begin recording the Emperor's voice at about 11.30 p.m.

After this had been done, the engineers reported that the recording was almost inaudible. The Emperor then recorded his message for a second time. There followed some discussion as to whether a third effort was called for, but the Emperor was spared this additional burden.

It was well after midnight before the broadcasting engineers had finished packing up their equipment.

Unfortunately no prior thought had been given as to how and where these recordings, each consisting of two discs, should be stored for safe custody overnight.

Eventually they were given to an Imperial chamberlain who put them in two small canvas brief-cases which he then placed in a safe.

As will be seen, they remained there undisturbed, despite the frantic searches which were to be made for them during what was left of the night.

At about 2 a.m. on *Wednesday the 15th August* the press offices in Tokyo received a communiqué. This gave an account of the signing by the Emperor, earlier in the evening, of the Imperial Proclamation, announcing the capitulation. This was 'embargoed' for publication until after the Emperor's broadcast at midday the same day.

During such times on the Tuesday as he had not been engaged in Cabinet meetings, the War Minister, **Anami**, had been constantly approached by army officers trying to persuade him to give the Army a lead in rejecting any idea of capitulation. Among these was his brother-in-law **Takeshita**, who worked in the War Ministry.

Word of these undercurrents of discontent reached the Emperor, who offered to speak to these dissident officers personally if that was felt necessary. **Anami** assured the Emperor that His Majesty could count on the loyalty and obedience of the Army.

At 2.40 p.m. on the Tuesday **Anami** and a number of other senior Generals signed an order which enjoined the Japanese Imperial Army to obey the Emperor's decision.

Later in the afternoon the War Minister addressed the officers of the War Ministry in his office, impressing upon them the necessity for obedience to the wishes of the Emperor.

It was midnight before the War Minister, having taken his leave of the Prime Minister and having done all that he could to hold the officers of the Army in check, retired to his official residence.

Between 2 and 3 a.m. on Wednesday the 15th August he was relaxing, drinking sake with **Takeshita**.

Despite numerous appeals for support during that night from those dissident officers who, as will be seen, had 'mutinied', the War Minister declined to encourage them.

In the early hours of the morning, and with solemn and agonising ritual, **Anami** committed suicide by cutting his carotid artery with a dagger.

The real danger to the successful accomplishment of the decisions taken by the Emperor and his Government were not to become apparent until the early hours of the morning of *Wednesday the 15th August*.

While the Emperor was recording his broadcast message at about midnight on the Tuesday, three separate groups of Japanese officers, whose activities and intentions were fortunately not known to each other, were planning in different ways to ignore the Emperor's decision to capitulate.

Quite apart from the actions of these three groups of 'plotters', many Japanese naval and air bases, to which rumours of the impending capitulation had not yet penetrated, were preparing in their normal fashion to attack the Allied Forces at sea off their coasts, with whom they genuinely believed they were still at war.

The huge **Atsougi** Naval Air Station near Yokohama had been the training base for hundreds of *Kamikaze* suicide pilots. Seven thousand aircraft ready for combat were still there with enough supplies and stores to continue the struggle for two years.

Naval Captain Yasouna **Kozono** spent the Tuesday night successfully exhorting the officers of the 302nd Air Corps to fight on under his command whatever the Emperor might say.

Also at Yokohama, a Captain commanding a detachment of the Imperial Guard, Takeo **Sazaki**, with somewhat less success, was urging his fellow-officers to support him in his intention to assassinate the Prime Minister and 'liberate Japan from all evil influences'. In his condemnation of the impending capitulation, **Sazaki** referred to the fact that many of Japan's armies were undefeated in the field and, more ominously, that there were hundreds of thousands of P.o.W.s still in Japanese hands.

By 4 a.m. on the Wednesday **Sazaki** had made modest progress in his one-man crusade. With thirty-seven adherents, some being soldiers of the Imperial Guard and some students, he was driving from Yokohama to Tokyo, bound for the Prime Minister's official residence.

It was nearly dawn by the time **Sazaki** and his followers had reached their objective. There they opened fire with machine-guns on the main entrance of the Prime Minister's official residence. They did not know that the Prime Minister had decided to spend the night in his private residence.

Some of the Prime Minister's staff escaped by the back door and set off to warn their master. Having learnt from the doorkeeper that the Prime Minister was at his private residence, **Sazaki** set fire to the official residence and drove off with his rabble.

The Prime Minister only just escaped from his private residence before **Sazaki** arrived and set that on fire too.

To round off this foray, **Sazaki** successfully set fire to the house of Baron Kiichiro **Hiranouma**, the President of the Privy Council, without ascertaining whether the Baron or anyone else was inside. The Baron's house was razed to the ground.

It was after 7 a.m. before the rebels started their return journey to Yokohoma.

Sazaki then went 'underground' for fourteen years and was ultimately pardoned.

By far the most important, and for a time the most successful, of these focal points of disaffection was formed by a group of officers drawn from the War Ministry itself and from the Imperial Guard detachment at the Palace.

At about midnight on the Tuesday, at which time the Emperor was recording his broadcast, a group of officers were waiting in the Officers' Mess of the Imperial Guard at the Palace to be received by Lieutenant-General Takeshi **Mori**. The moving spirit among these 'plotters' was Major Kenji **Hatanaka** of the War Ministry. Other officers of the War Ministry, including two Colonels, and officers of the Imperial Guard were also involved.

This group was hoping to persuade General **Mori** to agree to take the Emperor into 'protective custody' and thus to provide a rallying point for the many dissident officers throughout the Armed Forces.

Shortly after 1 a.m. on the Wednesday, three of these officers entered General **Mori**'s office. **Hatanaka**, who was one of them, shot General **Mori** dead with a revolver; another officer decapitated with his sword Lieutenant-Colonel **Shiraishi**, the General's brother-in-law, who happened to be in the General's office taking his leave at the time.

Forged orders which had already been prepared were then issued, stamped with the murdered General's seal.

It was not long before the mutineers, who had cut all communications with the outside world, were in complete control of the Palace compound.

A number of persons, including the Director of Information Services, his personal staff, the President and other representatives of the Japanese Broadcasting Service, as well as the engineers who had recorded the Emperor's address, all of whom were still within the Palace limits, were 'taken prisoner' and flung into a small outhouse under heavy guard.

At about 2 a.m. the mutineers issued a communiqué to all press officers in Tokyo. It was to the effect that the Imperial Japanese Army had successfully effected a *coup d'état* and that the war would continue.

This reached the press offices while an air-raid alert was in force. It also reached them at the same time as the 'official' communiqué describing the signing by the Emperor earlier that evening of the Imperial Proclamation announcing the capitulation.

As all the electric current was cut off during air-raid alerts, the editors of *Asahi Shimbun* decided, by the light of candles, to prepare two editions, one announcing 'peace', the other 'war'. Which edition would be distributed would be decided later.

The mutineers had two main objectives. One was to keep the Emperor in 'protective custody' and to deny His Majesty contact with any of his 'evil advisers'. The other, and more pressing, was to find and destroy the recordings of the Emperor's broadcast which had been made at midnight.

Interrogations of all the 'prisoners' and of others within the Palace compound led the mutineers to conclude that the recordings were still on the premises. Thorough searches of every part of the Palace were made but the recordings were not found.

The mutineers also realised that if their coup was to succeed they would have to secure support from at least one quarter and preferably two. Emissaries were therefore sent to the War Minister and to the Commander-in-Chief of the Eastern Army in Tokyo, General Shizoukichi **Tanaka**. Neither of these appeals bore fruit.

Anami, as has been recorded, was preparing for his suicide; **Tanaka** was waiting for further information before preparing to crush the rebellion.

At about 4 a.m. the mutineers were becoming anxious at the lack of response from the War Minister or the Commander-in-Chief of the Eastern Army. They therefore decided to appeal to the Japanese Armed Forces and the Japanese civilian population direct. If they could not find the recordings of the Emperor's address, at least they could—or so they hoped—put their case across first.

A large detachment of the Imperial Guard was therefore despatched to the broadcasting station and some of the accompanying officers attempted to go on the air. For various technical reasons this proved to be impossible, though their leader **Hatanaka** made another, equally unsuccessful, attempt at 5 a.m.

The Imperial chamberlains had had an exciting and disturbed night. Concealed from the mutineers in medicine cabinets and underground passages, they had played a game of 'hide-and-seek' with the enfuriated soldiery, reminiscent of a Restoration farce. At about 5 a.m. one of the chamberlains discovered that the mutineers had failed to cut a direct telephone line to the Ministry of Marine. A naval A.D.C. to the Emperor was able to telephone to the Ministry a brief account of all that had happened during the night.

At ten minutes past five in the morning General **Tanaka** arrived at the Palace, and in effect, the rebellion was over, though the ring-leaders were still at large and active.

From 7.30 a.m. it was continuously announced from the broadcasting station that the Emperor's address would be broadcast at 12 noon.

The precious recordings, which at one time were believed to have been lost, were ultimately found and safely transported to the broadcasting station between 10 and 11 a.m.

Later that morning the irrepressible and elusive **Hatanaka** and another of his associates were distributing tracts outside the Palace. Between 11 a.m. and 12 noon they committed suicide on the lawns which surrounded the outer wall of the Palace. Others of the mutineers also committed suicide, one of them by the side of the coffin in which the body of the murdered General **Mori** was lying in state.

There was one final incident to mar the solemnity of the Emperor's unprecedented broadcast. Just before 12 noon a Lieutenant of the Japanese Military Police on duty at the broadcasting station ran amok. Threatening to kill everyone in sight, he attempted to enter the studio and prevent the broadcast. He was overpowered just in time.

Of such stuff is history made.

Appendix III

(See footnote on page 235)

The following is the exact text of an 'open letter' addressed to 'the English Government' which was drafted in English by the Japanese and circulated to P.o.W.s in Miyata Camp (Fukuoka War Prisoners Camp No. 9) 'for signature' on or about the 11th August 1945. It was never despatched or even signed.

To. The English Government.
Sirs,
    We somehow feel a sort of pleasure at hearing Premier Churchill and his party were beaten all to sticks by the Labour Party headed by Attlee at the recent general election. Life as a P.o.W. in Nippon for the last four years has indeed been a great sacrifice to us. And so, if Mr. Churchill could further continue to fight against Nippon it would be too much for us to bear anymore. Our prisoners' feeling is also the same as that of the English people in general who longing for peace preferred Mr. Attlee, Pacifist, to Mr. Churchill war pilot of England. If we look 'straight' at the total blow sustained by England up to now, it is quite clear that further continuation of the war against Nippon would certainly prove to be a complete suicide and ruin of England herself. And so, before it is too late to heal herself of the blow the English Government should devote itself to the management of the internal questions putting awhile external war problems aside. As the present internal crisis it is indeed the wisest policy for England to recover from the said blow and nourish redoubled energy and fresh force to resume her post-war offensives. Otherwise she will be sure to fall between two stools. Originally the war itself against Nippon seems to be one of the follies and impossibilities both from a military and political stand point of view. Hoping for making Nippon kneel down before the Anti-Axis countries is just like a mid-summer dream yearning for something beyond their reach. Because, Nippon has a mysterious kind of supernatural power which is no [sic]

match for Anti-Axis forces. At present Nipponese war preparations against the Allies are, as far as we can see, as firm as a rock and literally and absolutely invincible both in various places within the Greater East Asia Co-prosperity Sphere as well as in Nippon proper. The Nipponese Army is essentially a Divine Crusade but on the Contrary the Anti-Axis forces are more or less a cats paw of a small number of covetous and hegemony-maniac international capitalists. And so the conclusion of itself of the present war is as clear as day. Availing ourselves of Mr. Churchill's retirement we do hope that the English Government and other Anti-Axis Governments would suspend hostilities against Nippon Government as soon as possible and that we may be able to return home at once. Furthermore we also entreat our families relatives and acquaintances at home to ask the English Government to be as sympathetic with us as to call us back immediately at any cost.

Respectfully yours,
From all P.o.W.s in Camp 9. **Fukuoka**
Chief Representatives

Britain   Canada   Australia   America   Holland

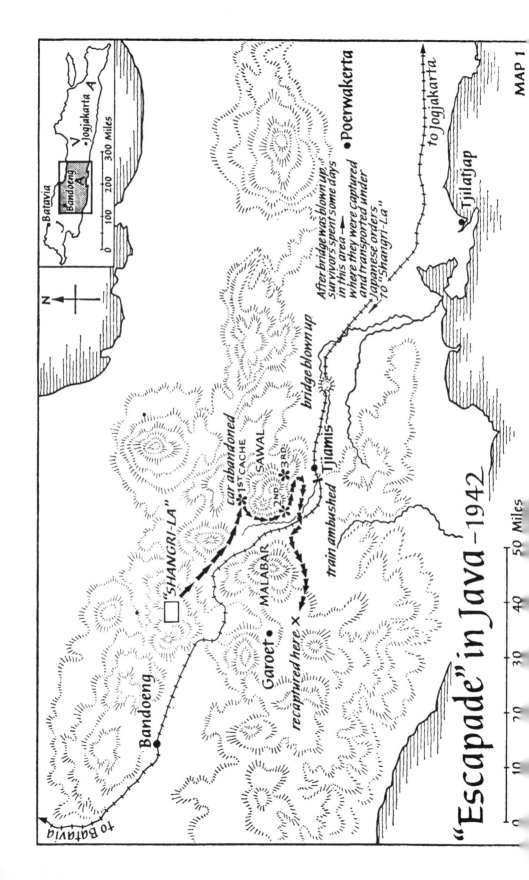

"Escapade" in Java – 1942

MAP 1

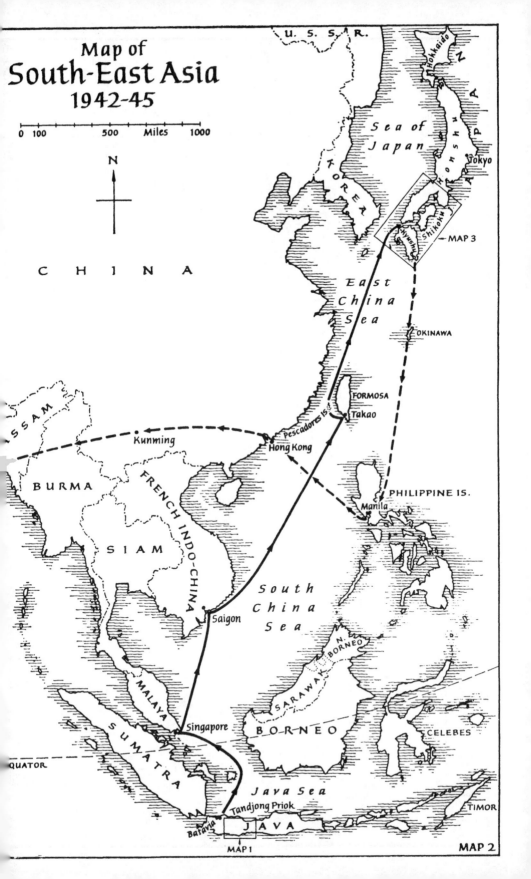

Map of
South-East Asia
1942-45

0   100   500   Miles   1000

N

U. S. S. R.

C H I N A

Sea of Japan

Tokyo

KOREA

East China Sea

MAP 3

Hokkaido

Honshu

Shikoku

Kyushu

OKINAWA

FORMOSA

Takao

Pescadores Is.

Hong Kong

ISSAM

Kunming

BURMA

FRENCH INDO-CHINA

SIAM

PHILIPPINE IS.

Manila

South China Sea

Saigon

N. BORNEO

SARAWAK

BORNEO

CELEBES

MALAYA

Singapore

SUMATRA

QUATOR

Java Sea

Tandjong Priok

Batavia   J A V A

TIMOR

MAP 1

MAP 2

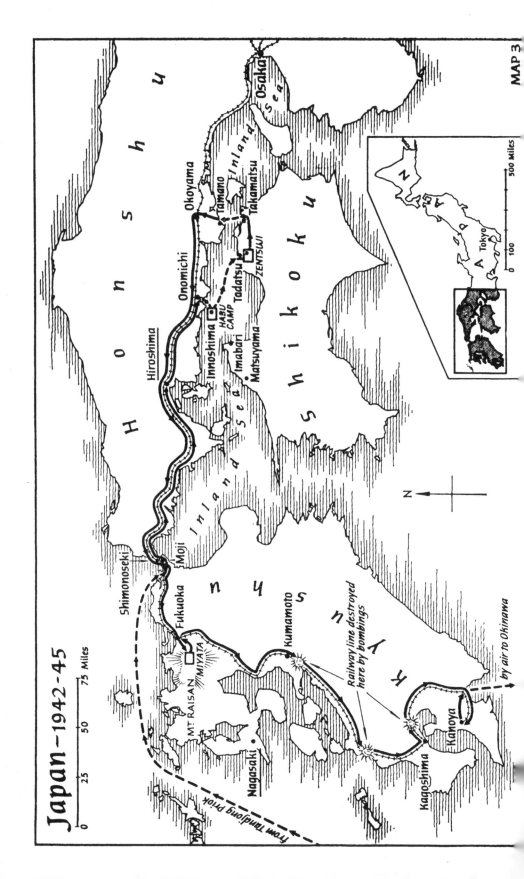

Japan – 1942-45

MAP 3

0   25   50   75 Miles

Shimonoseki

from Tandjong Priok

Fukuoka

MT. RAISAN   MIYATA

Nagasaki

Kumamoto

Railway line destroyed
here by bombings

Kagoshima

Kanoya

by air to Okinawa

K y u s h u

Moji

I n l a n d   S e a

Hiroshima

Onomichi

Innoshima
HABU CAMP

Imabari

Matsuyama

Tadatsu
ZENTSUJI

Okoyama

Tamano

Takamatsu

I n l a n d   S e a

Osaka

S h i k o k u

H o n s h u

N

Tokyo

500 Miles

0   100